ROBERT FROST
The Trial by Existence

ROBERT FROST
The Trial by Existence

ELIZABETH SHEPLEY SERGEANT

HOLT, RINEHART AND WINSTON *New York*

Published simultaneously in Canada by Holt, Rinehart and Winston of Canada, Limited.

An excerpt from Chapter 5 appeared in the May, 1960, issue of *The Atlantic* under the title "England Discovers Robert Frost."

Library of Congress Catalog Card Number: 60–8792

87810–0110
Printed in the United States of America

Published, June, 1960
Second printing, July, 1960
Third printing, January, 1961
Fourth printing, September, 1961

Acknowledgment is warmly offered to many individuals and publishing houses for permission to make quotations:

Mrs. Lascelles Abercrombie for quotations from "Ryton Firs" from *Twelve Idylls and Other Poems* by Lascelles Abercrombie (Martin Secker, London, 1928).

Van Wyck Brooks and E. P. Dutton and Company, Inc.,

by Olivia Howard Dunbar. Copyright, 1947, by the University of Chicago.

Harriet Fox Whicher for quotations from "Out for Stars; a Meditation on Robert Frost" from *Poetry and Civilization: Essays by George Frisbie Whicher*, Collected and Edited by Harriet F. Whicher (Cornell Univ. Press, Ithaca, N. Y., 1955).

Roland Wood for quotations from the introduction by Robert Frost to Frost's play *A Way Out*. Copyright, 1917, 1929, by Robert Frost (The Harbor Press, New York, 1929).

I wish to acknowledge also my indebtedness to the publishers of various magazines, journals, and newspapers for permission to quote from articles:

Amherst College for excerpts from the Robert Frost issue of *Touchstone* (February 1939). *The Amherst Graduates' Quarterly* for "Education by Poetry," by Robert Frost (February 1931). *The Amherst Student* for "Everybody's Sanity" by Robert Frost (1936). *Biblia*, Princeton University Library, for quotation from "Poverty and Poetry," a talk given by Robert Frost at Haverford College on October 25, 1937 (Vol. IX, No. 1, February 1938). *The Christian Science Monitor* for "Poetry of Amy Lowell," by Robert Frost (May 16, 1925). *Daedalus:* Journal of the American Academy of Arts and Sciences, for "On Emerson" by Robert Frost (Vol. 88, No. 4–1959). *The Dartmouth Alumni Magazine* for quotations from "Freshman Days," an interview by Edward Connery Lathem (March 1959). *The Harvard Alumni Bulletin* for a letter from Robert Frost to Dean Briggs (September 10, 1897) and for excerpts from "The Frost Festival and a Sequel" (February 12, 1955). Copyright, 1955, by Harvard Bulletin Inc. University of Massachusetts, for quotations from the "Address by Robert Frost," printed in Massachusetts State College Convocation (October 18, 1934). The University of Michigan for brief quotations from university publications and from an article by Frances Swain, "The Robert Frost of the Whimsies Evenings" from *The Inlander* (April 1925, Vol. 5, No. 4).

CONTENTS

ACKNOWLEDGMENTS

This book is dedicated to Robert Frost, and to the goodly number of his friends who have made the writing possible by sharing their memories, their knowledge, and their criticism of the selective record I have tried to make of the poet's life.

Among those who must be first named (though twice or thrice as many more are remembered with gratitude for their contributions) are Mrs. Joseph W. Ballantine, Robert Frost's eldest daughter Lesley; Mrs. Theodore Morrison, his friend and secretary; Mrs. George F. Whicher, the widow of one of Frost's closest associates in the English Department of Amherst College; Charles R. Green, Librarian *Emeritus* of the Jones Library, Amherst; F. B. Adams, Jr., Director of the Pierpont Morgan Library; E. C. Lathem, Assistant Librarian of the Baker Library, Dartmouth College; the poet David McCord of Harvard University; Mrs. Sue Bonner Walcutt, one of Frost's students and daughter of his friend, the late Professor Campbell Bonner, at the University of Michigan; Joseph Blumenthal of the Spiral Press; Dr. Jack W. C. Hagstrom, a former Amherst student of Robert Frost's, who has contributed valuable bibliographical material; and three friends who have read the book from the standpoint of the writer—Mrs. Agnes de Lima, May Swenson, and Thornton Wilder.

For source material I am greatly indebted to research libraries, named later; to Professor Lawrance Thompson, a recognized authority on Robert Frost and author of *Fire and Ice,* for the use of his chronology to 1925 and for brief study of his files at Princeton University; to C. Waller Barrett, who opened his Robert Frost collection to me for research and quotation; to Mrs. Ballantine, for quotation from the Frost children's composition books; to Mrs. H. K. Painter of Minneapolis, who has gathered her vivid childhood recollections of Mrs. William Prescott Frost, Jr., Robert Frost's mother and her teacher; and to Mrs. Samuel F. Schneider of Ann Arbor for permission to quote from reminiscences and letters of her father, the late Professor Morris Tilley.

Robert Frost has with unbounded generosity allowed me to quote from his writings, poetry and prose, published and unpublished, youthful and mature. This permission includes professional correspondence, many letters to personal friends, a few letters from his wife Elinor. Some letters, always named in the text, are in library collections, others in the archives of friends or their families.

From the *Complete Poems of Robert Frost* I have quoted without limitation, and I have also been permitted to quote in full two recent unpublished poems: "Auspex" and "Away" (Christmas 1958); and from two recently published poems: "One More Brevity" and "Kitty Hawk."

An example of Frost's school-day verse (Class Hymn, 1892, Lawrence High School) and an unpublished "Fragment," written probably in the next year at Dartmouth College, are noted in Part One.

Of Frost's light verse, usually written for friends, I have quoted "Couplet," an unpublished couplet for Mrs. Thomas W. Lamont; "A Correction," written for the Whichers; and from "John L. Sullivan Enters Heaven," written for Sara Teasdale, Vachel Lindsay, and Louis Untermeyer—both published.

Several poems from the privately printed, posthumous *Franconia,* by Marjorie Frost Fraser, the poet's youngest daughter, are included.

From Robert Frost's published prose (not yet collected) I have quoted from introductions to books, from articles and essays often buried in college periodicals, and from a few published letters notably to Harriet Moody and Mark Van Doren.

Of his unpublished prose other than letters, the documents quoted are the high-school valedictory: "A Monument to After-Thought Unveiled," and quotations from a notebook of his early married years.

In addition to acknowledgments made above I wish to express warmest thanks to each of the following persons for some special contribution to my study of Robert Frost:

From the colleges, Professor Reuben Brower and Professor *Emeritus* Ernest Hocking of Harvard University, Professor (and poet) John Holmes of Tufts University, Professor *Emeritus* Roy Cowden of the University of Michigan, Professor *Emeritus* Otto Manthey-Zorn of Amherst College, Viola C. White, former Curator of the Abernethy Library of American Literature, Middlebury College, Professor Basil Willey of Cambridge University.

From friends of the poet's and writer's world, Mary S. Cooley, Eleanor Farjeon, Michel Farano, the late Ferris Greenslet, Mrs. Alfred Harcourt, Mark A. De W. Howe, Takechiyo Matsuda, Frederic G. Melcher, Marianne Moore, Mrs. George J. Openhym, Howard G. Schmitt, Mrs. Kenneth Stewart, Jean Starr Untermeyer.

From several former editors of Robert Frost's at Henry Holt and Company, the Hon. Lincoln MacVeagh, Richard H. Thornton, William M. Sloane, 3d; and from A. C. Edwards of the present firm and my own editors, Harry Shaw and W. I. Bradbury.

In addition I wish to acknowledge with appreciation the grants received from the Pierpont Morgan Library and the John Simon Guggenheim Memorial Foundation; and to thank the MacDowell Colony for furthering the writing of the book over the past five summers.

Also I wish to thank Nancy Barnett and Mrs. Louise Lawn, who gave all the secretarial assistance they could spare from their busy lives, and Sarro who guarded my writer's quiet at home.

I wish to thank the following libraries and their curators for their courteous assistance in giving me access to materials in their manuscript collections bearing on the life and work of Robert Frost.

The Abernethy Library of American Literature, Middlebury College, Middlebury, Vermont: for access to letters of Robert Frost to William Stanley Braithwaite, Thomas Bird Mosher, and Marguerite Wilkinson.

The Baker Library, Dartmouth College, Hanover, New Hampshire: for access to letters of Robert Frost to Sidney Cox and Thomas Bird Mosher.

The University of Chicago Library, Chicago, Illinois: for access to letters of Robert Frost to Mrs. William Vaughn Moody; and to the Harriet Monroe Modern Poetry Collection of this library: for access to his letters to Harriet Monroe.

The Houghton Library, Harvard University, Cambridge, Massachusetts: for access to Robert Frost's letters to Amy Lowell.

The Henry E. Huntington Library, San Marino, California: for access to Robert Frost's letters to Herbert Hayes Ward and Susan Hayes Ward, editors of *The Independent*.

The Jones Library, Amherst, Massachusetts: for access to Robert Frost's high-school writings, and many other records and archives.

The Firestone Library of Princeton University: for access to correspondence of Robert Frost with Henry Holt and Company.

INTRODUCTION

Every year Robert Frost sends to friends and associates an original Christmas card—it does not always arrive before the Fourth of July—bearing a poem sometimes new, sometimes old. The card of 1949 reprinted a notable poem which had first appeared in *New Hampshire* in 1923:

ON A TREE FALLEN ACROSS THE ROAD
(TO HEAR US TALK)

The tree the tempest with a crash of wood
Throws down in front of us is not to bar
Our passage to our journey's end for good,
But just to ask us who we think we are

Insisting always on our own way so.
She likes to halt us in our runner tracks,
And make us get down in a foot of snow
Debating what to do without an ax.

And yet she knows obstruction is in vain:
We will not be put off the final goal
We have it hidden in us to attain,
Not though we have to seize earth by the pole

And, tired of aimless circling in one place,
Steer straight off after something into space.

At the end of the card sent to me Frost wrote, in his handsome, fastidious script:

You will find nothing new here unless from having an old poem forced on your attention for a second reading. The best line in it, if you ask *me* is

But just to ask us who we think we are

Who in Hell are we? That is the question for all over seventy-five. . . .

At his Vermont farm, the previous summer, I had talked with him enough about his unique life to discern in it a kind of repetitive drama of blockage, pause for reflection, daring self-direction and self-renewal that made the symbolic statement of the poem a clue to Frost's individual way.

He had told me that, as a very young man, close to poetry but not close to people with his poetry, he knew more of himself than he was able to prove to anyone except the girl he married at the age of twenty-one. Before long a tree had fallen across the road of the pair, and both pleaded for time to think things over on a farm. They didn't put it that way, but it was the gist of the matter.

Ten years and more passed and again a poet, still unheard, was halted in his runner tracks. There was no market for the slowly accumulating poems, the amount by then, R.F. said, of three books. Farming, doubled by secondary-school teaching, had not solved the living problem of a family with four children. So, with a flash of bravado, or was it discovery, the poet had sold his farm and sailed off into space—to England, where he had no connections save with the great poetry of English literature, and no goal but to "write and be poor."

Two years and more later, Frost returned to his native land with two small volumes of verse, *A Boy's Will* and *North of*

Boston, and a critical reputation that established him immediately as one of the most significant and original poets in the dawning American poetic renascence; and as it soon turned out, in the unfolding revolutionary movement of twentieth-century poetry.

Just before this return, early in 1915, I read my first Robert Frost poem, "The Death of the Hired Man," which appeared in the *New Republic,* then a new journal. This felicitous "eclogue," in freely treated blank verse, had conversational tones especially convincing to the ears of New Englanders who had long found wearisome the conventions of the Golden Age poets. Then the Holt editions of the two books were in print for our delight. I remember Willa Cather's fervent enthusiasm, and Amy Lowell's proud, possessive one—she had discovered Frost in London.

For ten years more, I knew only the poetry. Then in 1925, the *New Republic* asked me to write a literary portrait—its subtitle was "A Good Greek out of New England"—which was to be the germ of the biographical memoir that follows.

Robert Frost at this period was teaching at Amherst College, and summoned me to come up for a few days of talk. Mrs. Frost had found me a boarding place and received me gently. Her fine head, with its coiled braids and classic Puritan features, clearly framed a mind. She was an old hand at protecting her bard, but once she had assessed me as an intellectual being, she welcomed me to a brownish, book-lined, fire-placed living room that I now but vaguely recall. I had brought along the five small volumes of poetry in print at that date. These little books lay, like a pile of gold, between the poet and me on a hard sofa, and Frost would pick one up, turn to some special passage, and then say:

"Just let me keep this, will you and I'll write in it?"

And the book would be returned next day with an unpublished poem he was keeping for a later volume on the flyleaf, and penciled annotations which amounted to a rich, spicy and complete statement of his aesthetic philosophy, about which he was articulate and aphoristic. Here are a few samples:

In making a poem you have no right to think of anything but the subject matter; after making it no right to boast of anything but the form.

Make of this one ["The Mountain"]. I'll stand by you. Has no equal of mine in form but "Stopping by Woods" and "An Old Man's Winter Night."

Poetry is gloating. Dreams the fact. First talk-song I was ever aware of ["Mowing"].

Robert and Elinor Frost at that moment were just on the royal turn of fifty, and both possessed their singular and arresting New England beauty. In the wife it had been purified into an almost desperate calm, a hint of melancholy and somber pessimism, as if she had paid a price for sustaining and protecting her genius. In her vaguely shadowed presence Frost then seemed a cheerful skeptic, complex, elusive as an airborne spirit, though so related to earth.

A rascal haze of Yankee humor, mischief, wit played about him. He especially wanted to speak and yet not to be pinned down. If I quoted him back to himself he might say, no, that wasn't quite it, it was in fact the opposite. He seemed to be the center of converging lines of light, which made for paradox. He enjoyed confusion, though ever searching for form.

> Pan came out of the woods one day,—
> His skin and his hair and his eyes were gray,

Yet these two, so different in their natures, were a pair, alike and together, even in their differences—by turns casual and happy-go-lucky; or ravaged by vicissitude and dread of illness, of which there had been so much in their lives and their children's.

One day as we walked to the college course on Emerson that Robert Frost was giving—he was offering me a sample of his college teaching—he told me that the reading trips which often took him from home were a special worry to Mrs. Frost; she seemed not too glad of what Shakespeare called "that bubble, reputation." She had liked best to be the only one to know who he was. When *her* secret got out, when others were let in on it, she wasn't sure she was any happier. As he took me back through the mellow old town after the class, the poet-professor was full of his Amherst students.

They give me, often, phrases I can use in a poem. Like 'Sakes, It's only weather.' in "The Runaway." But I don't use dialect, you know. . . . Don't forget [and I didn't because he had written almost the same words into my *Selected Poems*] it was never my special aim to keep to any particular speech, unliterary, vernacular, or slang. I lay down no law to myself there. What I have been after from the first, consciously and unconsciously, is tones of voice. I've wanted to write down certain brute throat noises so that no one could miss them in my sentences. I have been guilty of speaking of sentences as a mere notation for indicating them, I have counted on doubling my meaning with them. They have been my observation and my subject matter.

Is poetry just license to spoil good prose? [He further meditated.] A poem must at least be as good as the prose it might have been. The sentences must go into it as unchanged in size and shape as the words. You are rhyming phrases and sentences, not just words.

I know what I want to do most. I don't do it often enough. In "The Runaway" I added the moral at the end, just for the pleasure of the aggrieved tone of voice—Shall I say it for you? [Say it he did, right out there on the porch of my boarding house.]

THE RUNAWAY

Once when the snow of the year was beginning to fall,
We stopped by a mountain pasture to say, "Whose colt?"
A little Morgan had one forefoot on the wall,
The other curled at his breast. He dipped his head
And snorted at us. And then he had to bolt.

We heard the miniature thunder where he fled,
And we saw him, or thought we saw him, dim and gray,
Like a shadow against the curtain of falling flakes.
"I think the little fellow's afraid of the snow.
He isn't winter-broken. It isn't play
With the little fellow at all. He's running away.
I doubt if even his mother could tell him, 'Sakes,
It's only weather.' He'd think she didn't know!
Where is his mother? He can't be out alone."
And now he comes again with clatter of stone,
And mounts the wall again with whited eyes
And all his tail that isn't hair up straight.
He shudders his coat as if to throw off flies.
"Whoever it is that leaves him out so late,
When other creatures have gone to stall and bin,
Ought to be told to come and take him in."

'Whited eyes,' 'shudders his coat'—that's what I liked to write.
Once I made those lines I was lost.

So was the writer of the portrait lost, aware, as she returned
to New York, of all that would inevitably be missed.

"Keep the crooked straightness, whatever you drop," the
poet wrote me. "A crooked straightness in character is my
favorite just now—an absolutely abandoned zig-zag that goes
straight to the mark."

After that, when I occasionally saw Robert Frost, or more
rarely heard from him in a letter, there always seemed to be
a metaphor, or image, or intellectual hypothesis in his mind
used to test other minds and perhaps his own. Shortly after
the republication of his portrait in my collection *Fire Under
the Andes* (1927), the theme stated in the last sentence of a
letter I received was the battle between the human spirit and
life as it runs away to waste. He referred first to friends he
was losing "through no fault but their own," then ended with
a potent figure. Later I found it, with excitement, very little

changed in the duologue, "West-Running Brook" (1928) and in the triumphant love poem "The Master Speed" (1936).

They [the friends] run away with someone else's wife and then avoid me as if it was my umbrella they had stolen. Now what do you suppose is the psychology of that? And some of them get into such tragic messes that I feel as if it was my proverbs failing me and not just my friends. And still I can't say that I didn't always know it was coming. My prophetic soul told me I was in for it forty five years ago come yesterday on the cliff house beach at San Francisco. Is it not written in a poem of mine. The one thing I boast I can't be, is disillusioned. Anything I ever thought I still think. Any poet I ever liked I still like. It is noticeable, I go back on no one. It is merely that others go back on me. I take nothing back. I don't even grow. My favorite theory is that we are given this speed swifter than any stream of light time or water for the sole purpose of standing still like a water beetle in any stream of light time or water off any shore we please.

This image of a personality maintaining itself by will, or destiny, or temperament, or an obstinate drive of personal direction at high tension *against* the stream of time, gaining its stature by *not* going along with the stream, stirred my imagination and never seemed contradicted by my rare meetings with Robert Frost. For what I cared most about in him was his difference from the brisk and driving urban men of the industrial age, engaged in competitive, material, or purely intellectual pursuits. But even the poetry, which started with the particular and ended, as great poetry does, with the universal, did not illumine the whole of R.F.'s life or mind. I kept on feeling teased by how "the whole thing" had come to pass.

It was in New York in 1946 when he dropped in on me for tea, before a reading of *A Masque of Reason,* that I suddenly heard myself take courage to ask him if I might again talk to him about his life and poetry, with a view to making a new and more biographical study. There seemed to be nothing recent of the sort in print; the good Gorham B. Munson biography dated back to the twenties.

"All right," Frost said easily, "Mrs. Morrison will let you know when to come to Vermont."

Time passed and I rather guessed he had forgotten. Willa Cather died in 1947, and I began working on the memoir that J. B. Lippincott published in 1953. Then, quite unexpectedly, in the spring of 1949, Mrs. Morrison, Mr. Frost's secretary and friend, wrote proposing that I come to Vermont in midsummer. Frost, with his *Complete Poems* "out," had a little time to spare for me.

So with the rashly named *Complete Poems* in my right hand and my nascent Cather manuscript in my left, I went to stay in the bare little village of Ripton, with two old Vermont ladies, Miss Agnes Billings and Mrs. Homer Noble. From the latter Robert Frost had bought his farm and cabin several miles above, among the verdant peaks, back of the Middlebury College Bread Loaf School of English.

For a month and more K.M., in her kindness, drove down several times a week to take me up to the farm or log cabin for a long talk with R.F., which usually wound up at some festivity connected with the English School and later, the Writers' Conference; or at a picnic or more formal meal with R.F. and the Morrisons and their friends, many of them poets or scholars.

The material discussed with Mr. Frost was of three kinds—poetical, biographical, and research-directed. On the poetry side, usually of an evening, and how lucky I was, how good it is to recall, we went straight through the lifetime collection, the ripe green volume: a thick one, though written only at the rate of ten poems a year, so the poet maintained. He might—or might not—say something about the origin, date of writing, form; more rarely meaning, for he wished to leave that to me and made no "exegesis." Occasionally he read a poem or a passage aloud, citing a favorite word, phrase, voice tone, image, or metaphor. Twenty-four years earlier he had done the annotating of the smaller books himself for me. Now he asked me to write his comments into the big book; and confirmed this, when I left, by writing on the flyleaf "To Elsie from Robert with all the annotations, August 1949 Ripton, Vt."

On the side of his life, Frost with a modesty, simplicity, and toughness that I revered, gave in his Yankee idiom a happy-sad, humorous-skeptical, episodic narrative full of discontinuities, anecdotes, and hard, frank facts about his San Francisco childhood; his Lawrence, Massachusetts boyhood and adolescence; his Harvard College interim; his New Hampshire farm and teaching years at Derry. He concentrated at this time largely on his first fifty years, since I was to some degree familiar with the last twenty-five.

My dilemma was that he enjoyed the telling and reminiscing only if I took no notes. This was partly because he said a great deal more than I could set down about a living subject, partly because he preferred to make the occasion a little excursion, a sort of "interval" where, in the fastness of New England, old friends strolled together in a cordial and "treesy" setting through a poet's life.

Obviously, when I began the book I should have to test out the notes I wrote down after the talks, by verifications from him, extensions, and all the research possible. At the time the poet indicated the libraries and collections that had essential documents and—a generous gift indeed—set me free to quote the material and also quote his poetry. That same summer, I was able to visit the Abernethy Library of Middlebury College where Miss Viola White was then Curator, and take a first look at the valuable Robert Frost collection.

It was five years later, in 1954, the year after the publication of *Willa Cather: A Memoir,* that I settled down to the serious undertaking of writing the present book, with a fellowship from the Pierpont Morgan Library and, later, a Guggenheim Fellowship. The many further consultations with my great subject—who, for all his patience, does not, as he once said on a Christmas card, enjoy being a subject all the time, like a Briton—during these years of his growing fame have taken place largely in Vermont and in New York City. I count one visit to Cambridge, one to meet him at the home of F. B. Adams, Jr., in Princeton; another day of fog at my cottage on the green edge of the Hudson, where the waves are never silent and the birds pause lightly on their way north to Vermont.

In distinction to the 1949 talks I have been permitted, in those of the 1950s, to take immediate notes and to verify manuscript and facts through queries to Mrs. Morrison. The quotations from the poet's *spoken* words are thus largely drawn from my notes. Where they are less sharp and idiomatic than Robert Frost's own, I must take the blame. In one instance only, the dialogue with Ellery Sedgwick in Part II, he dictated the exact words. In another, he wrote a brief paragraph about a classmate of his Dartmouth College days, whose memory he cherishes.

Robert Frost has been noticeably happier, as his circle has widened and widened, to talk of the clear-cut faraway and long-ago of his life than of the fluid, confusing years of fame and contemporary activity. Parts IV and V, so far as facts and details go, are selective and somewhat abstracted. Throughout the book I have interrupted direct narrative with the symbolic, quasi-autobiographical language of Frost's poetry which, so much more pointedly and subtly than any prose translation or interpretation of my own, expresses what he has made of his life experience.

The difficulty of translating Robert Frost is sharply apparent in the field of foreign languages. Though a major figure among world poets, Frost is one of the least translated. This is sometimes explained as being a matter of meaning: Frost is a militant nationalist, not a "one-worlder." He is an "optimist," not transfixed by fear or despair. His way of taking nature, too, is neither the romantic way, suffused with sub-jective mood, nor usually, the most modern way of taking it as a complete otherness to man and his concerns. Frost identi-fies to a leaf, puts his arm around a tree when he feels like it. He even dares guess how flowers feel, although in "The Most of It" he does painfully disidentify with the landscape of a lovely lake until a great buck makes the animal connection. But isn't the chief difficulty of translating Frost into a foreign tongue a matter of voice tones? The "vocal image" is far harder to convey in a foreign tongue than the visual. "Spring Pools" and other poems where Frost's fine visual imagination prevails are easier to translate than, say, "Blueberries." Can a French schoolboy or a scholar put the Yankee tones and images of those spicy anapestic couplets into Alexandrines?

The only complete translation, so far, is in German, though a dozen European countries in their anthologies and journals, and the Persians, perhaps, and the Japanese, surely, have be-gun to translate and estimate Frost seriously. *A Boy's Will*, translated by Ichiro Ando, appeared in Japanese in Tokyo in 1959 (*World's Famous Poems*, Vol. XI, Kenkyusha, 1959). A critical biography by the same author is included in his series of five studies of "world poets": (*Critical Biographies: Robert Frost*, Heibonsha, 1959).

This last, in my hands, reads backward of course. The "backispiece" is from a photograph of R.F. at ease in his Morris chair in the Ripton cabin, with one of the Morrisons' little dogs, and in loose garments a Zen Buddhist would ap-prove. Facing it is a holograph reproduction of "Stopping by Woods on a Snowy Evening."

Of still greater appeal to the non-English speaking will no doubt be the movie of Robert Frost, taken in the summer of 1959 in Ripton for distribution in eighty countries and thirty-five languages.

In my selections from Frost's poetry I have wanted to quote brief lyrics in full, but have often found other poems too long. I regret that I have frequently had to quote lines or stanzas rather than wholes. This is true, also, of the letters and documents I have freely cited as more appropriate and objective evidence on the life of a man among us than final summations by myself.

For Robert Frost's generous permission to quote from some of his hitherto unpublished letters—and from a few others that have appeared in print—I am most grateful. Pithy, humorous, or serious like his poetry, these letters, some already in libraries, were nevertheless not written for posterity or punctilio. They were addressed very intuitively and casually to a particular friend or purpose, flowing often from Frost's brisk sense of immediacy rather than from his meditative spirit. Yet that is only a half-truth, denied by his original thinking on poetry and teaching and politics in his major correspondence.

With their minor idiosyncrasies of spelling and punctuation, Robert Frost's letters or excerpts from them are printed here *verbatim ac litteratim*.

It is understandable to a friend, though scary to a writer, that the subject of this book decided not to read it. (He did look at the early chapters of Parts I and II.) So I am doubly indebted to certain devoted members of the poet's family and intimate circle, who have, in their several realms, contributed to my undertaking.

In spite of all this, my narrative is necessarily unfinished and imperfect. Some of the dates noted may be queried: the poet himself is doubtful about dates. He has kept few records, except in his head. The book will not tell all that the reader wants to know about one of the most beloved poets and sages of our midtwentieth century. For Robert Frost was born long, long ago—nine years after the end of the Civil War, in a period when two American opposites, North and South, were struggling to become one again. It is often said of him that he possesses the stability and optimism of the Victorian age. In fact, his childhood, boyhood, and early youth were in some ways the least stable periods of his life. He had rather to surmount them. So I suspect that a positive view of life and a perpetual struggle for balance and wisdom were partly innate, partly the end result of what he sometimes calls "the trial by existence" and sometimes "a lover's quarrel with the world."

PART I

THE POET UNHEARD

1874–1912

CHAPTER 1

A PECK OF GOLD
1874–1885

A PECK OF GOLD

Dust always blowing about the town,
Except when sea-fog laid it down,
And I was one of the children told
Some of the blowing dust was gold.

All the dust the wind blew high
Appeared like gold in the sunset sky,
But I was one of the children told
Some of the dust was really gold.

Such was life in the Golden Gate:
Gold dusted all we drank and ate,
And I was one of the children told,
"We all must eat our peck of gold."

Children rarely ask themselves what they are. Unlike one of the grandsons of William James, who at the age of three dared his mother to prove herself "real"—"You might be a dream parent"—Robert Frost, though exposed to the raw and raucous and bawdy-gay aspects of a frontier town, seemed to preserve his innocence in this gold-dusted San Francisco where he was born on March 26, 1874. Whatever "influences" other than love of his parents surrounded him in that

3

birthplace house on Washington Street, near the corner of Leavenworth, it was as if he knew them not. His childhood was essentially tragic, but he did not query it. "The tale of earth's unhonored things" came to him very young, possibly dedicating him to poetry and imagination, adding that vague melancholy which seems to have accompanied him through life. The pessimism common to all poets of our age, in him undefined and patient, is overcome in Frost by positive human faith, by what he likes to call "prowess" and earth confidence.

Robert Frost has always cared to look at and live with mountains. Strange that one whom we are now bound to think of as a White and Green Mountain man should have had for his first "specimen" that California volcano Tamalpais, which emerges like a mountain in a Japanese print from the redwoods and the clouds of Marin County. Or did he choose for his own the Mount Diablo range? Or the tawny, rolling hills of Contra Costa County? All these were across the bay, as an eye roved on and on, following land in movement, sea water of changing blues, and foggy distances. Such landscape is education, all unconscious and instinctive, for a poet's sensibility and his observation.

Views taken from Telegraph Hill or Russian Hill, set down in period print and etching, reveal the town as it was in Frost's childhood: the enclosed port on the bay side thick-crowded with the matchstick masts and airy rigging of three-masted schooners, the indented baylets filled with smaller craft of every conceivable origin. As you looked down from the hills into the city itself, it appeared closely built with homes of native brick, on narrow streets, and with high, yellowish, many-windowed urban dwellings that were largely destroyed in the terrible earthquake and fire of 1906.

Robert Lee Frost, as he was christened, in deference to his father's Copperhead sympathies, had parents of high intelligence and striking individual characteristics and fates.

William Prescott Frost, Jr., his father, born in 1850, son of a Lawrence, Massachusetts, mill overseer of the same name, came of nine generations of rural Frosts, Dorset and Cornwall men originally, who had fought the Indians up and down the north-of-Boston coast; and from Colcords on his grandmother Frost's side, who were also considerable and conservative New Englanders.

The elder W. P. Frost (Robert's grandfather) sent his son to Harvard at a time when a student could choose between reading eight books of Caesar and committing two to memory. In college, the young fellow—who had tried to run away and join the Confederate army—did brilliantly, made money through a tutoring school of his own, cut some capers too, which amounted to escapades, but graduated *cum laude* in 1872 with a Phi Beta Kappa key. He had saved a little money for his future.

A restless youth, with a deliberate grim panache, he decided again to break with New England tradition, migrate to California, and make his way in law or journalism. The days were not far back when respectable Connecticut businessmen, gone West to make sober fortunes, had taken their share—through monte, faro, and the roulette wheel—of the piles of gold and silver coin in the elegant saloons and gambling houses of San Francisco. Tales of the fortunes made, of the fair ones presiding over the coin and their nude counterparts on the walls, still circulated in New England after the Civil War.

Since teaching was one of his available gifts and he wanted money, the New Englander paused on his way West at Lewisburg, Pennsylvania, to take on a school, Bucknell Academy, and it was this that settled his fate in marriage. A Scottish girl, Isabelle Moodie, who had been teaching mathematics for seven years in a high school in Columbus, Ohio, had been summoned to join his staff. He promptly fell in love with her, wooing her with a seventeenth-century quatrain by James Graham, first Marquess of Montrose. The old poet says his father often quoted it at home:

5

He either fears his fate too much,
Or his deserts are small,
That dares not put it to the touch
To gain or lose it all.

Isabelle had not deliberately chosen her path in life—she was one to be chosen by fate. Born in 1844, left an orphan at eight by the death of her father, an Edinburgh sea captain, she had been brought across the water as an immigrant by her grandmother, to live with a Scots uncle in Ohio. (She liked to tell her children about the marvels of her landing in Philadelphia and how a kind sailor had offered her an American peach—she had never seen a peach—and how it was "too bonnie to eat.")

Belle Moodie was bonnie too. Her pure, indeed ravishing young profile, which we know from a daguerreotype—long nose, full, firm, well-cut lips, sparkling, humorous blue eyes—spoke for itself. Her virtuous Scottish traits, her fine intelligence, her contrasting religious temperament, mystical and Gaelic-poetical, and perhaps, even, her six extra years made her bait for the easy-going, daring, bluffing yet Puritan-based nature of a buccaneer in search of a future. Once Belle's heart and hand were won, he left her with her people in Columbus and went on to San Francisco, where he found a job on the *Bulletin*. From his first year on the coast till his last, Frost's father worked on several newspapers—first the *Bulletin*, then the *Post*,—he was city editor and manager—then the *Bulletin* again. A brilliant wild fellow, he thoroughly enjoyed the mental turmoil of the pressroom, even when the *Bulletin* editors had to barricade themselves to avoid the gunfire of stock-market men with wounded feelings.

No wonder Isabelle Frost felt herself battling with the incalculable in this still raw city on the Pacific, where her husband carried a revolver and wild boys ran in the streets. Seemingly ill-mated and certainly ill-fated, the couple were always moving; sometimes they lived in a house, sometimes in a hotel. The wife was a careless housekeeper (this was her weakest point) and her mate a nomad. But the worst of it was that Robert Frost's father's intellectual interests had a way of succumbing to the fascinations of games of chance, and he also frequented the saloons where the game of politics was played. There he fell into the drinking way, "a bad boy who never stopped being one," as R.F. put it to me when he first told me his childhood story. Plenty of things in her Far-West environment Isabelle Frost doubted and feared, but most of all the condition of a husband never drunk but always "out of sorts."

Born a Scotch Presbyterian, Isabelle as a young woman in America, her son says, had been greatly drawn by the intellectual and spiritual currents roused by Ralph Waldo Emerson and his Unitarianism. But in her San Francisco domestic trials Belle turned, and permanently, to the mystical Swedenborgian faith, which had the story and the wonder that her imaginative nature seemed to need. Indeed the closest counsellor in her private and inner life was the Reverend John Doughty, a black-bearded Swedenborgian of Worcester, Massachusetts, and Harvard provenance. Later, Doughty was to draw to church and Sunday school with their mother the two children born to this couple. Belle's husband did not go to church. Robert Frost, though no churchgoer today, has had a lifelong interest in theology, and friends among the clergy of many faiths. How much does this trend derive from family talk and from the black-browed mystic who was nearly scalped by Indians on his early trip West from Massachusetts?

Rob was only two when, before the birth of her second child Jeanie Florence, in 1876, Isabelle Frost fled cross-continent to state her marital case to her unknown in-laws: solid, stiff New Englanders, highly respectable folk with money in the bank. But she was rebuffed, refused credence, blamed. If (the elders said) their clever son, who had come out of Harvard with honors, was going to the devil, surely it was Belle's fault. Why hadn't he married the Lawrence girl, a girl who loved him, whom he jilted, who had died and been mourned by all?

7

The Scots wife had her girl child in Lawrence in June; then, retreating, spent a religious summer with a woman friend in Greenfield, Massachusetts; halted in Ohio to see her own people; resignedly journeyed back over the interminable prairies in the slow coaches which R. L. Stevenson described in *Across the Plains.* Isabelle Frost was helped with her tiny children by a kind woman she'd found in Columbus, who would stay with her in San Francisco for four years. This was Blanche Rankin, soon "Aunt Blanche" to Rob and Jeanie.

After her rebellious trip East, Belle Frost, her son says, in the manner of Victorian women, never queried her marriage. She accepted her husband and his ways and learned to deal with them. She had also to worry about the tuberculosis which he had acquired—she believed from the strain of a six-day foot race during her absence, in which, in spite of a head start, he was defeated by one Dan O'Leary.

Mrs. Frost's intellectual and artistic interests now revived. There was an occasional drama to see, especially *The Count of Monte Cristo,* played by James O'Neill, the father of the famous playwright, who brought his company to San Francisco. James O'Neill and W. P. Frost became congenial friends and Rob some years later consulted O'Neill about becoming an actor himself. But the closest family friends were the Henry Georges. The famous author of *Progress and Poverty* worked at one time in the composing room of the *Bulletin* and soon converted the Frosts to the theory of the single tax.

Isabelle Frost occasionally reviewed books for her husband's paper; her son recalls their covers but never looked inside. He remembers, too, his mother's poetic trances. His father, he says, knew but two pieces of poetry, the James Graham quatrain already cited, and the end of Bryant's "Thanatopsis." But his mother loved romantic poetry. When she was inspired, her Scotch reticence fell away, and she would let down her thick brown hair which fell to her feet, and recite Poe's "The Raven," or it might be "Annabel Lee":

It was many and many a year ago,
  In a kingdom by the sea,
That a maiden there lived whom you may know
  By the name of ANNABEL LEE;
And this maiden she lived with no other thought
  Than to love and be loved by me.

Does this remind the reader of one of Frost's tender early poems, "Love and a Question," written in the same ballad form?

A Stranger came to the door at eve,
  And he spoke the bridegroom fair.
He bore a green-white stick in his hand,
  And, for all burden, care. . . .

It was not, however, the boy but his little sister who stood on stools and spouted poetry. The man thinks the boy could not read at all before he was ten. His parents considered Rob an outdoor boy. His own view of himself too was that he was a walker, a racer, athletic like the father he tagged after and worshipped.

One of Robert Frost's own poems, "At Woodward's Gardens," based on a childhood memory, nevertheless grants himself as a boy an exploratory curiosity, even a mind:

A boy, presuming on his intellect,

it begins, is the story of how a boy tried out some monkeys at the zoo with a burning glass and found that monkeys are not men.

It's knowing what to do with things that counts.

One of the great gifts of San Francisco to its citizens is the backdrop of primeval forest and mountain and valley or ocean beach that is accessible even to the humblest. In summer the Frost family had their share of it, always choosing a new and fascinating place to go to that a gifted, curious child was bound to remember.

For instance, there was the summer at Nicasio when Rob was five: he rode horseback—he still loves horses and colts—and was hit over the head with a croquet mallet by a little girl who accused him of cheating. Another summer they spent at San José, where Rob had his first but not last experience with a witch—here a Spanish tea witch, who read tea leaves as fortunes. During the summer at the farm on the Napa River, a raw-boned Mrs. Bragg was concerned about some animal that was eating her eggs.

"I took pleasure," Frost recalled, "in pecking holes in the eggs with a nail because I liked the table talk about what animal could be doing this."

The matter of lying or cheating was one of importance to Rob's Victorian parents and vaguely to him also, for he clearly lived already in his imagination to some degree. He built a bridge over a brook and said a rabbit ran over it—did he make this up, he wonders now? During a summer in the Sierra foothills back of Santa Cruz, he went off by himself, cutting through deep woods to see a boy whose father had made a tank hewed out of a big tree to hold spring water. As he returned alone over a bridge, an eagle tried to carry him off—or so he told his parents. He liked to stir up a sensation and is actually unsure today whether this melodramatic event happened or not. In any case he has written a poem about it, published here for the first time:

AUSPEX *

Once in a Californian Sierra
I was swooped down upon when I was small
And measured but not taken after all
By a great eagle bird in all his terror.

* Copyright © 1960 by Robert Frost.

Such auspices are very hard to read.
My parents when I ran to them averred
I'd been rejected by the royal bird
As one who would not make a Ganymede.

Not find a barkeep to the gods in me?
I have resented ever since that day
When any but myself presumed to say
That there was anything I couldn't be.

As he grew older, the problem of make-believe stirred Rob's thinking and his conscience. He used to say to himself with remarkably adult insight that he would be happy if he could have one single day when he did not *lie* or *pretend to himself*. It was all right if he *knew* he lied.

This blue-eyed boy, who according to the parental view had no intellectual interests, as he grew tall, thin, wiry, was considered delicate, perhaps of tubercular trend, and was kept out of school "for his health." The favorite and darling of a politician father, he was introduced, green and innocent, into the brash male world, through buggy rides over the hills, campaigning for Grover Cleveland, and eating lunches at Levy's on Bush Street.

"What's the matter with saloons?" Robert Frost asked a lady who "hoped they'd not return" after the repeal of the Volstead Act. "I was brought up in them."

Though he loves the "happy-sad blend of the drinking song," Frost, however, has never liked drink; says that "if his stomach hated it as much as his mouth he would have died of the first mouthful."

In spite of this close companionship, Rob was severely, even cruelly punished for errors in manners and other minor sins. He did not resent it, thinking, he says, that all fathers were like this: keeping their boys out of school for company, beating them for things they couldn't help—like losing a dime in the crack of a pavement while bringing beer from the saloon.

On this occasion Rob was taken into his mother's arms and prayed over, before the dreadful duty of confessing to his father. For once he was let off, drawn onto the couch where the sick man lay, and forgiven. Tomorrow, like a good son, he'd be hurling silver dollars at the ceiling of saloons, in the attempt to drive in thumbtacked cards bearing the name of W. P. Frost, Jr., Democratic candidate for tax collector. What wonder that the poet has a persistent interest in American politics. But he still marvels that at ten years old he was allowed to run alone anywhere, all over the rough city of San Francisco.

His father would send him to that seat of corruption, the City Hall, as a messenger with documents. He would even dispatch Rob to ring dubious doorbells, to ascertain whether the registered voters lived where they said they did.

"Of course," said R.F. with a twinkle, "it would be Republican voters on the election lists I would have to look up. My father was not concerned about the Democrats having a fair record!"

No doubt, because of this singled-out destiny, Robert Frost was something of a hero with the "bad" boys of the streets—the ones his mother feared for him. They took him on as foot-loose, school-free joiner of their exploits—at least by day. Rob was not allowed out at night. He remembers an expedition to the country with an older boy (who later became a criminal), raiding for fruit. Returning disappointed, without spoils, he was ordered to climb a fence at a slaughterhouse they were passing, where pigs in process of assassination were loudly squealing. Up he went over the fence, with lucky celerity pushed a slick squirmer into his fruit bag and bobbed back undiscovered. His companion then led him to a Chinese washhouse, sold the pig for ninety cents, and handed Rob fifteen of the illicit pennies, "which I accepted unresentfully."

The boy, the man reports, feared and suspected in his heart that he was a coward, and in this random fashion kept trying out his own courage. Once he dared a companion called Franklin that he could beat him running twenty times around the block for fifty cents. Something of drama and publicity, as with his father's six-day foot race, attended this effort. Each boy had a different block and a yelling crowd of spectators. Franklin (the elder) won.

At this period in San Francisco, even the enlightened regarded the Chinese down Washington Street as inferior yellow folk with pigtails, beyond the pale of civilization. The boys enjoyed standing outside the washhouses, listening for the hiss of the Chinaman's spit as he ironed the white man's shirt front. When W. P. Frost's friends, including his own father and mother, came out from Massachusetts for a visit, the journalist-politician would hire a policeman to accompany them to the underground "opium dens," ominous with decay, and evil fumes. Opium was smuggled and sold openly in San Francisco at this period, Frost remembers.

The old poet's heart still warms to recall the grand, proud family trip to Oakland in 1884, to see Father off in top hat and frock coat, as delegate to the Democratic National Convention that nominated Hancock. But San Francisco went Republican, in spite of plenty of frontier trickery at the polls, and W. P. Frost was not elected.

It was after this that the elder Frost grew sicker, and took his lanky boy with him to the stockyards to watch him drink warm fresh blood. This horrendous practice was, at the time, a recommended cure for consumption. Cures were never *not* talked about at the Frosts. Someone called "Count Matteo" had discovered something, or perhaps they should all go to "the Islands" for Father's health?—the Sandwich Islands, of course.

R.F. has indelible memories of the last summer of his father's life, spent at Sausalito, on San Francisco Bay. The little family of four camped in tents not far below what used to be the Yacht Club, along with a jolly, rowdy crowd of Bohemian newspapermen who came out from the city. Rob was aware of his mother's unease and sadness in this company

13

of topers and jokers, who made a ceremony of "burning their sins" on a funeral pyre on the beach.

The saddest, most striking memory, however, was that of his father's reckless, desperate swims, far out into Sausalito bay, leaving the agonized ten-year-old on the beach, a lonely watcher. The flaunting search for physical energy turned quickly to spent force: the swimmer, scarcely able to reach shore again, arms and legs gone, dragging to the tent for his "medicine bottle."

> And the mind whirls and the heart sings,
> And a shout greets the daring one.

Wildness, mystery, and meaning were surely associated for Rob with the Pacific Ocean. In giving me the background for his noted poem below, R.F. mentioned the mighty storm he had witnessed at the Cliff House at the age of five or six. It lingered in his mind as grandeur, darkness, and portent. In 1892, while at Dartmouth College, he experimented with some of the lines of what became the poem, but did not publish it till thirty-six years later, in *West-Running Brook:*

ONCE BY THE PACIFIC

The shattered water made a misty din.
Great waves looked over others coming in,
And thought of doing something to the shore
That water never did to land before.
The clouds were low and hairy in the skies,
Like locks blown forward in the gleam of eyes.
You could not tell, and yet it looked as if
The shore was lucky in being backed by cliff,
The cliff in being backed by continent;
It looked as if a night of dark intent
Was coming, and not only a night, an age.
Someone had better be prepared for rage.
There would be more than ocean-water broken
Before God's last *Put out the Light* was spoken.

Robert Lee Frost was eleven years old when, on May 5, 1885, his father (then thirty-four) died in his own home, in the arms of an older man, a faithful political friend and backer, Colin Boyd, a Scotsman.

As the reckless fellow lay, conscious of his fate, he made his son promise never to go into the streets to play at night: a promise that was kept.

"I never spoke of my father for years after he went: I couldn't."

And binding all is the hushed snow
Of the far-distant breaking wave.

CHAPTER 2

A RECORD STRIDE

1885–1893

Robert Frost says now and then "men tell me I have no straddle," and chuckles, recalling this "record stride"—the distance from the Pacific to the Atlantic which he measured so young. The memory lives in a poem, probably written in the early 1930s, about a pair of old boots that stood in the closet of his farmhouse bedroom in South Shaftsbury:

> I touch my tongue to the shoes now
> And unless my sense is at fault,
> On one I can taste Atlantic,
> On the other Pacific, salt.
>
> One foot in each great ocean
> Is a record stride or stretch.

American children do not feel that stretch today. But think what it was like in 1885 to travel three thousand-odd train miles, accompanying a coffin that had smothered and extinguished a florid, beloved, and enigmatic personality. Wasn't Robert Lee Frost already exposed to the drama of his sensibilities? Seven years later, in his high-school valedictory, he wrote some memorable phrases about death: memorable in their tone and wording, even though there might be some reminiscence of Tennyson, Arnold, or even Bryant's rhetorical "silent halls of death."

There are men . . . who go to death with such grey grandeur that we look back upon their past for some strange sorrow, such as does not fall to others. . . . They seem like Merlins looking ages from their deep calm eyes. With what awe we stand before the mystery of their persons.

There were factual and miserable as well as awesome things to think of on the journey East: the last insurance premiums unpaid, twenty thousand dollars lost. A mother, a widow, with two young children, dependent (but for her own powers) on the mercy of elder relatives not her own—why, the old poet now wonders, didn't she go to Ohio where those who loved her and recalled her fine record as a high-school teacher of mathematics could have found her a suitable opening? Certainly when the body of the father was buried in the Frost family lot in the Lawrence graveyard which crowned a hill above the smoky industrial mill town where the spindles kept up their perpetual spin, the trial by existence closed upon the little family group of three. The color of life, so high in San Francisco, had faded into the wan and gray.

The Lawrence Frosts were aware of duty and the ties of blood but on the whole querulous, disparaging—why didn't Belle Frost inform them about the unpaid premiums? They'd have paid them! And they were old—people in their sixties were old in 1885—and "purse-proud," as New England parlance went. Robert's grandfather was the complete opposite, seemingly, of the grim-gay renegade, his son. When Frost speaks of his grandfather today, he looms as a sort of fateful, archetypal image in the background of his adolescent and young life: an image of severity and power, gigantesque.

It was his mother's courage, faith, and independence that passionately commanded the boy's love and loyalty. She was not one long to fit in with the household of Great-Aunt Sarah Frost Messer, where they first lived in Amherst, New Hampshire, after a brief stay with the grandparents; or to adapt herself and her children's lives in Lawrence to those of Great-Uncle Elihu Colcord (Robert's grandmother's brother) and Great-Aunt Lucy Frost Colcord (his grandfather's sister).

So in the spring of 1886 the brave widow found herself a district school to teach, and a modest lodging where she could be alone with her children, now transferred from a Lawrence school to her instruction. This was in Salem, New Hampshire, just over the state line. Belle may have been glad of that. She remained a nomad, as in San Francisco, moving from tenement to farmhouse wing as she could. Her pay was nine dollars a week and the school year was thirty-six weeks. This was all they had, except for Rob's minor earnings.

The Houghton Library of Harvard University has a photograph of Belle Frost outside the Salem school with her thirty-four pupils. The fresh young beauty of the early picture is gone: a long, sad face, with hollow cheekbones, fine eyes and nose, hair somewhat flurried and ragged, expression regardless of self but concerned and alive. If you look for two special children, you will find, close beside the teacher, a well-featured ,boy, somewhat aware of the world, in a stiff straw hat; and in the front row a subtle little girl lost in a dream, her long hair, by repute gold-red, billowing down like a waterfall. This is Jeanie, the bright temperamental sister who never married, became a teacher, but lost her mind in middle life and died.

Rob remained at the Salem school until he was ready for high school, and perhaps because of his mother's original teaching methods—she seated the children according to their abilities, instructed them individually, and read aloud to them—began to shoot forward intellectually, and prove "good in nearly everything."

The first book he recalls reading to himself is associated with work he was doing for a farmer. He took it as a matter of course, as a young boy, that he should get one little job after another to help his mother. He borrowed *The Scottish Chiefs* from the farmer's wife, a dog-eared copy. Flopping down in the sweet smother of new-cut hay, he lost himself

18

in the history and romance of the Highlands. But he didn't finish the book, because he "knew the end."

Much of his mother's reading aloud to the children at home had a Scotch background. Busy as she was, and no hand to "housekeep," she never failed to find time to read to her youngsters the tales of George MacDonald, the poems of Robert Burns and Walter Scott. One of Isabelle's aunts, she told her children, knew the whole of "The Lady of the Lake" by heart and on some childhood trip of theirs to Loch Katrine said it all in a boat on the lake.

When Rob had heard the bay of the "deep-mouth'd bloodhound" resounding up the rocky way, it didn't matter if there were only onions and potatoes for lunch or "the halesome parritch, chief o' Scotia's food" for breakfast and maybe supper.

"That Rob can do anything," my mother used to say [Frost recalled as he sat by his cabin fire]. I'd sometimes complain or run off to go swimming, but on the whole I guess I liked to try myself out in a job. I was curious about life. I liked working with rough characters—they did me no harm [he said defensively. After all, he'd fraternized with them from childhood].

One year when I was twelve I worked in a shoe shop, inserting nails into holes in the heels of shoes. I held the nails in my mouth (Mother did not realize that) but I never inhaled or swallowed any. Then next year, I was thirteen, I worked behind a big machine run by a big man—that process was really dangerous for a child but I didn't let her know or lose a finger.

Frost's poetry shows little evidence of the interest in the growing industrial world to which he was considerably exposed, north of Boston, through his family connections and his own adolescent jobs. His boyhood effort to help an old farm codger grind a blade ("The Grindstone") reveals an almost daemonic emotion about this primitive piece of farm machinery. The single poem in which a mill process is concretely (and exquisitely) described is a poem of rebellion from industry ("A Lone Striker"). To know where the dream and observation of the farm helper developed into the dream of the poet one must go to the farm poems like "A Tuft of Flowers" and "Mowing."

> The fact is the sweetest dream that labor knows.
> My long scythe whispered and left the hay to make.

In discussing this period when jobs and books began to enlighten and enlarge him, Frost told me of a book that came along when he was fourteen and in high school. His mother read it to the children—Bellamy's *Looking Backward*, a romantic story of a Bostonian who had a sleep of fifty years and awakened in an ideal socialistic world.

This fitted right into the Henry George tradition and inspiration in the Frost family and may have been recommended by George, who always looked up his old friend Belle when he came to Boston, visited her in her widow's home, and persuaded her to attend his single-tax banquets in Boston. This connection counted for a great deal with the devoted, hard-working teacher, drew her back to her youth and her socialist convictions.

Robert, recalling young Rob listening to Bellamy, says that the youth was rather bored and found himself forced to cogitate on the social order:

I discovered from Bellamy that socialism is everybody looking after Number Two. My criticism was the same then as now; just as conservative. It's harder to look after Number Two than Number One, for how do you know what Number Two wants?

Frost's individualism was inherent, and when he read Henry George's book subsequently, with considerable admiration, he still, as his later political-philosophical poetry shows, stuck to his own ideas. He was exposed on his first visit to England, before World War I, to the same trend:

In London I knew Beveridge—he that started the whole cradle-to-grave welfare system under which all governments now groan

20

and sink. I found him this spring (1957) sitting in the House of Lords!

No [reflected the poet, getting up to open his screen door to the scratch of a minute and favorite schnauzer], I'd hesitate to abolish poverty myself. Too much good has come of it. If it's going to be abolished, let Mrs. Roosevelt do it!

Frost was a poor boy indeed when, in the fall of 1888, he matriculated at fourteen at the Lawrence High School, an uncompromising brick building in the middle of town. Salem neighbors were critical because it meant the expense of a train ride back and forth to the larger place. But the grandparents welcomed the plan; Grandmother Frost cut down for Rob one of her husband's suits, and Grandfather Frost furnished the commuting ticket. The boy's success in school was immediate, and Great-Uncle Elihu Colcord rewarded him with a "boughten" suit, his first as a teen-ager. For four years Rob Frost became the "regular feller" he never was before or after, taking his place ambitiously as scholar and leader. His prominence was based on intellectual and literary powers largely dormant till then, as well as on personality and personableness. One of his personal gifts, his mother felt, was that he could "adjust" the troubles of others—he could see both sides of a question.

R.F. recalls two periods of suffering for exactitude in high school. One improved his spelling, which has never been perfect because his ears apprehend more than his eyes do. The second furthered his Greek and Latin, through Miss Newell, a teacher of iron fiber who allowed no temperamental variability. The boy grew passionately interested, as it proved for a lifetime, in Latin poetry and verse forms.

He also grew interested in girls. By his second year began the major attraction between himself and Elinor Miriam White, who was to become his wife when he was twenty-one. Elinor's father was a Universalist minister who had deserted the pulpit and become a woodjoiner. He claimed descent from

Peregrine White and other ancestors who fought at Lexington and Concord. There was some early New England history between the two of them, Robert and Elinor. Elinor was a brilliant scholar, intrepid soul, and guileless beauty; she was not yet convinced of her lifetime fate; kept Robert "on tenterhooks," as they said in the nineties, and at arm's length.

Was it at least a little because of Elinor's emotional place in his mind and heart that Rob Frost in 1890 began to write poetry and publish it in the Lawrence High School *Bulletin*? It happened quite unexpectedly. He had been reading Prescott's *The Conquest of Mexico* in his history class, learning about Cortez, when suddenly the same afternoon, he wrote "La Noche Triste," a generous-hearted, heroic narrative poem in ballad form, based on an incident befalling a group of Indians, who "just might have turned the tide for themselves" —so Frost commented—but didn't. He felt poignantly for these Montezumas.

He has been quoted as to how it came about, on the way home from school:

"I recall how there was a wind and a darkness. I had never written a poem before, and as I walked, it appeared like a revelation, and I became so taken by it that I was late at my grandmother's."

Then he straightway sat down at her kitchen table and wrote the poem, just so, with no hesitation, as he had conceived it in his mind on the road. Next day he took it to the editor of the school paper, Ernest Jewell of the class of 1890, who published it, with a fragment, also signed Robert Lee Frost, called "Tenochtitlan," in the high-school *Bulletin* of April, 1890.

Now he was really started in his very own deep groove— though of course not yet aware of anything so momentous— and released from the tormenting inner question as to whether he could write or not. After all, his father had been a practicing journalist and had written a life of their San Francisco neighbor, General Rosecrans, of Civil War repute; and his mother too had said her minor say in print.

22

A month later, in May, 1890, Rob Frost again published in the high-school paper "The Song of the Wave," a poem with a taking lilt and a personal notation of nature. The singer is one with the wave in its motion from sea to shore. In his junior year, in 1890–1891, the *Bulletin* published in May one poem only, "A Dream of Julius Caesar," a study of personality arising from classic studies and hero worship. This immature work, which can be examined in the Jones Library at Amherst, Massachusetts, has, in spite of a host of echoes and stock phrases, the passion that makes a poem and considerable skill in form.

Look too in the *Bulletin* for December, 1891, for a prose essay on the ancient site of Petra, on Mount Hor—and then remember Frost's beautiful poem, "The Mountain" (inexplicably called Hor), which is a blend of many mountains. In this, his senior year, 1891–1892, Rob was himself elected editor of the high-school *Bulletin;* very much in character, however, he became impatient of the tardiness of his contributors, so wrote all the contents of one issue under assumed names and resigned.

Schools at this time, Frost told me, had tests but didn't give students the marks.

I didn't know I was head of the class of 1892. In the second year they began to play it on me. In the third year it became a school issue and I was in distress. There was a rivalry between the Greek and Latin teachers, and Elinor bobbed up in the last year as a rival. The head of the school was a very cultivated man, Greek and Latin scholar; aware of the "higher uncertainties." I had him only in Greek and Roman history. This head of school came to me, smoked as a ham, scholarly and lazy—very pleasant.

"Do you realize," he said to me, "that Miss White is catching up—she may get the valedictory?"

I said: "Give it to her now." No, he wouldn't, but called it a tie. So Elinor, too, gave a speech.

My further thoughts were: the valedictory would come in handy later. I was beginning to be literary, on my own. But I had no tendency to ape any other writer. . . .

My idea was—tackle the subject—say it the best you could—make your own troubles and get out of them. Nobody around me had thoughts. I scorned opinions from the beginning. I wanted ideas; wanted to use a figure.

In his valedictory, Robert Frost spoke to an extraordinarily subjective theme, "A Monument to After-Thought Unveiled," somewhat magniloquently expounded. The passages chosen reveal how many mature-immature after-thoughts his mind had already grasped:

. . . Not in the strife of action, is the leader made, nor in the face of crisis, but when all is over, when the mind is swift with keen regret, in the long after-thought. The after-thought of one action is the forethought of the next.

It is when alone, in converse with their own thoughts so much that they live their conventionalities, forgetful of the world's, that men form those habits called the heroism of genius, and lead the progress of the race. This, the supreme rise of the individual—not a conflict of consciousness, an effort to oppose, but bland forgetfulness, a life from self for the world—is the aim of existence. . . .

The poet's insight is his after-thought. It is of varied heartbeats and converse with nature. And the grandest of his ideas come when the last line is written.

Life is an after-thought: how wonderful shall be the world? that is the after-thought of life . . .

Any good Frostian knows that Robert Frost today disclaims being either an extravert or an introvert; he's "just a plain Vert from Vermont." But how did those future industrialists and businessmen among his class brethren, who admired him in school and sharply criticized him later, take these very inward comments?

Elinor White's valedictory essay had for subject "Conversation as a Force in Life."

Already, perhaps, she dreamed that the very best conver-

sation, the most elusive and least recordable, was indeed to
be a daily force in her own life.

The Lawrence *Daily Bulletin* for July 1, 1892, carried a
story of these high-school exercises, with vignettes of the
two star performers in their striking young charm.

The class hymn set to "music by Beethoven" was also
written by Robert Lee Frost:

> There is a nook among the alders,
> Still sleeping to the cat-bird's "Hush";
> Below, a long stone bridge is bending
> Above a runnel's silent rush.
>
> A dreamer hither often wanders. . . .

We get a Narcissus image of this "dreamer," not too atti-
tudinizing to be impressive already, in an early poem "The
Quest of the Orchis," published in the *Independent* in 1901,
the year of his grandfather's death. The poem was lost track
of for many years. Below, an excerpt from the final version,
"The Quest of the Purple-Fringed" published in *A Witness
Tree* in 1942.

> Yet further I went to be before the scythe,
> For the grass was high;
> Till I saw the path where the slender fox had come
> And gone panting by.
>
> Then at last and following him I found—
> In the very hour
> When the color flushed to the petals it must have been—
> The far-sought flower. . . .
>
> There stood the purple spires with no breath of air
> Nor headlong bee
> To disturb their perfect poise the livelong day
> 'Neath the alder tree.

I only knelt and putting the boughs aside
Looked, or at most
Counted them all to the buds in the copse's depth
That were pale as a ghost.

Then I arose and silently wandered home,
And I for one
Said that the fall might come and whirl of leaves,
For summer was done.

Summer was really done for the high-school demigod.

But he was still a flounderer, he has told me, neither gird-
ing his loins for a practical career nor having a faith deep
enough to launch him into an artistic one.

Who was he? That was, when graduation was over, Rob's
after-thought, a vague overwhelming doubt. It was his grandmother's decision, not his own, that he should go to Dartmouth
College in the fall of 1892, for four years as she supposed and
planned. His mathematics teacher had recommended Dartmouth, and his grandmother feared the Harvard drinking.

"In fact, I hated liquor. If I ever got drunk in my whole
life it was to make somebody sorry for something he had
done to me."

But why go at all? Rob wondered. What was a college education? To him? Elinor White had no doubts at all on her
own score; off she marched to St. Lawrence, a Universalist
college in New York State. Perhaps that helped Rob to move
north to the elm-shaded college town of Hanover.

The old buildings of Dartmouth—the oldest, Dartmouth
Hall, completed in 1791—made an immediate appeal to Rob
Frost. In a very real sense, he told me, he was stepping into
his future when one day he walked into a certain romantic
arched door, the Romanesque door of the then Library, Wilson
Hall.

Tuition was low [the poet recalled for me], $90 a year. Mine
was only $10 because I had won a fellowship, and because I was

a monitor and because I did not stay even a whole term. My room in Wentworth Hall was $26 a year, and my board was $2.50 a week.

There was no drinking at all—if we wanted an orgy, we sat up all night with a box of Turkish paste.

I was invited into a fraternity—Theta Delta Chi—and joined up. One of my "rich" classmates paid my initiation fee. But somehow I was no fraternity brother.

No housekeeper either; the rooms in Wentworth were heated by open coal stoves. I never emptied my ashes—just let them pile up on the floor till they reached the door. My mother had to send up my high-school friend, Carl Burrell from Lawrence, to dig me out.

I had a large indifference to my teachers. I guess I wanted to be a teacher myself and be on top—not underneath the system. Instinctively, I suppose.

What Rob Frost, the freshman, was immediately let in on —though, he says, "without much self-approval"—was "rough-housing" with a gregarious mass of adolescents.

Preston Shirley . . . was my greatest and only very intellectual friend at Dartmouth in 1892. Though a frail boy and always a sufferer from ailments, he was the life of the place in many ways, full of old family and Dartmouth traditions, the more roughhouse the merrier. . . . My escapades were always his escapades. We sat up all night carrying on and saying good-bye to each other the night before I ran away. He was the only person I said good-bye to when I ran away. . . . He never missed the chance to take part with his fists in the savage rushes (so-called) of those wild days. I liked them and he liked them. Our high old talks about religion, politics, and history were almost as turbulent. These are fond memories.

The "wooding up" of unpopular professors—a sort of foot-pounding on old floor boards till a great dust arose in the classroom and the teacher fled—and the "salting down" of freshmen with rock salt were all in the collegiate day's work. Frost recalls one occasion, a battle royal following one of the weekly Rhetoricals for seniors, when the Acting President

27

himself had to run out of the chapel to escape the oncoming battle of flying cushions, wooden stools, and clouds of salt-laden dust.

The best psychological reference for this type of rebellion would seem to be the stiff puritanical curriculum and directives for Dartmouth freshmen in 1892: attendance at sixteen exercises of prescribed studies a week, daily college prayers, and public worship on Sunday forenoon.

Robert Frost in talking with me recalled taking only Latin, Greek, Mathematics.

No, I can't remember any English—except maybe when the professor we called "Clothespin" Richardson encouraged us to read

"Where music and moonlight and feeling are one."

Shelley, isn't it? I liked that. I liked discovering on my own Palgrave's *Golden Treasury*. [He bought a paper copy at a bookstore.]

This last, as Frost has often said, was one of the two most crucial experiences of a literary and poetic kind in his student life. And he told me of the other:

I happened into the old library, and found on the magazine rack a copy of the *Independent*, with a poem on the front page. It was a sort of threnody called "Seaward," by Richard Hovey, a friend of Bliss Carman and a celebrated Dartmouth graduate. The subject was the death of Thomas William Parsons, translator of Dante's *Inferno*, friend of Longfellow.

This experience [Frost told me] gave me my very first revelation that a publication existed, anywhere in my native land, that was a vehicle for the publication of poetry. There was even an editorial about this poem, which I read with rapt amaze. So when later I had a poem, "My Butterfly," I of course sent it to the *Independent*.

Dartmouth's Baker Library still has the copy of the *Independent* that gave Robert Lee Frost his determinant: Number

2294, November 17, 1892. So we may assume that it was about that time that poetic ideas and half-unconscious hopes and purposes began to germinate and sprout in the proud, hobbledehoy lad whose poetry was to become an American classic in his lifetime.

In an interview with E. C. Lathem, Assistant Librarian of Dartmouth's Baker Library ["Freshman Days" published in the *Dartmouth Alumni Magazine,* March, 1959], Robert Frost elaborated:

Somebody talks about rededication and dedication, and nobody really dedicates himself till long afterward. He doesn't dedicate himself, he gets dedicated. He finds himself deep in something and long before he's aware of committing himself. And he's never aware of his taking his life in his hands to go forward to do something or do or die, you know, unless it's to battle or something.

I didn't think anything like that. I just had it coming on me. I can't tell how it came, this wish to have something: write things and get them printed.

What were the immediate signs of genius? An aversion to routine and a trend to nonchalance and reverie. Rob fell more and more into long walks, night and day walks in the fine woods and hills that surround Hanover. Night walks were never scary to him—it was in a house that he felt afraid sometimes. His unsocial way puzzled the Theta Delts, and he was finally visited by a delegation of wags who asked what he did in the woods—*all alone.*

"I gnaw wood," was his reply.

The records of the dean's office show he did not take his term examinations. He left without notice to the dean or good-by.

I was glad to seize the excuse (to myself) that my mother needed me in her school, to take care of some big, brutal boys she could not manage.

That wasn't the real reason [R.F. added]. I had decided I was up to no good at Dartmouth, so I just went home to Methuen. I did take hold of my mother's school, bought some rattans and caned those unruly boys good and plenty. . . . Then I took a job on electric lights in the mill. . . . I'd spent just about a term at college.

My mother did not reproach me. She believed in any honest work.

But that I should so treat a grandfather—one who had sincerely offered a college education to a promising valedictorian—put me out of all repute in Lawrence. A cloud of puzzlement hung over me as an obstinate, indecisive young fool.

The poem "Bereft," published in the *New Republic* as late as 1927 and collected in *West-Running Brook* in 1928, bears Frost's note "As of about 1893." This does not mean, R.F. says, that it was written in 1893, when he decamped from Dartmouth, but that it was based on memories of that year. Certainly it might be taken as close to the temper of the college student who hadn't made a go of things or fitted into the ideas of his elders.

BEREFT

Where had I heard this wind before
Change like this to a deeper roar?
What would it take my standing there for,
Holding open a restive door,
Looking down hill to a frothy shore?
Summer was past and day was past.
Somber clouds in the west were massed.
Out in the porch's sagging floor,
Leaves got up in a coil and hissed,
Blindly struck at my knee and missed.
Something sinister in the tone
Told me my secret must be known:
Word I was in the house alone
Somehow must have gotten abroad,
Word I was in my life alone,
Word I had no one left but God.

Where had he heard that wind before? Certainly it is the same portentous wind of doom and darkness he heard as he wrote his first high-school poem and immortalized in "Once by the Pacific." R.F. says that this last poem was actually written at Dartmouth, as a fragment. "Some of the final lines are a survival." E. C. Lathem has identified them:

> The clouds were low and hairy in the skies,
> Like locks thrown forward in the gleam of eyes.

"Once by the Pacific" is, however, an entirely different poem [he told Lathem] except for a couple of remembered lines. (I do *that* sometimes: I steal a couplet out of something that I throw away.) And I managed to do it, I always fancy, so you wouldn't know there was any joint in it, you know; it comes in so natural. . . .

[Another that seems to date back to his Dartmouth period is, Mr. Frost is quoted as saying,] one of the first *North of Boston* things, now preserved at the Huntington Library in California. It's an attempt to do "The Black Cottage" in rhymed verse. I gave it up and then [later] suddenly wrote it. . . .

About the same time [R.F. told me] I wrote another fragment that never came to be a poem. This shows I was still, at Dartmouth, a Californian at heart. I still thought the future of the world lay out there:

> Europe might sink and the wave of her sinking sweep
> And spend itself on our shore and we would not weep
> Our cities would not even turn in their sleep.
> Our faces are not that way or should not be
> Our future is in the West on the other Sea—

One complete and truly final poem, printed for the first time in *A Boy's Will* in 1913 but presented to his Harvard English A course in 1897, had its first fragile, germinal roots at Dartmouth, though it was not written till some time later. It is, in mood, the direct opposite of "Bereft." The two together seem to reveal the essential duality of Robert Frost, the artist, of which he became fully aware only in his slow-coming maturity. They tell far more about him than this adolescent at the time knew of himself.

In "Bereft," the poet is rebelliously fighting the dark side of life and of his own nature, the loneliness and even hate he must meet to find himself. He is awed by what he must work out with God. In "Now Close the Windows," given below, he has blessedly discovered that the solitude within his own nature in its very exclusions, even from bird songs, can be serene, positive, fecund and joyous in its creativity of the spirit:

NOW CLOSE THE WINDOWS

Now close the windows and hush all the fields:
 If the trees must, let them silently toss;
No bird is singing now, and if there is,
 Be it my loss.

It will be long ere the marshes resume,
 It will be long ere the earliest bird:
So close the windows and not hear the wind,
 But see all wind-stirred.

CHAPTER 3

BOND AND FREE

1893–1900

Love has earth to which she clings
With hills and circling arms about—
Wall within wall to shut fear out.
But Thought has need of no such things,
For Thought has a pair of dauntless wings. . . .

Within a year of his retreat from Dartmouth in 1893, Rob
Frost wrote and published a poem, "My Butterfly" (1894),
and in another year, fulfilled his early, star-crossed love in
marriage. This swift overcoming of mighty obstacles sprang
surely from his overwhelming psychic need and from the
roots of personality and individual genius. A shy, lonely,
vague boy, with no worldly resources, no conscious sense of
destiny, his latent force helped him to find his own way against
the world's convictions.

Close as R.F.'s mother was, she did not, R.F. says, awaken
to the implications of his poetry writing. Elinor White was
away at college. In the eyes of paternal relatives and ex-school-
fellows, Rob the brilliant valedictorian, rejecting college, re-
fusing his grandfather's offers to set him up in business, doing
elementary teaching and minor mill jobs, was turning drifter
and ne'er-do-well.

Let that pass, he thought. His "laziness" was proverbial,
even with himself, but he had a hunch that it meant some-

thing. He was bound to "pursue his own headstrong folly without interference."

During the summer of 1893 Rob's strong-minded grandmother died. His teaching over, he had some summer time with Elinor, who had completed her freshman year at St. Lawrence as a first-class student. She was a beauty, too, and a dear friend. When she went back for her sophomore year, Frost has told me, he began to work as a light fixer in the dynamo room of the Arlington mill, half way between Methuen, where his mother had taken another school, and Lawrence.

His business at the mill was to keep a sharp eye on the arc lights to replace the carbon they fast consumed. For this, the agile youth shinnied up tall ladders and fitted himself into perilous angles, peering down through the machines and belts to quip with his fellow workers. When the day was bright and the lights were out of use, he still climbed up there to a private hideout under the great belts, with a pocket Shakespeare that he read constantly for pleasure. An old Lawrence friend and contemporary, "Ed" Gilbert, then a fellow worker, recalled for me once during a reminiscent talk on the telephone his Shakespearean intervals with Robert Frost during the night shift. With a second copy borrowed from an office shelf, he and Rob would read the great plays together, he said, breaking off into the deep confidences of subjective youth, sometimes expressed in Shakespearean diction.

Against this background a youth of nineteen, still working in a mill, wrote "My Butterfly. An Elegy," his first poem to reach professional publication.

"I wrote it," R.F. told me, "all in one go in the kitchen of our house in Tremont Street. I locked the door and all the time I was working, Jeanie my sister tried to batter it down and get in."

Even as he wrote it he had "sensed in a way that something was happening. It was like cutting along a nerve." He read me the first two stanzas to illustrate:

34

MY BUTTERFLY

Thine emulous fond flowers are dead, too,
And the daft sun-assaulter, he
That frighted thee so oft, is fled or dead:
Save only me
(Nor is it sad to thee!)
Save only me
There is none left to mourn thee in the fields.

The gray grass is scarce dappled with the snow;
Its two banks have not shut upon the river;
But it is long ago—
It seems forever—
Since first I saw thee glance,
With all thy dazzling other ones,
In airy dalliance,
Precipitate in love,
Tossed, tangled, whirled and whirled above,
Like a limp rose-wreath in a fairy dance.

The first stanza—well, that's nothing. But the second—it's as good as anything I've ever written. It was the beginning of *me*.

"Its two banks have not shut upon the river;"

I got something there, and I knew it. But especially the last figure:

"Like a limp rose-wreath in a fairy dance."

That's like a blush. Never thought of that before. Poetry is like a cry, I've said. But it's like a blush—you can get something you didn't know you had.

Frost has said that the manner of a poet's germination is like that of a waterspout at sea. He has to begin as a cloud of all the other poets he ever read.

That statement applies in some respects to "My Butterfly"; yet Robert Frost has retained the poem in his *Complete Poems*

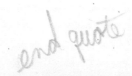

not just because it was his first published poem but because it came to him as a series of revelations, and in a classic form, the ode. This form he has used inventively in poems of maturity, like "Storm Fear" and "After Apple-Picking." It was, in part, because it was an ode, R.F. thinks, that it was accepted by William Hayes Ward, the editor of the *Independent*, who (wrongly) inferred that the unknown contributor was under the influence of Sidney Lanier.

The Huntington Library, which bought the files of the *Independent* from Herbert Hayes Ward (the son of William and husband of Elizabeth Stuart Phelps), has six letters from Robert Frost to his first editors, written from Lawrence and Boston in this fateful year 1894. They reveal some remarkable aspects of the mind of a poetic youth, half dreamy and adolescent, half on fire, and sustained most of all by its flashing insights. Obviously the letter that follows, with its curious Thoreauvian ring, had had a predecessor but this is the first in the collection:

Lawrence Mass., March 28. [1894]

Editor of The Independant.

Dear Sir:

The memory of your note will be a fresh pleasure to me when I waken for a good many mornings to come; which may as well confirm you in the belief that I am still young. I am. The poem you have is the first of mine that any publication has accepted. At about the same time however, that I sent you this, I disposed of three others in a similar way in other quarters. As yet they are not returned. As for submitting more of my work, you may imagine I shall be only too glad to avail myself of your kindly interest. Nevertheless since I have but recently discovered my powers, I have, of course, no great amount of verses in store and furthermore, being still inexperienced of myself, I cannot easily tell when I will have. But I shall not forget my obligations.

If you mean what might be called the legitimate education I have recieved when you speak of "training" and "line of study," I hope that the quality of my poem would seem to account for far more of this than I have really had. I am only graduated of a public high-school. Besides this, awhile ago I was at Dartmouth College for a few months until recalled by necessity. But the inflexible ambition trains us best, and to love poetry is to study it. Specifically speaking, the few rules I know in this art are my own afterthoughts, or else directly formulated from the masterpieces I reread.

I sincerely hope I have done nothing to make you overestimate me. It cannot be, though, for rather than equal what I have written and be satisfied, I will idle away an age accumulating a greater inspiration.

There is no objection to using my name with the poem.

Yours

Robert Lee Frost
Tremont St.,
Lawrence, Mass.

Lifelong characteristics of R.F. here emerge: humor with a Puritan twist; he won't consent to be overestimated; "inflexible" determination to go his own way and take his own time about it; "afterthoughts" as in his high-school valedictory. Doesn't his whole body of poetry derive from afterthoughts about concrete observations of nature and man's nature? Or from intensive, subjective sensual-sensuous experience scarce realized at the time, like his impassioned participation in the airy love life of the butterflies?

Another thing that emerges from the first letter is that the editors of the *Independent*, Dr. Ward and his sister and assistant, Miss Susan Hayes Ward, were asking searching questions with a view to the moral and intellectual improvement of the rebellious Rob. The young poet felt awe before the culture of a brother and sister versed in Sanscrit and the classics, descended from a Congregational clergyman of Plymouth, New Hampshire, and a Hayes of South Berwick, Maine—north-of-Boston to their roots. The rebel, however, felt his spine stiffen when Dr. Ward exhorted him like a grandfather to get more education, to go back to Dartmouth. He did not need another grandfather. But he did need the *Independent* and he needed Miss Susan Ward, a robust spinster with a warm heart and fine mind, who wrote him comments on the poems he sent in and provided a wise and human intellectual influence at a time when he was badly in want of critical advice and recognition.

"Learn to spell the name of our magazine," they told him, and the poetling "Who koulde songes make and wel endite" tried to laugh, and improved his spelling. His eyes must be sharper to the physical shape of words. Young Frost's ears never failed him. He heard in his mind's ear every word of a poem he wrote.

It is known that sometime in the spring of this year 1894, R.F. gave up the mill work suddenly, as if under a new star, and found himself another elementary teaching job. As I heard the story, the youngster had arrived late, after the noon hour, and finding the mill doors closed, shouted:

"You can't do this to *me!*" and went off.

A poem first printed in 1933 as a Borzoi *Chap Book,* then published in *A Further Range* in 1936, seems autobiographical. An excerpt from "A Lone Striker" is given below. The worker arrives tardily at the factory and is locked out for half an hour, "his pittance docked," "rebuked and unemployed."

> And yet he thought he saw the scene:
> The air was full of dust and wool.
> A thousand yarns were under pull,
> But pull so slow, with such a twist,
> All day from spool to lesser spool,
> It seldom overtaxed their strength;
> They safely grew in slender length.
> And if one broke by any chance,
> The spinner saw it at a glance.
> The spinner still was there to spin. . . .
>
> He knew another place, a wood,
> And in it, tall as trees, were cliffs;
> And if he stood on one of these,

'Twould be among the tops of trees,
Their upper branches round him wreathing,
Their breathing mingled with his breathing.
If—if he stood! Enough of ifs!
He knew a path that wanted walking;
He knew a spring that wanted drinking;
A thought that wanted further thinking;
A love that wanted re-renewing.
Nor was that just a way of talking
To save him the expense of doing.
With him it boded action, deed. . . .

I hazard a guess that the next letter to Miss Ward came after the "deed." The faulty spelling persists.

Lawrence Mass., Apr. 22, 1894

Dear Miss Ward,

It is just such a letter as you wrote me that I have been awaiting for two years. Hitherto all the praise I have recieved has been ill-advised and unintelligent; all the criticism, this general one upon the rueful fact that I, once the friend of so and so, should have at last turned poetaster. So that something definite and discriminating is very welcome. My thanks unlimited! Yet this consideration is hardly due me. Take my word for it that poem exaggerates my ability. You must spare my feelings when you come to read these others, for I haven't the courage to be a disappointment to anyone. Do not think this artifice or excess of modesty, though, for, to betray myself utterly, such an one am I that even in my failures I find all the promise I require to justify the astonishing magnitude of my ambition.

You ask to know more of me. This is certainly very tempting. It might well throw one into a talking trance which nothing could dispell but a reversal of the charm. . . .

When I am well I read a great deal and like a nearsighted person follow the text closely. I read novels in the hope of strengthening my executive faculties. The Polish triology "With Fire and Sword," "The Deluge" and "Pan Michael" are engaging me at present. Thomas Hardy has taught me the good use of a few words and, refering still to me, "struck the simple solemn." And as opposed to this man, Scott and Stevenson inspire me, by their prose, with the thought that we Scotchmen are bound to be romanticists—poets. Then as for poems my favorites are and have been these; Keats' "Hyperion," Shelley's "Prometheus," Tenneson's "Morte D'Arthur," and Browning's "Saul"—all of them about the giants. Besides these I am fond of the whole collection of Palgrave's. So far everything looks auspicious. But it is necessary to admit that I teach "orthography" in a district school: . . . so wholly uncongenial is the work that it has become for me a mere test of physical endurance. For several weeks now when not teaching I have spent my time lying around either conciously sleeping or unconciously waking and in both cases irresponsibly iratable to the last degree. It is due to my nerves—they are so susceptible to sound. Consequently the prospect is not bright— for the immediate future at least. When in this condition I can neither read nor write: nevertheless I find a few hours for study and, as I say, I always entertain great hopes. . . .

Yours by right of discovery

R. L. Frost.

Teaching was clearly a noble profession to Miss Susan, who regarded the naïve confession of boredom and superiority as deserving of censure. That a young man of twenty should lie around! That his ears should wince! In the interval she has spoken her mind.

Lawrence Mass. June 10 1894

Dear Miss Ward,

It is clear this letter must be in the nature of a defence. Since last I wrote I hope I have aged enough not to seem so callow and distasteful as I used: at any rate I have been thoroughly overhauled in search of affectations.

Yet even as I am, my inclination would be to give thanks immoderately for that volume of Lanier's poems. As you expected I have been very much interested in the memorial; and I have been enthused over what I conceive to be Lanier's theories of art. I wish I had the Elizabethan knack of expressing gratitude.

Will you allow me to correct several wrong impressions I seem to have given you? My pride sees nothing degrading in teaching.

40

We provincials affect Bohemianism—experience, give us experience! I have sold newspapers "on the streets of" San Francisco and worked in the mills and on the farms of New England. My pride is peculiar.

And my friends! how have I betrayed my friends! True, they have not encouraged me much as a poet: but if I were so accomplished as to be able to improvise a few heroic metres for them by the campfire next summer, be sure they would appreciate me. Written poetry is rather ineffectual after all, unless artists are the readers of it.

It has been painful for me trying to induce a passion like the one that is the spirit of my poem. I am afraid I cannot revise the thing. I am greatly dissatisfied with it now. Do you not think it would be well to suppress it. If I am not overworked this summer I promise to write you something better by far. Nevertheless I have cancelled one line, altered two, and now the whole is at your disposal. . . .

Really

Robert L. Frost

His doubts of his poem must have been ignored, as indicated in his next letter, still preceding the publication of "My Butterfly."

Boston Mass. Aug 22, '94

Dear Miss Ward;

Surely you have not recieved my last letter. I shall be sorry if it is too late to arrange to meet you. Write to me at least.

For I percieve that my childishness in regard to poem (said poem) may have become wearisome. It is very trying to be noticed, you know. But give me another chance: I may have disqualified myself for a political career by one foolish act but I cannot have for a literary one: all the cannonized afford me consolation.

I am learning to spell.

I am writing better poetry.

It is only a matter of time now when I shall throw off the mask and declare for literateur mean it poverty or riches.

You are amid real poetry, I presume; and I can imagine that a conventional verse or stanza and the familiar see-saw of phrases in antithesis, would distemper you.

Sincerely

Robert L. Frost.

Boston, Mass.
35 Cambridge St.

Elinor again went off to St. Lawrence, for her junior year, thinking poorly of him.

In Elinor's second year at St. Lawrence College I had seen very little of her [Frost explained in 1957]. In the summer of 1894 she took a job with a composer in Boston. Then she came home but when I called on her she did not want me to come in —the president of her college was there. He thought I was a fool! I must have looked awful to Elinor. I looked worse than unpromising—everybody was broken up by the way I *looked*. I had no sense of being defiant—I just went this vague way. . . .

As a result of that evening I quit—I was persuaded at last that Elinor did not love me. I went off to Boston for a day and was really convinced. Since then I have never believed that life would turn out right. I still today feel I could lose everything and not be surprised.

I came back to Lawrence to find that my mother was having a religious meeting in her schoolroom, as she often did. I stopped in and sat down in a back seat. Fifteen or twenty people were there. Mother called out to me, put in my hand a letter from Elinor, calling me back. She went through college in three years and then you wonder what settles these things. . . .

He for his part was tossing off his little jobs as a juggler plays with balls—like a fellow who didn't even *want* to amount to something, even though trying to sell a Shakespeare Reader.

The young fellow said to himself he couldn't blame them or argue them out of their worries. But he had to "show" them, somehow, especially his girl. So he went to a job printer in Lawrence, to engage the printing at his own expense of his first book.

Twilight, it was called. There were but two copies, one for

42

the beloved, one for self (the type being then distributed). The book had covers of pebbled leather and pages of fine linen paper. It contained five poems, "My Butterfly" and four others that have not been preserved in the *Complete Poems:* "Twilight," "Summering," "The Falls," and "An Unhistoric Spot." *

Thoroughly fixed in his purpose, jubilant, for he was celebrating his first real demonstration that inner hope and outer fate could match up, Robert started off in a fine October glow for Elinor's college. But his young lady was in offish mood, surely thinking of another lad, and under the spell of professors who, like the president of St. Lawrence, preferred to laugh at a mill-hand poet. The poems were read aloud and scorned around the halls of learning.

The rebuff, for rebuff it was, struck to the poet's innermost heart. Bleeding and betrayed, he tore up his own copy of his first opus, and "ran away," "out of time," out of his head almost, into unknown country—not north to the familiar White Mountains but south, south, south. Look at the handsome fellow, scalded by denial of worth, breaking his way through the azaleas and dogwoods of that hilly country, lashing his blazing blue eyes full of tears from the twigs and blossoms, doing minor jobs for bread, breaking his pride all the way.

While gone, nobody knew where, no address, no news (only in 1957 did we learn his whereabouts from his long poem "Kitty Hawk"), "My Butterfly. An Elegy" by Robert Lee Frost appeared November 8, 1894, conspicuously printed on the front page of the *Independent,* and was duly delivered in Lawrence. But the young poet was not there to receive it and gloat. He did this on his return in a letter dated from Lawrence, December 4, 1894.

Dear Miss Ward,—

Now that you have ceased expecting to is the time you hear from me. The occasion is, or was, the appearance in print under

* One copy of *Twilight* still exists, and one poem, "The Falls," has been reprinted by a collector.

your supervision of my first poem. I am going to thank you. Four weeks ago and until Friday last I was in Virginia, North Carolina, and Maryland, very literally and without address, so that I have not been aware of my own doings as expressed in the phrase I "published a poem." That is the point or points;—I thank you tardily because I for my part have been out of time a little while, and thank you because you and not I published a poem, a work that certainly requires qualities I lack. And the poem does look well—don't you think it does?

Before proceeding further I percieve I must assume an attitude or else endanger the coherency of my remarks, for my natural attitude is one of enthusiasm verging on egotism and thus I always confuse myself trying to be modest. It is my rule to be despondent to be dignified (or coherent) and I might be cynical for the same purpose, but really unless it be enthusiastically I am at a loss to know how to comfort myself on the present occasion. You see I am just returned from experiences so desperately absorbing that I am nothing morbid now and can enjoy the poem as freshly as if it were but lately written and I had not since wasted eight months in ineffectual aspiration.

Yes, I think sound is an element of poetry, one but for which imagination would become reason. I justify the use of dialect in this way; it contributes to the illusion (perhaps) and gives the artist the courage of his imaginings. Kipling says nearly all he says under the influence of sound. I am so fond of sound that I was wishing the other day he would write some more poetry. Listen to that!—when we generally read poetry because we are in the business and it is written.

I have one or two poems to send you when I find time to revise them.

Sincerely

Robert L. Frost.

And the poem does look well—don't you think it does? Evidently both the Wards were touched by that innocent query and eager for more backing for their protégé. Miss Ward arranged an exciting meeting at Boston's new North Station to deliver the fifteen-dollar check for "My Butterfly."

This was the first step toward what developed into a creative friendship. Dr. Ward who had, R.F. thinks, already invoked the approval of Bliss Carman, a poetry adviser to the *Independent*, wrote also for moral support to Maurice Thompson, another writer of the day—since forgotten as poet but remembered as the author of *Alice of Old Vincennes*. Thompson's letter of reply to Ward, which all moralistic advisers of young genius should think over, has survived:

Crawfordsville
Indiana

Dear Dr. Ward:

You asked me to look at the poem, "My Butterfly," in this week's paper, by Mr. Frost.

I am a trifle dizzy over the election, feel as if a hogshead of salt had rolled over me; but I am not stupid enough yet to fail to see the extreme beauty of that little ode. It gives me a pang to know that its author is poor. To be a poet and be poor is a terrible lot. What hope is there? I have felt the gag in my teeth whenever I wanted to sing—and I'm not much of a poet—a gag that can speak and say to me: "No! go grind for bread! Let the rich men like Tennyson and Swinburne and Lowell and Browning and Holmes do the singing; what right has a poor man to waste his time and breath with song?" But all the same were I a rich man that young Frost should not leave school "for financial reasons." Going back to the poem "My Butterfly," it has some secret of genius between the lines, an appeal to sympathy lying deep in one's sources of tenderness; and moreover its art is singular and biting, even where the faulty places are almost obtruded. My wife read it aloud to me the other evening when my eyes ached after too hard a day's work; and it made me ashamed that I could feel discouraged when I thought of the probable disappointment in store for young Frost all his life long. If I had a chance to say my say to him I should tell him to forget that he ever read a poem and to never pen another rhyme. . . .

Always sincerely yours

Maurice Thompson

10 November 1894

A little later when, with Christmas, Elinor White came back for vacation a heavy storm occurred, one that the human eye and ear have no instrument to record. This settled things once and for all time. Elinor returned for her last college term engaged to Rob, firmly, in the old-fashioned way. She had the certainty of graduating this, her third year.

What Robert had been doing was a bit of reporting on the Lawrence *Sentinel*. It did not suit him: too much "prying into the affairs of others." By March he was teaching again in a district school in Salem. This led up to a summer of tutoring boys. By fall, 1895, Rob's mother had opened a private school on Essex Street, Lawrence, a courageous attempt for personal expression. The engaged couple both taught there as her assistants.

One of the reticent love lyrics which appear scattered through the works of Frost, from youth to age—in which the beloved is evoked and characterized in terms of a gesture, a smile, a mood, or a tone of voice—seems to suggest the subtle atmosphere of committed-uncommittedness, half dream and half desire, of this year of waiting.

MEETING AND PASSING

As I went down the hill along the wall
There was a gate I had leaned at for the view
And had just turned from when I first saw you
As you came up the hill. We met. But all
We did that day was mingle great and small
Footprints in summer dust as if we drew
The figure of our being less than two
But more than one as yet. Your parasol
Pointed the decimal off with one deep thrust.
And all the time we talked you seemed to see
Something down there to smile at in the dust.
(Oh, it was without prejudice to me!)
Afterward I went past what you had passed
Before we met and you what I had passed.

But the decimal became a unit in late December, 1895, when Robert Frost and Elinor White were married. Their passionate shy union hoped for eternity and in fact lasted forty years.

R.F. recalls that he had in hand at this time in addition to "My Butterfly" six unpublished poems, some superior to the one chosen by William Hayes Ward for the *Independent*. According to a list made by Genevieve Taggard, these were: "The Flower Boat," "Now Close the Windows," "Waiting— Afield at Dusk," "Hannibal," "The Trial by Existence," and "Revelation."

"And, I think," added Frost, "'A Tuft of Flowers,' but maybe that was a few years later."

All Rob had to give Elinor when they married was himself, the young lover and husband, and himself the poet, who had something like a cold crystal, an otherness at the center of his being. The two, poet and lover, were not separable; Elinor knew this, married it, accepted it with all the deprivation, sorrow, joy, and pride such an endowment offers a wife.

On the material side, life continued denuded, vague, indeterminate, humbling, and baffling. But Elinor read every poem; that was her intimate joy. She asked no gifts from Mammon. Rob was hardly aware of her sacrifice. The only other woman he had known intimately was still fighting a hard battle for meager existence. He instinctively trusted a woman's strength and intelligence. Never had he had, up to this time, a penny of his own earnings.

"I did not miss it. Money was Mother's affair."

So the newly wedded pair, as 1896 began, lived with Mrs. Frost at her new private school, continuing their teaching and sharing in the common family purse. Mrs. Frost's assistant was her daughter Jeanie. The school was wholly a family undertaking.

An illuminating (unpublished) memoir-portrait by one of the pupils of this school who attended it for all the six years

47

of its peripatetic life, Clara Searle (Mrs. H. K. Painter of Minneapolis), recalls the young couple in their teaching roles:

Under Robert Frost himself I studied arithmetic. Two rooms across the center of the house formed the classroom. There must have been about twenty pupils. Above the fireplace was a blackboard, on which were written each day poems, short and long. Into notebooks we copied the poems and we learned them by heart. At one end of the room, a few chairs faced a desk backed by three long windows of a bay, and there our arithmetic class of four or five assembled. A door from the family dining room opened directly into this bay; our arithmetic was the first class of the morning, and as we sat and waited, the door finally opened and the blue-eyed young man seated himself casually at the desk. The aroma of toast still associates itself in my mind with arithmetic . . .

"I can't understand it, I can't, I can't!" I insisted stubbornly and with some heat.

"Yes, you can, Clara Searle, if you want to, but you have made up your mind that you won't see it," came back at me with some impatience and a great deal of truth.

Mrs. Robert Frost became my French teacher then, and the brown sparkle of her eyes, her gentleness and sweetness made the French lessons a joy . . . I have known and learned from many inspiring teachers . . . but the four who made that school are by themselves apart. Holding them together, holding the school together, calmly, quietly, with the light of humor in her eyes, stands that single, careless, spare figure, beloved of the little child.

The main figure, the "great teacher," Robert Frost's mother, is keenly and tenderly described in an earlier passage of the same memoir:

. . . Her frame was angular, rather loosely knit, the type of figure we associate in a man with Lincoln. Her face and head I still see, the large, broad brow of the thinker; the eyes deep-set, somewhat cavernous, blue, with a humorous, kindly twinkle; a large, generous mouth. The heavy graying hair was coiled at her neck, and always a stray lock detached itself. There were eye glasses that never stayed put. It was the day of shirt waists and skirts, whose union was supposed to be concealed by a belt, a belt that always had an urge to move from its prescribed location.

I had particular reason to remember her patience and understanding. . . . [Any difficulty] at school would be followed by a visit to my home [from the teacher]. I see, as clearly as when I peered through the front window, the gate open, the angular, black-clad figure, with the fat little dog, Keno, come leisurely up the walk.

"What's Clara been up to now?" was on my father's lips, and an uneasy conscience disturbed me. She came in pleasantly, sat quietly and casually in the rocking chair. It was always the same chair, and Keno always settled comfortably for a quiet nap. So great was her patience, her understanding . . . that the visit was a pleasure even to the repentant child. When the discussion was over, and I remember that I was a partner in it, she would smile affectionately at my urgency, take me in her lap and sing, in her low voice, the innumerable verses of "The Frog who would a-wooing go, Whether his mother would let him or no."

From this mother, who in her school treated every child as an individual, used no obvious discipline, gave rewards that introduced the child into the world of literature, Robert Frost must have drawn some of his own later powers and methods as a teacher. But elementary teaching was not really his calling and poetry was always getting at him from behind his back.

I didn't make the world [R.F. told me when discussing this period, in Vermont in 1949]. I didn't feel anybody owed me a job. I knew by now there would be lulls in poetry and then pick-ups. I had to proceed with my own headstrong folly without interference.

But I was a puzzle to everyone, I didn't know at all what I was up to. But I liked to write poems, I knew I could write a little poem, even when I had no sense of destiny or direction.

Evidence of Frost's inner conflict is visible in a letter to Miss Susan Hayes Ward, about a month after the wedding.

Dear Miss Ward,

Perhaps you had better not waite any longer. I have done my level best, in the time that has elapsed since last you heard from me, to make good my promise as a poet. But I fear I am not a poet, or but a very incomprehensible one.

The enclosed are an excuse for writing to you, nothing more. You will not find what you want in them, although it is not for me to say anything against them, who have learned to be thankful for little things.

Do not think but what I would have been glad to hear from you anytime these six months, but of course I could not expect to. Possibly I may now when you come to understand the good and sufficient reasons for my long silence.

Robert Lee Frost

Address: Central Bldg.

Another letter was sent just after the Fourth of July.

You are to hear from me now only because school is closed and I am quite rested having slept more or less soundly for a whole week night and day. Well I did what I tried to do so that the future is not so uncertain though it is not with success as it is with failure which is final, while success to a coward is only suspense, the most awful of tortures. . . .

I verily believe there is such a thing as not knowing whether you have opened your lips or not. Speech is a strange thing and however little thought preceeds it, it is still distinct from thought and the proof is that the one may be utterly at variance with the other and the thought be no less definite.

But to the point. If it is not too late I am anxious to avail myself of your kindness and publish one more poem before I die. . . .

The next may refer to "The Birds Do Thus," a poem printed in the *Independent* of August 20, 1896.

You were very considerate in the matter of the title. I presume the other poem as emended was not satisfactory. Will you let me know?

There are other things I would like to know. Write me if you are not too busy.

We are about to move down town again to open school. I am becoming dangerously interested in that concern, to the exclusion I fear of things more lofty. (DON'T BELIEVE HIM). . . .

But I must hear from you directly before I continue. I have lost touch with mankind and must approach the individual circumspectly.

Remember me to Miss Hetta please. Tell her that I am botanizing will I nill I. You make the laws and an enthusiast here is found to enforce them. I am overwhelmed with books on the subject. Mrs. W. S. Dana and I don't know who all!

Be sure to write.

R. L. Frost

Eliot, the Frosts' first child, was born a month after this letter (September 25, 1896). Rob did not inform Miss Ward till December and made the announcement casual:

Don't think because I haven't written I haven't once thought of you all this time. I have thought of you often and as often tried to write to you but in vain. It is just possible you do not understand this: all I can say is *I* do, though to no purpose. . . .

As nothing that happens matters much and as most of my thoughts are about myself I am always at a loss for likely subject matter. I am the father of a son if that is anything. . . .

"Caesar's Lost Transport Ships" appeared in the *Independent* for January 14, 1897. Frost did not preserve either this or "The Birds Do Thus" in his later collections. Elinor had given up her contribution to the school before Eliot's birth; Rob's continued through the spring of 1897.

But in the summer of that year the couple with their baby found an old house at Salisbury Point, and began to burn their brains as to "what next"? Rob knew he had to do something more decisive.

Now R.F. himself continues the story in the *Harvard Alumni Bulletin* for February 12, 1955:

"Along in 1897 (it must have been)," he remembered himself one day as a sedentary poet, reading Tacitus in the attic. "How was I going to earn a living? All of a sudden it occurred to me: Why couldn't I go to college and become a teacher?"

Possibly his poem "Warning," printed September 9, 1897, in the *Independent* emboldened him to write to Dean Briggs:

Lawrence Mass. Sept 11 [1897]

Dear Sir,

You are the one it seems for me to submit my case to if you will be so kind as to consider it. You will discover the propriety as I proceed.

I desire to enter Harvard this fall, if possible a candidate for a degree from the outset. It came to me as a surprise only the other day that I might reasonably hope to do so consequently I find myself somewhat unprepared for examination. This is the great difficulty I graduated from the Lawrence High School as many as five years ago (having in 1891 passed examinations for admission to Harvard occupying seven hours for which I hold a certificate.) It is true that since that time I have been teaching school and tutoring more or less in Latin Algebra and Geometry. Still my studies are all at loose ends. In particular I have neglected my Greek. If proficiency in English were any consideration, I make no doubt I could pass an examination in that. You will find verses of my inditing in the current number of the Independent and others better in back numbers. I might possibly pass in French also and in Physics and Astronomy for that matter but in Greek I fear not. You'll say it doesn't sound very encouraging.

Another embarrassing circumstance is the fact that once upon a time I left Dartmouth without having applied to the proper authorities of that paternalism for an honerable dismissal. I stood not upon the order of my going but went incontinently—for reasons I am free to explain. I assure you the matter will bear looking into.

This is the whole case not very clearly or succintly stated. The question is what will you advise me to do. Let me say that if I enter college it must be this year or never. It will be hard if a fellow of my age and general intelligence (!) must be debarred from an education for want of technical knowledge representing less than two months work. All I ask is to be admitted. I don't care how many conditions you encumber me with I will take the examinations if you say so, or I will enter as a special. I am anxious to hear from you soon. Rev. John Hayes of Salem or Rev. W. Wolcott of this city will answer questions with regard to me.

Respectfully

Robert L. Frost

Harvard's response was favorable, so the self-prepared examinations were obviously well passed. Rob's grandfather agreed to pay his tuition and his mother-in-law took a house in Boston to help out with their living problem. Rob's father-in-law did not "get on" with him; there was no affinity between them, but Rob always had the support and affection of Mrs. White.

So Robert Frost entered Harvard in the fall of 1897 as a freshman. His chosen college subjects were Latin and Greek and Philosophy and his professors in classics were F. C. Babbitt and Clifford H. Moore. In English A (which he tried to get out of), he was under Alfred D. Sheffield, brother-in-law of a younger poet who was to be a challenge in his maturity, T. S. Eliot.

The lanky Rob, with the long, moody, starry countenance, startled Sheffield when he handed in "Now Close the Windows."

"Did you write this for my class?"

"No." He had substituted his unpublished poem for a daily theme and perhaps mentioned others already in print.

"So we have published poetry, have we?" The tone did not please. Yet Sheffield was a man of parts and when, years later, he met his ex-student on the street, stopped and said:

"You have made a place for yourself. It is well-deserved."

What Rob Frost, the freshman, might have hoped for at Harvard, the recognition of a court of peers, could not come to him in a required freshman course. He did not do well in it. He was, in fact, too mature for English A and hated it.

Yet things as a whole went pretty well—"reasonably so,"

he told me. He got high marks in the classics, and received a Detur, coveted Harvard honor. He remembers two fellows who sat near him in his Latin class. At one end of the bench was a Negro student; at the other a Southerner, a future financier named Catchings. Robert and Catchings would sometimes go out to the country together and read Terence for pleasure.

On the whole, Rob did not want to know people at Harvard and attributes this to shyness. He was old for a freshman, he was married—unusual for freshmen or any other undergraduate in those days—and reserving himself for his individual life.

In the sophomore year, though I had won a big scholarship, nothing went well. I know now why—Harvard had taken me away from the question whether I could write or not. I did a little teaching in a North Cambridge public school the first year. The second, I kept leaving during the term to look after my mother's school in Lawrence, which soon came to an end. It just might have been a success [he said with the veiled look of pathos his eyes assume when discussing the forlorn hopes of the past].

A feeling of suspended animation came over me, [says the causerie in the *Harvard Alumni Bulletin*]. I was restless, and didn't seem to be liking things again.

I got very sick, terribly so [he told me], as if something were very wrong with heart or stomach. Trouble in the solar plexus. So I resigned from the sophomore class at the end of March, to the Dean's regret. The doctor thought I would die. He sent me home to die.

Before he left, his daughter Lesley was born in Boston on April 28, 1899.

For the second time Rob Frost had run away from a college, in an anticlimactic way and, in his words, "a spring-fever sort of puzzlement" possessed him. The young couple with two tiny children retired to raise chickens in Methuen, where Rob's mother had lived and where there were relatives. Wearing, no doubt, an air of abstraction, Rob mixed the mash and

54

gathered the eggs and wrung the necks of the pullets. Or did he?

That autumn, Robert's gallant mother became very ill with cancer, went to a sanitarium in Pennacook, New Hampshire. Then in July, 1900, his first-born, Eliot, died. Elinor's passionate maternal sorrow filled the house as with some darkness no man could understand.

Yet, being completely in the "earthly room" at this time, thrall to love and her fate as mother and wife, Elinor was the one who solved the puzzle of what to do about a living. Downing her pride, in her high Puritan way, she went to Rob's widowed Grandfather Frost. Would he buy them a farm? One they had found for themselves, only twelve miles from Lawrence, in West Derry, Rockingham County, New Hampshire. Thirty acres rather run down and poor, but with orchard, fields, pasture, woodland, and spring. A one-man, one-horse farm. It cost $1,800. If Rob could get well enough to farm and write poetry, he might achieve this in Derry.

"Shall I give you a year?" [My grandfather asked me about then]. "I know what you are up to" [he meant poetry]. "Will you settle down if I give you a year to try this out?"

I struck a great auctioneer's pose and dared him with:

"Give me twenty, give me twenty!"

And that [said R.F.] is just what it took.

CHAPTER 4

INTO MY OWN
1900–1912

INTO MINE OWN

One of my wishes is that those dark trees,
So old and firm they scarcely show the breeze,
Were not, as 'twere, the merest mask of gloom,
But stretched away unto the edge of doom.

I should not be withheld but that some day
Into their vastness I should steal away,
Fearless of ever finding open land,
Or highway where the slow wheel pours the sand.

I do not see why I should e'er turn back,
Or those should not set forth upon my track
To overtake me, who should miss me here
And long to know if still I held them dear.

They would not find me changed from him they knew—
Only more sure of all I thought was true.

This lonely and revealing poem published late in Robert Frost's life in Derry (the *New England Magazine,* May, 1909) suggests in metaphorical terms the meaning to a sensitive spirit of the self-chosen and almost compulsively isolated life. It is the poetic answer—the one Rob could not give to the Dartmouth boneheads as to what he was doing "alone in the woods."

Frost has told me that this poem represents his first desire to escape from something, his fear of something. As Willa Cather still harbored, while writing in New York, the irrational fear that she might die in a Nebraska cornfield, so Frost perhaps irrationally dreaded to be captured by the spinning mills of Lawrence or hauled back into living dependently under the tutelage of elder relatives.

I recall a conversation with him in the twenties about the word "escapist." He objected to the negative meaning. The point he said was: what are you escaping from? Possibly something that is strangling you. What are you escaping to? Possibly something you need and must have. He and Elinor were ready for a desert island when at the turn of the century in 1900 they settled on the Derry farm.

IN NEGLECT

They leave us so to the way we took,
  As two in whom they were proved mistaken,
That we sit sometimes in the wayside nook,
With mischievous, vagrant, seraphic look,
  And *try* if we cannot feel forsaken.

The scornful dare to fate stirred the springs of life and poetry. Friends and relatives in Lawrence, if they came at all, did so to protest that a brilliant mind was being buried in earth. They saw a bare cupboard and a halfhearted farmer who dreamed down the furrow—not the touching, flowing poems that were later to reveal how truly were the years of obscurity a matrix for the poet's long life and eventual great body of poetry.

That *A Boy's Will* would come of this farming venture, and *North of Boston* and *Mountain Interval* and parts of their successors, the bewildered man of twenty-six could not himself even guess, much less know. The starting point and the commitment were to the human life itself. Here, abandoning the provisional, he was tied to a concrete destiny, which became all the more fixed and final when his mother died in November, 1900, a month or so after their move to the farm. She was only fifty-six years old.

In sending Miss Susan Ward a copy of *A Boy's Will* from England, Frost wrote:

. . . a good book in spots, I don't need to tell you. The beauty of such things as Into Mine Own, My November Guest, Dream Pang, Mowing, and Reluctance is that they are not post-graduate work nor post-post-graduate work but the unforced expression of a life I was forced to live.

"I am the most unconscious thing," the old poet still exclaims. "I never know where I am while things are going on."

The facts of his day labor engrossed him. The gently rolling hills and winding valley contours of Derry made him happy. The farmhouse had no modern conveniences, but its average, modest, pleasant familiarity—the usual bay-window front, typical side porch, and ell running back to the barn were New England to the core and could accommodate a real family which, almost as quickly as a "real" farmer's, had four children.

Very different, certainly, the farmhouse was from the "Ghost House," the "vanished abode," where the poet says he used to dwell with "mute folk" who shared the "unlit" place with him. The ghost house had a "cellar in which the daylight falls" and stood

> On that disused and forgotten road
> That has no dust-bath now for the toad.
> Night comes; the black bats tumble and dart;

Yet they sometimes took drives on forgotten Derry roads that had forgotten farms. Frost recalls one they came on, early in their Derry life, with a black "tarn" beside it (for convenient suicide) and what a pang it cost the poet not to have chosen it! Their actual human house overlooked from a rise a traveled road, once the famous coach road from Concord, New Hampshire, to Boston, forty-two miles to the south. Passing farmers, jogging by in their wagons, could look up and see a child or two under the apple trees or, by night and into the small hours, a warm glow from the kitchen windows that roused speculation. A stone wall to the east separated Frost's domain from his French Canadian neighbor's.

> My apple trees will never get across
> And eat the cones under his pines, I tell him.

Farmer Frost knew he had to keep Poet Frost going somehow. Their agreement was delicately fraternal. The cow was milked at one P.M. and midnight, to give the Poet the halcyon nocturnal hours when most farm men slept heavily to rise early. This was deliberate, and had its lifelong price and effect.

After the last chore as the house, hushed now, became his thought and dream domain, Rob sat by the kerosene lamp to read his Shakespeare or his Virgil's *Eclogues*. Maybe something was written down in a handy five-cent copybook in which he created "by the year," not by the day or month. No impatience. Just a quiet creative gloom, such as you find in "Into My Own" where the vastness of the woodland seems to approximate the inner unconscious mind of the speaker. If the mood grew adverse, why out into the night to wrestle with it in a tempestuous walk; or just to smell the spicy spruce or the new-mown hay before blowing out the flame of the lamp, climbing up to bed.

> "A boy's will is the wind's will,
> And the thoughts of youth are long, long thoughts."

Robert Frost's *A Boy's Will*, published first in England in 1913, is no literal or even symbolic autobiography of his last adolescent years and his first years of marriage in Derry. Yet the subject-speaker, the "I" of the lyrics, a young man under a spell, has a clear and sensitive identity. The prose gloss—dropped in later editions and in the *Complete Poems*—is a sort of permission or even invitation to confuse the hero with the author. In any case the poems enlarge and give a warm glow to the hard facts of the human story.

The book has appealing self-portraits. Take the one in the last part of "To the Thawing Wind":

> Burst into my narrow stall;
> Swing the picture on the wall;
> Run the rattling pages o'er;
> Scatter poems on the floor;
> Turn the poet out of door.

Or again, the last stanza of "The Vantage Point"—a poem that, in an early version called "Choice of Society," was enclosed in a letter to Miss Ward in August, 1907. Here the early riser at dawn, instead of hastening to his cornfield, has sought a slope where "the cattle keep the lawn" and reclines amid "lolling" juniper to view far off the homes and the graves of men.

> And if by noon I have too much of these,
> I have but to turn on my arm, and lo,
> The sun-burned hillside sets my face aglow,
> My breathing shakes the bluet like a breeze,
> I smell the earth, I smell the bruisèd plant,
> I look into the crater of the ant.

"Gloats, I say," he wrote in my book beside the last lines. At this time poetry is gloating and not skeptical social criticism as in the late ant poem, "Departmental," written in the middle thirties.

The not quite artless, bareheaded blue-eyed young man with the wind-tossed hair, described only by association or reminiscence on the reader's part—recall, for instance, the youth we met in "The Quest of the Orchis"—can be discerned, as he grows older, in a whole series of lyrics. If he strides to the village to get some meager groceries for Elinor, his mind is on the "Rose Pogonias" in the high meadow, on the "desolate deserted trees" of November, or the ferny roadsides of August. He must cross West-Running Brook along which the first Scotch-Irish settlers of Derry grew and washed the flax they spun into linen for General Washington's army; and, hard by, stare at an old black cottage to which was also attached in due course an historical American story. Both the cottage and the brook had the makings of very fine later poetry.

This young man's sensuous perception of the seasons and all their fruits and moods singles him out. His love—he is now married—shall have for bird

> The meteor that thrusts in with needle bill.

or, as the apple orchards bloom, the bees

> The swarm dilating round the perfect trees.

Stars, winds, rains, snows, all to bring home to his dearest or to call her forth:

> And it seems like the time when after doubt
> Our love came back amain.
> Oh, come forth into the storm and rout
> And be my love in the rain.

The reader knows a little more about him than about her, the beloved "you," who is waiting at home. Yet we catch the wife, recognizably, in an enchanting, evasive poem:

GOING FOR WATER

> The well was dry beside the door,
>   And so we went with pail and can
> Across the fields behind the house
>   To seek the brook if still it ran;

Not loth to have excuse to go,
  Because the autumn eve was fair
(Though chill), because the fields were ours,
  And by the brook our woods were there. . . .

Each laid on other a staying hand
  To listen ere we dared to look,
And in the hush we joined to make
  We heard, we knew we heard the brook

A note as from a single place,
  A slender, tinkling fall that made
Now drops that floated on the pool
  Like pearls, and now a silver blade.

Here again "poetry is gloating."

"You have to be secretive to secrete anything," Frost sometimes says. The beloved is fully described nowhere. It is her
feeling aura that we apprehend in his verse. The love lyrics
and ballads suggest her tender dependence and trust, and the
young husband's heart-torn uncertainty as to how far he can
shield her innocence from the intrusion of life's dark ways.

LOVE AND A QUESTION

A Stranger came to the door at eve,
  And he spoke the bridegroom fair.
He bore a green-white stick in his hand,
  And, for all burden, care.
He asked with the eyes more than the lips
  For a shelter for the night,
And he turned and looked at the road afar
  Without a window light.

The bridegroom came forth into the porch
  With "Let us look at the sky,
And question what of the night to be,
  Stranger, you and I."
The woodbine leaves littered the yard,
  The woodbine berries were blue,

Autumn, yes, winter was in the wind;
   "Stranger, I wish I knew."

Within, the bride in the dusk alone
   Bent over the open fire,
Her face rose-red with the glowing coal
   And the thought of the heart's desire.
The bridegroom looked at the weary road,
   Yet saw but her within,
And wished her heart in a case of gold
   And pinned with a silver pin.

The bridegroom thought it little to give
   A dole of bread, a purse,
A heartfelt prayer for the poor of God,
   Or for the rich a curse;
But whether or not a man was asked
   To mar the love of two
By harboring woe in the bridal house,
   The bridegroom wished he knew.

Does one need to know more about the young lovers and their thistledown happiness than "Flower-Gathering," with its double quatrains, tells between the lines?

FLOWER-GATHERING

I left you in the morning,
And in the morning glow,
You walked a way beside me
To make me sad to go.
Do you know me in the gloaming,
Gaunt and dusty gray with roaming?
Are you dumb because you know me not,
Or dumb because you know?

All for me? And not a question
For the faded flowers gay
That could take me from beside you
For the ages of a day?

They are yours, and be the measure
Of their worth for you to treasure,
The measure of the little while
That I've been long away.

These three lyrics have in them the magic identifications of early love, which the human race has cherished in its poetry since poetry began. But there is a poignant love sonnet in *A Boy's Will* in which the lovers have become separate beings again, and gaze at one another with dawning intuition of their differences.

A DREAM PANG

I had withdrawn in forest, and my song
Was swallowed up in leaves that blew alway;
And to the forest edge you came one day
(This was my dream) and looked and pondered long,
But did not enter, though the wish was strong:
You shook your pensive head as who should say,
"I dare not—too far in his footsteps stray—
He must seek me would he undo the wrong."

Not far, but near, I stood and saw it all
Behind low boughs the trees let down outside;
And the sweet pang it cost me not to call
And tell you that I saw does still abide.
But 'tis not true that thus I dwelt aloof,
For the wood wakes, and you are here for proof.

In addition to her childbearing, her slavery to domestic routine, her motherhood, her wifehood, Elinor Frost was her husband's Egeria and strove to live the woman's sheltering role of keeping him in touch with human feeling when under the spell of poetic frenzy or aloofness. This must have been hard at the moments when there were only potatoes in the cellar, or when the few poems Rob braced himself to send out to a few magazines, maybe once a year, returned with "Rejected" stamped in red on the tender poem itself. This happened to "Bond and Free," R.F. remembers, during this period. He kept the poem secret for many years thereafter.

For the first eight years in Derry, Rob Frost was not away once from home after eight in the evening. In all that time he and Elinor were not invited out for a single meal at a neighbor's. When they moved to the farm, he felt, he has told me, that he did not need or want "people." There were good people down the road, the Lowes and the Berrys and the Websters, ready and glad to "change works" with him, but he shunned them. A beautiful ode, which in form shows his growing liberation as a poet, reveals how a more human need first came to him.

STORM FEAR

When the wind works against us in the dark,
And pelts with snow
The lower chamber window on the east,
And whispers with a sort of stifled bark,
The beast,
"Come out! Come out!"—
It costs no inward struggle not to go,
Ah, no!
I count our strength,
Two and a child,
Those of us not asleep subdued to mark
How the cold creeps as the fire dies at length,—
How drifts are piled,
Dooryard and road ungraded,
Till even the comforting barn grows far away,
And my heart owns a doubt
Whether 'tis in us to arise with day
And save ourselves unaided.

That unexpected last word "unaided" has a tremor. Frost is scared. He must have the assurance that in danger, physical danger, somebody—some male of the species—will come to his help. So, after all, the neighbors in the clearings are real. He only thought he could ignore them.

A *Boy's Will* has still another poem that adumbrates the theme of fellowship with other men.

THE TUFT OF FLOWERS

I went to turn the grass once after one
Who mowed it in the dew before the sun.

The dew was gone that made his blade so keen
Before I came to view the leveled scene.

I looked for him behind an isle of trees;
I listened for his whetstone on the breeze.

But he had gone his way, the grass all mown,
And I must be, as he had been,—alone,

"As all must be," I said within my heart,
"Whether they work together or apart."

But as I said it, swift there passed me by
On noiseless wing a bewildered butterfly,

Seeking with memories grown dim o'er night
Some resting flower of yesterday's delight.

And once I marked his flight go round and round,
As where some flower lay withering on the ground.

And then he flew as far as eye could see,
And then on tremulous wing came back to me.

I thought of questions that have no reply,
And would have turned to toss the grass to dry;

But he turned first, and led my eye to look
At a tall tuft of flowers beside a brook,

A leaping tongue of bloom the scythe had spared
Beside a reedy brook the scythe had bared.

The mower in the dew had loved them thus,
By leaving them to flourish, not for us,

Nor yet to draw one thought of ours to him,
But from sheer morning gladness at the brim.

The butterfly and I had lit upon,
Nevertheless, a message from the dawn,

That made me hear the wakening birds around,
And hear his long scythe whispering to the ground,

And feel a spirit kindred to my own;
So that henceforth I worked no more alone;

But glad with him, I worked as with his aid,
And weary, sought at noon with him the shade;

And dreaming, as it were, held brotherly speech
With one whose thought I had not hoped to reach.

"Men work together," I told him from the heart,
"Whether they work together or apart."

Beside this poem in my *Selected Poems* Frost wrote:
"*A Boy's Will* told how I was scared away from life and
crept back to it through this poem. I was speaking literally."

So it was actually a poem, not a crop or an ear of corn at
the County Fair, that made Rob Frost known in Derry as a
man among men.

"Got me my first real job. I have never earned a cent except by and through verse. For my first twenty years of it
I earned a total of $200. Whole family owe their life to this
poem and they'd better believe it."

This succinct comment refers to a day, probably in the
spring of 1905, when Farmer Frost found the local grocer
assessing his old horse for the grocery bill. By this time he
had besides Lesley a son Carol, born in 1902; Irma, born in
1903; and Marjorie, new-born in March, 1905.

The year 1905 was an important one to him as poet because, besides an occasional lyric, he had discovered an entirely new vein in himself. In that year he wrote, he has told me, three long poems that dug deep into the mature human fate, and proved later in *North of Boston* to be among his most original contributions to American poetry: "The Black Cottage," "The Housekeeper," and "The Death of the Hired Man." Nobody saw them, for the poet-farmer did not send them out to editors, with the exception of "The Black Cottage"; that last in the innocent hope that "it might fit on Decoration Day."

"Virgil's *Eclogues* may have had something to do with them. Some poem I had heard of and never read [*Piers Plowman*] influenced me by what I imagined it to be."

The further Robert Frost went with the long dramatic, colloquial poems in blank verse, the less did farming like his mean subsistence for children or brain children. So the grocer posed a question he had to answer practically. Teaching was in his blood. An old school stood on the village hill—Pinkerton Academy, symbol of the undying intellectual hopes of New England farmers.

Robert Frost had now some friends among the superior Derry men: Charles Merriam, a minister, friend of his mentors the Wards; and John C. Chase, a businessman and thirty-third-degree Mason. Mr. Merriam, not quite incidentally, asked Robert Frost to read "The Tuft of Flowers" on a certain ladies' night at the Derry Village Men's Club. The young man, far too shy to get on his feet, handed it to his ministerial friend, who made the poem of fellowship very moving. The school teachers were there, including Miss Sylvia Clark, who has described the occasion in a Robert Frost issue of the New Hampshire *Troubadour*. Suddenly it was perceived by all that in the modest, queer, dreamy, aloof fellow who farmed rather ineffectively in West Derry they had someone they did not know they had, possibly the stuff of an English teacher.

It is believed that it was in the spring of 1906 that Robert Frost began to teach a little at the typical native institution of red brick with Romanesque-Gothic windows, central tower, and air of dignity and decorum. The Academy was a good two-mile walk from his farm. The poet thinks this first teaching was interrupted by pneumonia. But by fall the quondam farmer was enrolled as a regular part-time English teacher on the basis of $200 a year for two classes a week. A full-time position, which he did not desire, would have paid $1,000. After all, he wrote Miss Susan Ward on November 4, 1907, there were also the apple trees:

One of my apple trees, standing stock still and rooted, earns more money in a year than I can earn with all my locomotion and artistic detachment.

The core of the new job, to him, was that he had five free days at home. As he told Robert Chase:

"The only thing we had plenty of [at the farm] was time and seclusion. I couldn't have figured on what this life would give me in advance but it was right as a doctor's prescription."

From then on, for the rest of his days, like the majority of American males who have grown up to be earners at maturity or sooner, Frost lived in two worlds. In the light of his long life, as it developed, this discipline of teaching, in spite of the desperate emotional stresses it caused him at times, strengthened his human and poetic fate. Confronted with a fact—"not something that is going to be, something that *is*," he has defined a fact—he accepted its implications and effects.

In the playful little early poem "Revelation"—presented, Frost tells me, in English A at Harvard—he wrote:

> We make ourselves a place apart
>   Behind light words that tease and flout,
> But oh, the agitated heart
>   Till someone really find us out. . . .
>
> But so with all, from babes that play
>   At hide-and-seek to God afar,
> So all who hide too well away
>   Must speak and tell us where they are.

The prose gloss line for this poem in the Table of Contents of *A Boy's Will* is:

"He resolves to become intelligible, at least to himself, since there is no help else."

"The Trial by Existence," the poem that follows "Revelation" in the book is, according to the gloss, an effort to know what the subject thinks about the soul—and was published on October 2, 1906, in the *Independent*. I quote the first of nine stanzas, which might have been inspired by memories of the poet's first hero, his own father.

> Even the bravest that are slain
>   Shall not dissemble their surprise
> On waking to find valor reign,
>   Even as on earth, in paradise;
> And where they sought without the sword
>   Wide fields of asphodel fore'er,
> To find that the utmost reward
>   Of daring should be still to dare.

Apparently it had not occurred to Robert Frost, when he submitted the poem to the *Independent,* that the published poem would be read by his fellow teachers. He wrote Miss Ward in dismay:

West Derry N. H. Dec. 26. '06

My dear Miss Ward,

. . . I had just begun teaching at Pinkerton Academy when my poem about the heretofore turned up in the school library. Its effect was startling. From the moment of its appearance, all the teachers abruptly broke off all but the most diplomatic relations with me. Put to it for a reason, I thought at first that my poem had led them to question my orthodoxy (if not my sanity.) Then I thought that a flock of teachers would be more apt to loathe me for mispelling Derry than for grafting Schopenhauer upon Christianity. Mr. Merriam says that I was twice wrong. I had made myself unpopular by the simple act of neglecting to give Pinkerton the credit for harboring the poet that wrote the poem. It was too funny. But while it lasted and I was still guessing, I was rather miserable. . . .

Frost has told me that he felt none too secure in his job at first. The programs and ways of the Academy, to a son of Belle Moodie, were old-fashioned and formalistic, and Rob made no effort to conform. Moreover, he had no degrees, and he had no backers yet but Mr. Merriam and Mr. Chase.

Pinkerton teachers were expected to take turns at leading morning chapel. The very thought of doing this turned Rob Frost's knees to water. Besides, chapel was too early for his late-rising habits. So he just skipped it and found himself running at a clip up those high brick stairs to reach his first class on time.

In the classroom his original flavor and savor soon made him notable. He never assigned work, asked pupils to write out of their own ideas and lives, stressing "what was common to experience but uncommon to expression." His individual thoughts on the duties of an English teacher reversed the usual order. For the first duty was to self, the second to books, and only the third to students.

Frost has told me a Pinkerton classroom story which I have also heard related of his later teaching work at Amherst—possibly it happened twice. He had asked for some written work. But when he came in and found the big pile of themes on his desk, his native "orneriness" (or as he likes to put it "indolence") overtook him. These were his words:

"Anything here anyone wants to keep?"
They shook their heads "no." So I asked them again and they said "no" again.
"All right. If you don't value them enough to keep them, I don't value them enough to want to read them."
And I threw them all into the wastepaper basket.
"I'm no perfunctory reader of perfunctory writing."

This is an early example of R.F.'s method of "scaring a class so they want to find out what you've got to say." On the whole he was genial, kindly, friendly, informal with his classes. He aroused latent dramatic gifts at Pinkerton by giving and admirably directing *Macbeth* and several other Shakespeare plays. He took his Pinkerton boys on botanical and philosophical walks, sharing their interests like baseball and bears' dens, and even their personal problems. He joined them sometimes as pitcher or coach on the baseball team—at the risk of being "brushed off" for his thirty-odd years, and has remained an ardent baseball fan ever since.

He also asked his pupils questions about life, perhaps because he asked himself crucial questions and sometimes got poems in reply. "Pan with Us" gives the skeptical answer to what a new-world poet, in the early 1900s, thinks about art (his own). Pinkerton may have forced the young man to ask himself what he thought about science: here he got one of the most mature and subtle of the poems in *A Boy's Will*, "The Demiurge's Laugh." This poem is mentioned to Miss Susan Ward in a letter of October, 1906.

. . . I have been ambitious to get some of my larger thoughts into shape for you; but it seems they wont be driven—not at least by a sick man. There's one about the Demiurge's Laugh (good title) which if I can take it by surprise some day ought to be made to mean something. . . .

THE DEMIURGE'S LAUGH

It was far in the sameness of the wood;
  I was running with joy on the Demon's trail,
Though I knew what I hunted was no true god.
  It was just as the light was beginning to fail
That I suddenly heard—all I needed to hear:
It has lasted me many and many a year.

The sound was behind me instead of before,
  A sleepy sound, but mocking half,
As of one who utterly couldn't care.
  The Demon arose from his wallow to laugh,
Brushing the dirt from his eye as he went;
And well I knew what the Demon meant.

I shall not forget how his laugh rang out.
I felt as a fool to have been so caught,
And checked my steps to make pretense
It was something among the leaves I sought
(Though doubtful whether he stayed to see).
Thereafter I sat me against a tree.

This poem might have caused confusion among teachers and been less popular than the casual ephemeral verse called "A Number One Sundown: Written by Request" and dropped on Miss Sylvia Clark's desk. This sprightly and dignified old lady, in her eighties, who did the honors of Derry for me in 1954 and even took me to the former Frost farm—reluctantly, because it was then littered with junk and labeled "Frosty Acres"—has enjoyed her role of recalling the unknown years of one who, as she said, "would be heralded as one of the country's greatest poets before many years had elapsed." But when I ventured to ask her how her friend Robert Frost looked, back in 1906, she answered with octogenarian crispness:

"I don't particularly remember.

"He was at first to me one of several young men teachers at the Academy whom my mother would invite to lunch sometimes. . . . My father was the village doctor—always away on his rounds. Often at the Frosts' too—they were always getting sick. My mother had literary tastes—she was interested in the young men teachers."

Did Rob Frost, I wonder, ever suddenly let loose one of his brilliant, shimmering webs of poetic talk-thought at the doctor's wife's village symposium? Was she, like Susan Hayes Ward or Gertrude Stein, one of the older women who start young men's ideas moving? Miss Sylvia didn't divulge and when I asked her about Mrs. Robert Frost, she again answered crisply:

"I do not remember her clearly—a young woman with a lot of little children . . . she was never around; one didn't see her."

For good reason: lovely Elinor had no baby sitters or complaisant nearby relatives; she never could get away, not for a church fair or an absence of a single night. The four children, largely educated at home and on the *ABC* side by herself, were always underfoot. Lesley, first to go to school, was already nine when the parental decision to send her was made. A secret rivalry, which the children felt, hid beneath the situation. The farmer-teacher-poet must be primary with his wife; she must be first with the children; nor could Elinor set aside her grief. It stayed with her and cast her down.

"I understand it," said Lesley Frost Ballantine loyally. "To lose a child—dreadful; a mother *cannot* get over it."

Moreover, Elinor Frost bore and lost in four days a sixth child, Elinor Bettina, in the early summer of 1907, about a year after the birth of baby Marjorie. In Lesley's childish yet older daughter's private composition book, I caught a touching impression in poetry of a visit to an upper room where mother and new baby lay.

"Home Burial," perhaps the greatest of Frost's eclogues, is of course no literal picture of any one episode in Robert's and Elinor's marital history. They had lost Eliot, and their relatives had lost children. As a composite of the poet's broader experience, the poem reveals, in depth, how a pair of married lovers may be pulled apart by the shared hurt consciousness that a man and his wife can find no common ground on a stark peak of mutual loss.

HOME BURIAL

He saw her from the bottom of the stairs
Before she saw him. She was starting down,
Looking back over her shoulder at some fear.
She took a doubtful step and then undid it
To raise herself and look again. He spoke
Advancing toward her: "What is it you see
From up there always—for I want to know."
She turned and sank upon her skirts at that,
And her face changed from terrified to dull.

He said to gain time: "What is it you see,"
Mounting until she cowered under him.
"I will find out now—you must tell me, dear."
She, in her place, refused him any help
With the least stiffening of her neck and silence.
She let him look, sure that he wouldn't see,
Blind creature; and awhile he didn't see.
But at last he murmured, "Oh," and again, "Oh."

"What is it—what?" she said.

                              "Just that I see."

"You don't," she challenged. "Tell me what it is."

"The wonder is I didn't see at once.
I never noticed it from here before.
I must be wonted to it—that's the reason.
The little graveyard where my people are!
So small the window frames the whole of it.
Not so much larger than a bedroom, is it?
There are three stones of slate and one of marble,
Broad-shouldered little slabs there in the sunlight
On the sidehill. We haven't to mind *those*.
But I understand: it is not the stones,
But the child's mound—"

                    "Don't, don't, don't, don't," she cried.

She withdrew shrinking from beneath his arm
That rested on the bannister, and slid downstairs;
And turned on him with such a daunting look,
He said twice over before he knew himself:
"Can't a man speak of his own child he's lost?"

"Not you! Oh, where's my hat? Oh, I don't need it!
I must get out of here. I must get air.
I don't know rightly whether any man can."

"Amy! Don't go to someone else this time.
Listen to me. I won't come down the stairs."

He sat and fixed his chin between his fists.
"There's something I should like to ask you, dear."

"You don't know how to ask it."

"Help me, then."

Her fingers moved the latch for all reply. . . .

A dog-eared five-cent copybook, now in the possession of an American collector and unpublished, has given me some quotations that follow, and some hints at what the writer Rob Frost was thinking, feeling, doing in the Derry years. There are no dates. The handwriting is smudged pencil. The children seem very much with him and he writes little realistic-fantastic stories about them or for them—not fairy stories but embryonic tall tales like his Michigan tall tale "Paul's Wife." He notes a queer name, Toffile—a French-Canadian corruption of Theophile, that he gave later to the husband of "The Witch of Coös." R.F. also set down occasional insights such as he tosses off in his public readings in old age.

I hate most the fellow who makes common stories of the plight of man.

He came out of the heavy mist and contemplated the terms and accepted them. They were as they are now: a little more pleasure than pain by actual count—the pleasure of being alive.

Thought advances like spilled water along dry ground. Stopping gathering, breaking out and running again.

The Ultimate Essay (Attempt) Metaphor. May not be far but is our farthest forth. Only accumulation of ages. Balance expected missed and compensated for.

We have a playful glimpse of Lesley in an early version of a poem called "The Message the Crow Gave Me for Lesley," later published in *Mountain Interval* in 1916 as

THE LAST WORD OF A BLUEBIRD
AS TOLD TO A CHILD

As I went out a Crow
In a low voice said, "Oh,
I was looking for you.
How do you do?
I just came to tell you
To tell Lesley (will you?)
That her little Bluebird
Wanted me to bring word
That the north wind last night
That made the stars bright
And made ice on the trough
Almost made him cough
His tail feathers off.
He just had to fly!
But he sent her Good-by,
And said to be good,
And wear her red hood,
And look for skunk tracks
In the snow with an ax—
And do everything!
And perhaps in the spring
He would come back and sing."

Lesley Frost Ballantine was seven when her father began
his teaching. From the age of five she had been encouraged—
it was the chief part of her education, she asserts—to write
daily in a composition book something she had observed or
experienced. Metaphor was explained, figures of speech were
praised, by Father himself.

The little girl did not, however, know that her father was
"a poet." Often he read the children poetry, sometimes a poem
of his own. Lesley might commit one to memory. But she did
not know Papa made it. How would one know? He had no
desk. He never told them.

"I played with them more than most fathers," the old poet
said a bit wistfully. "Spring flowers are so slow to come in

New England. One year I made some out of paper and put them down the roads on April Fool's Day. . . ."

"We never felt poor or deprived, or that we were dressed differently from others," Lesley stoutly declared. She noticed her own clothes first when she was ten and went to a child's birthday party.

"We made our own Christmas presents for our parents. They were always these books we wrote in. . . . They made our presents. . . ."

Mrs. George F. Whicher of Amherst has recalled a talk with Mrs. Frost about one of the Derry Christmas Eves when Elinor sat up with Rob, who was carving little wooden animals for the children. There was a pig for Carol. But about two or three o'clock on Christmas morning the father decided the pig needed a pen, and went on sitting there, carving, whittling till daylight.

"Did you go to bed?" Mrs. Whicher asked Elinor.

"Oh no—I sat there with him. I went to sleep as I rocked and woke at dawn . . . I found that Rob had just finished the pen!"

In looking back on it, Lesley thinks their life in Derry was like that of the Brontë family:

We lived in a similar isolation and world of our own, and a similar ferment. Father Brontë was not a tyrant, as people say— no more than our father—both cared about and fostered their children's writing. The only trouble is we Frosts weren't geniuses like the Brontës. We should have been!

In the worn old notebook of Frost's, which looks as if it had lived a long life stuffed in a pocket during farm labors, there is a characterization of Carol.

THE LORD PROTECTOR

Once there were three little girls who were afraid of almost everything when they were away from home, engines and electric cars and automobiles and road rollers and bears and giants and cannons. But when they were at home they felt perfectly safe because they had a little brother there just a little bit smaller than they were who was a great hero. He always walked about with his chin close in to his neck and his fists in the pockets of his new trousers. He kept almost whistling. All about the yard, like bones in front of a lion's den, were scattered the sticks and clubs that none but he could wield and the carts and boxes and things he had broken by not playing with them gently enough. When he heard a wagon coming down the road, he would come to the barn door to let people see that he was on guard. As long as they went by it was all right. He had a terrible smile, a terrible smile. He made the three little girls feel perfectly safe even at night.

Another Carol story, at least five pages long, and fantastic, describes how the little boy kissed everybody good-by, and climbed into the nut tree,

. . . going quickly round and round the trunk where the branches were best until he was out of sight. He was out of hearing too before any of us thought to ask him when he would be back. . . . We were afraid that he would not risk climbing down by starlight and we would have to stay under the tree all night.
That was the way it turned out. . . .

Finally after days when all farm chores were neglected, there came down from the nut tree, one by one, three old gray men with white pointed beards and red pointed hats.
Carol had found them conferring about how high the sky was. When at last the little body himself appeared out of the tree, his cap missing, he told the family all about it.
Another realistic-fantastic story relates how a fence post went to pick checkerberries for Irma, while she held its wires. Of baby Marjorie there is just a glimpse, hidden away in a thicket, reading stories from leaves.

I asked Lesley Ballantine if she took care of the younger children for her mother. She supposed so, but had not been aware of it.

79

We were all together all the time, indoors and out. We had no playmates among neighbor children. Our house was isolated. We were a little scared all the time—tramps!—all but my mother. My father had a gun, as he should have had—a revolver. But he never killed anything—never an animal. He tried to cure us of our scaredness by bribing us to walk down the dark road to the Berrys' at night alone. He would take a ten cent piece, put it way down that road on a stump and say the first child to go could have it. Also he constantly took us walking at night.

In "The Fear," a *North of Boston* eclogue, such a walk with a child is described (but the fear was not in the walkers). In a fanciful poem, written in Derry, published much later, we see another way the poet-father dealt with children's fears.

LOCKED OUT
AS TOLD TO A CHILD

When we locked up the house at night,
We always locked the flowers outside
And cut them off from window light.
The time I dreamed the door was tried
And brushed with buttons upon sleeves,
The flowers were out there with the thieves.
Yet nobody molested them!
We did find one nasturtium
Upon the steps with bitten stem.
I may have been to blame for that:
I always thought it must have been
Some flower I played with as I sat
At dusk to watch the moon down early.

The father encouraged physical prowess in his children. They were brought up not just to be walkers but athletes. As they grew older, they climbed enormous trees and ropes, had trapezes in the barn. Carol had the strongest muscles. Lesley, a great runner and first-rate skater, almost qualified for the Olympics later. These physical feats were a feather in her cap when she went to the Derry school. Also, she had a bicycle!

Frost tells me that tramps really did come through the country, asking for food and lodging. He would sometimes allow them to sleep in the barn or the kitchen—but slipped a bolt inside the house. In one of our talks he said:

I remember one night when I was playing with the children on a blueberry knoll, I was reading them something rhetorical like "Ye Mariners of England" through a self-made megaphone, when a tramp came by and went to the pump for water. He was on his way from Sidney, Australia, to London to see his wife. He'd left her in her father's care because he thought her father could take better care of her than he could. . . .

Frost's interest in far places and queer characters was real, but he made his own journeys, then, through favorite books, and read them aloud to the family in the evenings. Lesley mentioned Prescott's *The Conquest of Mexico,* Melville's *Typee* and *Omoo,* Hudson's South American books, Hakluyt's *Voyages,* books on Arctic exploration, the *Odyssey,* Darwin's *Voyage of the Beagle.* And, of course, *Walden,* which R.F. compares to *Robinson Crusoe.*

Lesley attributes her interest in politics to the tremendous discussions between her mother, a dyed-in-the-wool Republican, and her father, a Cleveland Democrat.

The father and mother were always mild with the children. They had Victorian standards and Puritan inhibitions—for instance, sex was never mentioned or explained in any way, even on a farm.

Travel in a minor but significant sense came to the Frosts for reasons of health after 1905. Disturbances of the chest—grippe, bad colds which Rob took easily, finally in 1906 and 1907 pneumonia—frightened Elinor and him too because of his father's tuberculosis of the lungs, and his own suspected consumptive trend as a child. What plagued him most was hay fever.

He wrote to Miss Ward, in a letter already quoted (October 29, 1906):

81

. . . Since the ragweed dusted, I have done nothing and written nothing—except my own epitaph provisionally like this:

> There was a poor mortal believer
> Who gave way to a thought of hay fever:
>   He coughed like a cold
>   Till over he rolled,
> And went into the hands of a receiver.

A very false gallop of verses which I achieved in despite of my invention and which I insert here with some hesitation, it having met with no especial success in the family. . . .

It was either that summer or the following, R.F. told me, that he first took a bag and went up to Bethlehem, in the White Mountains, because he had heard that Henry Ward Beecher, a hay-fever sufferer, had done so. He found thirty hotels plumb full of boarders who had come for fishing and climbing and blueberry pies.

I was in the drugstore looking round, when I met a man named Fitzgerald. His hotel was full up but he recommended his cousins, the Lynches. The Lynch farm stood high out of the village, to the north—quite a walk. But I had nothing against that. The house viewed on all creation. Lynch was a gloomy old Irish patriot who had lost money in Ireland, signing a note for a brother-in-law. He hated England. Mrs. Lynch was quite a character but before long she agreed to let me bring Elinor and the children; gave us a couple of rooms upstairs and a share in the kitchen. There were lots of Lynches and lots of Fitzgeralds and we liked them and they liked us.

We went in August every year from then on till we sailed to England, and back there afterward. It was right down that road that the boy in my poem "Out, Out" lost his hand. . . . That's a poem I never read in public—too cruel. [The title from *Macbeth* implies it.]

Journeys had then to be made by trains and "trolleys," and when the Frosts changed at Holyoke they appeared in the poet's later back-look like one of those casts of clumps of Victorians, which stood in some of Derry's best parlors:

A ROGERS GROUP

How young and unassuming
They waited in the street,
With babies in their arms
And baggage at their feet.

A trolley car they hailed
Went by with clanging gong
Before they guessed the corner
They waited on was wrong.

And no one told them so
By way of traveler's aid,
No one was so far touched
By the Rogers Group they made.

Yet no doubt they were as touching and charming as in the group around the pony, at Bethlehem, in our illustration. Certainly, once at the Lynches', little and big Frosts were released into a high, free mountain world. It was from Bethlehem in the summer of 1907 that the poet wrote his old friend Miss Ward, who had some time since retired from the *Independent* and might have been staying in South Berwick, urging a visit from her that was later made.

. . . You are really not very far from us over across the mountains as the light flies in the morning. People here go down to the surf at Old Orchard and return the same day like Freedom rejoicing in each of the two mighty voices, one of the Sea, one of the Mountains. . . .

In November he wrote a letter of immediate reminiscence:

. . . How long ago and far away Bethlehem is already. Our summer was one of the pleasantest we have had for years. But it is almost hard for me to believe in the reality of it now. I have been that way from boyhood. The feeling of time and space is perennially strange to me. I used to lie awake at night imagining the places I had traversed in the day and doubting in simple wonderment that I who was here could possibly have been there and there. I can't look at my little slope of field here with leaves in the half dead grass, or at the bare trees the birds have left us with, and fully believe there were ever such things as the snug downhill dinning room with the view over five ranges of mountains, our talks under the hanging lamp and over the fat blue book, the tea-inspired Mrs. Lynch, baseball, and the blue black Lafayette. There is a pang there that makes poetry. I rather like to gloat over it.

The pang that made poetry increased; in 1909 Rob Frost tried to get his Pinkerton hours reduced—just at the moment when it was suggested that he might become principal of Pinkerton Academy! He pushed that off with:

"You don't really want me—no degrees! That would not look well in your prospectus."

The new principal, Mr. Silver, an alumnus with degrees, at once observed Robert Frost's original classroom methods, took him to a state teachers' convention to give a speech; this marked him for advancement by Morrison, state superintendent of schools. Morrison called him the best teacher in New Hampshire—something Frost, at heart, less and less wanted to be. For one year the family, deserting the farm, moved up to a house in a group of fine old mansions in East Derry, near the Academy. But in the fall of the next year, 1911, they moved on north with Principal Silver to the State Normal School in Plymouth, on the edge of the White Mountains, where the former English teacher was now scheduled to teach psychology and education to budding schoolmarms.

"For one year, just one," Frost agreed, making the point final to himself, if not to Silver. He had stored their furniture and was thinking of selling the farm, for the ten years' holding required by his grandfather's will had now given him title to the property—something that might help out his poetry, if he found a way to manage.

Meanwhile Plymouth offered the stimulus of change in curriculum: from the very first day Robert Frost rejected the stuffy old volumes of the required *History of Education.*

"Take them to the basement," he told the girls, "we won't use them. Instead we'll get a few books that have lighted teachers down the ages—Plato, Rousseau and others."

The last little poem in *North of Boston,* "Good Hours," was written in Plymouth in 1912.

> I had for my winter evening walk—
> No one at all with whom to talk,
> But I had the cottages in a row
> Up to their shining eyes in snow. . . .

The poet needed the talk now, more than the cottages full of good folk who retired by ten P.M. and soon, in fact, he found a literary friend, his first of the male species: a young high-school teacher just out of college, who took to him like a son and was passionately concerned to understand the hows and whys of his elder's personality and his poetry. This was Sidney Cox, later professor of English at Dartmouth, whose letters from Frost, quoted occasionally in future chapters of this book, form one of the treasures of the Baker Library at Dartmouth.

In an essay recalling the Plymouth days, Cox described in the New Hampshire *Troubadour* the many long walks he and R.F. took together, in snowy woods and over the intervals:

When we returned from those walks he would take me to the drugstore for a glass of white grapejuice (it might have been then that he told me that in the years of eagerness and frustration he had tried heavy drinking to see if it would help with the poetry and found that it did not). Other times he took me home with him for a dinner of leg of lamb. When the kids had gone to bed he would read from thin, attractive volumes of poetry. . . . Once he recited Thompson's "The Hound of Heaven," his uniquely vibrating voice a flexible instrument for the speech music of many emotions. Tones, he said, pauses and rushes and intensities of sound are more revealing than the definition value of the words. "Lycidas," he said, sympathetically read aloud would be stirring and charming if heard through a wall that muffled all the words. He had once recited "Lycidas," he said, all of it, alone on the summit of Mount Lafayette.

This instinctive force of poetry, so long pent up, made him feel insecure in Plymouth: something was prodding him from within to shake off the harness of teacher.

A letter of December 19, 1911, to Miss Ward from Plymouth shyly offers a gift and hints at forthcoming change:

I don't know where you are, nor how you are, nor how you are at present disposed toward minor poets. And I have been such a laggard in letter writing that I don't believe I deserve to know. Well then take this book of manuscript verse as a peace offering. I thought it might be nearer right in the circumstances than anything I could buy in the book mart. It represents, needless to tell *you,* not the long deferred forward movement you are living in wait for, but only the grim stand it was necessary for me to make until I should gather myself together. The forward movement is to begin next year.

Another letter was written on December 28:

. . . And though getting along in years like other folks, I still find myself young enough to hate and abhor giving up what I have once really set my heart on. So I am coming to have a spoken word with you, if no more than a word. And this as of obligation; for how are we going to continue to read each other's letters satisfactorily unless we renew in memory from time to time the image of the living voice that informs the sentences. . . .

Then, the afterthought in a letter, dated by Frost "circa Jan. 15 1912":

It wasn't to be expected that I would get back to business the minute my train arrived; and I didn't. And that was not because I can't move as fast as a train when I am on a train, but because it is so much further from the literary to the psychophysical than it is from little New York to Plymouth. I have been a constant sufferer since my visit with you from that Where-was-I-when-I-left-off or What-did-I-say-last feeling as I should have made complaint before if I had felt constrained to write you before I got safely and thoroughly home. I must tell you that one day—I couldn't for the life of me say how afterwards—I actually turned a recitation in the History of Education into a recitation of irrelevant verse. But there's no harm done, perhaps even some good. At anyrate Elinor and I think so. It will never be counted against you with us that you have encouraged my poor Muse with interest when you couldn't with praise. . . . Sonnet on the next page for my Moth and Butterfly book.

The sonnet referred to, then called "In White," was an early version of "Design," a darkly skeptical and important later poem of Frost's, sometimes wrongly regarded as a masterpiece of his sixties.

Frost shortly [February 10, 1912] wrote Miss Susan of a strange experience in the woods. Some of the world's great geniuses (Goethe is one of them) have recorded similar meetings with their own images at a moral or mental cross-roads in life. Was the nonmystical Frost for once subject to an illusion, born of a gloom-doom mood? What matter, since it seems to have been the seed of a most celebrated poem, "The Road Not Taken," written, he has told me, in 1914 in England.

Two lonely cross-roads that themselves cross each other I have walked several times this winter without meeting or overtaking so much as a single person on foot or on runners. The practically unbroken condition of both for several days after a snow or a blow proves that neither is much travelled. Judge then how surprised I was the other evening as I came down one to see a man, who to my own unfamiliar eyes and in the dusk looked for all the world like myself, coming down the other, his approach to the point where our paths must intersect being so timed that unless one of us pulled up we must inevitably collide. I felt as if I was going to meet my own image in a slanting mirror. Or say I felt as we slowly converged on the same point with the same noiseless yet laborious stride as if we were two images about to float together with the uncrossing of someone's eyes. I verily expected to take up or absorb this other self and feel the stronger by the addition for the three-mile journey home. But I didn't go forward to the touch. I stood still in wonderment and let him pass by; and that, too, with the fatal omission of not trying to find out by a comparison of lives and immediate and remote interests what could have brought us by crossing paths to the same point in a wilderness at the same moment of nightfall. Some purpose I doubt not, if we could but have made out. I like a coincidence almost as well as an incongruity. . . .

The moment coincided with a major decision taken about this time to go off somewhere where it was possible to be poor and write poetry. The teaching road now offered better prospects than ever before, provided that school teaching was the goal. But Frost was driven to admit that it was not the goal.

We'd had the usual domestic parleys about this, idle ones, the only kind we Frosts ever engaged in. Elinor, after making that first big resistance—before I married her—to being swept into my good-for-nothing life accepted everything. First we'd thought of Vancouver as a refuge. But somebody told us it was too expensive. Then I suggested England.

"Yes, let's go over there and sleep under thatch!" cried Elinor. [Lesley recalls that her mother was standing at the ironing board in the Plymouth kitchen at the time.] Ever since I found the little book at Dartmouth I'd wanted to visit the land of *The Golden Treasury*. "Let's toss a coin," I proposed. The coin chose England. So we began really to move to sell the Derry farm.

Silver thought I was going to Hell, I was so offhand and careless about uprooting four children and leaving a school where I was in good standing as a teacher and earned $1,100 a year. (In Derry it had never been over $1,000.) Silver said I could never come back to the school if I swerved away from New Hampshire now.

I had no letters of introduction, I knew not one soul in England.

But I felt impelled to lose myself among strangers, to write poetry without further scandal to friends or family.

Silver couldn't get it at all but he was kind. Put the children on the train. I had gone on ahead to Boston, to buy the steamer tickets. They cost me $60.00 each—$120.00 between us—with the children going free. I had in hand $1,100, the price the farm brought after the mortgage was paid. Then there'd come in a small allowance from my grandfather's estate, $800 a year; that would last out another two-three years. We could risk it. I was wasteful of money, like my mother.

Frost has often said publicly that "The Road Not Taken" refers less to himself than to Edward Thomas, a dear friend made in England—the closest friend he ever had; a poet almost created by Frost's recognition that he *was* one. But the poem's last lines and indeed all its substance have, as I see it, a subterranean connection with his experience on that Plymouth wood road, and with the inner compulsion that in 1912 at the age of thirty-eight sent him forth to try a new fortune on strange shores.

> I shall be telling this with a sigh
> Somewhere ages and ages hence:
> Two roads diverged in a wood, and I—
> I took the one less traveled by,
> And that has made all the difference.

PART II

THE ROAD TAKEN

1912–1916

CHAPTER 5

AND THE WORK IS PLAY
FOR MORTAL STAKES

October 1912 – April 1914

Surely poetry is the hard-won communication of those who all
but despair of being able to tell anything of the compelling drama
of their sensibilities.

Thornton Wilder

OUR NEW HOUSE

We got out of the train in Beaconsfield station. It was all new
to us, and we walked up the road, and through many roads.
There weren't many people in the street. "I must go into the
groser's," said papa, "and tell him to come in the morning." Papa
went in and we waited at the door. The groser said a lot of things,
and papa said, "You come in the morning," and he said "Yes,"
and we went on our way and papa went up to the bakers. We
went up to our house. The rest got away ahead of Carol and I.
Pretty soon papa came up behind us. I ran back to meet him, but
Carol went with the rest. Papa pointed to our house and I saw
people putting "fernercher" in our house. [The child had instantly
caught the English pronunciation!] The others had gone in already. Papa unlocked the side door, and he put the key on a nail.
We went through that room into the hall. Then we went into a
big bedroom, and then into a small one, and then into the sitting
room where the furniture was. Then we went out through the
hall into the kitchen. There were some men washing the room.

It was aufully dirty. Mama and the children had gone out in the garden, so we went out too. There was a hothouse, a summer house, and some dead flowers. We looked around and then we went in and placed some of the furniture around.

This is probably Irma's account, from the English composition book given the Frost parents at Christmas, of her "new house" at Beaconsfield, Buckinghamshire. Her father's early impressions are given in a letter to his oldest literary friend:

Dear Miss Ward:

Perhaps I ought not to conceal from you, as one of the very few mortals I feel in any sense answerable to, that I am in the mood called aberrant. Psychology holds me no longer. What have I taught for, anyway, but to confute my well-wishers who believed I was not enough of the earth earthy to be above a fool? And now that I have proved myself as a teacher in two departments of learning without benefit of college, my soul inclines to go apart by itself again and devise poetry. Heaven send that I go not too late in life for the emotions I expect to work in. But in any case I should not stay, if only for scorn of scorn—scorn of the scorn that leaves me still unnoticed among the least of the versifiers that stop a gap in the magazines. The Forum gives me space for one poem this year; the [Youth's] Companion for two. The Independent, longest my friend, has held one of my poems unprinted now these three years. So slight is my consideration. I may be too old to write the song that once I dreamed about ("The tender touching thing")—at least I can achieve something solid enough to sandbag editors with.

Here we are between high hedges of laurel and red-osier dogwood, within a mile or two of where Milton finished Paradise Lost on the one hand and a mile or two of where Grey lies buried on the other and within as many rods as furlongs of the house where Chesterton tries truth to see if it wont prove as true upside down as it does right side up. To London town what is it but a run? Indeed when I leave writing this and go into the front yard for a last look at earth and sky before I go to sleep, I shall be able to see the not very distant lights of London flaring like a dreary dawn. If there is any virtue in location—but don't think I

94

think there is. I know where the poetry must come from if it comes.

Sincerely yours always

Robert Frost

September 15 1912

Robert Frost's English experience, which within two and a half years established his place in modern poetry in a final way, stands out as dramatic in the very manner that a Frost poem is dramatic. It begins innocently with the arrival of a little country family from New Hampshire, without money or connections, in great, dark, brooding, historic London. One evening spent rashly at the five-hundredth performance of *Fanny's First Play* by Bernard Shaw: the poet might have to turn playwright. Then poetic forces take over, sweeping all to a conclusion hardly suspected till the surprise ending is reached.

Yet was it wholly a surprise? Today we discern that the lonely poet was overwhelmingly ready for his first book. Though three years of total dearth in magazine publication had preceded the year 1912, three of the most lovely lyrics of *A Boy's Will* were published at home, just as he was preparing to cross the Atlantic. "October," in the *Youth's Companion* of October 3; "My November Guest" in the November *Forum;* and "Reluctance" again in the November 7th *Companion*—as Frost evasively named the young people's magazine in England.

These lyrics stand separated in the little book that was to come, yet to the thoughtful reader they make a triad, a set of three, with some likeness to a musical chord. In "October" the poet celebrates, in almost Keatsian vein, the luscious charms of autumn, and bids them linger; in "My November Guest" he sorrowfully and firmly takes the arm of muted yet appealing winter; in "Reluctance" through his nostalgic drifting mood, both accepting and rejecting, he admits some sort of end.

If "Reluctance" had been his last word the mighty wave from below, sweeping a poet toward a rich fulfillment in England, could scarcely have failed to break into storm and shipwreck. But the poet told me that when he said "good-by" to Superintendent Silver and normal schoolteaching in Plymouth, he had unexpectedly heard himself utter a sturdy phrase from Paul's first Epistle to the Corinthians:

"Quit you like men."

He had repeated the admonition to himself on shipboard, and on the second morning in London he set forth, not to show the children the "sights" like Westminster Abbey and the Tower but to run down a list of country cottages near London, where the canny Frosts would grow subsistence vegetables to save money to prolong their English stay. On a hunch he went to the "Country Walks" columnist of *T.P.'s Weekly*—an ex-policeman, he told me with eyes a'twinkle—and in a few countryman's explorations on foot found them the real right place.

Elinor Frost, fragile though she was, took on the perils of British housekeeping without a murmur. (Picturesque brick stoves were hard to heat.) The mother had brought along her rocking chair in the hold of *The Parisian* and sat in it as close as she could to the fireplace doing her darning and thinking of colds, pneumonia, chilblains, and poetry. The father, also a fancier in respect of chairs, sat opposite in his own Derry Morris chair, similarly crated and brought to Merrie England in a packing case.

The chair I could write in [he recalled for George Whicher many years later] had to have just the right arms to support a shelf stolen from the closet and not to interfere with my elbows.

No question of school for the children: their education was to grow out of the concrete and practical comparisons they were busy making between New England and Old England. Lesley's composition book is full of them. Nothing about ancient Norman churches or Elizabethan houses with dark beams. She describes the stony British soil, so different from the many-colored earth of New Hampshire, so intractable to the shovel when dried out; the active children in their rubbers caked with an inch-thick platform of clay-mud; the old, old man in a torn gray shawl, and burst-out boots with hanging threads who, when met on the road, keeps demanding of their father—a nonsmoker—"baccy" and matches.

As for Rob, properly chaired, R.F. says that his first real impulse as poet in exile was to dig a handful of manuscript poems out of the bottom of the family trunk and lay them in a pile by the fireplace.

I have never written poetry every day as you know. It was just every so often that I would weed out this pile or do something to a poem. One evening I found myself sitting on the floor by the fireplace, burning what I could spare. These were poems of youth, written separately, between 1892–1912, not in a design to be together.

They were all of the period when I thought I preferred nature to people, quite at the mercy of myself, not always happy. They represented a sort of clinical curve. I put the [unburned] poems in my pocket, and next day realized that they had a unity, could be a book [A Boy's Will].

The poetry itself represented evasiveness, furtiveness. The boy in the poems couldn't be publicly a poet. He was too shy . . . I wrote some prose lines to tie them together. Thirty-some poems. Lesley typed them for me on our old Blickensderfer.

I decided to take them to the policeman columnist—my only English friend; I hadn't met anybody yet. I thought he might know about smaller publishers. It didn't even occur to me to go to the bigger ones.

The policeman said: "Little books like that cost the author about fifteen pounds." I declared I'd never publish a book at my own expense. Then he proposed Elkin Matthews. I said Matthews was a "vanity" publisher. Then the policeman suggested David Nutt and—recalling that I'd noticed something of W. E. Henley's under this imprint—I felt that might be the place.

So I found the Nutt office, said I had some poems, and wanted to see David Nutt. A strange lugubrious lady, a Frenchwoman, appeared in deep black weeds saying: "I will speak for David Nutt."

Nutt was dead, but I did not know this or that Mrs. Nutt had also lost her son David by drowning. I just left the manuscript with her.

In three days I had a card to come in. I went. The book was accepted!

She never told me anything, though—the relict. Whether she admired the book or why, or who advised her to admire and publish. To have nobody in England to advise or confer with was baffling.

Frost's state of mind is further expressed in a long letter to the Portland, Maine, publisher, Thomas Bird Mosher, whose small finely printed volumes of verse he had admired and read at home. Mosher had evidently asked him for a volume:

. . . The Dea knows I should like nothing better than to see my first book, *A Boy's Will,* in your Lyric Garland Series. It even crossed my mind to submit it to you. But under the circumstances I couldn't, lest you should think I was going to come on you as the poor old man comes on the town. I brought it to England in the bottom of my trunk, more afraid of it, probably, than the Macnamara of what he carried in his. I came here to write rather than to publish. I have three other books of verse somewhere near completion, "Melanism", "Villagers", and "The Sense of Wrong", and I wanted to be alone with them for a while. If I ever published anything, I fully expected it would be through some American publisher. But see how little I knew myself. Wholly on impulse one day I took my MS. of *A Boy's Will* to London and left it with the publisher whose imprint was the first I had noticed in a volume of minor verse. . . . I suppose I did it to see what would happen, as once on a time I short-circuited a dynamo with a two-foot length of wire held between the brushes. What happened pleased me at first—in the case of the MS., I mean. I am not so sure how I feel about it now. David Nutt made me a proposal on a royalty basis. I have signed no contract as yet, but after what has passed, I suppose I am bound to sign, if pressed, almost anything that doesn't seem too one-sided. I expect the publisher will drive a hard bargain with me: who am I that he shouldn't have a right to? One thing that disconcerts me, however, is the eleventh-hour claim he makes on my next three or four books, verse or prose. I wish I knew what you would say to that. I suppose I ought to be proud to be so much in demand: the embarrassment is so novel in my experience. But won't it seem traitorously un-American to have all my first work come out over here? . . . Why couldn't you have spoken two weeks sooner and saved me all this perplexity? It seems to me you owe me something in the way of helpful advice for not speaking. Perhaps I can stave off that contract till I can get an answer from you. Have I made a serious mistake in going to David Nutt? Do you know anything about him (or her, if I may drop the business fiction)? Am I too far committed to draw back? I am nearly the worst person in the world in a muddle like this.

The contract was nevertheless signed—at 12½ per cent. No down payment. It was getting to be Christmas time and no extra cash in sight. The children, carrying out their Derry habits, went in a swarm to the grocer's back room, to barter with their three or four pennies each of spending money, for old wood to make one another presents.

Frost has noted for me an English-winter lyric he wrote in Beaconsfield, but whether at just this time I am not sure.

A PATCH OF OLD SNOW

There's a patch of old snow in a corner
    That I should have guessed
Was a blow-away paper the rain
    Had brought to rest.

It is speckled with grime as if
    Small print overspread it,
The news of a day I've forgotten—
    If I ever read it.

Lesley, the old poet told me, recalls the first winter in Beaconsfield as one of real hardship in their family life. But her father disagreed. Theirs, at least, he said, was not the misery of the beautiful little timbered cottage of the English country laborer who had no pigs, no cow, no hens, as Yankee farmers had: lived on tea, bread, and sugar, giving the baby weak tea from a bottle with a nipple. The English poets they came to know also lived like the rustics.

"But we had, with our extra American pennies, eggs, meat, milk. I ought to know—I did a great deal of our cooking!"

Frost's revolt against the subservience of the English laboring countryman and his acceptance of class restrictions was eloquent, indeed indignant. Some of his British friends were ruffled by his views. The tough independence of the hill people with whom the American had neighbored for a decade haunted him. Not a man of the native American characters he was concerned with as he wrote his second book but shot quail or partridge in the fall of the year or at will fished a trout brook in spring. Not a child but had her favorite berry patch.

His village neighbors in Beaconsfield had no fish or game unless they had a poacher in the family. Their little girls went berrying in peril of having their baskets dumped by the game warden who also claimed the birds wounded by the gentry's guns and scattered into the bushes. In Herefordshire, where they lived in 1914–1915, a bucolic couple boasted that they "had only two girls on the street." The subtle, free-flung liberties practiced by farmers' families as in Frost's poem "Blueberries"; the dangerous conflict between the pride of the man hired for haying and that of the farmer unfamiliar with the hired man's code had no parallel in the English class system.

This early winter of 1913, when A Boy's Will was in press but not out, was restless and lonely. Mrs. Nutt remained unapproachably Delphic, and introduced her American poet to nobody. Frost, in 1949, told me how he first found, entirely on his own, a little center of Georgian poetry. He liked the Georgians because they too had discarded the nineteenth-century poeticisms and made poetry of the harsh tragedies of common folk, in common speech.

I used to steal off to London for an occasional day and wander about the streets. One dark morning, early in the New Year, or maybe it was late in December, I found myself pausing before the window of a shop where a clerk was arranging volumes of current poetry. A notice announced the opening, that night, of Harold Monro's Poetry Bookshop. I went in and asked if I might return for the evening. The assistant told me the guests were "Invited." But I might try.

Like any other American, Rob Frost had a couple of photographs taken after he had placed *A Boy's Will*. So we today can understand why nobody scowled at the Yankee with tossed fair hair, Grecian profile, deeply plunged speaking blue eyes, long upper lip, finely molded sensuous mouth, who looked about him with a shy, vulnerable air. He had made his way shyly through the crowd of poets and patrons of the arts to a seat on a stairway beside a charming British lady who promptly inquired:

"Are you a poet?"

"I accept the omen," replied the stranger who hardly looked older than the "I" of *A Boy's Will*.

"Have you a book?"

"No!"

The lady, the wife of Ernest Gardiner, an archeological scholar (who later introduced the Frosts to the Beveridge circle) had, however, taken his measure and so had F. S. Flint, a British poet who lived in London and had allied himself with Ezra Pound's budding group of Imagistes. Flint asked the American (Frost has told me) after a reading by John Drinkwater, if he knew Ezra Pound.

"No."

"Well, you *should*," commented Flint; and just a few days later R.F. received, in Buckinghamshire, a card:

Ezra Pound, Number Ten Church Walk, London.
At home sometimes.

I didn't like that very well [Frost ruminated in his mildest manner].

Several months passed. Then one day, maybe in March, finding myself in Kensington near a sign 'Church Walk' I pulled out the card from my vest pocket and knocked at the door.

Ezra was at home, taking a bird-bath; and scuttled into an ornate purple Oriental dressing gown. He showed annoyance that I had not been more attentive to his summons. Immediately wormed out of me that David Nutt was publishing my first book of verse. He said:

"We'll go over to the press and get a copy." I had none myself, as yet, but go we did and Pound (not I) took possession of the first copy of my book. I had to walk back to his lodgings with *him* holding *my* book.

He began reading it at once, pulling at his beard with me there, standing on one foot. After a bit I caught a chuckle. Maybe he was getting it? Presently he said:

"You don't mind OUR liking this?"

"Oh no—go ahead and like it."

"You'd better find a book to read," Pound advised me.

Next he said:

"I guess you'd better run along home. I'm going to review your book."

This simple statement must have, like a lightning flash, illuminated a whole new landscape for Robert Frost. Since 1894, when he published "My Butterfly," nineteen years had passed, and he had printed but fourteen poems in all. Never in that long stretch had his poetry received formal critical notice. Pound's review would carry authority, and would appear on home ground. For Pound had constituted himself the London-American-expatriate adviser of Miss Harriet Monroe's promising Chicago review, *Poetry: A Magazine of Verse,* which had been launched just as Frost took flight.

Frost had, in fact, recently sent Miss Monroe a batch of

102

poems that she had rejected. (Later, she said that this had happened because she was away on a trip.) Now, seemingly, she was to have forced upon her a review of *A Boy's Will*. Pound assured his new discovery that Harriet, though an old maid, was far less of a one than the editors of *Harper's, Scribner's,* and the *Atlantic Monthly*.

Pound wrote to Alice Corbin, a poet who was then Miss Monroe's assistant editor:

> . . . Have just discovered another Amur'kn (Robert Frost). *Vurry* Amur'k'n with, I think, the seeds of grace.
>
> Sorry [he said in a letter to Harriet Monroe] I can't work this review down to any smaller dimensions. . . . it's our second scoop for I only found the man by accident and I think I've about the only copy of the book that has left the shop.
>
> I'll have along some of his work, if the book hasn't used up all the best of it. . . .

I always speak of Ezra with praise [Frost commented] for having been so quick and kind, for his haste to speak of my poetry before anyone—anyone before him or beside him. But when his review came to me in England—in May 1913—mind you, *my first American review*—the piece was so personal that Elinor cried. But it was generously intended, I have always felt grateful to Ezra for the start he tried to give me. He continued generous, he reviewed me justly, even after we'd acutely quarrelled and disagreed, as we did in a very short time.

Certainly Robert Frost in 1913 did enjoy, at first, being singled out by an American poet who, however eccentric, was making an unusual mark in literary London. One who, like himself, did believe that "poetry is the thing" and that it lives, as an art, through flux and changes of manner.

Don't forget our first moment together—Pound's and mine—was happy, even romantic. Pound showed me London's Bohemia —he was boyish about it. He presented me with two little books of his verse, *Personae* and *Ripostes*. The last had recently appeared. I liked them and said so—then he backed off—

"If you value them. . . . But it's all old stuff. I shall not go back to it."

But I liked them. This was what Ezra was to me before he got to writing *Cantos*.

Pound and Frost were in happy agreement about another American, as Frost records in his Preface to E. A. Robinson's *King Jasper*:

The first poet I ever sat down with to talk about poetry was Ezra Pound. It was in London in 1913. The first poet we talked about, to the best of my recollection, was Edwin Arlington Robinson. I was fresh from America and from having read *The Town Down the River*. Beginning at that book, I have slowly spread my reading of Robinson twenty years backward and forward, about equally in both directions.

I remember the pleasure with which Pound and I laughed over the fourth "thought" in

> "Miniver thought, and thought, and thought,
> And thought about it."

Three "thoughts" would have been "adequate" as the critical praise-word then was. There would have been nothing to complain of, if it had been left at three. The fourth made the intolerable touch of poetry. With the fourth, the fun began. . . .

[Now Frost and I were in Ripton talking.] Pound presented me to William Butler Yeats and to another man of influence, Ford Madox Ford (Hueffer), formerly editor of the critically powerful *English Review*. These two were at this time his chief English friends—he had quarrelled with many of the rest. Yeats and I did not hit it off personally, especially after my fight with Pound, which happened very soon . . . truth is I had begun to make friends of my own in the Georgian group—Harold Monro of the bookshop was a poet himself, but still more the publisher of this group with his Georgian anthology and his review *Poetry and Drama*.

There was another place I got invited to meet poets and critics —St. George's Restaurant. There, having tea, I met Wilfrid W.

Gibson, Lascelles—he said it like tassels—Abercrombie; also (I think) my closest English friend, Edward Thomas.

For these associations Pound reproached me in this wise:

"If you *will* frequent the purlieus of literature!"

[Frost continued] Pound had a personal hate for Abercrombie. He said to him (if you want the story): "Stupidity beyond a certain point becomes a public affront. I hereby assume the public's quarrel in your case. My seconds will wait on you." Abercrombie —a charming fellow rather like an American—and a fine poet, laughed it off by proposing, since he had the right to name the weapons, that they should be unsold copies of the author's works at a hundred yards.

Robert Frost stubbornly refused the chance offered by Pound, to sit as learner at established great men's feet, and instinctively sought, instead, these English poets who were still making their own way and open to his strong bent and his immense gift for talk. When he met Robert Bridges, who became Poet Laureate of England in 1913, he listened attentively to Bridges' views on the application of classical prosody and quantities to English metrics—and wrote home, as we shall see, a totally opposite theory of his own, which became all the more clear-cut and vocal for the rivalry he felt with an "authority."

Pound's adherence to the concise and the concentrated in poetry, as evidenced in his creation at about this time of the group called Les Imagistes, did not offer novelty: it was not far from Frost's own conciseness.

As John Livingston Lowes said, in his *Convention and Revolt in Poetry:*

Given a rich vocabulary and the artist's sense for words, and metre will oppose little opposition to the *mot juste*. The diction of Mr. Robinson and Mr. Frost—to leave William Shakespeare and a few others out of account—is quite as exact, in the full Imagist sense of the term, as the diction of H. D. or Richard Aldington, and the blank verse doesn't halt for it either. I am talking of artists, of course. Neither free verse will save, nor metre damn, the others.

I asked R.F., when he was discussing his early relation to Ezra Pound, whether the latter had tried to correct his verse.

He tried to, he asked me to join the little group of Imagistes who shortened one another's poetry: F. S. Flint, T. E. Hulme, H. D. and Richard Aldington. The poets were interesting. Flint, especially, became a friend I have kept to this day. But I had to work alone. Pound, to illustrate what it should be, took a poem of mine, said: "You've done it in fifty words. I've shortened it to forty-eight." I answered, "And spoiled my metre, my idiom and idea."

Frost's ability to balance his lack of reputation and worldly sophistication against his inner knowledge that he had already achieved a personal and original form, especially in the blank-verse poems that soon became *North of Boston,* reveals a stout and heartening self-belief. Yeats could not be his god or model. Frost was closer, in spirit, to Thomas Hardy's conception of man and nature than to Yeats' or Pound's. Like Hardy, he saw the background of nature as dangerously chaotic, beyond man's reasoning but not beyond man's power to impose his own design upon. Where Yeats viewed nature, as a poet may, as a sort of backdrop, Frost lived in it concretely, almost as a naturalist with an eye for the neglected and the seemingly insignificant but fertile detail.

But Frost was lucky and knew it in having come to England in the middle of a poetic renascence. The year 1912 had produced de la Mare's *The Listeners,* which he admired; Abercrombie's *Emblems of Love;* Masefield's *Dauber* and *The Daffodil Fields* of 1912 and 1913. These poets had influenced Wilfrid Gibson, turning him away from his early pseudo-Tennysonian verse toward the tragedy of the common lot of mankind. His *Daily Bread* and *Fires* were collections of the same period.

The lovely opening of Ralph Hodgson's *The Song of Honor* could almost have been written by Frost: another who did not cast off tradition but cared about "the tune."

I climbed the hill as light fell short,
And rooks came home in scramble sort,
And filled the trees and flapped and fought
And sang themselves to sleep. . . .

Actually, Robert Frost's closest friendship in England was with Edward Thomas who, when they met in February 1913, was not known as a poet but thought of as a superior hack writer and excellent critic of other men's poetry.

Frost's unpretentious book, which sold for "one and six" (a shilling sixpence), appeared early in April, and as this was London, notices promptly appeared. The first was an anonymous review by Edward Thomas in the London *Athenaeum* for April 5. It was then reviewed or noticed over several months in other leading literary reviews like the London *Times Supplement, Poetry and Drama,* the *English Review,* the London *Bookman,* the *Academy,* and the *Nation.*

These voices built up to a critical *succès d'estime* for Robert Frost. He had been named a true poet in a truly critical literary world.

Frost took pride in sending along a gift of his first volume to at least two Americans who had sponsored his poetry: to Miss Susan Ward, saying that the verse she alone, for years, had recognized was drawing the attention of Yeats, Newbolt, Ernest Rhys, Ezra Pound, and May Sinclair; to Ernest C. Jewell of Lawrence, who had printed his first poem, "La Noche Triste," in the high-school paper. This letter to Jewell tells something important about Robert Frost:

The Bungalow
Beaconsfield
Bucks
England
May 6, 1913

Dear Jewell:—

The book I am sending will tell you what I am about this year. I don't expect you wholly to approve of my venture and yet I don't know—perhaps you may see the wisdom of it, all things considered. You always believed in me as a—what shall I say?—as an intelligence and as an honest man, I think, at least in intention. And perhaps you believed in me as a poet. I never was quite sure of that. But really I am going to be justified of my poetry before the end. I have hung off long enough. I wasn't going to pass forty without having had it out with myself on this score. . . .

An excerpt of a unique copy of Pound's review in *Poetry*, as Frost enclosed it in a letter to Sidney Cox, is given below; note that Pound took his chance there to omit, in print, parts of Frost's lines, and that the poet also deleted words of his critic and added comments in ink!

I had withdrawn in forest, and my song
Was swallowed up in leaves ["that blew alway," omitted]

There is another personality in the realm of verse another American, found, as usual, on this side of the water, by an English publisher long known as a lover of good letters. David Nutt publishes at his own expense *A Boy's Will,* by Robert Frost, the latter having been long scorned by the "great American editors." [R.F.: the author's surmise—inference from my sad look.] It is the old story.

Mr. Frost's book is a little raw, and has in it a number of infelicities; [R.F.: this is the superior person who objected to "Trial by Existence."] underneath them it has the tang of the New Hampshire woods, and it has just this utter sincerity. It is not post-Miltonic or post-Swinburnian or post-Kiplonian. This man has the good sense to speak naturally and to paint the thing, the thing as he sees it. And to do this is a very different matter from gunning about for the circumplectious polysyllable. . . . One reads the book for the "tone," which is homely, by intent, and pleasing, never doubting that it comes direct from his own life, and that no two lives are the same.

He has now and then such a swift and bold expression as

["And] The whimper of hawks beside the sun."

He has now and then a beautiful simile, well used, but he is for the most part as simple as the lines I have quoted in opening or as in the poem of mowing. He is without sham and without affectation. . . .

Since in the small London literary world everything that happens in spring or early summer gets about, Frost was soon aware, in the spring of 1913, that an aggressive Boston poetess, author of *A Dome of Many-Colored Glass* (a sentimental work in regular meters) had arrived, determined to fill with her abundant person every gap in the American-English poetic hierarchy. Frost avoided meeting Amy Lowell, he says, at this time, perhaps because he did not care for her poetry, or because Ezra Pound was boasting of her:

"When I get through with that girl, she'll think she was born in free verse."

Amy, a sudden convert, gave herself over as Frost had not to being indoctrinated with Pound's Imagiste theories, and started writing the new free verse way, as was shown in *Sword Blades and Poppy Seeds* (1914). Frost had met T. E. Hulme, reckoned the first of the Imagistes, and was interested in his ideas, but less in his practice. Indeed, he began to weary of all these cliques and movements. He was himself writing and revising blank verse—in his own original way, he felt confident, but he was leaving that to be said by the English poets and critics he trusted, who were now asking to see the "talk" poems in manuscript. The ones he had "strewn along," as he put it to me, "with the lyrics I was writing between 1902 and 1912." Mrs. Nutt had made him sign a contract for the new volume, and I am told by F. B. Adams, Jr., that she announced it in her 1913 catalogue as *Farm Servants and Other People*. Over this in the catalogue Frost had written in his unmistakable script, *New England Hill Folk*. He had rejected another English suggestion to call it *Yankee Eclogues*.

We get the poet's own explicit comment on his poetic technique in *North of Boston* in another letter to Thomas Bird Mosher:

Dear Mr. Mosher:—

I like the decision with which you speak and am content to let you prefer "Reluctance" to anything else I have written. Nevertheless the book contains a dozen poems that are at least good in the same kind and for the same reason. In "Mowing," for instance, I come so near what I long to get that I almost despair of coming nearer.

I am made too self-conscious by the comment on my first book to think of showing another like it for some time. If I write more lyrics it must be with no thought of publication. What I *can* do next is bring out a volume of blank verse that I have already well in hand and won't have to feel I am writing to order. I had some character strokes I had to get in somewhere and I chose a sort of eclogue form for them. Rather I dropped into that form. And I dropped to an everyday level of diction that even Wordsworth kept above. I trust I don't terrify you. I think I have made poetry. The language is appropriate to the virtues I celebrate. At least I am sure I can count on you to give me credit for knowing what I am about. You are not going to make the mistake that Pound makes of assuming that my simplicity is that of the untutored child. I am not undesigning.

You will be amused to hear that Pound has taken to bullying me on the strength of what he did for me by his review in *Poetry*. The fact that he discovered me gives him the right to see that I live up to his good opinion of me. He says I must write something much more like *vers libre* or he will let me perish of neglect. He really threatens. I suppose I am under obligations to him and I try to be grateful. But as for the review in *Poetry* (Chicago, May), if any but a great man had written it, I should have called it vulgar. It is much less to my taste than the shorter reviews in *Poetry & Drama* and in *The English Review*. The more I think of it the less I like the connection he sees between me and the Irishman who could sit on a kitchen-midden and dream stars. It is so stupidly wide of the mark. And then his inaccuracies about my family affairs! Still I think he has meant to be generous.

I wish sometime if you know Robinson you could put me in the way of knowing him too—*sometime*, if it comes right. Not a month ago I was asking Miss Sinclair if she shouldn't have put him ahead of Moody and Torrence in her article of a few years back in the *Atlantic*. She said that Robinson was the only one of the three she still cared for.

You *know* I want you to use my poem in your catalogue.

Sincerely yours

Robert Frost

About my book in America. I shall do nothing for the present. Seymour of Chicago was out here from London to talk about it. Mrs. Nutt is going to have to be very much consulted in the matter. These are things I don't know very much about. R.F.

Soon after this the whole Frost family needing, as usual, a summer jaunt, entrained for a fisher's cot in a lonely Scottish fishing village, King's Barn, that faced the great curve of the Firth of Forth. Mrs. Ernest Gardiner had recommended it, and sure enough the charming Yankee had soon met, on the beach, one of his own kind, E. C. Smith, a distinguished Scottish scholar. Within another day or two, the legend goes, the poet who got carried too far from shore by a current while swimming was rescued by the Scotsman's speed in organizing a human chain of rescuers. Frost says he had climbed on a rock and was never in real danger. Smith aided him in other ways: by having nice children, who became fast and durable friends of his own children; by reading "The Death of the Hired Man" and liking it; by presenting him to Laurence Binyon, another English poet and writer of influence.

It was inspiriting to find in the *Academy*, as late as September 15, another review, which says in part:

We wish we could fitly express the difference which marks off *A Boy's Will* from all the other books here noticed. The poems combine, with a rare sufficiency, the essential qualities of inevitability and surprise. We have read every line with that amazement and delight which are seldom evoked by books of modern verse. . . . We do not need to be told that the poet is a young man: the dew and the ecstasy—the audacity, too—of pristine vision are here. . . . No one who really cares for poetry should miss this little book. . . . We have not the slightest idea who Mr. Robert Frost may be, but we welcome him unhesitatingly to the ranks of the poets born, and are convinced that if this is a true sample of his parts he should presently give us work far worthier of honour than much which passes for front-rank poetry at the present time.

. . . I give you fair warning [Frost wrote Mosher on October 28], I am going to have my moderate success in these islands. The signs are not wanting. . . . Binyon had me to lunch the other day with Bridges. When I can get rid of this house I am to go to Gloucester to live, to be with Wilfrid Gibson and Abercrombie. I am out with Pound pretty much altogether and so I don't see his friend Yeats as I did. I count myself well out, however. . . .

These Englishmen are very charming. I begin to think I shall stay with them till I'm deported. If I weren't so poor I should plan to stay five years anyway.

How little did Frost dream, as he wrote to his young teacher friend in Schenectady, New York, that the world's mask of peace and tranquillity would break in August of 1914, less than a year after he'd made his five-year plan, and would confound all poets and their hopes. No premonitions are to be found in the pregnant letter that follows:

The Bungalow
Beaconsfield
Bucks
Jan 19 1914

Dear Cox

Absolve me of trying to make you think of me as hobnobbing with the great over here . . . I'm far from important enough for the likes of the Poet Laureate to have sought me out. I'm simply going to tell you about him because I happen to have eaten at the same table with him by an accident. I was visiting Laurence

112

Binyon (see anthology) when Bridges turned up. I have a right to tell you how the king looked to the cat that looked at him.

He's a fine old boy with the highest opinion—of his poetry you thought I was going to say—perhaps of his poetry, but much more particularly of his opinions. He rides two hobbies tandem, his theory that syllables in English have fixed quantity that cannot be disregarded in reading verse, and his theory that with forty or fifty or sixty characters he can capture and hold for all time the sounds of speech. One theory is as bad as the other and I think owing to much the same fallacy. The living part of a poem is the intonation entangled somehow in the syntax idiom and meaning of a sentence. It is only there for those who have heard it previously in conversation. It is not for us in any Greek or Latin poem because our ears have not been filled with the tones of Greek and Roman talk. It is the most volatile and at the same time important part of poetry. It goes and the language becomes a dead language the poetry dead poetry. With it go the accents the stresses the delays that are not the property of vowels and syllables but that are shifted at will with the sense. Vowels have length there is no denying. But the accent of sense supercedes all other accent overrides and sweeps it away. I will find you the word "come" variously used in various passages as a whole, half, third, fourth, fifth and sixth note. It is as long as the sense makes it. When men no longer know the intonations on which we string our words they will fall back on what I may call the absolute length of our syllables which is the length we would give them in passages that meant nothing. The psychologist can actually measure this with a what-do-you-call-it. English poetry would then be read as Latin poetry is now read and as of course Latin poetry was never read by Romans. Bridges would like it read so now for the sake of scientific exactness. Because our poetry must sometime be as dead as our language must Bridges would like it treated as if it were dead already.

I say you can't read a single good sentence with the salt in it unless you have previously heard it spoken. . . . Words exist in the mouth not in books. You can't fix them and you dont want to fix them. You want them to adapt their sounds to persons and places and times. You want them to change and be different. I shall be sorry when everybody is so public-schooled that nobody will dare to say Haow for What. . . .

The sense of achievement goes far to help a new voice to declare itself. Theories do not create true and major poems; rather poems actually written and printed engender the theories, under the spur of contending rival minds. All Frost had to point to, in print, when he met Bridges first, in the fall of 1913, was his book of lyrics, which had in it certain echoes of the past that he later repudiated. He must have wished that "The Fear" and "A Hundred Collars," poems in his new vein, with no Victorian echoes, had already appeared, as they did in *Poetry and Drama* for December, 1913.

In his autobiographical volume *From Another World,* Louis Untermeyer notes that coming there upon the contribution of one Robert Frost, among poems by the English Georgians, Abercrombie, Rupert Brooke, W. W. Gibson, he had imagined this "Frost" to be one of them—until he was overcome by the accent:

. . . what Englishman . . . could have written those two poems? ["The Fear" and "A Hundred Collars"] . . . there was something beneath local color and far beyond background here; something which, in its very inflection, fixed identity . . . American. It was the accent of common speech and, at the same time, the accent of uncommon poetry. What was more, this was blank verse; yet it was a blank verse so different from the traditional English medium that it had acquired a whole new tone and direction.

A month or two later the confusion was explained. I learned what has since been enshrined in every American textbook: that Frost's career had been founded on contradictions.

Untermeyer and Frost did not meet until Frost returned to his native land in early 1915. But as an anthologist and poet in his own right, listening for new voices, Untermeyer had been "alerted" and was waiting to become a member of R.F.'s intimate circle.

More recognition of his conversational approach to blank verse came to the American poet through "The Housekeeper," published on January 15, 1914, in the *Egoist*. This "eclogue" had been written in Derry nine years or more earlier. Perhaps American editors raised in the Puritan tradition had balked at the theme of the common-law wife, who, wearied of not being offered marriage, went off to a man who did espouse her, leaving behind her a monumental mother, a woman too sizable to be moved quickly out of an untenable situation.

The theme was not unlike some of W. W. Gibson's. The English poet, a man of humble origins, wrote truly, in simple diction, of the rough lives of English working people whom he knew at first hand. That was his attraction for Robert Frost in 1914. Yet today, Frost's humor, his objectivity, his intellectual grasp in poems like "The Housekeeper" or "The Code —Heroics" mark off these "talk" poems as little masterpieces, whereas Gibson's poems are largely forgotten.

Miss Monroe had accepted "The Code—Heroics" for a February, 1914, issue of *Poetry*. Pound had kept pricking her, and it did seem time that something should appear in Frost's native land. If England liked him so well, would America still say no? Frost had let Ezra, his "enemy friend," send "The Death of the Hired Man" to Willard Huntington Wright of the *Smart Set*. "As you know the thing I'm most anxious for you to print is that poem of Frost's, . . ." wrote Pound.

Rejected . . . well, he would try the *Atlantic Monthly*, himself, with six poems sent directly to the editor, Ellery Sedgwick, who came back with:

"We are sorry that we have no place in the *Atlantic Monthly* for your vigorous verse."

"Damn them," said Frost, "a few months later these editors were falling over themselves to get me: *When were they right?*"

Because books of poetry brought so little to the publisher, Mrs. Nutt seemed jealous of any modest receipts he might get from magazines:

She acts as if she thought I was up to something [Frost wrote Sidney Cox, on March 3]. Last time I saw her she told me frankly she thought I had no right under my contract to traffic in my poetry before I brought it (the book manuscript) to her.

But Frost could be obstinate and he needed moving money to resettle in the West Midlands. He did not, however, think of going until he had handed in the manuscript of *North of Boston*. Lesley was typing it, and occasionally showing him a page of her own prose that he could commend. He boasted that she could now read a whole page of Caesar without looking up more than a word or two, and she showed pride in her father's achievement and growing prestige. A girl so full of beauty, sparkle, and competence was a treasure also to her mother. Elinor had broken through her Puritan habits to some extent; when she could get to a London party, she held a cigarette in her fingers.

As for the poet, "who never saw New England as clearly as when he was in Old England," he could not tie down his creative moments. It was about this time, early in 1914, while tramping the muddy yard at the Bungalow, that he suddenly, he says, wrote a new poem, not to be included in *North of Boston*. This was the now so famous and beloved "Birches," with its cold and crystal memories of another kind of wintry world:

BIRCHES

When I see birches bend to left and right
Across the lines of straighter darker trees,
I like to think some boy's been swinging them.
But swinging doesn't bend them down to stay
As ice-storms do. Often you must have seen them
Loaded with ice a sunny winter morning
After a rain. They click upon themselves
As the breeze rises, and turn many-colored
As the stir cracks and crazes their enamel.

116

> Soon the sun's warmth makes them shed crystal shells
> Shattering and avalanching on the snow-crust—
> Such heaps of broken glass to sweep away
> You'd think the inner dome of heaven had fallen. . . .

The autobiographical end reveals R.F.'s continuity with his own fate, his power to be intensely moved, in manhood, with what he had learned as a high-school boy:

> . . . Earth's the right place for love:
> I don't know where it's likely to go better.
> I'd like to go by climbing a birch tree,
> And climb black branches up a snow-white trunk
> *Toward* heaven, till the tree could bear no more,
> But dipped its top and set me down again.
> That would be good both going and coming back.
> One could do worse than be a swinger of birches.

Though he must have recognized its excellence, Frost just salted the poem away. "Birches" was a happy discovery, leave it at that, something to bring him home when the time came to face a third book. The Yankee liked to hoard his poetry. Money he spent, poems he kept in the bank, acquiring interest.

. . . I make them in haste and repent of them at liesure [he wrote Marguerite Wilkinson, an anthologist-professor, in 1919]; I dont know that I would have taken the liesure I took if the editors and such hadn't forced it on me. They took care [he said bitterly] that I should take time to judge my own work. Not that I like to judge it . . . I'm still fearfully afraid of committing anything to print. . . . A book on publication day is what Sherman said war was.

Sometimes he would revert to "The Wood-Pile" which a poetic observer he knew well had discovered "out walking in the frozen swamp one gray day."

> . . . I thought that only
> Someone who lived in turning to fresh tasks

117

[What I have most aspired to be, R.F. wrote in my book]

> Could so forget his handiwork on which
> He spent himself, the labor of his ax,
> And leave it there far from a useful fireplace
> To warm the frozen swamp as best it could
> With the slow smokeless burning of decay.

The handwritten footnote in my book reads:

Eclogues exerted some influence. Hard to trace my origins.
First thought I heard the voice from the printed page in Virgilian
eclogue and Hamlet. (Been influenced by what I have supposed
Piers Plowman to be.)

Sometimes the poet's eyes were on the far New England
mountain that "held the town as in a shadow." His new book
was a book of people, not of nature. Yet all the hillfolk neighbored with peaks—some pointed like Lafayette from Franconia, some long and rangy like Monadnock from Peter-
borough. You can't recognize this region's people without
their glimpses of the black bodies of mountains cutting into
the sky:

> . . . I saw through leafy screens
> Great granite terraces in sun and shadow,
> Shelves one could rest a knee on getting up—
> With depths behind him sheer a hundred feet.
> Or turn and sit on and look out and down,
> With little ferns in crevices at his elbow.

Some have thought that "After Apple-Picking" derived in
its richness from the rich tended orchards of Herefordshire,
a true cider country, where Carol, the tall stripling with his
father's eyes and charming smile, loved to sort and wrap
superlative English fruit for market. In fact, the manuscript
had been surrendered before the move and the supremely fine

118

ode on apples and trancelike sleep—which perfects the form used in "My Butterfly" and "Storm Fear"—grew out of the unpruned, unsprayed meager orchards of Derry. In Frost's *North of Boston*, "The Wood-Pile," "The Mountain," and "After Apple-Picking," all three largely written, he told me, before he went to England, stand as landmarks of habitual attention and action to New England folks staring into dark abysses or shrewdly counting their blessings. All these Yankees had climbed their mountains to drink at a spring, had built their wood piles and gone drowsy with their apple-picking.

AFTER APPLE-PICKING

My long two-pointed ladder's sticking through a tree
Toward heaven still,
And there's a barrel that I didn't fill
Beside it, and there may be two or three
Apples I didn't pick upon some bough.
But I am done with apple-picking now.
Essence of winter sleep is on the night,
The scent of apples: I am drowsing off.
I cannot rub the strangeness from my sight
I got from looking through a pane of glass
I skimmed this morning from the drinking trough
And held against the world of hoary grass.
It melted, and I let it fall and break.
But I was well
Upon my way to sleep before it fell,
And I could tell
What form my dreaming was about to take.
Magnified apples appear and disappear,
Stem end and blossom end,
And every fleck of russet showing clear.
My instep arch not only keeps the ache,
It keeps the pressure of a ladder-round.
I feel the ladder sway as the boughs bend.
And I keep hearing from the cellar bin
The rumbling sound
Of load on load of apples coming in.

For I have had too much
Of apple-picking: I am overtired
Of the great harvest I myself desired.
There were ten thousand thousand fruit to touch,
Cherish in hand, lift down, and not let fall.
For all
That struck the earth,
No matter if not bruised or spiked with stubble,
Went surely to the cider-apple heap
As of no worth.
One can see what will trouble
This sleep of mine, whatever sleep it is.
Were he not gone,
The woodchuck could say whether it's like his
Long sleep, as I describe its coming on,
Or just some human sleep.

Frost's dream, as Robert Penn Warren said in a fine essay
on this poem, is a reliving of the literal experiences of apple-
picking. Always, if he uses the dream world as symbol, Frost
brings it back to earth and its meanings.

We shall make a week of it in London before we drink silence
and hide ourselves in cloud [Frost wrote to Cox on March 26]. I
sold some poetry to *Poetry and Drama* and I propose to take it
out in room rent in the upper floors of the Poetry Shop in Devon-
shire St Theobalds Road London W.C. . . . The fellow that runs
it and edits the quarterly I speak of is a poet and all about him
are the poets my friends and enemies. Gibson had a room there
for the year before he married the proprietor's secretary. Epstein,
the futurist sculptor, the New York Polish Jew, whose mind runs
strangely on the subject of generation whose work is such a
stumbling block to the staid and Victorianly but who in spite of
all is reckoned one of the greatest living geniuses, will be across
the hall from us. All the poets will be in and out there. It will be
something that Lesley of the children will be sure to remember.

We mean to do the city for the youngsters as much as I am
capable of doing a city or anything else. There must be a great

deal to see in London if one will look for it. There is the Tower and—well there simply must be something else. I must get a guide book.

I really do take an interest in the historical places. I didn't fail to notice that I passed the scenes of two battles Evesham and Worcester when I was travelling the other day. But I don't know what I would have done if I had been set down in either of them. It thrilled me enough merely to see the names on the stations. I got as much out of seeing Dumferline town from the train as from straggling around Edinburgh Castle for a day. The best thing in Edinburgh Castle was the Black Watch on parade. Places are more to me in thought than in reality. People are the other way about. (Probably not so—I am just talking.)

A week in London to a Frost was long as a year. London, like Lawrence, was an industrial city. Living more like that of the Lake Poets lay ahead and the Frosts gloated in the prospect. Gibson, who dwelt in a thatched house of ancient origin, The Old Nail House, at Greenway, north of Dymock, had found them a half-timbered, "small holding" homestead, a real farmer's house, Little Iddens, at Ledbury, a mile or two from his own. Abercrombie lived to the southeast of Dymock, in a thatched house, The Gallows—an easy walk for R.F.

As for Dymock, a small hamlet with a Norman church in Herefordshire, near the Gloucestershire border, its very name was derived from a primeval past: "Swineherd's hut" in old Welsh. Near by was the Forest of Dean—it sounded like the Forest of Arden. The Georgian poets, Gibson, Abercrombie, Rupert Brooke, and John Drinkwater had, in 1914, begun to publish their own quarterly, *New Numbers*, in Dymock. Lesley had thought she would follow suit with a children's magazine.

It was hoped, too, that Edward Thomas whom the Frost children had instantly loved, when he visited them at Beaconsfield, for the pathos of his Welsh songs, for the beautiful melancholy of his sensitive tender face, for his many-pocketed coat, full of birds' eggs and other fruits of the wilds, would come during the summer with wife and children. The year

121

1914 was going to be, as Lesley wrote on the cover of a fine big composition book,

An Important Year.
by
Four Children.
Dedicated
To
Papa and Mamma.

CHAPTER 6

ALL SIMPLY IN THE
SPRINGING OF THE YEAR

Easter 1914 — February 1915

Light has killed the winter and all dark dreams,
Now winds live all in light,
Light has come down to earth and blossoms here,
And we have golden minds.
("Ryton Firs" by Lascelles Abercrombie)

Let me try what I can say in a few words about where we are
[Robert Frost wrote Sidney Cox]. The important thing to us is
that we are near Gibson; we are far from any town. . . . We can
go almost anywhere we wish on wavering footpaths through the
fields. The fields are so small and the trees so numerous along the
hedges that, as my friend Thomas says in the loveliest book on
springtime England, you might think from a little distance that
the country was solid woods.

We are now in the country, the cider country, where we have
to keep a barrel of cider for our visitors and our hired help or
we will have no visitors nor hired help. So we are in the way of
adding drink to cigarette smoking in the record of our sins. Even
Elinor gets drawn in. . . .

In coming to Little Iddens, Robert Frost had, in a sense,
returned to his youth as he lived it in Palgrave's *Golden Treasury* at Dartmouth. Pastoral England had early been his in

the spiritual sense, and now here it was in the earth sense. The county of Hereford as Edward Thomas said is "the most delicately rustic of them all." In Ledbury he and his family too flowed joyously forth into the landscape. Even a poem or two were written outdoors.

Regular hours for meals stopped, if they had ever existed. Elinor satisfied the family hunger with simple cold foods set out in the living room or carried into the lanes and woods. When Lesley Ballantine recalls Little Iddens today, the words "cowslips!" "picnics!" burst rapturously from her lips.

> And travellers in lanes [wrote Abercrombie]
> Catch the hot tawny smell
> Reynard's damp fur left as he sneakt marauding
> Across from gap to gap:
> And in the larch woods on the highest boughs
> The long-eared owls like grey cats sitting still
> Peer down to quiz the passengers below.

The light that blossomed in the meadows along the half-hidden river Leadon between Easter and Whitsuntide and flowed up under the Ryton Firs, where the Abercrombies and their children lived "under thatch," was the reflected glow of thousands and thousands of daffodils. Just glimpsed and they were gone, as Robert Herrick, one of R.F.'s favorites, had said in a mood very like that of "Reluctance" in "To Daffodils":

> Fair daffodils, we weep to see
> You haste away so soon . . .

Frost claimed legitimate ancestry in this poem, as he explained in a letter to Sidney Cox:

The sentence is everything—the sentence well imagined. See the beautiful sentences in a thing like Wordsworth's "To Sleep" or Herrick's "To Daffodils"

Remember, a certain fixed number of sentences (sentence sounds) belong to the human throat just as a certain fixed number of vocal runs belong to the throat of a given kind of bird. These are fixed I say. Imagination cannot create them. It can only call them up. It can only call them up for those who write with their ear on the speaking voice. We will prove it out of the Golden Treasury some day. . . .

Words are only valuable in writing as they serve to indicate particular sentence sounds. I must say some things over and over. I must be a little extravagant too.

Sometimes Rob wandered "lonely as a cloud" amongst the blooming orchards that followed the daffodils, cherry, plum, pear, apple, dropping a rain of petals on a soil streaked with red marl. Sometimes he helped Lesley, Carol, Irma (the little Queen, Lesley called her) and Marj, nine, in the planting of potatoes and green things under the brick walls of Little Iddens. When Edward Thomas came, as he did twice that spring, drawn ever closer to his rare American friend, he led them all out to hear "the first abundance of the day-long calling cuckoos . . . the first nightingale song . . . twitched away by gusty winds."

Frost had very rarely written poetry in the diffusion of outdoors. But it was at Little Iddens, he assures me, "under a plum tree" that he wrote

TO EARTHWARD

Love at the lips was touch
As sweet as I could bear;
And once that seemed too much;
I lived on air

That crossed me from sweet things
The flow of—was it musk
From hidden grapevine springs
Down hill at dusk?

I had the swirl and ache
From sprays of honeysuckle
That when they're gathered shake
Dew on the knuckle.

I craved strong sweets, but those
Seemed strong when I was young;
The petal of the rose
It was that stung.

Now no joy but lacks salt
That is not dashed with pain
And weariness and fault;
I crave the stain

Of tears, the aftermark
Of almost too much love,
The sweet of bitter bark
And burning clove.

When stiff and sore and scarred
I take away my hand
From leaning on it hard
In grass and sand,

The hurt is not enough:
I long for weight and strength
To feel the earth as rough
To all my length.

Contrast the mood of this love lyric of Frost's sentient maturity with the cloudlessness of "The Pasture." He has told me that he first placed the young love poem—unlisted in the Contents—in the front of *North of Boston* as a link for the reader between *A Boy's Will* and say, well, a man's will, though these may not have been the poet's exact words. Still unlisted "The Pasture" faces us on page one of the *Complete Poems* as if to prove that the innocent love of two is the well-spring of all poetry.

THE PASTURE

I'm going out to clean the pasture spring;
I'll only stop to rake the leaves away
(And wait to watch the water clear, I may):
I sha'n't be gone long.—You come too.

I'm going out to fetch the little calf
That's standing by the mother. It's so young
It totters when she licks it with her tongue.
I sha'n't be gone long.—You come too.

Yet the self-same lovers, in their life process of growth do surely seem to reappear, bowing their heads as in prayer before the wonder of new earth life, in a sonnet written at Little Iddens but no more than "To Earthward" English in subject matter:

PUTTING IN THE SEED

You come to fetch me from my work tonight
When supper's on the table, and we'll see
If I can leave off burying the white
Soft petals fallen from the apple tree
(Soft petals, yes, but not so barren quite,
Mingled with these, smooth bean and wrinkled pea;)
And go along with you ere you lose sight
Of what you came for and become like me,
Slave to a springtime passion for the earth.
How Love burns through the Putting in the Seed
On through the watching for that early birth
When, just as the soil tarnishes with weed,
The sturdy seedling with arched body comes
Shouldering its way and shedding the earth crumbs.

Rob Frost liked to rise late, especially if he had been on a solitary night walk, or groping by matchlight to find a rare Spleenwort fern by a bridge over the Leadon, in the company of a friend and legal adviser of his poet friends: a Gloucester solicitor who proved to be one of Britain's leading amateur botanists, as well as a lover of poets and poetry, John W. Haines. In a letter to an American collector, which I have seen, Haines says that Frost, after his return home, sent him the Spleenwort's American cousin, "to symbolize that basically English and American were the same language."

127

Frost had heard so much of Haines in advance that Haines says he had expressed the hope that the solicitor "would read *A Boy's Will* aloud to himself before they met." The connection has persisted and Frost visited Haines in his English home both in 1928, on his first return trip with Elinor and Marjorie, and again in 1957, when Lesley's daughter, Lesley Lee Francis, who had come from her work at the American Embassy in Madrid to be with her grandfather, was his companion.

Haines has described the first meeting in a retrospective sketch:

It was in one of the flowery country lanes north of Dymock that I met a thick-set man of my own age, and medium height, with blue eyes and beautifully sensitive mouth, and asked him if he knew where a Mr. Robert Frost lived. . . . I had been botanising, and was carrying my vasculum . . . and Robert Frost's eyes froze on to that tin, whilst he explained that he also was a botanist, as indeed I had known from his poetry. With this link between us, for something like a year we met and wandered over May Hill, the Leadon Valley, and the ridges of the Cotswolds, hunting flowers together, and talking ceaselessly of poets and of poetry.

What they searched for were Lady's Tresses, Little Teasel, and Spreading Campanula, a harebell as rare as those orchids most loved by Frost in Derry, the Rose Pogonias.

When the Yankee sat out, as he did, in the cobbled space behind his house, facing the broken line of hills and mountains that stretched to Wales, writing on his knee, probably with a rug spread over it, or talking with the Englishmen about how a poet should write, as Wordsworth said, with his eye on the object but also with his ear on the speaking tones, he seems to have chosen May Hill as his special mountain. It was but six miles away and a thousand feet high. There was an inn at its foot where a countryman's lunch of cheese, bread, and cider could be had. And its top, when talk was going, especially with Thomas, became a true haunt of the muses.

Until April 18, 1914, English publication date of *North of Boston,* a grim doubt brooded in the background of blossom and birdsong. The American poet was no longer unknown, but not yet known for his most original and most ripe expression. With scarcely a dissenting voice, however, the critics discovered a classic. Some of the poets with whom Frost had walked and talked, notably Thomas, Abercrombie, and Pound, were among them. But those who knew him not spoke forth the same recognition.

When R.F. talked with me in 1949 of this moment, he bade me take careful note that *North of Boston* sealed his fate twenty years, almost to a day, after that gloomy hour of his retreat from Harvard, when his grandfather offered to stake him for one year of poetry-writing.

"Give me twenty!" he had cried.

"God heard me."

Was he, R.F., elated by his English success? I ventured to ask at Ripton.

"Not elatable. Too old!" he flashed back like a youth.

The English reviews of *North of Boston* can be given here only in brief excerpt: The first from a review in the *Daily News* by Edward Thomas:

This is one of the most revolutionary books of modern times, but one of the quietest and least aggressive. It speaks, and it is poetry. . . . These poems are revolutionary because they lack the exaggeration of rhetoric, and even at first sight appear to lack the poetic intensity of which rhetoric is an imitation. Their language is free from the poetical words and forms that are the chief material of secondary poets. . . . Many, if not most, of the separate lines and separate sentences are plain and, in themselves, nothing. But they are bound together and made elements of beauty by a calm eagerness of emotion. . . .

This last characterizing phrase has survived and so has another by the same critic—not yet visible to his own world as a poet—used in an unsigned review in the *English Review* (August, 1914):

Only at the end of the best pieces, such as "The Death of the Hired Man," "Home Burial," "The Black Cottage," and "The Wood-Pile" do we realize that they are masterpieces of deep and mysterious tenderness.

Abercrombie's unsigned review in the *London Nation*, printed in June, 1914, was like its author, more intellectual, and we are reminded that after the end of the Great War, Abercrombie gave himself over to books on the technique of poetry and eventually became lecturer in poetry at Oxford.

His method—we cannot quarrel with it, because in its final result it nearly always accomplishes something remarkable—is to invite us to assist, first, at his careful and deliberate laying of the material for a poetic bonfire; the skill is interesting, and the stuff is evidently combustible; and suddenly . . . we find that a match has been put to the pile. It burns out, as a rule, rather quickly; but while it is burning, substance and fire are completely at one, and at the end we are not left with embers, but with the sense of a swift and memorable experience. . . .

The critic observes that the New England country life portrayed seems harder and lonelier and also more reflective and philosophic than English rustic life:

. . . it is life that has time to look at itself as well as to look about itself. How much of this is due to Mr. Frost's interpretation of New England we, on this side of the Atlantic, can hardly say; but, if internal evidence goes for anything, life has seldom been made into literature with as little manipulation as in this book. . . .

The *Nation* article—actually much fuller and longer than the excerpt quoted—was copied during this 1914 summer in the Boston *Transcript* and did Frost the extra service of arousing interest for *North of Boston* in Boston. This mattered to him supremely; there had been something troubling to him, as his letters to Sidney Cox and Thomas Bird Mosher show, in acquiring a reputation first abroad. It was thus gratifying

130

that his enemy-friend, Pound, curtly demanded a review copy which would bear fruit in Miss Monroe's *Poetry* for December, 1914, as *American Georgics*.

Amy Lowell had also discovered his book. She recounts how it happened in her essay on Robert Frost in her critical collection *Tendencies in American Poetry* (1917) where Frost and Robinson, his fellow New Englander, fared better than the Middle Westerners.

I had passed the Summer of 1914 in England, and there I had heard much talk of *North of Boston*. I well remember purchasing the little green volume at the Poetry Book Shop, and spending an evening reading it with ever increasing delight. On my return home, I suggested its publication to no less than two publishing houses, but the suggestion met with no response, and with its subsequent issue by Messrs. Henry Holt and Company I regret to say that I had nothing to do. . . . Mr. Frost's reputation was suddenly made. . . . A paper usually so hostile to American verse as *The Times* [London] wrote: "Poetry burns out of it, as when a faint wind breathes upon smouldering embers." . . .

Frost, knowing that Mrs. Nutt had his affairs in hand—a high hand at that—and must be as he put it "in on" anything that was done toward American publication, had no inkling that a celebrity he didn't know, or then much want to, had his active, interfering benevolence toward his book. Gossip about her quarrels with Pound (who had but a year earlier converted her to free verse and made her an Imagiste) had reached the Dymock poets, of whom he was now counted as almost one. The cousin of James Russell Lowell was capturing some of Pound's *Les Imagistes* (with an "e") poets for her own proposed American collections, entitled *Some Imagist Poets* (without an "e"). Richard Aldington, his wife H. D., F. S. Flint, D. H. Lawrence she was luring away into a movement, centered in her Victorian mansion Sevenels, in the heart of Brookline's rich estates. Pound called the new movement "Amygisme" and wrote his friend Harriet Monroe:

131

"Too bad about Amy—why can't she conceive of herself as a Renaissance figure instead of a spiritual chief, which she ain't?"

But Amy Lowell was temperamentally a chief if not a chieftain; well born, rich and powerful and dictatorial, she did become at least publicity leader and effective promoter of a branch of the modern American poetry movement with which, almost willy-nilly, Robert Frost, the individualist, was loosely associated. When the Great War brought the English poetic renascence to a tragic close, as it did in the next few months of that year 1914, the movement, in England guided by men, seemed to leap the Atlantic like wildfire, and started to flame on far less cultivated ground under the leadership of women.

So Amy Lowell's ardent discovery, in London, of a Yankee poet "writing the only true bucolic poetry in America today" had eventually realistic and favorable repercussions for Robert Frost.

The one-candle-lighted poetry evenings of Little Iddens—which Lesley Frost Ballantine has mentioned as part of the pattern of that summer—conjure up for me a row of children sitting on the floor, listening with eight sharp ears that had already heard many fine poems, viewing with eight bright scrutinizing eyes the personalities and peccadilloes of the reading poets. There is no evidence of children in Gibson's "The Golden Room," a poem of the twenties in which the retrospective picture of the Dymock poets is drawn with fond nostalgia. But Miss Eleanor Farjeon, who came to join the Thomases, in a delightful memoir on Edward Thomas speaks of children as ever-present, and Frost says Abercrombie called him *Tête d'Armée*, with his band of four.

The four young Frosts had rejected Ezra Pound: "he didn't like children and thought poets shouldn't be burdened with them." They were entranced by Thomas. They admired Abercrombie, whom their father admired. I wonder if Abercrombie ever read them "Witchcraft: New Style," an authenti

132

Robert Lee Frost at six months.

William Prescott Frost, Jr.
poet's father.

Harvard A

Isabelle Moodie Frost . . . "Belle,"
Frost's mother.

From a daguerreotype, family source

Mrs. Prescott Frost at her Salem, New Hampshire, school. Rob, to the right of his mother, is wearing a stiff straw hat; Jeanie, third left, bottom row, has long hair "billowing down like a waterfall." *Circa* 1886–87.

Robert Lee Frost as ser
class poet and valedi
rian, Lawrence H
School, 1892.

Elinor Miriam White, sen-
ior, Lawrence High School,
1892, who shared honors as
valedictorian with Robert
Lee Frost.

Lawrence High School, "an uncompromising brick building in the center of town."

Robert Frost wrote his first published poem, "My Butterfly: An Elegy" in the kitchen of the Tremont Street house. The poem was published in 1894.

The young Frost family at the Lynch farm, Bethlehem, New Hampshi
circa 1909. The group around the pony includes the poet; his younge
daughter, Marjorie; Mrs. Frost; Lesley, the eldest daughter; Irma; a
Carol.

Family so

Robert and Elinor Frost at Plymouth, New Hampshire, in 1912.

Courtesy Lesley Frost Ballantine

Robert Frost in England at the time of the publication of *A Boy's Will*, 1913.

Jones Library, Amherst, Mass.

In the spring and summer of 1914 the Frosts lived in a half-timbered homestead, "Little Iddens," at Ledbury, Herefordshire, England.

From Dymock Down the Ages *by the Rev. J.E. Gethyn-Jon* *published by H. Osborne, Gloucester, Great Brito*

...ert Frost, as he re-...ed to the Dymock re-..., fresh from his Oxford ...Cambridge honors, in...

...y the Rev. J.E. Gethyn-Jones

Edward Thomas.

From The Life and Letters of Edward Thomas *by John Moore, published by Wm. Heinemann, Ltd., England*

Back from England in 1915, the Frosts found this house in Franconia, New Hampshire.

Robert Frost at his home-made writing board at Franconia farm, *circa* 1915. He built a platform under his Morris chair to protect his feet from the cold.

Frost and his son Carol in Franconia, *circa* 1916–17.

it of the poet by Ullmann, *circa* 1925.

Elinor and Robert Frost in the Old Book Room, Maddox House, Rockfo
College, Illinois, in 1935.

Courtesy Frederic G. Mel

The 1941 Bread Loaf Writers' Conference. Left to right, back row, Edward Weismiller, Theodore Roethke, William Carlos Williams, Louis Untermeyer, Robert Frost, Theodore Morrison. Seated in front, Charles Edward Eaton, Richard Ellman, Cedric Whitman.

Courtesy Bread Loaf Writers' Conference

Robert Frost playing cat's cradle on a cracker box in South Shaftsbury, 1935.

Courtesy Jerome A. Johnson

Playing jackstraws with his daughter, Lesley, and two grandchildre
Elinor and Lesley Lee Francis, at the Ripton log cabin, *circa* 1945.

Jacob Lofman, Pix,

The poet and Gil
Homer Noble Farm
1952.

Jones Library, Amher

A recent portrait of the poet by Lotte Jacobi.

Courtesy Lotte Jacobi

Away

Now I out walking
The world desert,
And my shoe and my stocking
Do me no hurt.

I leave behind
Good friends in town.
Let them get well-wined
And go lie down.

Don't think I leave
For the outer dark
Like Adam and Eve
Put out of the Park.

Forget the myth.
There's no one I
Am put off with
Or put out by.

Unless I'm wrong
I but obey
The urge of a song:
I'm bound away!

And I may return
If dissatisfied
With what I learn
From having died

Robert Frost

"Away," Robert Frost's Christmas poem, 1958.

and powerful character piece, though not as major as their father's later "The Witch of Coös"?

By this time the Frosts, young and old, must have sought out the crossroads in the Dymock woods where poor Sarah Ellis, demented and driven to suicide by the "Dymock Curse," was buried with a stake through her heart. And must have seen the seventeenth-century lead tablet of the Curse, now in the Gloucester museum, carved with Sarah's name, written backward, and with the hieroglyphs of the demons invoked to "make this person to Banish away from this place and countery Amen to my desier, Amen."

Gibson, a shy reserved man, the young Frosts liked. But his sing-song voice was comical to Lesley. He may have read "The Stone," one of his familiar tragic poems about a poor girl of the people who had lost her young lover:

> "And will you cut a stone for him,
> To set above his head?
> And will you cut a stone for him—
> A stone for him?" she said.

"If you can't control your giggles," Elinor told Lesley, "just tiptoe out of the room as if you had something very important to do."

Lesley always had something important to do—she was a born doer. It was important to her to get out her little monthly magazine regularly—in fact there were twelve issues of one copy each, compact, shipshape, with maps and water-color or crayon illustrations—some by Irma, who had gifts in this direction—and concrete observations of nature, always real and not sentimental in the Frost family. Just as *New Numbers* had its resident contributors, and its contributors who came and went in Dymock, as did Drinkwater and Rupert Brooke, so Lesley brought in contributors to her magazine from London and Scotland—the E. C. Smith children whom she and her father visited in Scotland for a week in July, 1914, and the children of Mrs. D. D. Mairs, of the London School of Economics, later Lady Beveridge.

Davies, reckoned the leading unsophisticated nature poet of England at this time, often came to Dymock also and somehow rubbed Frost the wrong way, though the American admired his simple lyrics, like "The Example" which contrasts so innocently with the complexities and formalities of his own butterfly ode.

THE EXAMPLE

Here's an example from
   A Butterfly;
That on a rough, hard rock
   Happy can lie;
Friendless and all alone
On this unsweetened stone.

Now let my bed be hard,
   No care take I;
I'll make my joy like this
   Small Butterfly;
Whose happy heart has power
To make a stone a flower.

He (Davies) sells upward of 100 pounds worth of small poems in a year [Frost wrote Sidney Cox]. His success seems to have hurt him a little and its not strange that it has when you consider his origin. Six years he tramped in America till he fell under a freight car and lost a leg. Then he came home and stumped about selling shoe strings and penny rhyme sheets. Then my friend Adcock discovered him and the rest has followed—recognition from Shaw Conrad and everyone else that counts. The poems in the Anthol are a fair sample of what he can do. No one at the present time can get those flashes in a line as he can. His note is Elizabethan. No one doubts that he is a very considerable poet, in spite of several faults and flaws everywhere. But his conceit is enough to make you misjudge him— . . . His is the kind of egotism another man's egotism can't put up with. . . . He set about encouraging Lesley to write about nature. It would be good practice for a child. He admitted that he had used it up as copy. Lesley is old enough to have to struggle to keep a straight face in such circumstances. There now, he said, see that little bird, that little green one, I wonder what kind he is. Says Lesley It's a sparrow and it isnt green, is it? And Davies stumped into the house. He doesn't really know nature at all. . . .

Edward Thomas, Frost told me, had quite another approach to Lesley's nature knowledge and observation. When she said to him that a swallow in flight looked like a bow running away with an arrow, he asked if he might use this fine simile in a poem.

The great, the glorious meaning of the summer for Robert Frost "the tender, touching thing" lay in Thomas' arrival at a neighboring farm, with his wife, Helen, a laughing earth woman, and his three children with Welsh names. Mervyn, the eldest, was near Lesley's age and the youngest a baby. The two families and Eleanor Farjeon, a dear friend of Thomas', and a granddaughter of Joseph Jefferson, ardently joined their playtimes, while the two men moved off into heart to heart, mind to mind, spirit to spirit relationship in which there seemed to be but one issue—the inner genius that commanded poetry.

From de la Mare's introduction to Thomas' *Collected Poems* of 1921 one senses that Thomas, but for his voice, was almost Frost's double in some aspects of personality; for instance, talk that could be listened to for its own sake.

His smile could be whimsical, stealthy, shy, ardent, mocking, or drily ironical; he seldom laughed. . . . His voice was low and gentle, but musical, with a curious sweetness and hollowness when he sang his old Welsh songs to his children. I have never heard English used so fastidiously and yet so unaffectedly as in his talk. *Style* in talk, indeed, is a rare charm; and it was his. You could listen to it for its own sake, just as for its style solely you can read a book. . . . His learning was of men and things at first hand rather than of facts at second or third; . . . What he gave to a friend in his company was not only himself, but that friend's self made infinitely less clumsy and shallow than usual, and at ease. . . . To be with him in the country was to be in one's own native place, . . .

Frost wrote to Amy Lowell in 1917:

I don't know that I ever told you, but the closest I ever came in friendship to anyone in England or anywhere else in the world I think was with Edward Thomas who was killed at Vimy last spring. He more than anyone else was accessory to what I had done and was doing. We were together to the exclusion of every other person and interest all through 1914—1914 was our year. I never had, I never shall have another such year of friendship.

He also told Harold Roy Brennan what happened between them, in a letter of 1926 cited by R. P. Eckert, in his biography of Thomas:

Edward Thomas had about lost patience with the minor poetry it was his business to review. He was suffering from a life of subordination to his inferiors. Right at that moment he was writing as good poetry as anybody alive, but in prose form where it did not declare itself and gain him recognition. I referred him to paragraphs in his book *The Pursuit of Spring* and told him to write it in verse form in exactly the same cadence. That's all there was to it. His poetry declared itself in verse form, and in the year before he died he took his place where he belonged among the English poets.

Here is a Thomas poem R.F. is fond of:

IF I SHOULD EVER BY CHANCE

If I should ever by chance grow rich
I'll buy Codham, Cockridden, and Childerditch,
Roses, Pyrgo, and Lapwater,
And let them all to my elder daughter.

The rent I shall ask of her will be only
Each year's first violets, white and lonely,
The first primroses and orchises—
She must find them before I do, that is.
But if she finds a blossom on furze
Without rent they shall all for ever be hers,
Whenever I am sufficiently rich:
Codham, Cockridden, and Childerditch,
Roses, Pyrgo and Lapwater,—
I shall give them all to my elder daughter.

The Great War had been creeping up on these poets for some months. The American Frosts were less aware of it than their British poet friends. On June 28 Archduke Ferdinand of Austria and his Archduchess had been assassinated by a Serbian at Sarajevo. All the European powers were, by complex treaty guarantees, involved, and as some of us remember, Sir Edward Grey, England's foreign minister, was, all through July, 1914, negotiating for conference and mediation in an effort to avoid the threatening general European war. Germany, nevertheless, closed her ears, declared war on Russia August 1; on France August 3; and marched into Belgium in violation of her neutrality on August 4. That same day Britain declared war on Germany.

Although Rupert Brooke, who was just twenty-seven on August 3, and the most romantic and striking figure among the four contributors to *New Numbers,* immediately volunteered, the war was reported at first in Dymock as not too serious, likely to be over by Christmas. But sharp anxieties swiftly grew. Chandler, the farmer with whom the Thomases were lodging, a former army sergeant, was called to Hereford and enrolled to fight in France. The British Expeditionary Force arrived there August 16. The battle of the Marne began on September 6. Brooke was commissioned in the Royal Navy and took part in the heroic expeditionary force to Antwerp, after Germany occupied that city on October 9.

Immediately in August the Dymock poets and their friends,

who had supported themselves however meagerly by manuscript reading and critical work for London reviews, received notice that there would be no more articles and reviews to write or manuscript to read until the war was over.

As for the Frosts, worried for their English friends, they were unpleasantly startled by suspicious attitudes on the part of rustic neighbors. The American's New Hampshire accent was queried, and a few stones were thrown at his unshaded windows.

> But let there never be curtain drawn
> Between you and me.

he wrote in "Tree at My Window" in 1927. Moreover he was always going off suddenly and returning without explanation. He might be a Hun—Russians with snow on their beards had been spied in local trains.

Frost found the same sort of irrational suspicion in Mrs. Nutt. When later on, at long last, she invited him and Elinor to dinner and he inquired how the book (after all much in view) was doing she retorted:

"Just like you Americans—all dollar chasers!"

"But Mrs. Nutt, I am not asking about the money—I only want to know if people like the book."

Again she called me a dollar chaser and I said:

"If you call me a dollar chaser I'll go home and keep America out of the War!"

Within a fortnight after England's declaration of war Robert Frost was, in fact, thinking of going home and wrote Sidney Cox to that effect on August 20:

You must think I have been and gone to war for the country that has made me a poet. My obligation is not quite as deep as that. If I were younger now and not the father of four—well all I say is, American or no American, I might decide that I ought to fight the Germans simply because I know I should be afraid to.

138

The war is an ill wind to me. It ends for the time being the thought of publishing any more books. Our game is up. There will really be genuine suffering among the younger writers. My friends have all been notified by the editors they live on that there will be no more space for special articles and reviews till the war is over. De la Mare (greatest of living poets) has just lost twelve or fifteen hundred a year by being dropped by the publisher he read MS for.

So we may be coming home if we can find the fare or a job to pay the fare after we get there. I don't mean to complain. I like the war and the idea of abolishing Prussia, if there is any such thing.

The book was lucky in one respect. It may not have had time to sell much; at least it had made its mark with the reviewers. . . . No book of verse has had as much space given it for a good while.

They [the reviews] have all been ridiculously favorable. *The Times* has talked of the book three times. I understand that there has been an article in the *Boston Transcript* based on the *Nation* article. *And* the Plymouth (N. H.) Public Library has bought me. And I have had a letter from Stowe Vermont which showed that the book had penetrated to that village behind a mountain. . . .

We are here or in this neighborhood till we sail for home. Probably that means for some time. We are going to share house with the Abercrombies for the winter to cut down expenses for both families. . . .

The letter from a Mrs. Henry Holt in Stowe, Vermont, mentioned to Cox, and soon to Mosher, was recalled later in New York as fateful. But at the time Mrs. Nutt's arrangements for American publication were her own. The Yankee poet felt left out of the whole business and indeed was so. Later, in another letter to Cox, follows a paragraph taking grave things lightly, yet aspiring to a future that actually came to pass:

We grow more and more concerned for our future. The prose I sometimes talk of writing for bread and butter would simply bring me nothing now if I wrote it. I may have to go home soon. The difficulty there is that the expense of getting home would

139

leave me under the necessity of getting a job for a while till I got on my feet again. I should awfully like a quiet job in a small college where I should be allowed to teach something a little new on the technique of writing and where I should have some honor [just a little bit] for what I suppose myself to have done in poetry. Well, but I mustn't dream.

Then there is one more letter to Cox, a sort of postscript casual as a bomb-shell:

This is only to say that Henry Holt will supply the book in America. Will you write that on any circulars you have still to send out?

They say the Germans have made the whole Atlantic unsafe. This raises questions for me

1) Do I dare to go home now?
2) Won't it be more dangerous to go every day we delay?
3) Won't it be impossible to get money across to live on pretty soon?
4) Do I dare to stay?

Perhaps you think I am joking. I am never so serious as when I am.

If you never hear from me again, write Henry Holt & Co. Publishers New York on the circulars and let it go at that

That Frost was no dreamer or temporizer when confronted with a world tragedy is clear. But he could live on two levels, and the walks and talks with Thomas went on for another moment, brief as a summer day. Both poets—for Thomas was now one in spirit and soon in fact—wrote poems later about their final unbroken English hours. *This England,* one of the very last prose pieces of Edward Thomas, quoted below, richly describes the Herefordshire setting which moved both poets so deeply by its quiet beauty and peace. Yet the American was aware that he must seek his long future in the other hemisphere, and the Englishman—who was but thirty-six years

140

old at this time—knew already that his half-plan of going back to New Hampshire to settle near the Frosts would yield to the need to enlist in the English army and die for all that England was and stood for.

It was a part of the country [wrote Thomas in his essay, *This England*] I had never known before, . . . But now I was here for the third time since the year began. . . . Here I had the consummation of Midsummer, the weather radiant and fresh, yet hot and rainless, the white and the pink wild roses, the growing bracken, the last and best of the songs, blackbird's, blackcap's. Now it was August, and again no rain fell for many days; the harvest was a good one, and after standing long in the sun it was gathered in and put in ricks in the sun, to the contentment of men and rooks. All day the rooks in the wheat-fields were cawing a deep sweet caw, in alternating choirs or all together, . . .

Three meadows away lived a friend, and once or twice or three times a day I used to cross the meadows, the gate, and the two stiles . . . There, at another stile, the path ceased. . . . The little house of whitened bricks and black timbers lay a few yards up the road, . . .

How easy it was to spend a morning or afternoon in walking over to this house, stopping to talk to whoever was about for a few minutes, and then strolling with my friend, nearly regardless of footpaths, in a long loop, so as to end either at his house or my lodging. It was mostly orchard and grass, gently up and down, . . .

If talk dwindled in the traversing of a big field, the pause at gate or stile braced it again. Often we prolonged the pause, whether we actually sat or not, and we talked—of flowers, childhood, Shakespeare, women, England, the war—or we looked at a far horizon . . .

Whatever road or lane we took, once in every quarter of a mile we came to a farmhouse . . . under the trees stood a thatched cottage, sending up a thin blue smoke against the foliage, and casting a faint light out from one square window and open door. It was cheerful and mysterious too. No man of any nation accustomed to houses but must have longed for his home at the sight, or have suffered for lacking one, or have dreamed that this was it. . . .

141

It seemed to me that either I had never loved England, or I had loved it foolishly, aesthetically, like a slave, not having realized it was not mine unless I were willing and prepared to die rather than leave it as Belgian women and old men and children had left their country. Something I had omitted. Something, I felt, had to be done before I could look again composedly at English landscape . . .

Shortly after the Thomases left, the Frosts gave up Little Iddens and moved to The Gallows at Ryton Dymock, Gloucestershire where Elinor at last fulfilled her wish to live "under thatch." A poem of later date recalls this charming old house, and hints that domestic moods and tensions followed:

THE THATCH

Out alone in the winter rain,
Intent on giving and taking pain.
But never was I far out of sight
Of a certain upper-window light.
The light was what it was all about:
I would not go in till the light went out;
It would not go out till I came in.
Well, we should see which one would win,
We should see which one would be first to yield.
The world was a black invisible field.
The rain by rights was snow for cold. . . .

The poem describes the birds that flew out from their holed-in nests, as the elbow of a poet in dark meditation or domestic quandary brushed or frightened them. Then it goes on:

They tell me the cottage where we dwelt,
Its wind-torn thatch goes now unmended;
Its life of hundreds of years has ended
By letting the rain I knew outdoors
In on to the upper chamber floors.

142

This was the cottage where Robert Frost wrote one of his most noted poems, "The Road Not Taken," which, at his public readings, as I have said earlier, he often introduces as "more about Edward Thomas than about me." Rightly enough, for Thomas, all his life, lived on the deeply isolated, lonely and subjective "way less travelled by" which Frost had chosen in youth but had half deserted through the fate that gave him recognition at forty. At that point he faced, and wanted to, the more double and complex destiny of traveling both roads. He and his poetry too had a stake in the world of people. From this same cottage, in October, he wrote to Sidney Cox, enclosing some circulars about *North of Boston* which he hoped Cox could "scatter." He was centrally concerned to achieve a reputation native, not just British.

Another letter went from Ryton Dymock to T. B. Mosher in November about the time of the first disastrous British Battle of Ypres.

Dear Mr Mosher

. . . Mrs Nutt bears you no good will as I found out when I tried to get her to look at some of your book work. Some people are best not stirred up.

You would have been too late for my book anyway. Someone else took it some time ago, I am informed. I want to thank you for your interest just the same.

I see you have begun reading de la Mare. And you find him not a "free verster." Some careless reviewer had let you in wrong as to his classification. I knew you would like him when you gave him a fair trial. The nineties produced no single poem to put beside his "Listeners [1912]." Really the nineties had very little on these degenerate days when you consider. Yeats, Jo(h)nson and Dowson they had, and that is about all. De la Mare and Davies are the equal of any of them in lyric and Abercrombie (whom I mustn't praise too much for he is in the house with me) leaves them all behind in the sublime imaginative sort of thing. I wonder you haven't discovered Davies. He seems in your line.

This war mars all for the like of us, but it does so much worse for a million others that I don't feel justified in worrying let alone complaining. . . .

This Mosher correspondence was important to Frost. One more letter, this one from the Abernethy Library collection, confirms the significant fact about his American future in publishing.

Ryton Dymock
Gloucestershire Eng
December 27 1914

Dear Mosher

I meant to make it perfectly clear to you how sorry I was that I couldn't see my books named in your catalogue. I venture to say it would make less difference to me than to you if they didn't sell. My first care is that the poetry shall be right. For ten or fifteen years that was all I thought of. Lately I have begun to care a little about placing it where it will stand the least chance of being lost. I feel the responsibility for it that one does for a grown-up child: I want to give it a fair start in life. . . .

Dont you worry about Pound's or Abercrombie's causing me any purturbation of the orbit. I happen to be living in Abercrombie's house at present, but I really know him no more intimately than I do Davies or Gibson or Hodgson or any one of a dozen others. This is a small England and especially so speaking literarily. There are only a few poets in even the greatest countries (America, for instance) and if you know one you know, or can know, them all. Pound and I fell out nearly a year ago. But I see he still reviews me in *Poetry* (Chicago.) Pound is the most generous of mortals.

It turns out that my American publisher is Henry Holt. I have just learned the fact lately, and I don't know how it came about unless it was through someone of the name of Holt who wrote me an appreciative letter from Stowe Vermont in the summer. I think it is only North of Boston that is in question. . . .

In spite of his near-veneration for Mosher's publications, which were frequently pirated but always notable as examples of fine printing, Frost's only publishing association with Mosher was after the death of the old pirate in the skull cap whom he had stayed with, most pleasurably, in Portland, Maine, sometime after his return from England. This was an introduction to *Dartmouth Verse 1925*, published by the Mosher press.

As 1915 came in and the war went on, Frost again wrote to Sidney Cox:

. . . The war has been a terrible detriment to pleasant thinking in spite of all I can do to approve of it philosophically I don't know whether I like it or not. I don't think I have any right to like it when I am not called on to die in it. . . . One of the most earthly wise of our time thinks the common soldiers do actually know what they are fighting for and he has said so in the only good war poem I have seen. (Thomas Hardy's my man.) There are many possibilities. The soldier may know. He may not know as in Southey's "After Blenheim." He may be at fault for not knowing, deficient in national imagination. He may be the larger for not knowing: he may have been a fool always when he thought he knew, playing into the hands of captains and kings. . . .

A last letter went to Cox on February 2, 1915.

Dear Cox
No more letters here, please. We sail for home by the St Paul from Liverpool Feb 13.

Even the trees, standing in a row near The Gallows, seemed to urge the American to uproot himself again.

THE SOUND OF THE TREES

I wonder about the trees.
Why do we wish to bear
Forever the noise of these
More than another noise
So close to our dwelling place?
We suffer them by the day
Till we lose all measure of pace,
And fixity in our joys,
And acquire a listening air.

They are that that talks of going
But never gets away;
And that talks no less for knowing,
As it grows wiser and older,
That now it means to stay.
My feet tug at the floor
And my head sways to my shoulder
Sometimes when I watch trees sway,
From the window or the door.
I shall set forth for somewhere,
I shall make the reckless choice
Some day when they are in voice
And tossing so as to scare
The white clouds over them on.
I shall have less to say,
But I shall be gone.

This poem, "written for Abercrombie" as Frost put it to me, is the "only one I wrote in England that had an English *subject*." One more, published also in *Poetry and Drama* for December, 1914, together with "Putting in the Seed" and "The Smile," had at least an English profile. For however much of New England it is, R.F. wrote it, he says, "after the bronze animals on the Albert Memorial."

THE COW IN APPLE TIME

Something inspires the only cow of late
To make no more of a wall than an open gate,
And think no more of wall-builders than fools.
Her face is flecked with pomace and she drools
A cider syrup. Having tasted fruit,
She scorns a pasture withering to the root.
She runs from tree to tree where lie and sweeten
The windfalls spiked with stubble and worm-eaten.
She leaves them bitten when she has to fly.
She bellows on a knoll against the sky.
Her udder shrivels and the milk goes dry.

These four poems in *Poetry and Drama* were Robert Frost's farewell offerings to the group of literary-poetical conversible Englishmen who had almost accepted him as one of theirs. (Not quite, he says nowadays, shaking his head. "No, not quite.") He left them sadly, shortly after reading their own final poetic offerings in the final issue of *New Numbers*, December, 1914. That review had lasted just one year.

Here were Rupert Brooke's five war sonnets which his friend Abercrombie considered the height of the war poetry of England. Brooke—especially W. W. Gibson's friend whom Frost knew but slightly, for Brooke had been away from England in 1913—had written the sonnets after his Antwerp war experience, while having winter training in Dorset. The fifth and universally familiar sonnet, called "The Soldier," which, now that war has lost its exaltation, reads sentimentally compared to Frost's later sonnet of almost the same title ("A Soldier"), seems to forecast Brooke's own death on a French hospital ship off the island of Scyros, in the Dardanelles, where he lies buried.

> If I should die, think only this of me;
>   That there's some corner of a foreign field
> That is forever England. There shall be
>   In that rich earth a richer dust concealed; . . .

Brooke died on April 23, 1915—St. George's Day and St. Michael's Day, as his friend Winston Churchill pointed out. When the Frosts heard of it, they were innocently watching for the first trilliums and the first lady's-slippers in Bethlehem.

CHAPTER 7

NO, THIS IS NO BEGINNING
February — May 1915

On February 13, 1915, with his family of five and Mervyn Thomas for six, Robert Frost, now publicly a poet, climbed on the deck of the *St. Paul*, a one-class boat dressed down for a war crossing from Liverpool. While they were at sea, the cresting sea that life had become to Frost, with its ever-vanishing and reappearing gleams of meaning, the Germans declared officially their submarine blockade of Great Britain. The youngsters quickly adjusted themselves to life preservers, lifeboat drill, and portholes blacked out at night.

Elinor and Robert, close under their old shawls on the deck, were happily aware of being together, the pair that was truly a pair, joined in an unending effort to adjust spirit to earth and earth to spirit. When Elinor cast herself into the wild waters of chance with her reckless, proud and instinctive mate, she did so companionably, fatefully. And now, victoriously! For could it be denied that they had won their human and poetic maturity in this English venture? Frost had been able to let off steam to Sidney Cox:

"The book is epoch making. . . . All I ask now is to be allowed to live."

One of the decisions on the ship was to buy themselves a new farm in high Franconia where they could, again, raise

148

vegetables and draw off for a period to think over what they had done.

Soon, very soon, they would be on their way north, to a silent mountain land of crystal chill, boundless moments, piercing stars. There, Robert and Elinor decided, Book Three would be born. They counted on American earth returning their love.

But the further the Frosts sailed westward, the more it worried this sturdy, singing man, "forever wild and young" (as Glenway Wescott once put it), that his reputation had come to him in England.

"That was as it happened," he said to Elinor, impressionable, consoling, but caught by his warring impulses, "that was as it happened."

Furthermore, Mrs. Nutt had still disclosed nothing of the arrangements she had made with Henry Holt and Company and paid him no royalties. In all they had spent $3,600 in two and a half years in England. It was gone. When I read "Immigrants," a verse fragment Frost later extracted from a poem he wrote for a Plymouth festival, I think of him on the *St. Paul*, standing by the foaming prow in the dark:

> No ship of all that under sail or steam
> Have gathered people to us more and more
> But Pilgrim-manned the *Mayflower* in a dream
> Has been her anxious convoy in to shore.

He had quitted him like a man (as he had bade himself when he left). He might have recalled with some irony the didactic verse from James Russell Lowell's "The Present Crisis" that all American children learned in district school in his mother's time as teacher.

New occasions teach new duties, Time makes ancient truth uncouth;
They must upward still, and onward, who would keep abreast of Truth.

149

Lo, before us gleam her camp fires! We ourselves must Pilgrims
    be,
Launch our *Mayflower*, and steer boldly through the desperate
    winter sea,
Nor attempt the Future's portal with the Past's blood-rusted key.

Poetry was the only American refuge Frost had found for
his verse while in England. The regular magazines had still
refused him, and even *Poetry* had not been welcoming except
to "The Code."

The *St. Paul* auspiciously docked on Washington's Birthday.
War was not yet looming over the New York skyscrapers. But
as the ship steamed past the Statue of Liberty immigration
inspectors came aboard and made trouble for Mervyn Thomas.
He must, they said, go to Ellis Island and probably be deported to England because he was still under sixteen. Very
little under. This was the welcome of the Land of the Free
to the son of an English poet-soldier.

Nor could the boy's American sponsor reassure them with
a bank balance. Robert Frost had literally only a bit of change
to jingle in his pocket, only his "high-hearted penury," as
Harriet Monroe called it, later on. But he swore by all his
gods that he would have Mervyn free by the morrow. They
would make out somehow.

The dockside of lower Manhattan was bleak and uncompromising as Lesley, fifteen, going on sixteen; Carol, twelve, going
on thirteen; Irma, eleven, going on twelve; Marjorie, nine,
going on ten (all young Frosts were born in spring or early
summer) formed with their handsome parents a gypsy huddle
on the stark downtown street. All were carrying hand luggage,
all were ready and resourceful walkers. They planned, Lesley
Ballantine recalls, to take the Fall River boat in the evening,
at that time the cheapest route to New England. Meantime
they headed uptown. Wanting a newspaper, Frost said in
telling the story, he turned his flock into an East-bound side
street. There, on the first newsstand, staring him in the face,

150

lay a copy of that brand-new weekly he'd heard about: the *New Republic* for February 20, 1915.

Inside, Robert Frost's *North of Boston* reviewed by Amy Lowell—second item in the Book section. If you have ever seen Robert Frost receiving a medal, an honorary college degree, a prize, you will remember the little smile, pleased, yet something skeptical and secret, almost derisive, that flits across his face at such a moment.

The legend, as told by Alfred Harcourt, in his privately printed volume, *Some Experiences,* is that the family walked straight across town to the East Side Elevated, bound for a day in the Grand Central waiting room. R.F. does not swear to this and has no concrete memory of what immediately followed his discovery that the leader of the Imagists, sister of Abbott Lawrence Lowell, was introducing him into the modern poetry movement of the U.S.A. His first American book, his first review in a highbrow weekly! No, he wasn't forgetting what Pound had already done for him.

Frost claims that he never reads reviews of his poetry and it may have been Elinor who held the pages open to the winds, as they walked along arm in arm, looking down the column in a snatchy, cursive way.

So, he was "photographic," "a recorder of a dim decaying New England," "lacked humor," pictured characters "unchanged by any personal mental process."

All the same, the review as a whole was laudatory:

One of the great interests of the book is the uncompromising New Englander it reveals. . . . And Mr. Frost has chosen his medium with an unerring sense of fitness. . . . He has not been seduced into subtleties of expression which would be painfully out of place. His words are simple, straightforward, direct, manly, and there is an elemental quality in all he does which would surely be lost if he chose to pursue niceties of phrase. He writes in classic meters in a way to set the teeth of all the poets of older schools on edge; and he writes in classic meters and uses inversions and clichés whenever he pleases, those devices so abhorred by the newest generation. He goes his own way, regardless of anyone else's rules, and the result is a book of unusual power and sincerity.

The mere revelation that his book was *out* gave Frost's feet the impulsion to get him swiftly to Henry Holt and Company, then situated at 34 West 33rd Street, between Fifth and Sixth Avenues. Mr. Holt himself was seventy-five years old, at this date, but young Alfred Harcourt, the live wire of the firm, manager of the trade department, was around. So Harcourt continues the story:

One day, just before we were to publish *North of Boston,* a rangy man of about forty, with an extraordinarily sensitive face, appeared at the door of my office and introduced himself as Robert Frost. His face flushed when I handed him the *New Republic* check.

The check is further explained in Harcourt's narrative:

One day in September [1914], I went to lunch with Harrison Smith and Sinclair Lewis at the old Park Avenue Hotel. They asked for news from Holt's office, and I said we were going to publish a book of poems by a new American writer that would sell at least 10,000 copies in its first season. There was a hoot of disbelief, and they wouldn't listen when I wanted to read some extracts from a set of sheets I had in my pocket. As I started back to the Holt office, I ran into Francis Hackett [the literary editor of the *New Republic*] in front of the old Holland House. We adjourned to the bar and he started talking about the *New Republic,* the first issue of which was rapidly taking shape. I asked him if they would print poetry. He said, "Of course, if it is good enough." I pulled the sheets of *North of Boston* out of my pocket and said, "Here it is. You would be smart to print a selection from this book in your first issue. We haven't any claim to magazine rights, but I'll take a chance on its being all right if you'll pay your usual rates for an extract." The next day he telephoned me that he and Philip Littell had read the poems and wanted to make a feature of "The Death of the Hired Man" in their first issue. The fee would be $80 or $90. When the book came out, they would give it a feature review by Amy Lowell.

On looking into the files I found "The Death of the Hired Man" in the *New Republic* issue of February 6, 1915—not in the first issue of November 7, 1914. The name of the poem is on the cover—but not yet the name of the poet.

Continuing his version of the story, Frost said that, with this good poetry money in hand, he made haste to wire the Irish Lynches, asking if he might send the family right up; then settled down to the long talk in which two men of earth and intellectual sympathy found common ground. For the first time Frost became aware of the happy significance, for a writer, of the author-publisher relationship which Mrs. Nutt had made so strange and insecure. One act of faith—Harcourt's and Holt's—was enough for him: he felt entirely ready to take the practical advice of the businesslike young man from Dutchess County, who had first seen New York City when he sailed down the Hudson with a load of apples.

The whole story of how *North of Boston* reached Holt's amused him. The Mrs. Henry Holt who wrote him in England from Stowe *had* sent the English copy with a warm recommendation to the head of her husband's trade department. Harcourt admitted that he had had the usual editorial distrust of the boss' wife, and had tossed the book into the wastebasket. Later, finding it still there, he'd taken a grudging look, and was instantly converted. An old friend of Harcourt's, a Vermont author on his trade list, Dorothy Canfield Fisher, was then asked to read the book. Her verdict was warmly affirmative.

So the Holts arranged to import a small edition of one hundred and fifty copies in sheets from Mrs. Nutt. She had made them pay roundly and they had announced the book in the fall catalogue in 1914 and published it then in tan boards. And now in March, 1915, the first strictly American edition—sometimes called the second American edition—in blue cloth, the cover stamped in gilt, was out. Frost was

suddenly glimpsing the end of his American obscurity and
isolation. Poetry had done it all! As he said later, in "Gathering Leaves":

> Next to nothing for use.
> But a crop is a crop,
> And who's to say where
> The harvest shall stop?

But Mrs. Nutt was, Harcourt admitted, making some
trouble. She had done nothing about an American copyright
and it might be some time before Holt's could obtain one.

As Alfred Harcourt explains in his book, and put it to Robert
Frost on Washington's Birthday, 1915, the greatness of the
poetry and the unfair way Mrs. Nutt had treated the poet—
binding him to five books, yet never giving a report of sales
or a penny of royalties—had, Harcourt felt, justified Holt's
action.

For a fact, Harcourt said, the magazine editors who had
refused Frost's verse were now avid to meet and publish him.
The Poetry Society was asking about him. The *New Republic*,
Francis Hackett, Philip Littell, Walter Lippmann, Herbert
Croly wanted him for a Round Table lunch before he left for
Boston. He would need all of them, and more, to make a new
world with.

Frost stood ready to follow Harcourt's lead, but must first
send the family up to Franconia, and get Mervyn Thomas out
of captivity. He was pledged to forward the boy to English
friends of his father in New England.

No doubt Elinor would have better enjoyed going to lunch
with poets and editors than taking her brood into the bitter
cold of an Irish mountain farmhouse. But it was for her to
make up to her children that their father loved poetry best
of all and had an impersonal fate bound up with it that some
of them were still too young to understand.

Frost has told me that when, the day after landing, he got
to Ellis Island he found that his charge Mervyn had been put

to bed, the night before, in a sort of cell, among thoroughly ambiguous characters, one of whom committed suicide that very night. The boy himself was already being examined in a quasi-courtroom—"judges three" asking intrusive questions of a scared adolescent and telling themselves, by no means *sotto voce,* to hurry up and get this over so we can go out to lunch.

Frost's indignation overflowed:

"Tell them you don't *want* to stay in a country like this," he had cried to Mervyn.

The judgment was that the English boy had to go back to England. So Frost, not trusting these "authorities" as far as he could throw a church by the steeple, appealed to Harcourt, who invoked the aid of the brilliant lawyer, Charles C. Burlingham. Burlingham gave Frost a letter to Fred Howe, Immigration Commissioner, and Howe, a man of sense and sensibilities, released Mervyn to the care of Robert Frost, a new and sudden celebrity in the American literary world.

Frost now had urgent business: income business in Lawrence and a need to revisit his high-school friend and editor, Ernest C. Jewell, to whom he had sent *A Boy's Will* from England.

From Lawrence, he wrote to Sidney Cox on March 2:

Dear Cox

Your letter was the first thing I read in America. In fact I read it before I was in America that's to say before I passed quarantine. You are always encouraging.

I wish I could afford to visit you at Scenectady and see you first and then anyone else you cared to bring along. . . .

You know that the Holts have my book out. Pretty cover. But the best of the Holts is that they are going to be a father to me.

Did you see what Amy Lowell had to say in the *New Republic* for Feb 20. She will pervert me a little to her theory, but never mind.

I am on the way to Bethlehem, New Hampshire. Write to me there in care of John Lynch. I wish we might be near you in the summer somehow.

On March 13, from Littleton, N. H. (Littleton, Bethlehem, and Franconia are adjacent villages), RFD No. 5, % John Lynch, he wrote again to Sidney Cox:

Write to me as soon as you can to say you got my letter from New York and understood my reasons for not going to Schenectady. I was aching to see you and almost hoped you would propose coming to us. You have a salary and can go and come as you please. When I got to Lawrence where I could ask for money (and might or might not get it) I had less than fifty cents left in my pocket. You can read Browning's "Up at the Villa" for a proper statement of why a man of my means might live in the country. As a matter of fact I like the country and might live there all the time of choice. At the present moment however I must live there of necessity. I am not rich enough to live even for a few weeks in the style you suggested in Schenectady.

I didn't get through New York and Boston without more attention that you may think I deserve from my fellow countrymen. The Holts are splendid. If you want to see what happened in Boston, look me up in the *Boston Herald* for Tuesday March 9 under the heading Talk of the Town. A number of my old editorial enemies actually asked me for poems. Let us weep before it is too late.

In the next letter, dated March 22, Frost told Cox he wouldn't be in jail or the poorhouse for five years or so. There was news through the Lawrence visit that a continuation of the $800 a year from his grandfather's estate would exhaust the principal in about five years.

. . . My only hope in those days [five years hence] will be my children or such of them as think well of me—don't judge me too hardly for having written poetry. There's Marj—she told Mrs. Lynch, I'm told, that I was a good one to write poetry and to bring up children. She's very likely wrong, but as long as she believes what she says—

And a word more to you my son. You are to dispense with further talk of disparity between us. I have never had such thoughts and I dislike having them thrust upon me.

156

Thus shamelessly I send you the *Herald* scrap. If the fellow who wrote it seems to know more of my goings and comings than he could without complicity of mine, the reason is because he is a lovely old boy and quite took possession of me while I was in Boston. When he wasn't actually with me like Mary's lamb he was keeping track of me by telephone. I believe he is doing for me on principle. He's got me on his conscience. The Ellery Sedgwick of the piece is mine ancient enemy the edtior of *The Atlantic*.

The *Herald* scrap, Boston journalism of 1915, reads in part:

Boston's literary sensation of the day has been the home-coming of Robert Frost. Three years ago a young New Hampshire schoolmaster went over to England, lived in retirement for a while, and published a volume of poems which won him many friends in a quiet way. Some time ago another volume of verse went to the same publisher and one morning Robert Frost found himself famous. His work was hailed as striking a new note in modern poetry. He was sought on every hand in the circles where literature values count and was acclaimed one of the elect—ranking with Masefield, Gibson, Abercrombie and others of that high grade in the younger generation of British poets.

. . . In due time copies crossed the water and appeared in the bookstore and the libraries. Readers began to discuss the remarkable work and ask, "Who is Robert Frost?" Nobody could say, in spite of diligent inquiry, and *Who's Who?* was silent.

"You'd better get hold of him," said a friend to the editor of *The Atlantic*—"he's another Masefield."

Then came the news that Frost had just landed in New York with his family, on his way back to New Hampshire, to take up farming again—he had been a farmer as well as a school teacher.

Last Friday they were discussing Frost at the monthly "shop talk" of the Boston Authors' Club; one of the members reading from his work, said that Frost was doing for New England in verse what Alice Brown, Mary Wilkins and Sarah Orne Jewett had been doing in prose. Another member announced that Mr. Frost was in Boston that day, and was dining that evening with Mr. Ellery Sedgwick and some literary friends. . . .

That dinner with the editor of the *Atlantic Monthly* was, I suspect, for R.F. one of the "crests" he reached in Boston. He was, all the while, secretly nursing the grievance which would project the dramatic scene that followed early in May, when he would confront his "ancient enemy" with three new poems as ammunition and with their power shoot himself an entrance into the *Atlantic's* walled garden. Yet Frost had his reservations about Boston "cut-glass dinners," as he called them. He knew himself to be the very man who, but now, had only fifty cents in his pocket, and even now had no secure backlog but eight hundred dollars a year for five years from the grandfather he couldn't bless.

If Josephine Preston Peabody (Mrs. Lionel Marks), a charming and generous lady whose lyre charmed Brattle Street, Cambridge, as Amy Lowell's more ornamental one Heath Street, Brookline, asked him (or if the more formidable Amy did):

"Frost, how do you like my poetry?"

and he didn't much, not very much, what could he say? His shrewd, empirical, subtle, leisurely talk and his simple, still unworldly-seeming personality concealed a very serious poet, counted by some a genius, needing an American living place. He recognized, with dismay, that he had to dig his heels in not to be swept away out of his Emersonian freedoms.

In England, as he had sensed in advance, you could be poor, live like a peasant, and, yet without any self-exploitation, be printed, read, reviewed, and get to the top of the list. Here it seemed that some of the women who were waving the banners of the forward march of poetry might enslave you. What would E. A. Robinson, the sardonic "old bachelor," do without women? It was said that Mrs. Marks had found him a publisher for "Captain Craig" and that Mrs. William Vaughn Moody of Chicago, though jealous for her dead husband's name, was helping him, too. Amy Lowell, for her part, was publicizing John Gould Fletcher even more than Robert Frost.

The sudden widening of Frost's circle had indeed its complexities. But one thing was sure. He had a gift for making a real intellectual friend at first sight. This is convincingly shown in a reminiscent letter to Charles R. Green, written by one of the guests at Mr. Ellery Sedgwick's "cut-glass dinner." The guest was the eminent Harvard professor of philosophy, Ernest Hocking, now emeritus, of whom R.F. says today: "We are thoughtful friends of long standing" and adds tenderly of Agnes Hocking, who died some years ago: "She was always poised to fly and quivering her wings."

Mrs. Hocking [wrote Professor Hocking] and I first met him about 1915 at a dinner given by the then editor of *The Atlantic* [Ellery Sedgwick] soon after his Frost's return from England. We had little chance to talk, at this dinner, though Frost had read some of John Boyle O'Reilly's poems and was interested in the fact that my wife was a daughter of O'Reilly. We had to leave early for a Lowell Lecture. Shortly after, at a railway station in Boston, my wife spied R.F. and spoke to him, saying that she had regretted not having asked him to tea. "When do you want me?" he said. "This afternoon". "I will be there". He came, and we began talking; he stayed the night, he stayed the next day and the next night. When I had to go to class, Agnes Hocking took him on; and when she had to get a meal, I took him on. We had a great time. In three days' time, we had done a fair two-years' job of ripening friendship. But during this time nothing had cropped up about his ever having been at Harvard.

Frost and Hocking discovered, only much later, that they had both been members of the Harvard class of 1901.

"Well, yes, I was in the class for fragments of two years [Hocking quotes Frost], and how I hated it."

Through Hocking, however, in the spring of 1915, R.F. was introduced to a scholar whose student in Logic he had been in college and found rather pompous. Professor Emeritus George Herbert Palmer had taught Ethics too in the famous group of philosophers that had included William James, Josiah Royce, and George Santayana. Now his ex-student was in-

159

vited ceremoniously to the grand old brick mansion on the edge of the Harvard Yard. It was full of famous manuscript collections—perhaps the first that Frost, now so close to bibliophiles and collectors, had ever taken thought of?

Palmer's views of poetry were not as interesting as his manuscripts. "In a democracy," he propounded to his new protégé, "the greatest poet should be the one read by the greatest number of people. If so, Edgar Guest is the greatest American poet!"

Shortly Palmer advised Frost solemnly that he must get down to really serious work, write an epic. He invited the younger man to settle next door to his summer home in Boxford. But Frost turned away. He had wanted no patronage from Pound, and certainly not from a pedantic professor.

It must have been a relief to Robert Frost when he at last met a poetic peer, Edwin Arlington Robinson. This happened in a conventional Boston setting, he says, and the evening did not warm up greatly till Robinson said (Frost recalls only this one sentence of the evening's talk):

"Frost, you look as if you needed a glass of bitters!"

Frost continued the story after E.A.R.'s death, in his introduction to E. A. Robinson's *King Jasper*.

There were Robinson and I, it was years ago, and the place (near Boston Common) was the Place, as we liked afterward to call it, of Bitters, because it was with bitters, though without bitterness, we could sit there and look out on the welter of dissatisfaction and experiment in the world around us. It was too long ago to remember who said what, but the sense of the meeting was, we didn't care how arrant a reformer or experimentalist a man was if he gave us real poems. For ourselves, we should hate to be read for any theory upon which we might be supposed to write. We doubted any poem could persist for any theory upon which it might have been written. Take the theory that poetry in our language could be treated as quantitative, for example. Poems had been written in spite of it. And poems are all that matter. The utmost of ambition is to lodge a few poems where they will

160

be hard to get rid of, to lodge a few irreducible bits where Robinson lodged more than his share.

Robinson's best poem, in Frost's opinion, was "Mr. Flood's Party." "The guarded pathos . . . is what makes it merciless."

Robinson must have had, that first evening, something to say of *North of Boston* and Frost of *The Town down the River.* Maybe they had both something to exchange about *The Spoon River Anthology*—the only rival poetry Frost's books had in the spring of 1915—which owed something to Robinson in lineage.

These two, Frost and Robinson, fellow New Englanders (often reported jealous of one another and, Frost implies, separated by their friends), felt, in fact, a great mutual respect. Both had had the courage to make a success out of many years of worldly failure. Robinson, after he deserted Gardiner, Maine, clung to cities and lived his summers as a detached, adulated, honored, frustrated, suffering bachelor at the MacDowell Colony; whereas Frost was always hastening back to the country, winter and summer, and living a familial and deeply involved, instinctive human life. Robinson, both poet and man, was a "heartacher" (as Frost has said), in spite of his wit and his comedy. Frost, in contrast, was somehow ever of good heart, even when his characters were caught in tragic circumstances.

Frost had, all through his English years, been hankering for the New Hampshire farmers, with their sparse lives and their laconic speech. In their winter rigs they were as familiar as his own hand, and he liked them best when

> The city had withdrawn into itself
> And left at last the country to the country . . .

The Notch still opened between two great mountains piled with snow. The stoves in their rooms at the Lynches' burned

161

red-hot only if Rob Frost split the wood; and he must make great circlings on foot, mud time or not, looking for their farm-to-be, and getting versed once more in northern New Hampshire country things. For instance, such experiences as led him to record, from Franconia memories of this season, "Evening in a Sugar Orchard."

A poem of sheer naturalistic nature, not a symbol in it. For similar realistic observation of water, running or frozen, compare "The Onset" and "A Hillside Thaw," both derived from Bethlehem-Franconia living.

This is the first stanza of "A Hillside Thaw":

> To think to know the country and not know
> The hillside on the day the sun lets go
> Ten million silver lizards out of snow!
> As often as I've seen it done before
> I can't pretend to tell the way it's done.
> It looks as if some magic of the sun
> Lifted the rug that bred them on the floor
> And the light breaking on them made them run.
> But if I thought to stop the wet stampede,
> And caught one silver lizard by the tail,
> And put my foot on one without avail,
> And threw myself wet-elbowed and wet-kneed
> In front of twenty others' wriggling speed,—
> In the confusion of them all aglitter,
> And birds that joined in the excited fun
> By doubling and redoubling song and twitter,
> I have no doubt I'd end by holding none.

"Aglitter" and "twitter" are examples of Frost's unconventional interest in words: his "lucky finds," he calls them, when he reads them to an audience.

Letters always following Frost up kept insisting on ties to the cultural world that cut across the deep ties to nature. While it was still March, 1915, he answered one from Braithwaite, the poetry reviewer of the *Boston Transcript* whom he had met down there.

Dear Mr. Braithwaite:

I've got as far as finding you the copy of Book I I promised you.
Perhaps as a busy man you wont resent my telling you what to
read in it if you are going to read at all. It is the list I always give
to friends I wish the minimum of suffering: pages 1, 2, 4, 7, 9, 14,
20, 22, 23, 25, 26, 34, 41, 42 (once printed in The Transcript), 45,
46 (8–18 line—first poetry I ever wrote that I could call my own—
year 1892) and 49. Don't read those unless you have to, but don't
read the others on any account. ["False, false," said Frost when I
showed him his own words. "What hypocrites we are!"]

The book is an expression of my life for the ten years from
eighteen on when I thought I greatly preferred stocks and stones
to people. The poems were written as I lived the life quite at the
mercy of myself and not always happy. The arrangement in a
book came much later when I could look back on the past with
something like understanding.

I kept farm, so to speak for nearly ten years, but less as a farmer
than as a fugitive from the world that seemed to me to "disallow"
me. It was all instinctive, but I can see now that I went away to
save myself and fix myself before I measured my strength against
all creation. I was never really out of the world for good and all. I
liked people even when I believed I detested them.

It would seem absurd to say it (and you mustn't quote me as
saying it) but I suppose the fact is that my conscious interest in
people was at first no more than an almost technical interest in
their speech—in what I used to call their sentence sounds—the
sound of sense. Whatever these sounds are or aren't (they are
certainly not of the vowels and consonants of words nor even of
the words themselves but something the words are chiefly a kind
of notation for indicating and fastening to the printed page) whatever they are, I say, I began to hang on them very young. I was
under twenty when I deliberately put it to myself one night after
good conversation that there are moments when we actually touch
in talk what the best writing can only come near. The curse of
our book language is not so much that it keeps forever to the same
set phrases (though Heaven knows those are bad enough) but

that it sounds forever with the same reading tones. We must go out into the vernacular for tones that havent been brought to book. We must write with the ear on the speaking voice. We must imagine the speaking voice. . . .

I like the actuality of gossip, the intimacy of it. Say what you will effects of actuality and intimacy are the greatest aim an artist can have. The sense of intimacy gives the thrill of sincerity. A story must always release a meaning more readily to those who read than life itself as it goes ever releases meaning. Meaning is a great consideration. But a story must never seem to be told primarily for meaning. Anything, an inspired irrelevancy even to make it sound as if told the way it is chiefly because it happened that way.

I have run on unpardonably. I couldn't write a whole biography; so I just had to plunge into the middle of things. I have pretty well jumbled the story of how I see my own developement and some of my theories of art. . . .

May I hope really to see something of you when I am in Boston again? I'd like to have a talk about poetry by ourselves alone.

Sincerely yours

Robert Frost

Such correspondence interrupted the search for the farm. At last the Herbert place was selected, a little farm two miles west of the village of Franconia, on the side of Sugar Hill, overlooking the Lafayette range and the Pemigewasset river in an alluvial "interval" like those referred to in Frost's poems.

In the long poem "New Hampshire" we seem to find the sales transaction described:

> Not even New Hampshire farms are much for sale.
> The farm I made my home on in the mountains
> I had to take by force rather than buy.
> I caught the owner outdoors by himself
> Raking up after winter, and I said,
> "I'm going to put you off this farm: I want it."
> "Where are you going to put me? In the road?"
> "I'm going to put you on the farm next to it."

"Why won't the farm next to it do for you?"

"I like this better." It was really better. . . .

So William Herbert moved down the road a small piece to a red farmhouse he'd had to buy to please a queer duck he now heard called a poet. Frost had agreed to pay $1,000— nothing required "down." But the title had to be cleared and some improvements made and, as time passed, Herbert came to the Lynches to say he'd heard that Robert Frost was "somebody," so wouldn't he pay a hundred more? Frost assented: $1,100 it was.

Frost had his eye on the upstairs bedroom over the porch he'd make into a study. It had a magnificent view of Mounts Lafayette, Liberty, and Cannon, which he would climb several times every summer with his children.

They were not settled in yet, though, when on May 5—the day after the sinking of the *Lusitania*—Frost made his first visit to a college, and faced his first town-and-gown audience at Tufts College, where he read before the Phi Beta Kappa Society three unpublished poems now among his most familiar and most beloved: "Birches," "The Road Not Taken," and "The Sound of Trees." He was scared but said the poems in his own poetic, realistic, unsentimental way that won immediate renown. Louis Untermeyer and he met in the flesh at this time and were, from then on for many years, often together and always in correspondence. There was a rich flow of wit and humor and poetic interchange between them.

Sylvester Baxter, with whom both were staying in Malden, urged Frost that this was the crest on which he should seek out Ellery Sedgwick in his sanctum on Park Street, Beacon Hill. Baxter arranged it for him. So Frost went with the three poems just read, burning a hole in his pocket.

Frost continued the story to me in these words:

"We are going to be your true friends. [Sedgwick began.] We are going to hold you up to your best. Have you any poems with you?"

165

I replied in an injured voice: "Mr. Sedgwick, I am not the kind of poet who goes around with poems in my pocket. But, as it happens, I have three right here that I've been reading at Tufts College."

He reached for them saying: "Let me have them." To be impressive, I took them out of my pocket and raised them high in the air.

"Are you sure you want them?"

He swallowed and said: "Yes." I came down into his hands with them.

I said: "I seem to be playing in luck."

Sedgwick said: "I haven't decided to use it." (We were only hostile friends.)

"Then you shouldn't have told me about it. You'll almost have to use it, for if you don't it will do me more good than if you do. I will tell the whole United States on you."

We both laughed a great deal (a hard laugh) as we carried on these conflicts and he generously used both the poems and the essay in the same number of the *Atlantic Monthly*. It was one of the best strokes in my favor that I've ever had. It made "Birches" in particular, one of my best known poems.

He never liked me afterward and neither did Harriet Monroe, for the reason, in her case, that she had refused all the poems I sent her till my reputation was established.

CHAPTER 8

MOUNTAIN INTERVAL
1915–1916

Mountain Interval, Frost's Book Three, published in November, 1916, was the true goal of the months that stretched ahead and exactly named the life that engendered the book which terminates Frost's "first period" as an American poet. Alfred Harcourt was devotedly interested in helping his "Simon pure" poet, as he called Robert Frost, to make out financially while he gave form to this collection. A battered copy of a letter (undated) from him to Robert Frost—which I have seen through the courtesy of Mrs. Harcourt—is given below:

Dear Frost;

Here's a check for $200. We are going to take our chances with Mrs. Nutt, and pay you what would amount to a royalty of 10% on our sales of *North of Boston,* and *A Boy's Will* in our own reprint. We expect to continue the honorarium unless we should be stopped. . . . We shall give you a report of sales on the 25th of each October and April.

Don't worry. You're going to be able to publish poetry and get your just dues. We'll go into all that when you come down. Of your troubles that I've heard, hay-fever is the worst.

Ever yours, Alfred Harcourt

167

The dedication of *Mountain Interval* when it appeared quite intentionally pointed the way back into the past for its sources:

TO YOU

WHO LEAST NEED REMINDING

that before this interval of the South Branch under black mountains, there was another interval, the Upper at Plymouth, where we walked in spring beyond the covered bridge; but that the first interval of all was the old farm, our brook interval, so called by the man we had it from in sale.

Both the "eclogues" of the book, "Snow" and "In the Home Stretch," concern a married couple—not the same one—who seem to be having an ideal existence together, when others leave them alone. In the second they are arriving on a late afternoon in their new-old farmhouse, amidst a confusion of goods dumped by the movers. The two exchange subtle marital reflections, intuitive and selfless.

"Dumped down in paradise we are and happy."

"It's all so much what I have always wanted,
I can't believe it's what you wanted, too."

"Shouldn't you like to know?"

                                    "I'd like to know
If it is what you wanted, then how much
You wanted it for me."

                        "A troubled conscience!
You don't want me to tell if *I* don't know."

"I don't want to find out what can't be known.
But who first said the word to come?"

                                    "My dear,
It's who first thought the thought. You're searching, Joe,
For things that don't exist; I mean beginnings.

168

Ends and beginnings—there are no such things.
There are only middles."

                                    "What is this?"

                                    "This life?
Our sitting here by lantern-light together
Amid the wreckage of a former home?
You won't deny the lantern isn't new.
The stove is not, and you are not to me,
Nor I to you."

                    "Perhaps you never were?" . . .

In life, as contrasted with art, however, the Robert Frosts
had lost the isolation and privacy they had known in Derry,
Plymouth, and Franconia, and even during their English sojourn. In his new Franconia home the poet found himself near
poets and writers who happened to live there—Raymond
Holden, a young poet whose work he liked and has followed
in a life-time sense dropped in frequently. Ernest Poole's back
line adjoined his own. City intellectuals like Justice Von
Moschisker turned up in Bethlehem hotels. Professors as diverse as Cornelius P. Weygandt of the University of Pennsylvania and Harold Goddard Rugg from nearby Dartmouth
College looked him up. Joseph Warren Beach came with his
family. Jean Starr and Louis Untermeyer, already fast friends
and of the same poetry world that Frost was joining and
creating, went up to visit him when they might.

This multiplicity of city folks (dudes as they used to call
them in New Mexico) puzzled and somewhat irritated the
Franconia country people with whom the Frosts had been
intimate in the past. Down the road at the Herberts' they
were pestered with telephone messages that must be relayed
to the Frosts. Finally Willis Herbert's father made a caustic
aphorism that has survived:

"Next time you sell a farm, son, find out beforehand if it's
going to be used as a farm or a park."

Frost, if one is to believe the poem that stands opposite "Meeting and Passing" in *Mountain Interval,* had a very much more elusive telephone service of his own.

THE TELEPHONE

"When I was just as far as I could walk
From here today,
There was an hour
All still
When leaning with my head against a flower
I heard you talk.
Don't say I didn't, for I heard you say—
You spoke from that flower on the window sill—
Do you remember what it was you said?"

"First tell me what it was you thought you heard."

"Having found the flower and driven a bee away,
I leaned my head,
And holding by the stalk,
I listened and I thought I caught the word—
What was it? Did you call me by my name?
Or did you say—
Someone said 'Come'—I heard it as I bowed."

"I may have thought as much, but not aloud."

"Well, so I came."

But the exciting world of literary rivalry and ambition cut into their precious separateness again, favorably, with the July, 1915, issue of the *Atlantic Monthly.* At last any good New Englander could read three beautiful poems of Robert Frost's and feel sure that they were all they should be because Edward Garnett, a distinguished English critic, had discovered *North of Boston.*

. . . The question first to ask seems to me whether a given author is a fresh creative force, an original voice in literature.

170

Such an authentic original force to me speaks from *North of Boston*. Surely a genuine New England voice, whatever be its literary debt to old-world English ancestry. Originality, the point is there. . . .

Garnett had much more to say; among other comments this one that may have set Harvard professors thinking:

. . . One may contend that "The Housekeeper" is cast in much that same gossiping style as Theocritus's idyl, "The Ladies of Syracuse," with its prattle of provincial ladies over their household affairs and the crush of the Alexandrian streets at the Festival of Adonis. And one may wager that this famous poem shocked the academic taste of the day by its unconventionality. . . .

By August 14 something extraordinary had happened to *North of Boston* in its homeland, something Harcourt had predicted. It was a best seller! This we know from a letter from Frost to William Stanley Braithwaite:

. . . Don't you think we could kill a week walking and talking? I am bursting with sounds I want to utter about the sound of poetry. Be careful how you refuse me. If you dont come I shall be sure it is because you are too nice to have anything to do with the author of a Best-seller (non-fiction) which is what I am told I have become. Isn't it—well hard to know how to take?

Braithwaite who was now busy with an anthology in which he wished to include several of Frost's poems ("honored enough if you will use two, honored beyond dreams if you will use three" wrote R.F.) had referred to a letter Pound had sent to the *Transcript* and Frost eagerly picked this up:

. . . No I haven't seen Pound's letter. What new terms of abuse has he found for your review? Why would you review him? He needs letting alone. The English have ceased to give him space in their papers.

Pound's letter, written from London in August, 1915, and reprinted in *The Letters of Ezra Pound,* is part of R.F.'s harvest of 1915 and shows that the tension between Pound and Frost had not abated.

To the Editor of *The Boston Transcript:*

. . . I note in *Current Opinion* for June a quotation from your paper to the effect that my friend Robert Frost has done what no other American poet has done in this generation "and that is, unheralded, unintroduced, untrumpeted, he won the acceptance of an English publisher on his own terms" etc.

Now, seriously, what about me? Your (?Negro) reviewer might acquaint himself with that touching little scene in Elkin Mathews' shop some years since.

Mathews: "Ah, eh, ah, would you, now, be prepared to assist in the publication?"

E.P.: "I've a shilling in my clothes, if that's any use to you."

Mathews: "Oh well. I want to publish 'em. Anyhow."

And he did. No, sir, Frost was a bloated capitalist when he struck this island, in comparison to yours truly, and you can put that in your editorial pipe though I don't give a damn whether you print the fact.

You might note *en passant* that I've done as much to boom Frost as the next man. I reviewed that book in two places and drew it [to] other reviewers' attention by personal letters. I hammered his stuff into *Poetry,* where I have recently reviewed his second book, with perhaps a discretion that will do him more good than pretending that he is greater than Whitman. E. L. Masters is also doing good work.

Amy Lowell and Frost were fast becoming easy friends.

There is an ominous note in your letter [Frost joked] that seems to tell me you are getting ready to throw me over as a poet of the elect ostensibly on the ground that I am become a Bestseller when really it will be because I haven't convinced you that I like your book. What's the use of my trying to say anything now when I am in a corner? You will be sure to ascribe my prettiest compliments to fear. . . . You know my little weakness for dramatic tones. I go so far as to say that there is no poetry of any kind that is not made of dramatic tones. Your poetry always

speaks. I wish sometimes you would leave to Browning some of
the broader intonations he preempted. The accent-on-the-you sort
of thing. But that's a small matter (or not so large as it might be);
the great thing is that you and some of the rest of us have landed
with both feet on all the little chipping poetry of awhile ago. We
have busted 'em up as with cavalry. We have, we have, we have.
Yes I like your book and all I lay up against you is that you will
not allow me a sense of humor. . . .

William Dean Howells, the revered Dean of American letters, now reviewed Frost's two first volumes in *Harper's* "Easy
Chair" for September, 1915.

. . . His manly power is manliest in penetrating to the heart
of womanhood in that womanliest phase of it, the New England
phase. Dirge, or idyl, or tragedy, or comedy, or burlesque, it is
always the skill of the artist born and artist trained which is at
play, or call it work, for our delight . . . here is the old poetry
as young as ever; and new only in extending the bounds of
sympathy through the recorded to the unrecorded knowledge of
humanity . . . with a touch as sure and a courage as loyal as if
the poet dealt with it merely for the joy of it.
But of course he does not do that. He deals with it because he
must master it, must impart it just as he must possess it.

How unpuritanical Frost was about play, how playful he
actually was as poet Howells failed to see. Frost had but one
meeting with Howells, a happy one, he has told me. Howells
sent him "The Mother and the Father," a blank verse poem
of his own, in dramatic duologue form, published in 1909.
This, though tending to the sentimental and solemn, has a
faint sturdy kinship with Frost's more inspired work.

Many of Frost's letters to Cox were directed to getting
certain original ideas about his poetry and his aims on paper
as well as into the consciousness of a disciple. Many passages
deal with the teaching of English—how it should be done, how
American colleges were doing it, where and how and wherein
Frost thought they failed.

One of the last letters from Dymock had said:

> . . . I have done what I have done and I believe I have made place enough for myself to be sure of a hearing for anything else I do. I ask no more. I should like now to go to a small college with the chance of teaching a few ideas. . . .

Frost had nevertheless many reservations about scholars and a poet's connection with scholarship. He has said throughout his life, that a poet should avoid the heavy burden of knowledge as such—should acquire and possess of scholarship only what he could carry like a stick that he swung ahead of him as he walked.

He had written to Sidney Cox on January 2, 1915, from England:

> Everything is research for the sake of erudition. No one is taught to value himself for nice perception and cultivated taste. Knowledge knowledge. Why literature is the next thing to religion in which as you know or believe an ounce of faith is worth all the theology ever written. Sight and insight, give us those. I like the good old English way of muddling along in these things that we can't reduce to a science anyway, such as literature love religion and friendship. People make their great strides in understanding literature at most unexpected times. I never caught another man's emotion in it more than when someone drew his finger over some seven lines of blank verse—beginning carefully and ending carefully—and said simply "From there to—there." He knew and I knew. We said no more. I don't see how you are going to teach the stuff except with some such light touch. And you can't afford to treat it all alike. I mean with equal German thoroughness and reverence if thoroughness is reverence. It is only a moment here and a moment there that the greatest writer has. Some cognizance of the fact must be taken in your teaching. . . .

Again Frost wrote to Cox on June 24, 1915, from Franconia:

> . . . I'm blessed if I don't believe sometimes that the whole subject of English was better neglected and left outside the cur-

riculum. School is for boning and not for luxuriating. We don't want much school even when we are young, that is to say, we want a great deal more of life than of school. And there is no use in this attempt to make school an image of life. It should be thought of as a thing that belongs to the alphabet and notation. It came into life with these. Life must be kept up at a great rate in order to absorb any considerable amount of either one or the other. Both are nonsense unless they mix well with experience. They are the past and the future, and the distant, and the problem is to bring them to bear a little on the present and the near, to make them make some difference even the slightest. Too much time spent on them is either an injury to the infant or a waste of time on the infant that refuses to be injured. Literature—I don't know where literature comes in, if it comes in at all. It is ever so much more of life anyway than of school. It is almost too emotional for school handling, almost too insubordinate and unconventional. The one thing that it is bound to be is what it is not told to be. Mind I do not say what it is told not to be, though there might be reason for its being that.

I write as I feel tonight. Some of what I say is true. Run it all through a De Laval separator.

I am up to my eyes in milk and such like farm produce. Hence this Georgic figure. And I'm too tired to be awake writing.

Bates College in Lewiston, Maine, was one of the first academic colleges (after Tufts) to offer an opening to read. Haggling over prices in the fall, by correspondence, was unpleasant. Frost had decided on seventy-five dollars as his fee. But he had to compromise on fifty dollars and expenses, when he finally got there on May 13, 1916.

It was never a question of what he was worth, he told them. He was probably worth nothing, he said, characteristically disarming them and arming himself. But it just came about that the unworldly were made self-seeking in self-defense. College presidents should know this, shouldn't they?

He went down Boston way at least twice in November, 1915. Once it was to see (and hear) a dramatic performance by the American Drama Society of two of his major "talk-poems": "Home Burial" and "The Death of the Hired Man."

During another trip, at a reading to friends at Browne's, the schoolmaster's, in Cambridge, he learned from Professor Palmer that Harvard had chosen him Phi Beta Kappa poet for the next June, 1916.

Then came bad news of a serious family crisis and he threw over everything to hurry back to be cook and nurse. Elinor had had a miscarriage. But she was well enough to write Miss Susan Ward a Christmas letter, in which she talked about the wonderful beauty of the snow-covered mountains.

". . . especially at sunrise. The sun rises directly over Mt. Lafayette just now, but the weather has been so bad lately, that we don't see it rise very often."

Amy Lowell sent up her *Six French Poets*, just out, and Frost found pleasure in being able to like it, with the daughter he had most raised and educated himself.

Thanks for this large—this spacious—book, and especially for the Paul Fort of it [he wrote Miss Lowell]. Between his French and your English I'm not sure that I don't come nearer some idea of him than ever I did of foreign poet before. . . . Do you know he's the only one of your six who shows with any vividness the sounds I am after in poetry. I'll tell you what we did with the Henry III. My daughter and I read it together, I with my head tipped one way following your English aloud she with her head tipped the other way following his French in silence, the book being open at two places at once you understand. And even under those unfavorable circumstances I brought tears of excitement to my daughters eyes. And she is a young thing.

Frost had discovered by now to what degree Amy Lowell's role in the American poetic renascence was, that of "Public Poet"—Louis Untermeyer's expression. Like Ezra Pound, he remarked, she rejoiced in minding other people's business. Her aim, she once said to me, with her disarming half-frankness, was to enslave all lives that touched her own, be they editors, publishers, poets, reviewers, cooks, waiters, or chauffeurs. From his youth Frost had his own techniques for avoiding enslavement—it started with his grandfather—and they stood him in good stead at this period when he was finding his poetic feet on his native soil. By no means would he acquiesce in Amy's demand that he use New England dialect, as James Russell Lowell did; as she did in her rather naïve rivals—so I have felt them—of Frost's *North of Boston* eclogues.

Frost and the children had concocted a "card" of their own make, in Franconia, for the Christmas of 1915. Lesley made a sketch of a snowy slope grown with firs and a sky with a new moon, above a poem written in R.F.'s own beautiful script: "Christmas Trees": the one in which a man refused to sell one thousand fir trees for thirty dollars for "trial by market," but did want to send one in a letter to a friend.

The "card" I have seen, which went to the mother and sister of Morris Tilley, a Michigan professor they had known in Franconia, says, in handwriting: *From Robert Frost and the children. And Mrs. Frost wishes to be remembered though she had no part in this nonsense.*

Midwinter was a time when the poet withdrew into his old self, dressed like an old tramp, stopped at a house when walking and said: "Do I smell coffee?"

The country people, so the niece of one of them told me in 1955, "didn't know who Mr. Frost was, yet." They liked to feed him and gossip with him. And there was nothing in these encounters to stop the poetry that sometimes came as he walked: the something ever so subterraneously half-glimpsed; some thought he had not been sure he'd had until he reached, say, that bush where the road closed for good turned off.

The poem in *Mountain Interval* that, for me, most deeply symbolizes and embodies what Robert Frost drew from his silent Franconia winters and, retrospectively, from his Derry winters is the poem whose very theme is winter, the winter of nature and of man.

AN OLD MAN'S WINTER NIGHT

All out-of-doors looked darkly in at him
Through the thin frost, almost in separate stars,
That gathers on the pane in empty rooms.
What kept his eyes from giving back the gaze
Was the lamp tilted near them in his hand.
What kept him from remembering what it was
That brought him to that creaking room was age.
He stood with barrels round him—at a loss.
And having scared the cellar under him
In clomping here, he scared it once again
In clomping off;—and scared the outer night,
Which has its sounds, familiar, like the roar
Of trees and crack of branches, common things,
But nothing so like beating on a box.
A light he was to no one but himself
Where now he sat, concerned with he knew what,
A quiet light, and then not even that.
He consigned to the moon, such as she was,
So late-arising, to the broken moon
As better than the sun in any case
For such a charge, his snow upon the roof,
His icicles along the wall to keep;
And slept. The log that shifted with a jolt
Once in the stove, disturbed him and he shifted,
And eased his heavy breathing, but still slept.
One aged man—one man—can't keep a house,
A farm, a countryside, or if he can,
It's thus he does it of a winter night.

"All a poet needs is samples [R.F. wrote in my *Selected Poems*], enough success to know what money is like. Enough to know what women are like. I believe in what the Greeks call synecdoche: the philosophy of the part for the whole; skirting the hem of the goddess."

The old fellow of the poem is a sample of those many aged New England countrymen who live on like old gnarled landmark apple trees, "keeping" a whole inert countryside in being, through their own quality of being. Yet there is something particular about this old man. Could he resemble Grandfather Jont Eastman, Carl Burell's grandfather, who lived for a time in the upper story of the young married Frosts' home in Derry? Just one "clomp" and one "creak" might have done it, when filtered through creative memory.

Surely this is a poem in which Frost achieved "the purification of his quality." He said in 1925 that "An Old Man's Winter Night" had no equal for form save "The Mountain" and "Stopping by Woods on a Snowy Evening."

I would add to this list "After Apple-Picking" and from *Mountain Interval,* "The Hill Wife," published in the *Yale Review* for April, 1916. This last strikes into the very heart of a domestic drama of loneliness, of madness—brief, tender, moving, and tragically concentrated.

In the five successive lyrics in ballad verse, a very young woman, living apart with her young farmer husband, has two shy, poignant utterances of her own—about her fear of loneliness, as expressed in her delicate observation of bird couples, and her fear of the stranger at the door. (This last reminds us of "Love and a Question" in *A Boy's Will.*) The other three poems describe without horror or strangeness how quietly the tragedy moved to its sudden end. The last lyric is quoted:

THE IMPULSE

It was too lonely for her there,
　　And too wild,
And since there were but two of them,
　　And no child,

And work was little in the house,
　　She was free,
And followed where he furrowed field,
　　Or felled tree.

She rested on a log and tossed
　　The fresh chips,
With a song only to herself
　　On her lips.

179

And once she went to break a bough
   Of black alder.
She strayed so far she scarcely heard
   When he called her—

And didn't answer—didn't speak—
   Or return.
She stood, and then she ran and hid
   In the fern.

He never found her, though he looked
   Everywhere,
And he asked at her mother's house
   Was she there.

Sudden and swift and light as that
   The ties gave,
And he learned of finalities
   Besides the grave.

"Besides" was, of course, vital to Frost's meaning. He has told me how irritated he was when a distinguished editor turned it into "beside."

Henry Holt and Company
34 West 33rd Street
New York

Dear Melcher [wrote Alfred Harcourt in January, 1916, to Frederic Melcher, then a book salesman in Indiana, describing the beginning of one of R.F.'s long friendships]:

I have two nice things to tell you.

Robert Frost was visiting me yesterday and was idly glancing through the *Publishers' Weekly*, a copy of which he had never seen before, when he happened on what you say in the last issue about *North of Boston* and *A Boy's Will*. He was so pleased that he wanted me to tell you. It was nice to have two friends meet that way in my home. I do hope you will have the pleasure of really knowing Frost in the flesh some time. I am still in a glow from the day with him.

Though it was nice to have your article and his visit fall together this way, I have something better still to tell you. He has enough new manuscript to make another book next fall. I have read it and it is finer than *North of Boston*, finer in form and in spirit. You will enjoy it when you see it.

I was a little afraid that since *North of Boston* was written in England under some stress of home-sickness, Frost might be slow in getting to writing here at home, but it has been coming rather fast of late and now I, at any rate, am sure that we have the Simon pure article, a real American poet. . . .

But Frost was by no means ready to surrender his manuscript. Thirteen poems—if you count the five parts of "The Hill Wife" separately—were published in magazines as the months passed. This, numerically and financially, was a new and happy experience. In the early part of 1916 he had, moreover, agreed to resume his "barding around" as he already called it. He read poetry or lectured in schools and colleges, in Hanover, Lawrence, Boston, Wellesley, New York, and other places. In March Frost wrote Harriet Monroe, enclosing "Snow," a long dramatic "talk" poem of *Mountain Interval;* comparable, though of lighter import, in its free, hand-drawn blank verse line, but not in tragic intensity, to "The Death of the Hired Man." He felt it a high spot in vocal imagination.

I should like awfully well to get not much less than two hundred dollars for it—if that doesn't take your breath away [he wrote Harriet Monroe].

Apparently it did take her breath away, for in a fortnight Frost wrote again:

My dear Miss Monroe,
    Greedy, I must seem. I don't want to be that even for the sake of variety. It would take too long to tell you in self defence how I figured it out that I ought to have two hundred for my "Snow."

A letter from Franconia to Miss Lowell of May 14, 1916, describes a man suspended uncomfortably between two cultures.

Dear Miss Lowell:

. . . I am sorry sorry but I can't really afford to make the trip to Boston for your meeting this week. . . . I hate to seem to stand outside of anything—I am always grieved when asked if I belong to the Masons or the Rebeccas to have to say No—and if I could be persuaded that I could do the Poetry Society any good or it could do me any harm I don't know but that I'd begin to save up money. . . .

But seriousness aside (I guess you'd think it was serious if all you had to keep an establishment on was an occasional ten dollars for a poem you only wrote for fun anyway). I shall hope to see you sometime a good deal sooner than I can promise to be at the Poetry Society to be reduced to the ranks.

I've been trying to tell Louis of New York, but I haven't got around to write it out yet, that I was asked to read poetry at the movies the other night to give the people time to get into their seats before the main part of the show began. I was advertised on the bills like this: Prayer by the Rev. Soambro. Poems by R.F. Pictures Life of Christ, 5000 feet. I was advertised first and invited afterwards. I wasn't there.

You may not believe that and if you don't you won't believe this: a neighbor got into the house on the pretext of wanting to sell me seeds. He began on me the minute he sat down with "How are the books coming on Mr. Frost?" Next he said "Poetry exclusively I believe it is with you?" Next very respectfully "What do you ask apiece for them?" And when I answered "Seventy-five cents and one dollar and twenty-five cents," he told me "Poole gets one dollar and fifty." Poole of "The Harbor" summers further up the mountain. All I ask is your sympathy.

Shall you be where I can find you in the middle of June?

The middle of June was the time when Robert and Elinor Frost, with their son Carol, went "down along" to stay with the Baxters in Malden while the poet read his eclogue, "The Bonfire," on Phi Beta Kappa Day at Harvard. Though Untermeyer described him as having "a stubborn scholar's face, masking the irrepressible poet's," he had not yet made his special place among the scholars and mounted platforms with trepidation. An added anxiety, discovered by consultation in Boston, underlay this whole experience.

Carol, who had had persistent chest colds, was diagnosed as having tuberculosis. This malady evoked stark memories for Carol's father, and rending fears for Elinor, always the Great Mother, mother of the race, her knees bearing the weight of her offspring at all times, especially in illness.

"The Bonfire," a poem about runaway fires and children—which had its origins in Derry and is listed as "of Franconia," won praise for Robert Frost. The last verse, contemporary to 1916, makes the analogy with the war that all the distinguished audience at Sanders Theater was thinking about. But in terms of a talk between father and children; in terms of a local conflagration, due to one man's careless bravado. "The Bonfire" begins:

> "Oh, let's go up the hill and scare ourselves,
> As reckless as the best of them tonight,
> By setting fire to all the brush we piled
> With pitchy hands to wait for rain or snow.
> Oh, let's not wait for rain to make it safe. . . ."

The poem, moreover, is not about the actual prankish fire the father urges on his offspring, but on one that he, Father, set sometime in the past to scare himself and the neighbors—and just barely managed to put out.

> ". . . Why wouldn't I be scared remembering that?"

> "If it scares you, what will it do to us?" [say the children]

> "Scare you. But if you shrink from being scared,
> What would you say to war if it should come?
> That's what for reasons I should like to know—
> If you can comfort me by any answer." . . .

Frost had also read at Sanders Theater a second poem that the critical world now esteems one of his masterpieces: "The

183

Ax-Helve." Ellery Sedgwick, with astute judgment, told him on the spot that it was the finer of the two and later claimed it for his magazine. The variety and power of Frost's human and poetic resources, the degree to which he was not alone a regional Yankee poet, was now becoming evident. Though every outward step had its price for him at home and otherwise, a more distant reading territory was already tempting his curiosity and his imagination for the following year 1917. This was the Middle West where, in Chicago, the two rival H.M.'s—spunky little Harriet Monroe, the creator of *Poetry,* and the formidable, international-minded Harriet Moody—presided over the "new" Middle Western poetry.

Frost never felt too happy in August, even in Franconia, thanks to his old hay-fever trend or its ghost; he could bear nothing like "clothes," and wore only a shirt and jeans no matter how many professors or judges turned up.

But visitors came and went that summer. Carol, faithfully following a stiff routine, was improving. Jean Starr and Louis Untermeyer shared the picnicking by waterfalls to the accompaniment of peerless talk. Jean Starr thinks that when they arrived for the first time, she in lipstick and rouge—for the war had now passed on to the literati what had before belonged only to the stage folk—she must have seemed a painted Jezebel to the Frost children. Such looks of dismay and repudiation, especially from Irma, who sat all day sewing or reading Jane Austen; her set was worn out by her! Elinor's lips were her own color; and the transfigured gaze of mother love that she fixed on her children, especially Lesley, enclosed them deeply in their old Puritan ways. In the snapshots taken by Jean and Louis, Elinor's purity of feature, her glints of humor, her head surrounded with long braids, stand out rare and fine. Robert, at forty-two, on the edge of a ravine, slim, athletic, looks still the young genius. But in Morris Tilley's snapshot, as he leans against a wall with Carol, his thought is brooding.

In *From Another World* Untermeyer describes the extraordinary moments when Frost was freed to talk at his best: his philosophic banter, his play of ambiguities, his symbolic figures and references, his reckless intemperance about his enemies, his eulogies of his friends, his play of opposites and double meanings, left breathless even his brilliant and volatile friend Louis. Talk that plunged, explored, and for all the poet's seeming conservatism disturbed innumerable prejudices, revealing a hidden subversive.

Jean Starr Untermeyer has written down for me a memory of her own. Elinor, Robert, and Lesley Frost were visiting the Untermeyers at their West Side apartment in New York, near the Hudson: a place that was becoming something of a poetic "salon" and hospitable home of ideas for the new poets and the new poetry.

"Robert," I questioned, "how is it that, though you had those twenty unrecognized years, years that must have tested you fiercely, and caused both you and Elinor much hardship, how is it that I have never heard you become bitter?" He looked at me in that quizzical way we all know so well, the lower lip pushed forward a bit and only the twinkle in the eye at odds with the gravity of his face.

"Well," he drawled, "with respect to poetry I have always felt like a man entrusted to carry a jar of precious ointment on his head: I didn't want to spill any of it; then, you know, one can never tell how the race will turn out till the end; then . . . then, I'm a lucky man; I've always been able to give full measure."

Has ever a man been able to give a better and more succinct account of himself? Even without all his poems, which have enriched my own thinking, I would have had to love him for that summing up.

Still the poems kept appearing: in October in the old *Independent*, "The Gum Gatherer" (*"There comes a day,"* said Frost, *"when the least mentionable can be mentioned."*) and "The Telephone"; in November, "Snow" in *Poetry*; in the

185

Atlantic Monthly, "An Encounter." "The Bonfire" appeared in the *Seven Arts*—the first number, November, 1916.

The *Seven Arts* was edited by a psychologist-writer James Oppenheim; his associate (fiction) editor was Waldo Frank, who soon discovered Sherwood Anderson and other then new names. Van Wyck Brooks, who had just published *America's Coming of Age,* took charge of criticism and essays; Untermeyer was poetry editor and critic; Robert Edmond Jones supervised the theater notes and brought in Eugene O'Neill. The opening manifesto sounded off buoyantly:

It is our faith and the faith of many, that we are living in the first days of a renascent period, a time which means for America the coming of that national self-consciousness which is the beginning of greatness. In all such epochs the arts cease to be private matters; they become not only the expression of the national life but (a means to) its enhancement.

Our arts show signs of this change. . . .

As "advisor" in poetry, Frost read a few manuscripts, but never attended an editorial meeting. Following "The Bonfire" he gave his prose play *A Way Out* for publication in February, 1917. His actual connection proved tenuous. The *Seven Arts* led into the Age of Sociology, and if there was one science (or pseudo-science as he would put it) that Frost already hated it was sociology. His childhood views on individualism had not altered. Randolph Bourne, writing his antiwar articles in this review was further from Frost spiritually than an editor of the old tradition like Miss Susan Ward.

To the latter the poet wrote in October, 1916, regretting that he and Elinor had not been able to visit her before her brother died—"before your circle broke," he puts it. He told her how busy he'd been all the year earning a living—"rather more of a living than I ever made before—you will be glad to hear that!" He will visit her "this winter when I am south-along. I shall hope to find you well and ready for a poem or two of not too new a kind."

The visit was made and out of it came "Wild Grapes," as I shall tell later.

Mountain Interval appeared in November, 1916. It contained enchanting lyrics, sonnets in several formal sonnet forms with Frostian variants—and of course the blank verse "Snow" and "In the Home Stretch"; *"poems of not too new a kind."* Starting with "The Road Not Taken," ending with "The Sound of the Trees" (Frost used the second "the" in the 1916 edition), the book is one of wholly country things and indeed, with few exceptions, New Hampshire things. But watch for a new Latin verse accent in the last line of "An Encounter." The poet, wandering through "a swamp of cedar," meets "a resurrected tree."

> A tree that had been down and raised again—
> A barkless specter. He had halted too,
> As if for fear of treading upon me.
> I saw the strange position of his hands—
> Up at his shoulders, dragging yellow strands
> Of wire with something in it from men to men.
> "You here?" I said. "Where aren't you nowadays?
> And what's the news you carry—if you know?
> And tell me where you're off for—Montreal?
> Me? I'm not off for anywhere at all.
> Sometimes I wander out of beaten ways
> Half looking for the orchid Calypso."

This hendecasyllabic accent from Catullus is one that Frost enjoys and used later in "For Once, Then, Something." We also find, as novelty, a little moral (or declarative) statement at the end of some sonnets, as in "Hyla Brook"—the brook named for the tree frogs which give spring its earliest and most haunting voice.

We love the things we love for what they are.

Or in its twin "The Oven Bird":

The question that he frames in all but words
Is what to make of a diminished thing.

"The Oven Bird" intones rather than talks, to quote the
poet, and those last two lines, he says, "have been used unjustly against New England." The criticism Frost most objected to, when it turned up in those days, was that he had
made New England country folk sad or mad. Actually he
spoke from the tragic background of the poet who writes
from the heart of the life that he knows and divines.

Mountain Interval was very much Elinor's book. Mrs.
George F. Whicher, the widow of a professor who was for
all his Amherst years a close friend and associate of Frost's
in the department of English, remembers a moment at Franconia, during a visit to the Frosts', perhaps in 1917. She was
assisting her hostess in making sandwiches, and found herself
able to speak out her own feeling for *Mountain Interval*.

"Don't you think it's beautiful yourself?"

Elinor Frost dropped her knife and clasped her hands.

"Beautiful," she said in a voice close to tears.

Another early believer, Mark A. De Wolfe Howe, Boston's
grand old man of letters, who had accepted the early work
of an unknown countryman for the *Youth's Companion,* because he, too, thought it beautiful, has told me that Frost, in
late 1916 sent him his three books, with new unpublished
poems written on the flyleaves. Frost then wrote apologizing
for his "impulsiveness" in showing poems not fully "aged" in
his notebook.

I usually keep my poems about me for some time before printing them. I found that easier to do in the old days when you were
nearly the only editor who would pay money for them.

And speaking of keeping poems a long time, there's a sonnet-
shaped thing in my new book called "Range-Finding" that you
(I think it was you) once wrote me a nice letter about as long
ago as 1906.

With gratitude for the way you helped me over those leanest years I am

Sincerely yours

Robert Frost

RANGE-FINDING

The battle rent a cobweb diamond-strung
And cut a flower beside a ground bird's nest
Before it stained a single human breast.
The stricken flower bent double and so hung.
And still the bird revisited her young.
A butterfly its fall had dispossessed
A moment sought in air his flower of rest,
Then lightly stooped to it and fluttering clung.
On the bare upland pasture there had spread
O'ernight 'twixt mullein stalks a wheel of thread
And straining cables wet with silver dew.
A sudden passing bullet shook it dry.
The indwelling spider ran to greet the fly,
But finding nothing, sullenly withdrew.

Frost has told me that he sent "Range-Finding" to Edward Thomas, at the British Front. Thomas wrote back that it was a surprisingly exact description of no man's land, the space between the firing-line trenches of facing enemy armies in the Great War. Frost had not needed to experience war to "see" and understand it from within.

Readers who know "Design," with its evil white spider that has wound a web about a moth, will compare it with the imagery of this wheel of thread in the foreground of a battle-field. I have come to feel that the web of strings is one of Frost's most characteristic poetic and metaphoric figures. Death was present in both these poems. Perhaps the web as Frost uses it is symbolically the web of life itself. All the poems in which it is found seem to have something deeply fateful about them.

Edward Thomas had fatefully enlisted in the Artists' Rifles

189

six months after his American friend returned to New Hampshire, and during any moment he could snatch for himself, in the midst of dreary camp training, had been writing poems. Some found their way happily to Franconia. Some—with the signed pseudonym "Edward Eastaway"—were dispatched by the author to the same English critical reviews in which he had written valued estimates of Frost's and other men's poetry, and all were refused, probably because they had been projected from Thomas' quiet, melancholy inner world, rather than from the seething war world that Britain had become. The repetition in Thomas' fate of Frost's own early experience of critical neglect wrung the American's vitals. Time had been on his side, but Thomas had none to spare.

But at last, at the end of November, 1916, the great news came from Thomas to Frost in Franconia that a volume, to be published under Thomas' own name by Selwyn and Blount, had been assembled and contracted for. He had dedicated it to Robert Frost, and was sending him the poems.

In Helen Thomas' autobiography, *As It Was World without End,* the final leave-taking, before Thomas, then a second lieutenant in the Royal Artillery, went off to Flanders, is described with anguished love. His haunting personal beauty, his fortitude in despair, his courage are rendered in this book, along with his tie to his earth wife, and to the children at the fireside. He left the poems, ready for the press, in his wife's hands, and walked away over the hill, forever, carrying in his pocket Shakespeare's *Sonnets* and, as Frost was to learn, an early copy of *Mountain Interval.*

A month later, on a certain cold, mid-December afternoon, Robert Frost made his first contact with Amherst College. The publication of *Mountain Interval* must have been a factor in the request that he read his poems there. The invitation had come from President Meiklejohn and from Stark Young who was a power in the English department. Frost reminded me of this connection with Stark Young—who was his host—when he spoke of the long, long tie forged by that particular reading.

190

The audience was small, town and gown, of course [Frost explained]. I felt scared enough till I noticed (I do notice) a man, German-built as to feature whom I picked right off—or he picked me, I don't know—as a poetry lover. He sat in the front row and he listened and he took pains to tell me, afterwards, that he especially valued "The Death of the Hired Man." His father had been one. This was W. R. Brown, a real estate man, a crony of mine till his death in early 1957. Another interest we had in common was Thoreau—I mean as a passion.

President Meiklejohn, after the reading on December 16, offered Frost an *ad interim* appointment for the second college term, to replace in the English department a professor who was going off to the legislature. This radical President, an experimentalist in education, brilliant and unconventional, had a way of taking sides with other brilliant people. He could, as President, accept a teacher who was no academic careerist and had no degrees, make him a full professor, and even grant him the unusual privilege—which Frost demanded—of brief absences to read his poetry elsewhere. The salary was $1,500 but the poet could augment it by readings—by "barding around," as henceforth he would describe it. So was the compact made, to go into effect after Christmas.

"Just one term," Frost told Elinor, "we can stand that."

Actually the decision to teach in a college—his first—was the end of the long-cherished hope that he could live only for and by poetry. In the forty and more years that followed he has never been able to separate himself for long from eager students—though, Frost adds, they were never very numerous. As teacher, he has always dealt with very few boys.

PART III

THE LESSON FOR TODAY

1917–1927

CHAPTER 9

ONLY MORE SURE OF ALL
I THOUGHT WAS TRUE

1917

The pattern of Robert Frost's life began, from January, 1917, to expand, change, and assume greater variety and a far broader connection with people. We know him so well now, in old age, as a very peripatetic man, almost a folk poet in his wide renown. He stands there on the platform, say at Columbia University, white-headed and stalwart at more than four score years, with fame clasping his slightly bent shoulders; a "sayer" who competes with "sarcastic science" herself in our Atomic Age America. One must look back to the Golden Age of New England, to Longfellow, to Emerson, to find any similar loved and potent figure in American letters.

But no such golden clouds surrounded or uplifted Robert Frost in 1917. When he mounted a platform to speak or read his poems he felt and—to some—seemed shy, sensitive, and elusive. It was certain that he dreaded also the impact of the stereotypes and systems of the scholars with whom he began to consort at Amherst College. Both teaching and speaking destroyed, for the time, his power "to write poetry with nobody looking on" as he had in England. His inner ear ceased to listen or to hear or to record the words of the spirit unless he had true solitude.

195

Thanks for your letter of praises [he once wrote from New Hampshire to Professor Carleton Wells, of Michigan]. When I get off here by myself I can hardly believe I'm the same fellow that faces crowds so heroically on nothing but tea and one raw egg. We're creatures of strange extremes.

Nevertheless, because of his willingness to suffer both the human and the poetic fate—a willingness clouded by doldrums and dearths, by hesitations and revolts—and because he suffered it in a high poetic manner, he assumed in the decade that began in 1917 greater human and poetic stature. He had untried inner powers that needed to be called forth to sustain his expanding fate. As the years passed, he could admit even that he had learned to get along better with Time. "I had all the time there was, as my grandmother used to be mean enough to say to my mother, who never had half enough, in her busy devotions." In the trial of the middle years, as we see them now, Frost was steadily winning, if only sometimes by the last throw of the dice.

"But to me it wasn't ever triumphant—it was just the 'Ups and Downs of a Donkey's Life.'" The old poet insisted on my understanding this. In fact his *New Hampshire* did not appear until seven years after *Mountain Interval*. As for the pattern that developed in his teaching, it was a sort of spiral that returned on itself, like the famous uroboros, the serpent that swallowed its own tail, fertilizing and giving birth to itself in a circular form.

Three years at Amherst College; then a period of twenty months for country retreat and verse; then two years at the University of Michigan; then back to Amherst for two years; then another return to Michigan. This latter had so assured itself as the decisive beginning of a lasting University appointment that most of the Frosts' Lares and Penates had journeyed along to Ann Arbor. But in one college year's time, exactly, the poet was loading everything on freight cars to jog back to South Shaftsbury and Amherst. A magnetic root of unplumbed strength had given the final pull, severing the Mid-

dle West from its colonist, restoring to New England its spiritually native son.

There was drama in these moves, an almost physical need
of adventure, change, and renewal; and it seemed sometimes
as if Frost embraced difficulties in order to conquer them or
to be helped out of them by his all-devoted friends.

"Everyone in the family liked change," Lesley has told me,
"except Marjorie." But the ironic French adage was true of
the Frosts:

Plus ça change, plus c'est la même chose.

Or to put it in the poet's own words at the end of "Into My
Own":

> They would not find me changed from him they knew—
> Only more sure of all I thought was true.

After the reading in late 1916 which had decided their
Amherst fate, a modest faculty house to sublet furnished for
the winter-spring term turned up for the Frosts on Dana
Street, where a row of professors lived under two pleasing
rows of shade trees. In the rather ambiguous period between
Christmas and New Year's, when the winter solstice keeps the
sun pallid, and fires and lamps assume their maximum glow,
a battered old car stopped at the bungalow on a cold late
afternoon. Mrs. Otto Manthey-Zorn, the wife of a German
professor now "emeritus," tells me that she watched from her
window next door a gypsy band—youngsters, animals, chickens in coops—tumbling out and spilling into the cold dark yard
and house. The strangers had a lost look that led her to run
over and see if she could help.

The "furnished" house had no blankets. The desperate poet
was shivering as he stoked the furnace; the lovely wife with
the encircling braids and classic face was in distress.

"He catches pneumonia so easily!" whispered Elinor.

Back rushed Mrs. Manthey-Zorn to tear the blankets off
her own beds and tell her husband he could sleep under his
overcoat that night. Thus casually and fortunately began one

of Frost's major Amherst friendships, in which the wives were as close as the husbands.

Soon "the children" (as they still humbly called themselves who had lived with genius and often felt eclipsed) were assorted roughly to their public school grades—if they cared to go. Taken in a row, they were now a tall thin ladder that mounted skyward like the ladder in the poem "After Apple-Picking," letting the fair blue of eyes shine through at the top. Their adaptations to education had an undocile ebb and flow. Carol, tall and spindling, charming, the very image of his father, brothered three heteroclite sisters and refused books. The two younger girls were still "in solution." Only Lesley, the top rung of the ladder—rash, brilliant, emotional and obstinate, sculptural in build and contour—wanted to exercise her mind in the grand style and shine as with her father's high marks and his classical tastes. Though on principle left behind in Franconia to finish her senior year, she was soon irresistibly with them on Dana Street, dominating and directing them as she followed the classical course at the high school.

Robert Frost was proud of this loyal, intractable girl who had read Caesar and Virgil under his tutelage, and started scanning Latin verse in England before she knew the grammar. Her reading of the *Aeneid* in her class marked her a poet's daughter, and brought obeisance from both her teacher and the previous star pupil who belonged to the only Jewish family in Amherst at that time. Lesley at once adopted her rival as close friend.

All was well enough in the family transplanted from mountain land to shady Academe. Yet as the poet looks back on the year 1917, he damns it as a "bad year," shaking his head. This was the year when his country took the great step of entering a European war as a world power; the year when he experienced grief and loss in the death of Edward Thomas; the year when the professing of English, with irresistible logic, devoured the leisure to write poetry. Three poems only appeared in magazines in 1917. It was the year when Frost discovered that one best seller in poetry did not always lead to another. It almost never does.

Mountain Interval, launched but a few months before the United States declared war on Germany, did not sell well after the first critical acclaim. So little, that Holt and Company, through Alfred Harcourt and Bristol, the quiet old treasurer of the firm, worked out a subsidy of $100 a month. Frost's aid from his grandfather's trust fund, which had totaled $6,000, doled out, was over sooner than expected. Though, thanks to President Meiklejohn's liberal views, the poet entered on his work with the dignity of a full professorship, his Amherst salary, even for the times, was a pittance. But when had he thought money a supreme value?

The first duty that Professor Frost assigned himself in Amherst College, just as 1916 ended, was to talk with Professor Churchill, the retiring incumbent, about the courses he must teach. They were three: Shakespeare; Pre-Shakespearean drama; English poetry based on Palgrave's *Golden Treasury.*

When the latter was discussed, Churchill said he had based his whole course, the first term, on one seventeenth-century poem, "A Garden," by Andrew Marvell.

"Must be a well-trampled garden," said Frost.

Churchill's reply was that he supposed you had to, *on principle,* spoil some great poetry to teach it.

Frost inwardly begged to differ. He knew he wanted ideas from his students, not exegesis. He wanted to bring pleasure and excitement into class, never boredom for himself or those he instructed.

"I'll never correct a paper for style," he told the boys when he met them. "I'm looking for subject matter, substance in yourselves."

"What we do in college is to get over our little-mindedness. Education—to get it you have to hang around till you catch on."

Sometimes they seemed to be catching on, sometimes they didn't. If not, Frost had to remind himself of the adage he often quotes in his old age—one especially pertinent in a war year: "No general but enters into battle on insufficient information. Nobody enters upon any enterprise but on insufficient information."

"Some are self-made outside of college; some are self-made in college; but all are self-made if made to any purpose," he told them. R.F. was self-made in every fiber of being and mind, and aware how deeply moved he was by his strong interests and major compulsions as a poet. He could not keep his own balance in a collegiate community unless he constantly adjusted the balances with his fellows and stuck to his own sense of "difference." For he had a difference, he recognized. In poetry, a "stride." He had found it and it belonged to nobody else. In life, a pattern that fitted nobody else, either.

Writing his notable preface to Edwin Arlington Robinson's *King Jasper* in 1935, after the death of the poet he had so greatly admired, Frost inquired:

. . . How does a man come on his difference, and how does he feel about it when he first finds it out? At first it may well frighten him, as his difference with the Church frightened Martin Luther. There is such a thing as being too willing to be different. And what shall we say to people who are not only willing but anxious? What assurance have they that their difference is not insane, eccentric, abortive, unintelligible? Two fears should follow us through life. There is the fear that we shan't prove worthy in the eyes of someone who knows us at least as well as we know ourselves. That is the fear of God. And there is the fear of Man —the fear that men won't understand us and we shall be cut off from them.

Frost had both fears and drew meaning from them.

Those early, semi-innocent Amherst teaching years—how can one figure the power and satisfaction they brought Robert Frost, as over against the rebellion that squeezed his soul dry when the lightning struck and he felt driven to go apart from

200

young men and devise poetry? Conflicts, Jung declares, are sources of fiery energy. We can't afford to be without them. Certainly in Frost could be discerned some igniting-nourishing process associated with cruel suffering and distress. He complained, protested, even moaned at the pain of dualism. He was slow to know what he thought about anything, but the struggle to find out, by taking time off to ponder, brought control and insight. These last killed off complacency, the worst enemy of professor and poet both.

The philosopher in Frost, ever-present, like the humorist, anywhere he lived, came helpfully to his rescue in the classroom. Detached, skeptical-playful, he would suddenly spoof the whole business of education and challenge the students: "What is education? What is poetry? Why is it written? Which of you know when I'm fooling and when I'm serious? Better find out." He would put on a Yankee drawl to say it.

Old fox! His way of suddenly taking cover amused and bemused them. It was one of his ways of "doing somp'm to 'em." Soon he showed signs of becoming, as Professor Elliott put it later on, "a prophet on his own campus." And that added luster to Amherst College.

The men only of Academe, those who made a lifetime career of their own advancement, might feel their prestige shattered by this lightsome Frostian approach. R.F. joined up with the solid and able among professors and scholars but from the very first he would not collaborate with the administrators and politicians. He would not, did not, go to faculty meetings —only three in a lifetime, he boasts. His chosen friends on the Amherst English faculty were exceptional men like George F. Whicher and George Roy Elliott (a later appointee), who, being professors given to writing, did not live only in the college, but lived also—though less than himself—in the world.

Don't get caught in campus politics, he would say to Whicher, as they walked at night together; don't rest on appointments alone—there's another horizon and something beyond. Frost could be fatherly, even with his equals, if the occasion warranted it. But mostly he was just human-companionable, brilliantly stimulating as talker, sometimes combative as friend, or suddenly communicative:

"I took out a poetic license to use the word beauty three times and I've not yet used it once."

In relation to students, an urgency would come upon Frost, he has told me, as he climbed the hill to where the towers of Amherst nestle among their sheltering trees. The unformed boy, a bundle of amorphous possibilities; the skinful of half-baked knowledge; the human creature making his touching struggle to find a true and honest expression in life gripped his mind and heart. The tool the poet used in teaching was words. But words that had become deeds "as in ultimatums and battle cries."

An exceptional student learned most, surely, from Robert Frost and came closest to him. Yet he was fair to the average, never gave a failure mark, rarely reproved or exhorted—save by silence or evasion—the reprobate or the inattentive. A student was on his own with Frost, he was his own master, his own business. Those who cared for real treasure in the classics, in English and American literature, or even in writing, and were ready to dig for it, he aided in every way he could. It was not the *amount* they read or wrote he cared about, however: it was how they took what they read, and how they thought what they wrote. Many a night did he sit up with anxious parents concerned to have a poet developing in the family. He did exhort writers to write and explained why and what he wanted back from them. Even if he scarcely read the product.

In the world of contemporary poetry as a collective movement, especially in the poetry groups that were forming or formed in New England, New York, and the Middle West at this period, a stubborn effort was made to enlist Frost as a registered leader and participator. But he was evasive and detached. Privately skeptical of the motives of the joiners who, he surmised, were often on hand to tout their own wares, he "played along" to a minor degree, so far:

. . . I want you to know [he wrote Miss Lowell in February, 1917] that I was elected a horficer of the Poetry Society [Vice-President of the New England Poetry Club, the NEPC], without my knowledge or consent. I think it best not to do anything to undo what has been done. But let things slide. My being elected in such an irregular way does not make me of the party of those who elected me that I can see. . . .

In fact he had not as yet attended a single meeting.

. . . I am sorry Mrs. Marks [Josephine Preston Peabody, President of the NEPC] has gone to war with you. What is the matter with her? She ought not to let herself be made unhappy by another person's success. Let's not be too hard on her. I understand she is seriously an invalid.

Frost could be very hard on those he disagreed with—but for a while only, as with Pound. He today regrets the things he said about Pound in letters—some now in libraries—pointing out that the acute stage of the conflict between them, once lived, passed away, and what remained in his mind was Pound's critical generosity to him as an unknown poet. He urged his friend Amy, "at the head of a fighting movement in art," to "forget it all and write poetry."

In the interest, in part, of this "fighting movement," which according to H. L. Mencken was threatening to make Chicago, with its *Poetry Magazine* and its Masters-Sandburg-Lindsay celebrities the literary, or at least the poetic, capital of the United States, Frost had proposed to Harriet Monroe to go to read there for one hundred and fifty dollars, "and take my chances on picking up a little more. The money would mean much—we won't say it wouldn't—but the great thing would be to see you and Vachel Lindsay."

Frost had had, through Harcourt, "something to do with" the publication by Holt's of Sandburg's *Chicago Poems* in 1916. He had heard tell of Sandburg's haunting voice and his twanging guitar, as of course of Vachel's vociferous chanting and knew (he told me) "he could not rival either Midwest erner in a 'platform show.'"

Yet Horace Gregory, in his life of Amy Lowell, presents the formality, distinction, and quiet assurance of Frost's early poetic readings as offering something of greater appeal Gregory's subtle impression of Frost as a poetic personality derives, I believe, from a subjective experience as enthralled listener, in the Milwaukee of his boyhood:

On his return in the first flush of becoming famous, Frost had a discreetly mannered yet boyish personality. . . . as he read aloud his dramatic narratives from *North of Boston* his voice often dropping to a whisper, had lyrical qualities that modulated rather than stressed whatever histrionics his lines required. . . In the years when many poets mounted the platform to read their writings aloud, Frost was a welcome exception to the rule of strained and overly dramatic performances. . . . At public read- ings a neatly tailored dinner jacket, worn with ease, accented a manner that was both engaging and precise. He was at the furthest removed from the image of a wild-eyed young poet or of a young provincial, fresh from the farm, wearing a "store-bought" suit of clothes to meet the club women who had come to hear him read his poems. His voice allowed his poems to speak for them- selves.

The editors of *Poetry* had begun to make plans for Frost to read his verse to the Arts Club at Chicago University and a couple of schools in March, 1917. Like most of the visiting poets, Eastern, English, or Asian—like John Masefield, like Rabindranath Tagore, the author of *North of Boston* was in- vited to stay with the widow of the poet-playwright William Vaughn Moody.

The rather magnificent "Harriet" (as she was called by all) had a comfortable, sizable mansion at 2970 Groveland Avenue, which by her own power of fantasy had been trans- formed from a rich lady's bourgeois home to an informal- formal nest of the Muses. There Frost would meet Padraic Colum, the vivid Irish poet and friend of Yeats; "the great-faced noble" Ridgely Torrence, and many others whom he later came to love—or dislike.

According to Mrs. Ridgely Torrence (Olivia Howard Dunbar) whose *A House in Chicago* is a lively, authentic, though uncritical portrait of Harriet Moody and her setting, there was almost no moment, from the tea hour till midnight, when large groups of people were not eating in Mrs. Moody's special salon, where a massive swing, her throne, upholstered in black velvet, hung from the ceiling. This "impressive woman of middle age, her face that of a wearied Buddha," was a professional caterer supplying through her Home Delicacies Company the best restaurants of Chicago; spending her mornings tasting sauces. Thus dishes for gourmets were offered her guests at home. They were served by a Hindu butler, stately and frock-coated, who bustled and bowed in and out, saluting his "lady" as "Mama" and all the male guests as "Papa."

When "Milary" first bowed in Robert Frost—Mrs. Moody had met him at the station with her imperial car, he says—he faltered (I have heard) at the door of the sanctuary; nervous, gray-white, and tired after his trip. Before a reading, Pan was never with R.F. unless he spent some hours totally alone. One of the *pro tem* daughters of the Moody household, then about seventeen, recalls that on that first evening Frost looked averse, and "all scrouged up." When provided, like the other assembling guests, with rich food at a little separate table, he just gazed in a baffled way at the ranged forks and spoons. Later, he remembers being summoned as an honored guest to sit with his maternal, all-embracing hostess in the velvet swing. The telephone kept ringing her away from him—once he heard her say: "Operator, give me Tagore, Bombay, India." He decided gloomily that Mrs. Moody wanted homage from him not just for herself but for her dead husband, the dramatist-poet.

When it was time to go to the reading, a swarm of women satellites appeared (he said), one holding Harriet's purse, one her coat, another her glasses. "She never moved without her swarm." "But," added Glenway Wescott, who has described to me how, as a young literary hopeful, he once occupied the second seat in the swing for a whole year, this benevolent woman, this Saint Harriet would "suddenly crush her female attendants to the wall." This image of bull-like power contrasts oddly with the girlishness Olivia Torrence notes; it showed in Harriet's laughter:

To know that you were responsible for the melting of a rather impassive figure into a charmingly responsive and gaiety-loving woman was exhilarating. As for you, though you had so recently been a tolerated stranger on your best behavior, you were now, in an hour, embarked on an actual intimacy. The truth was, of course, that when Harriet Moody found human material that was to her liking she lost no time in making it her own.

Despite Frost's measured way with womankind, this happened between him and his hostess. "Frost's playful extravagance in familiar talk delighted her." Soon, as the letters reveal, he was consulting her about the shall-I-stay-on-at-Amherst quandary. Can teaching be married with poetry? Through the following years the playfulness became friendship.

On April 9, 1917—Easter Monday in British terms—shortly after Frost's return to Amherst, the poet from whom he felt indivisible was killed at Vimy Ridge, near Arras, in the British spring offensive.

From the time of Edward Thomas' voluntary enlistment, Robert Frost had little hope of his friend's survival. Together they had shared in England the tremors and premonitions of a universal change leading to the triumph of Mars in our modern world. Together they had looked down

        . . . an avenue, dark, nameless, without end,

as the publication of another "self-made" poet's collected works hung in desperate balance. The English *Collected*

Poems, published in October, 1917, six months after Thomas fell at Vimy, were in press at that tragic instant, and it is doubtful whether the soldier knew that R.F. had arranged for publication of three poems by Edward Eastaway—"Old Man," "The Word," and "The Unknown"—in the February, 1917, issue of *Poetry.*

Frost's own relation to Thomas' death can be best understood through his poems. The first of these that might symbolically concern Thomas, "Not to Keep," was printed in the *Yale Review* for January, 1917. The verb "to keep" is one that Frost has used with special pathos and poignancy, though with varying meaning. Hark back to the old man who through his snow upon the roof kept—sustained or watched over—the winter night, and then follow the heart of the soldier's wife, who has her man—but not to cherish or detain from his fate.

NOT TO KEEP

They sent him back to her. The letter came
Saying . . . And she could have him. And before
She could be sure there was no hidden ill
Under the formal writing, he was there,
Living. They gave him back to her alive—
How else? They are not known to send the dead—
And not disfigured visibly. His face?
His hands? She had to look, to look and ask,
"What is it, dear?" And she had given all
And still she had all—*they* had—they the lucky!
Wasn't she glad now? Everything seemed won,
And all the rest for them permissible ease.
She had to ask, "What was it, dear?"

                                           "Enough,
Yet not enough. A bullet through and through,
High in the breast. Nothing but what good care
And medicine and rest, and you a week,
Can cure me of to go again." The same
Grim giving to do over for them both.

She dared no more than ask him with her eyes
How was it with him for a second trial.
And with his eyes he asked her not to ask.
They had given him back to her, but not to keep.

But now the news of death came: on April 27 Frost wrote Mrs. Thomas a letter from Amherst which no one but a great poet could have written:

Dear Helen:

People have been praised for self-possession in danger. I have heard Edward doubt if he was as brave as the bravest. But who was ever so completely himself right up to the verge of destruction, so sure of his thought, so sure of his word? He was the bravest and best and dearest man you and I have ever known. I knew from the moment when I first met him at his unhappiest that he would some day clear his mind and save his life. I have had four wonderful years with him. I know he has done this all for you: he is all yours. But you must let me crying cry for him as if he were *almost* all mine too.

Of the three ways out of here, by death where there is no choice, by death where there is a noble choice, and by death where there is a choice not so noble, he found the greatest way. There is no regret—nothing that I will call a regret. Only I can't help wishing he could have saved his life without so wholly losing it and come back from France not too much hurt to enjoy our pride in him. I want to see him to tell him something. I want to tell him, what I think he liked to hear from me, that he was a poet. I want to tell him that I love those he loved and hate those he hated. (But the hating will wait: there will be a time for hate.) I had meant to talk endlessly with him still, either here in our mountains as we had said or, as I found my longing was more and more, there at Leddington where we first talked of war.

It was beautiful as he did it. And I don't suppose there is anything for us to do to show our admiration but to love him forever.

Robert

Other things for other letters.

A poem distilled from this same intimate exaltation is "To E.T." which, however, did not appear in the *Yale Review* until April, 1920. Frost has told me that it was written in an hour of rest in the house of William Allan Neilson, when he first was President of Smith College. That the poet hesitated before the publication is made clear in a letter from Franconia to his colleague Whicher:

Franc   July   1919

Dear George

I am going to send you the E T poem to show you that it is something more than a mere project. The truth is it is probably as complete as it will ever be. I'm not keeping it back to go on with it. Perhaps I can tell you why I have hesitated over it. Edward Thomas was the closest friend I ever had and I was the closest friend he ever had; and this was something I didn't wait to realize after he had died. It makes his death almost too much to talk about in The Yale Review in the hearing of Wm. Lyon Phelps even at two years distance. Just one little poem however ought not to do any harm if I'm sure of my motives in printing it—and I think I am. They are practical, non-sentimental and sufficiently removed from my impulses (not motives) in writing it. I'm one person in writing and I'm another or if cornered can become another for purposes of publication. I've about reached the point where I am willing to wrong whatever may be wronged by publishing this poem. Some part of an ideal is sacrificed to some god in every deed done and the old formal sacrifice of one child out of so many to Moloch was no more than symbolic recognition of the fact. . . .

TO E.T.

I slumbered with your poems on my breast
Spread open as I dropped them half-read through
Like dove wings on a figure on a tomb
To see, if in a dream they brought of you,

I might not have the chance I missed in life
Through some delay, and call you to your face
First soldier, and then poet, and then both,
Who died a soldier-poet of your race.

I meant, you meant, that nothing should remain
Unsaid between us, brother, and this remained—
And one thing more that was not then to say:
The Victory for what it lost and gained.

You went to meet the shell's embrace of fire
On Vimy Ridge; and when you fell that day
The war seemed over more for you than me,
But now for me than you—the other way.

How over, though, for even me who knew
The foe thrust back unsafe beyond the Rhine,
If I was not to speak of it to you
And see you pleased once more with words of mine?

In both poem and letter Robert Frost is holding his friend
in the close here-and-now of mortal memory. He made, in
sonnet form in 1928, the more abstract, universal, and religious statement. With Thomas undoubtedly in mind, the
poem—one of his absolute masterpieces of technique—offers
a momentary, mystical vision into a "beyond" of the spirit.

A SOLDIER

He is that fallen lance that lies as hurled,
That lies unlifted now, come dew, come rust,
But still lies pointed as it plowed the dust.
If we who sight along it round the world,
See nothing worthy to have been its mark,
It is because like men we look too near,
Forgetting that as fitted to the sphere,
Our missiles always make too short an arc.
They fall, they rip the grass, they intersect
The curve of earth, and striking, break their own;
They make us cringe for metal-point on stone.
But this we know, the obstacle that checked
And tripped the body, shot the spirit on
Further than target ever showed or shone.

Still later, in 1936, through a sudden recall of a unique shared human experience that had wonder and magic in it, the spirit that had ranged so far rejoined its counterpart:

IRIS BY NIGHT

One misty evening, one another's guide,
We two were groping down a Malvern side
The last wet fields and dripping hedges home.
There came a moment of confusing lights, . . .
Then a small rainbow like a trellis gate,
A very small moon-made prismatic bow,
Stood closely over us through which to go. . . .
And we stood in it softly circled round
From all division time or foe can bring
In a relation of elected friends.

Thomas referred to the mythological rainbow in a letter to Eleanor Farjeon, printed with other excerpts and essays in a posthumous collection, *The Prose of Edward Thomas:*

I like your rainbow, but . . . mine that I saw with Frost seems like the first that ever was except that I knew it was a rainbow. I can't imagine a painter interfering with either. Mine was too much of a pure rainbow, a new toy discovered by Apollo, for anyone to paint. It was more for a mythologist clad in skins.

He wrote his poem "The Sun Used to Shine" about his walks with Frost perhaps in the very fertile period that followed the American's departure before his own volunteering in the army: in the period that produced also his anthology called *This England.* The poem begins:

The sun used to shine while we two walked
Slowly together, paused and started
Again, and sometimes mused, sometimes talked
As either pleased, and cheerfully parted . . .

211

Thomas visited Frost twice in Gloucestershire at The Gallows after he and his family had gone home and before the Frosts sailed. But it was for the American survivor to write the poems of elegiac lament for a dead friend: the only such laments in Frost's *Complete Works*. ("One More Brevity" may sometime be added.)

Oh I don't know about teaching after all [Frost had written to Amy Lowell on May 24]. When I am fifty, say—ten years from now—when the war is over. I want to write a few things first if I can only happen to.

As for you I suppose you go write on righting [he joked] all the time. I envy but don't blame you.

But in the end Amherst College asked Robert Frost to stay another year. The salary offered this time was $2,500, and R.F. accepted. In view of this inescapable obligation, the summer in Franconia passed all too quickly. In September the *Atlantic Monthly* published "The Ax-Helve."

A Yankee farmer, chopping wood in his yard, finds his ax stopped by Baptiste's expert intervention: the French-Canadian farmer (the same he had mended wall with) has noted a defective commercial helve.

Baptiste's dialect is used in "The Ax-Helve"—the only poem, Frost believes, in which he did use dialect:

> "Come on my house and I put you one in
> What's las' awhile—good hick'ry what's grow crooked.
> De second growt' I cut myself—tough, tough!". . .

> He liked to have it slender as a whipstock,
> Free from the least knot, equal to the strain
> Of bending like a sword across the knee.
> He showed me that the lines of a good helve
> Were native to the grain before the knife
> Expressed them, and its curves were no false curves
> Put on it from without. And there its strength lay
> For the hard work. . . .

If a farmer can sculpture a helve, a poet can evoke the artistic process in a burning image. That is what the poem is all about.

> But now he brushed the shavings from his knee
> And stood the ax there on its horse's hoof,
> Erect, but not without its waves, as when
> The snake stood up for evil in the Garden,—
> Top-heavy with a heaviness his short,
> Thick hand made light of, steel-blue chin drawn down
> And in a little—a French touch in that.
> Baptiste drew back and squinted at it, pleased;
> "See how she's cock her head!"

When R.F. reads this poem, as he does from his "evening" platforms, he often suggests by an introductory word that it is metaphorical-realistic, and can be understood on several levels.

He had begun to speak of the levels long ago, for I find written in his hand in my *Selected Poems* (1923):

"This is as near as I like to come to talking about art, in a work of art—such as it is."

I am as loath to use the word "great" as Frost to use the word "beauty," but surely this is a poem time will not easily get rid of. The poet must have found it easier to return to teaching with such an affirmation in print.

A sublet was found in the wood-surrounded town of West Pelham, several miles from the campus. But walking was like breathing to a Frost. The Manthey-Zorns, though no longer next door, remained intimates. Professor Manthey-Zorn recalls how often it fell to him to persuade the poet not to resign his teaching post. Direly and often, Frost threatened to do so, for the uncertain currents of the Meiklejohn administration would periodically rock the academic boat and make him seasick. But he would recover. . . .

Lesley, reducing them to only five, had gone off to Wellesley in the fall of 1917, convinced in advance that she would find no professor to equal the father who had since childhood played a major part in her education. The arrival of Thomas' *Collected Poems* from England stirred them all profoundly.

But the war was having an ill effect on American poetry and letters. Louis Untermeyer—now a close friend of R.F. and always turning up—playing with pacifism, as Frost felt and told him frankly, was up for trial for sedition with the other editors of the *Masses*. The *Seven Arts* was doomed to end with the one year 1917 because its "angel" had balked at Randolph Bourne's sociological antiwar articles. Still, Amy Lowell had brought out in October, as if poetry were all, her *Tendencies in Modern American Poetry*: critical-biographical studies of E. A. Robinson, Robert Frost, Sandburg, Masters and the Imagists John Gould Fletcher and H.D. The essays discussed in her dauntless fashion a group of American poets who could rival the French ones that the same author had presented in an earlier volume.

In the essay on Robert Frost—one of the best of the lot—Amy Lowell had presented him:

 . . . all compounded as he seems to be of the granite and gentians of our Northern mountains . . .

as writing:

The only true bucolic poetry being written in America to-day . . . true pastorals of the hill country in which he spends his life . . .

A few hundred miles [she said] was to contain all his poetic world, but these few hundred miles were to be deepened indefinitely by the delving of his own spade.

His eyes may see the soft rounded English country, . . . but the lines etched upon his heart are the articulate outlines of rock and hemlock. . . .

Mr. Frost writes almost as a man under a spell. As though he were the mouthpiece of something beyond himself, only conscious of the necessity of stating what is in him.

But in the latter part of the essay the author accuses Frost of having "no *ear* for their [New Englanders'] peculiar tongue"; of not *hearing* the Yankee dialect that James Russell Lowell, she herself, and Alice Brown plainly heard.

"Trouble with you, Amy," R.F. said to her privately, "you don't go to your back door enough."

Annoyance at her publicly setting up regional limitations to his poetry pushed R.F. to retaliate, in a half-spoofing letter of December 2:

. . . I must see you myself before long if only to put it to you while the business is still before the house why I am not by your own showing the least provincial, the most national of American poets—why I ought not to be anyway. Doesn't the wonder grow that I have never written anything or as you say never published anything except about New England farms when you consider the jumble I am? Mother Scotch immigrant. Father oldest New England stock unmixed. Ten years in West. Thirty years in East. Three years in England. Not less than six months in any of these: San Francisco, New York, Boston, Cambridge Lawrence, London. Lived in Maine, N. H., Vt., Mass. Twenty five years in cities, nine in villages, nine on farms. Saw the South on foot. Dartmouth. Harvard two years. Shoe-worker, mill-hand farm-hand, editor, reporter, insurance agent, agent for Shakespearean reader, reader myself, teacher in every kind of school public and private including psychological normal school and college. Prize for running at Caledonia Club picnic; 2 prizes for assumed parts at masquerade balls; medal for goodness in high school; detur for scholarship at Harvard; money for verse. Knew Henry George well and saw much at one time (by way of contrast) of a noted boss. Presbeterian, Unitarian, Swedenborgian, Nothing. All the vices but disloyalty and chewing gum or tobacco.

He got the Russell Loines Prize of the National Institute of Arts and Letters anyhow, and for the poem "Snow" which, bursting, as he knew, with New England voices and tones of voice, A.L. had felt inferior to the poetic dialogues of *North of Boston*. "Snow" it was, though, that brought the hard year 1917, the year that with E.T.'s death divided the past from the future, to some sort of reassuring ending.

CHAPTER 10

THE LOCKLESS DOOR

1918–1920

War issues were boiling and seething at Amherst College in 1918—Americans had died at Château-Thierry and the A.E.F. was preparing to win in the Argonne. As poet, Frost could struggle for uninvolvement; as man, he was tied fast into the fighting, the victory of the Allies, and then into the Armistice, the Peace of 1919. President Wilson was no favorite of his though; as he said, he had been politically an "unhappy Democrat since 1896." His Yankee father, the Confederate sympathizer, who had shown the little Robert Lee, on a map, the boundaries of the five nations into which the U.S.A. was bound to break up, had somehow bred as stout a nationalist as could be found. And a fighter, whether he went to war or not.

Lesley, inclined ever to go her father one better in the fighting spirit she inherited, and the restless love of change, had after one year left Wellesley, where her professors disappointed her. She was for becoming a flier, but there her parents resisted, and she had to be content to work in a factory which made propeller blades for airplanes in Marblehead, Massachusetts.

The rest of the family had moved in 1919 to a third Amherst domicile where they lived until March, 1920: an apartment

216

at the top of a comfortable house in the heart of town, rented from Miss Carrie Marsh. Strange for the solitary Frosts to settle on Main Street, between the Masonic Lodge and the Town Hall, pestered by the cacophonies of mystic rites—shooting their heads out of their windows, in protest, George Whicher amusedly observed. Frost wrote poetry here nevertheless; relieved strong inner feelings by drop-ins on W. R. Brown, the Thoreauvian insurance man, hard by in his office —and all the while dealt professorially with students in and out of the Army and Navy: students passionately taking sides in opposing currents of thought, which kept them through most of 1918 on the war griddle, then in limbo as the peace conference came on.

In a Robert Frost number of an Amherst publication, the *Touchstone* (February, 1939), based on the reminiscences of former students, it is made clear that Frost's formal teaching had, from the moment he began it, those capricious, informal moments which later became the very pattern of his pedagogy. He never "sat" but "lay" in a chair. He felt about his college classes "as a student does"—that is, he cut them when he could, made a point of always being four minutes late; yet did not like it if the students disappeared when he was five minutes late. He had "strong hates and prejudices," a "strong irritable anti-intellectualism"; yet he was not an "intellectual" but a "spiritual" who adumbrated something of the "fourth dimension." He was, they said, himself the man of fire and ice that he described in his poem. Yet he relished gossip, and showed himself a brilliant caricaturist of his best-beloved colleagues. He vastly preferred talks with students at his home to classes, and often started the latter by saying:

"Why do we have classes anyway?"

I remember [said E. Merrill Root of the class of 1917] that shock of wavy wild hair shaking down triangularly over the broad forehead; the ample, audacious nose; the large sensitive lips, usually puckered into a whimsical, half-whistling position; the eyes blue-grey, aloof yet alive, that seemed to sleep in eternity.

E. A. Richards of the class of 1921 wrote of his professor as "A Reality Among Ghosts":

I met Mr. Frost in 1918. Amherst was then part military camp, part college, and not very much of either, although we all did our best to go two ways at once. . . . we had no place in particular to head for, no place to go but where we were sent. . . . We were not *sure*, as young men ought to be. . . .

During those months it was good to be even remotely in acquaintance with Mr. Frost. . . . here was a man more deeply sentient, more solidly intellectual, with those qualities in finer and more equable balance than we had heretofore known, moving and living with us . . . and he lent us a sense of value and longevity in our thinking, . . .

We were glad to go to his house at ten or eleven at night and sit somewhat uneasily in his sitting room until he came in from some depth of the dwelling and sprawled out on a lounge. He read from this poet and that, throwing the book aside when he had reached what seemed to him the furthest reach of luminous expression in some particular poem. And then he would say what occurred to him in relation to that poem, going from there to the general considerations of poetry.

He never, or rarely, talked about his own work. . . . I dropped in one afternoon. I was welcomed by Mrs. Frost, one of the few completely beautiful women I have known. I walked into the vacant parlor and looked down at the half-finished manuscript of "The Runaway," which in later years I was to see and hear scores of people charmed by. And at those later times I thought to myself, "Well, I saw the runaway when he was only half born." . . .

. . . I must say the hardest job was to get him to say whether any of my stuff was bad or good. He did say at length, and the verdict . . . was hidden under such a half-kind, half-deadly phrase that the impact did not strike me until some hours later. Then it almost ruined me. . . .

When the student editors of the *Amherst Monthly* asked Frost for a poem for their June, 1918, issue, he produced the beautiful little pastoral (quoted in the Introduction) of which

Richards speaks—now one of Frost's most popular lyrics, known to every American college boy—about how an unfledged Morgan colt behaved in pasture on a cold winter evening. It has a complex metrical scheme and can be read either realistically as a poem about a colt or metaphorically as a poem about a boy, who might have affinities with the runaway in the poet himself. It made a tremendous local hit, the faculty tickled by the metaphor and the students ruefully catching on.

The *Touchstone* also printed reminiscences by young aesthetes or conservatives among students who during their college years had not appreciated Frost's poetry. His nonconformities of the true radical in the Emersonian sense were irritating to students still lured by nineteenth-century beauty. They hated R.F.'s realistic conversational technique, and groaned with one another over a brusque, humorous poem like "A Hundred Collars": almost a novel in itself, about "the Doctor" (a formal college professor) who had to spend an intimate night in the same bedroom in a dismal railway junction hotel with Lafe, a folksy, half-drunken collector for a local paper.

> The Doctor looked at Lafe and looked away.
> A man? A brute. Naked above the waist,
> He sat there creased and shining in the light,
> Fumbling the buttons in a well-starched shirt.
> "I'm moving into a size-larger shirt.
> I've felt mean lately; mean's no name for it.
> I just found what the matter was tonight:
> I've been a-choking like a nursery tree
> When it outgrows the wire band of its name tag.
> I blamed it on the hot spell we've been having.
> 'Twas nothing but my foolish hanging back,
> Not liking to own up I'd grown a size.
> Number eighteen this is. What size do you wear?"
>
> The Doctor caught his throat convulsively.
> "Oh—ah—fourteen—fourteen." . . .

219

In 1918 Robert Frost's life as poet expanded still further beyond academic confines: he was earnestly desired as a leader in the burgeoning poetry movement and was fearful of getting overinvolved.

The Amy Lowell–Imagist circle, the New York, the Chicago circles, once explored and reduced to their individual elements, yielded stuff that set fire to Frost's argumentative or poetical fantasy. The American public was eager for poetry.

We no longer [he wrote Miss Lowell] have to think so much of coaxing 'em along into objective existence. We've got 'em where we can jab it to 'em stiff without fear of having them all to create over again. They can stand art. And by the ton you've given it to 'em!

Louis Untermeyer, returning to this period in his autobiographical work *From Another World,* has recalled a gay evening early in 1918 when Robert Frost, Sara Teasdale, Vachel Lindsay, and he got together in New York. The delicate valetudinarian poetess, Sara, cast an illusionary spell over her adorer, Vachel. But it was not of love the three wrote when a poem on one theme was called for. Vachel would seriously have the subject John L. Sullivan, the famed Bostonian pugilist who had just died. Vachel's own offering, in "The Strong Boy of Boston," figures in his *Collected Poems.* But Frost's jocose piece, as quoted by Untermeyer, belongs to his occasional burlesques, written spontaneously to friends as trivia and not included in his published collections.

Consider the first verse of

John L. Sullivan Enters Heaven

(To be sung to the tune of "Heaven Overarches You and Me")

Sullivan arrived at the very lowest Heaven
Which is sometimes mistaken for the very highest Hell,
Where barkeeps, pugilists, jockeys, and gamblers
And the women corresponding (if there *are* any) dwell.
    They done queer things, but they done 'em on the level,
    And thus they escape the jurisdiction of the Devil.

220

This suggests comparison with other verses that have made their way into collectors' portfolios but not into print. Light verses of this type take one back to the adventures of Rob with his father in the bars of San Francisco—something from the fathers of the race, a sudden exuberance, in one who has remained half reticent Scotch Puritan all the while.

Another facet of Robert Frost's literary gift found expression through Amherst College early in 1919. His one-act play, *A Way Out* (printed in the *Seven Arts* in 1917), was presented at the Northampton Academy of Music on February 24, played by the Amherst Masquers, a college group, and directed very ably by himself. Brevity and dramatic surprise are as much of the essence of this play as of his murder poem, "The Vanishing Red."

In both irrationality rules; innocence (or is it dumbness?) in a lightning flash is tricked by power. In "The Vanishing Red," with its punning title, disgust or something deeper comes over a miller and he calmly dumps "the last Red Man of Acton" into the mill race. In *A Way Out* a sudden dramatic conflict breaks out between two escapists, both possessed by fear. Asa Gorrill, a timid hermit shacked up in the woods, is invaded by The Stranger, a brassy and ruthless shoe clerk who has just murdered, and is openly after the home and identity of the hermit. The men are opposites, yet doubles physically and somehow psychopathically. Their fates are clinched in a violent encounter. The play clicks at the end, like the ring on the miller's trap door, leaving in this case the query, "Who murdered whom?"

R.F. recalls that he was pushed to the wall and had to be protected by President Neilson against a mob of Smith College girls who had also given a play and bedeviled him in vain for his play's meaning. *A Way Out* remained unpublished for a decade and was then printed in a fine Limited Edition by Roland Wood—the chief mover and actor in the 1919 performance—at The Harbor Press.

The poet's introduction has his beautiful clarity yet yields no answer to his play's *double entendre*.

Everything written is as good as it is dramatic. It need not declare itself in form, but it is drama or nothing. A least lyric alone may have a hard time, but it can make a beginning, and lyric will be piled on lyric till all are easily heard as sung or spoken by a person in a scene—in character, in a setting. By whom, where and when is the question. By a dreamer of the better world out in a storm in autumn; by a lover under a window at night. It is the same with the essay. It may manage alone or it may take unto itself other essays for help, but it must make itself heard as by Stevenson on an island, or Lamb in London.

A dramatic necessity goes deep into the nature of the sentence. Sentences are not different enough to hold the attention unless they are dramatic. No ingenuity of varying structure will do. All that can save them is the speaking tone of voice somehow entangled in the words and fastened to the page for the ear of the imagination. That is all that can save poetry from sing-song, all that can save prose from itself.

I have always come as near the dramatic as I could this side of actually writing a play. Here for once I have written a play without (as I should like to believe) having gone very far from where I have spent my life.

Two other complete plays by Robert Frost exist in manuscript: *The Guardeen* and *The Art Factory*, the former written in England, the latter in Franconia or Amherst, not long after the poet's return. They have original Frostian qualities but are less headlong and tightly wrought than *A Way Out*. Frost has not—so far—cared to publish them.

In May, 1919, when the Peace Conference was over and done with and businessmen were considering what a new era might bring or portend, the acute Alfred Harcourt resigned from the Holt firm. Henry Holt, the elder, had retired and to his sons had not handed down comparable caliber and judgment. Harcourt, in his *Some Experiences*, explains that the tie broke for him because of a split in the realm of ideas between himself and the conservative, rather elderly group who had the business authority.

It had been Harcourt's pride that he had captured for Holt's, in the war years, the "new" poets—Frost, Sandburg, Louis Untermeyer, and others. Directly after the war, as he explains in *Some Experiences*, reaching out instinctively, astutely for interpreters and prophets of the new era, he bought in London for Holt's Bertrand Russell's *Proposed Roads to Freedom*. Because of its views of the Bolshevik revolution and in spite of its large sales, it was unpopular with the firm, and Harcourt left Holt's to found a new firm, where Maynard Keynes and Lytton Strachey would be happy discoveries. This was done largely through the support of Sinclair Lewis who had *Main Street* to offer immediately.

Harcourt Brace and Howe was set up in one ground floor room, with ten of Holt's business staff and a number of the Holt trade list detached and following along: as Louis Untermeyer, Carl Sandburg, the Benéts, and—so Harcourt hoped —Robert Frost. In any enterprise Frost is by temperament dependent on friendship. In every college and organization where he reads his poems today he has, he tells me, at least one personal and special friend who clinches his tie to the institution. Alfred Harcourt *was* Holt and Company to him, and he himself was at first, as a letter shows, inclined to be one of Harcourt's authors.

July 4, 1919

Dear Alfred:

It reads like a fairy story, you've got so nearly what you always wanted—so exactly I should say. I never look on at anything like that but I wish I was in it. Why wasn't I brought up to publishing instead of to writing so I could have added a fourth to your firm name. Perhaps it is long enough to say familiarly now. . . .

I suppose I should be more excited if I hadn't been looking for it to happen ever since something you said to me somewhere in a narrow street as we walked across town to lunch two or three years ago.

I shall hope to have a book on one of the earliest lists of the new firm. But we *will* try to have my affairs straightened out so that I won't have Mrs. Nutt hanging over me, however shadowily when next I publish, won't we? . . .

In fact, Henry Holt and Company would not release Frost's *A Boy's Will* and *North of Boston* to Harcourt, and as the poet "knew he had but one book in his system" and had also a loyalty he could not gainsay he wisely stayed where he was. He wished Harcourt Godspeed and remained a friend—but a Holt author. A message R.F. wrote Harcourt in 1951 on one of his Christmas cards, inscribed to "Alfred and Ellen," states the whole matter. He is thanking Alfred for his *Some Experiences:*

Dear Alfred:

It is the story of a natural-born great publisher and his successes. I am proud to have been one of your earliest. First came Dorothy [Canfield Fisher] then me, then Carl then Louis. I was down from the country in your office when you told Louis to go anthologizing and get rich. I think you suggested I should join him in the enterprise. You guessed right in so many fields against all doubters. I saw you single out Sinclair Lewis from the ruck of *Sat. Eve Post* writers to be a world-beating novelist. I was a visitor in your new office amid the excitement of the Economic Consequences. You had Keynes, Strachey and Lippmann in politics. You had Papini in religion. (And thereby hangs a tail I could tell of your generosity to the translator.) It seems strange that in the middle of all this you had a place in the heart of your business for a thing of such small profit as poetry. But you had. When the talk gets going all one way against big business in America I am apt to bring in for what it may be worth the record of my life with you and the others who have followed you in the big business called Henry Holt. It's a great debt I owe you.

Ever yours Robert.

Harcourt's immediate successor in the Holt firm was Lincoln MacVeagh, a man of Groton-Harvard background, a student of the classics, who left Holt's in 1923 to become president of the Dial Press; and in 1933 was appointed Ambassador to Greece. Later he served also in Portugal and Spain. Mr. Mac-Veagh from Portugal, where he is now retired, has sent me some notes pertinent to the official and friendly relationship he at once established with Robert Frost at Henry Holt in 1916:

It was in 1916 (or late in 1915) that I first met Mr. Frost, at a luncheon given by Mr. Roland Holt. Why I was included in the group I don't know, as I was no great shakes in the Company but only a member of the College Department. I could mean nothing to Mr. Frost at that time, and he may not recall the occasion, but it gave me a foretaste of his personal quality which I was to appreciate so much more fully later on. I remember Mr. Harcourt's enthusiasm over the success *North of Boston* was making, and Mr. Roland Holt's bumbling attempts to be the understanding patron. You perhaps know that privately he referred to Mr. Frost as "our b'gosh poet," an unhappy phrase which Mr. Frost himself soon heard about. . . .

When I rejoined the Holts in 1919 after two years in the army . . . Mr. Harcourt had made his break, and Mr. Bristol made me a Director and put me in charge of the Trade Department. . . . He almost at once required me to get in touch with Mr. Frost and try to keep him in the fold! What I was to say was left entirely to me. . . . He asked me up to Franconia where he and Mrs. Frost were then living, and there I spent some very pleasant days. Perhaps Mr. Bristol thought we were talking business, but we weren't! Instead we were "outwatching the Bear" (as so often since), talking philosophy, and like the characters in "The Star-Splitter," "saying some of the best things we ever said." Mr. Harcourt was a very able man, astute and experienced, and I was none of these things. I also felt that Mr. Frost was hardly a person to relish pressure of any sort, so I made my visit merely a "contact" one. In the sequel, Mr. Bristol got what he wanted, but Mr. Frost made up his own mind, without any urgings from me.

. . . Between you and me [Frost wrote his witty colleague Whicher from Franconia in 1919] I am having a lot of fun with

Hen Dekker syllables. You'd think I might be about something more profitable.

And we aren't farming much either.

And Elinor wouldn't let us hatch too many chickens.

Does Wilson at last stand revealed to you in his last message to Congress? . . . It seems he came not to bring peace but a League of Nations. Anyone who could use the word afraid as he does there! He is afraid we won't have to be afraid of European nations for sometime yet. Does he mean he's afraid we can't look for them to give us a fight worthy of our steel industry or rather chemical industry? Is it like Richard the Lion-hearted he talks. No I'm afraid he talks like a fraud. Afraid am I? . . .

Always yours

Robert Frost

The reference to "Hen Dekker syllables" is to one of Frost's finest explorations of the mystical—enough fruit for one summer, a whole poem this time, written in the meter of Catullus.

FOR ONCE, THEN, SOMETHING

Others taunt me with having knelt at well-curbs
Always wrong to the light, so never seeing
Deeper down in the well than where the water
Gives me back in a shining surface picture
Me myself in the summer heaven godlike
Looking out of a wreath of fern and cloud puffs.
Once, when trying with chin against a well-curb,
I discerned, as I thought, beyond the picture,
Through the picture, a something white, uncertain,
Something more of the depths—and then I lost it.
Water came to rebuke the too clear water.
One drop fell from a fern, and lo, a ripple
Shook whatever it was lay there at bottom,
Blurred it, blotted it out. What was that whiteness?
Truth? A pebble of quartz? For once, then, something.

Still for a moment the young god, looking through the flattering wreath of fern at his glorified image in the well water, in the spirit of the lad of *A Boy's Will,* Robert Frost half glimpses something that brings his mature philosophic mind into play. Is that whiteness Truth? Has it meaning? But is it there? The ironist once more leaves us to dally with the yea and nay.

Because poetry was coming into its own with him again, Frost made up his mind to resign from Amherst at the end of 1919, the first college term. Hungry for the smell of fields, tiring of the smell of books, wearying of what in "Birches" he calls "considerations"—as for example whether one who admired Meiklejohn for his originality and courage could tolerate certain obvious unfairnesses without being simply two-faced—he decided they would move back to Franconia in March, 1920. The decision made life a promise again.

All his days, Frost has made instinctive decisions that boil down to the need to yield to poetry. He once in a talk revealed this to his old Virginia-Michigan friend, Morris Tilley:

I suppose I have been guided in life so far by instinct to protect what I was or wanted to be. . . . I lost friends by leaving Harvard. I did not regret leaving, however, for I could not stay. I could not have explained, even to myself, why I didn't stay. I just had to go.

So it was when he left Dartmouth, when he took up farming, when he sold the Derry farm and went to England, and now when he left the little safe harbor of his appointment at Amherst College, and moved up to the snow mountains of Franconia. There it was cold enough to freeze your ears, but quiet enough to get his own impatient, abundant nature into what Tilley called "equipoise." Just the place to revert to favorite books—Shakespeare, Wordsworth, Turgenev's *Sportsman's Sketches,* and the *Odyssey.*

There is no strain in him at all [says Tilley in some Franconia notes on conversations with Robert Frost that go back to 1915]. He is rather like nature in his abundant outgiving, which is no effort to him, but obviously a joy.

Frost's blue eyes look out on the world with a kindly, dreamy expression. There is an expression of mildness in his countenance that radiates. I do not think that you could mistake the good feeling for man that is in his face. His manner is calm, attractive and of frank appeal. His personal view of everything is most pronounced.

Actually ten poems, a normal number for Robert Frost, were published in periodicals in 1920, this liberated, relaxed year—basic bricks for the next volume, *New Hampshire*.

In what environment and temperatures they were produced is suggested by a light verse Frost wrote to his friend George Whicher. Elinor had just written her friend Harriet Whicher that the thermometer stood at minus twenty, when Frost sent along

A CORRECTION

When we told you minus twenty
Here this morning, that seemed plenty.
We were trying to be modest
(Said he spitting in the sawdust),
And moreover did our guessing
By the kitchen stove while dressing.
Come to dress and make a sortie,
What we found was minus forty.

Franconia, N. H.

This verse had hung, framed, in Professor Whicher's study, unpublished until 1945, when another friend of R.F.'s, the poet David McCord of Cambridge, with his consent printed it in *What Cheer*, an anthology of British and American humorous and witty verse that McCord had "gathered sifted and salted."

Franconia always kept a very special meaning for Elinor and Robert Frost, partly because their youngest daughter Marjorie, who died prematurely, was so fond of it, so much a part of it, and wrote such delicate poetry about it.

The first poem of hers that her father quoted to me was:

IF I SHOULD LIVE TO BE A DOLL

When autumn birds have flown away
And left the snow to me,
The blueberry blue blue-jay
Still flits from tree to tree.

If I should live to be a doll
And sit with snow white hair,
I'll wear a blueberry blue blue shawl
And flit from chair to chair.

Still more touching, when only the little girl in the snow
was left to them, was the one Marjorie called:

FRANCONIA

Long, long ago a little child,
Bare headed in the snow,
Lay back against the wind—and smiled,
Then let her footsteps blow.

Lighter than leaves they blew about,
Until she sank to rest
Down where no wind could blow her out,
Deep in a mountain nest.

And to this day she's smiling there
With eyes alert and wild,
For she has lived on mountain air
And stayed a little child.

"Am I a nature poet?" Rob would ask, then answer himself:

"No, strictly untrue! All but very few have a person in them.
Why do I write poetry (they ask me, meaning instead of good
prose). Answer: 'To make poems different from each other.'"

What poems would R.F. have "said" to them by the Franconia fire which Elinor at least would have sensed in her
deepest perception as "different" from the poems in the first

three books, either in stanzaic pattern and rhyme scheme or in the very core of their meaning?

In form, "Dust of Snow," which came out later as "A Favour" in the *London Mercury* for December, 1920:

DUST OF SNOW

The way a crow
Shook down on me
The dust of snow
From a hemlock tree

Has given my heart
A change of mood
And saved some part
Of a day I had rued.

A person, and even a subtle self-portrait in that one. Still another person—though the same—in a bold, glorious poem, with a core of cosmic meaning also written in two-stress verse. This sings, in a reckless and passionate way, the journey of a poet's mind, and the acute listening of his ears through a wakeful night:

I WILL SING YOU ONE-O

It was long I lay
Awake that night
Wishing the tower
Would name the hour
And tell me whether
To call it day
(Though not yet light)
And give up sleep. . . .

Then came one knock!
A note unruffled
Of earthly weather,
Though strange and muffled
The tower said, "One!"

And then a steeple.
They spoke to themselves
And such few people
As winds might rouse
From sleeping warm
(But not unhouse). . . .

The excursion into the heavens, conjured up by the grave
"One" of the earthly clock; the connection it instantly makes
for the poet with the cosmic clock—the "world clock" as some
mystics have it—

With whose vast wheels
Theirs interlock . . .

suggests a divine harmony. Yet Frost had a little in mind two
Amherst clocks and must end with what he knows on earth:
man, still dragging down man and nation, nation. "Whatever
a man does in reality he himself becomes."

"Good-by and Keep Cold," published in *Harper's Magazine*
in December, 1920, was written in Amherst, Frost tells me,
and in its bucolic detail pronounced "pomologically correct"
by the Massachusetts Agricultural College—he was proud of
that. It has for human center a farmer (maybe amateur at
heart) who had to leave his young orchard to struggle along
because he didn't want always to climb a hill and liked his
sound, middle-aged repose at night.

GOOD-BY AND KEEP COLD

This saying good-by on the edge of the dark
And the cold to an orchard so young in the bark
Reminds me of all that can happen to harm
An orchard away at the end of the farm
All winter, cut off by a hill from the house.
I don't want it girdled by rabbit and mouse,
I don't want it dreamily nibbled for browse
By deer, and I don't want it budded by grouse. . . .

After some humorous lines of advice to the orchard, the poet ends:

> I wish I could promise to lie in the night
> And think of an orchard's arboreal plight
> When slowly (and nobody comes with a light)
> Its heart sinks lower under the sod.
> But something has to be left to God.

This fortyish level, less magical than the mood of "After Apple-Picking," seems to emerge from Frost's sanity, his ability to dismiss the past and move along with the known, living present. In a letter to Whicher, he can speak with tender realistic detachment of the tragedy of his own sister Jeanie, the one who in childhood spouted Burns' lyrics from a stool, who taught in her mother's Lawrence school, and late in life, when Frost was in England, put herself through the University of Michigan:

Franconia N. H.
April 12 1920

Dear George:

I had rather you heard it from me than in roundabout ways from other people that my sister has at last gone clearly insane. . . . She didn't know me when she saw me. It seems as if the poor girl had tried being everything, pro-German, pacifist, internationalist, draft-obstructor, and seditionist as a protest against the war; only to decide in the end that nothing would do her feelings justice but going insane. I dont know that I blame her. I admire the courage that is unwilling not to suffer everything that everyone is suffering everywhere. She has always been a sensibilitist and has now gone the way of the sensibilitist to the bitter end. It is a coarse brutal world, unendurably coarse and brutal, for anyone who hasn't the least dash of coarseness or brutality in his own nature to enjoy it with.

I don't know yet what hope there is for her, but it looks small.

I think of you more than I write to you. It wont be long before I see you again.

Ever yours

Robert Frost

Frost could do nothing to save Jeanie from her fate and had to settle down again to his poetry year. Miss Monroe evidently "wanted something":

If you don't like the way it sticks out in various directions like a fretful hedghog well enough not to bury it under a jarring heap of other people's poetry [he wrote her], please ask to exchange it for anything to eat wear ride or read in any of our departments. We are old friends and ought to be able to stand a little abuse from each other.

Harcourt had published *A Miscellany of American Poetry* in which eleven contemporary poets edited their own work: Frost had in this volume six current poems, including the little known "The Parlor Joke," a poem expressing hatred of urban life, never included in a final collection of his work. Braithwaite, too, was compiling an anthology and wanted some of the *Harper's* poems and "To E.T." Louis Untermeyer was publishing through Harcourt his first anthology, *Modern American Poetry,* with biographical notes on the poets, a book that still lives after many editions and transformations. Poetry was "booming." Whicher, something of a poet himself, "forded the Mohawk" to come up and talk things over and "compare progress" with his dear friend.

Part of the "progress" involved, surprisingly enough, a change of locale for the Frosts' farm. Franconia could never cease to hold their love—the poet would always, he then hoped, find a way to be there in hay-fever season, and did for a long time. Yet, somehow, he confided to me, his friends of many years among the country folk resented the sophisticated authors and professors who now drove up to his little place. In the cold winters after the war he had read poetry for the local Parent-Teachers Association in the high school. But by 1920, if the Village Improvement Society or the PTA asked for a benefit, it was held in a summer mansion. Agreeing to oblige if the true Franconians were invited, Frost found his country friends there as servitors only. That just didn't do.

Two worlds—confusing for the children, and everyone else.

"So," R.F. said with furtive eyes, "one morning in September [1920] I just piled them in the old car and by night we had a new roof over our heads—the entrancing stone house we'd admired in South Shaftsbury, Vermont."

Thus does a poet abridge forethought, deeds, down payments, and the like. It was true anyhow that the age of innocence was over; the world had compulsively and irresistibly broken through into the little family which Lesley, in her reminiscent vein, had compared to the unworldly, introverted Brontës. The last poem by Frost in the *Miscellany* of 1920 expresses it.

THE LOCKLESS DOOR

It went many years,
But at last came a knock,
And I thought of the door
With no lock to lock.

I blew out the light,
I tip-toed the floor,
And raised both hands
In prayer to the door.

But the knock came again
My window was wide;
I climbed on the sill
And descended outside.

Back over the sill
I bade a "Come in"
To whatever the knock
At the door may have been.

So at a knock
I emptied my cage
To hide in the world
And alter with age.

CHAPTER 11

HE LOADED AN OLD
STONE-BOAT WITH THE STAR
1921–1923

The Stone House, on its friendly farm acres in South Shaftsbury, worked out soon as a more human base for Robert and Elinor Frost, especially in winter, than the snowier, wilder, more spatial Franconia. Close to Bennington College and to a good Vermonter friend, Dorothy Canfield Fisher; not far from Amherst, its loyalties and intellectual ferment; within easy railroad reach of New York for the visits, both ways, that they counted on, the Stone House could also become in a poetry crisis their desert island. But the first months there were hard: the poet with his plant and tree qualities resisted transplantation. Sickness seized him. He wondered if he should have left Mount Lafayette.

Something in Frost's adventuring mind demanded that he now express in poetry the active, conscious process, philosophic in essence, that had come to his thinking through wider contacts with a world where not just poetry but history and science were outlining bold change. He had deep interest in both. Whether the view was backward or forward or acutely contemporaneous, the man of forty-seven was discovering more detached, ironic life meanings, seeking "deep stuff," going after it heroically. "The Census Taker," "The Star Splitter," and "A Star in a Stone-Boat," especially the last, belong to the new era:

> . . . for what I search
> I must go measuring stone walls, perch on perch;

It was many years since he had written, in Derry:

> Something there is that doesn't love a wall,

Even if he still doubted that good fences make good neighbors, Frost had himself found hard surfaces, barriers in daily living, that he was forced to measure and surmount. But even in a stone wall, one close to the constellations may feel his hand and arm electrified by the touch of a meteorite: a stony or metallic body that has fallen to earth from outer space. In "A Star in a Stone-Boat"—dedicated to Lincoln MacVeagh who had shared some of his firmamental moods—an imagined laborer has unknowingly built such a body into his wall:

> He did not recognize in that smooth coal
> The one thing palpable beside the soul
> To penetrate the air in which we roll. . . .
>
> He dragged it through the plowed ground at a pace
> But faintly reminiscent of the race
> Of jostling rock in interstellar space.
>
> It went for building stone, and I, as though
> Commanded in a dream, forever go
> To right the wrong that this should have been so.
>
> Yet ask where it could have gone as well,
> I do not know—I cannot stop to tell:
> He might have left it lying where it fell.
>
> From following walls I never lift my eye
> Except at night to places in the sky
> Where showers of charted meteors let fly.

Some may know what they seek in school and church,
And why they seek it there; for what I search
I must go measuring stone walls, perch on perch;

Sure that though not a star of death and birth,
So not to be compared, perhaps, in worth
To such resorts of life as Mars and Earth,

Though not, I say, a star of death and sin,
It yet has poles, and only needs a spin
To show its worldly nature and begin

To chafe and shuffle in my calloused palm
And run off in strange tangents with my arm
As fish do with the line in first alarm.

Such as it is, it promises the prize
Of the one world complete in any size
That I am like to compass, fool or wise.

Pretty low nature needed by the nature poet and the scientist
[R.F. ruminated in 1956]. Talk about inductive thinking, *a priori,
a posteriori*—Plato and Aristotle—Aristotle the father of modern
science—you kick something up from below and it sort of lodges
above—but you could make a case for there being nothing above
that had not come from below.

Did you ever think about that line of Wordsworth's,

> Bound each to each by natural piety.

Wordsworth probably meant *nature*—ever think of it that way
when you read it?

> My heart leaps up when I behold
> A rainbow in the sky:

He probably meant *nature* piety.

Frost's publisher had asked him, in the fall of 1920, to read
a few poetry manuscripts in return for his hundred dollars'
237

monthly stipend. He is still proud to have recommended John Crowe Ransom and Babette Deutsch. At Bryn Mawr College, where he read his poems for the first time, a group of clever girls touched by the sacred dew, the Reeling and Writhing Club (among them Kathleen Johnston, much later his secretary and friend) contrived a little poetry course with Frost, special and unique for themselves, that went on into the next year.

All the while he was sending out poems to magazines in response to requests and, as he jubilantly wrote Miss Monroe before Christmas, "I am cleaned out for the moment. But I am having some more at a great rate." Of these one of the fine ones was "The Pauper Witch of Grafton," which appeared in the Spring, 1921, book number of the *Nation*.

As woman, the "Pauper Witch," printed later in association with Frost's wicked major "Witch of Coös," seems to me closer to the "Hill Wife," than to the hag of Coös. The hill wife spoke her delicate irrational feminine thoughts to a man who was dumb to her need of his insight; that was her tragedy, for he had none till she was gone. The pauper witch—the story came out of a town history—a much tougher girl, was able to lead Arthur Amy, her husband, into abetting her just by being confident in her own female heart's knowledge. She "showed him signs" "off from the house as far as they could keep" [there is that word "keep" again] and he responded romantically.

> And I don't mean [she says] just skulls of Rogers' Rangers
> On Moosilauke, but woman signs to man,
> Only bewitched so I would last him longer.
> Up where the trees grow short, the mosses tall,
> I made him gather me wet snow berries
> On slippery rocks beside a waterfall.
> I made him do it for me in the dark.
> And he liked everything I made him do.
> I hope if he is where he sees me now
> He's so far off he can't see what I've come to.
> You *can* come down from everything to nothing.

238

All is, if I'd a-known when I was young
And full of it, that this would be the end,
It doesn't seem as if I'd had the courage
To make so free and kick up in folks' faces.
I might have, but it doesn't seem as if.

Frost's pencil marked the line

All is, if I'd a-known . . .

for my ear's attention, his notation of the true New England
vernacular versus Amy Lowell's cooked-up "dialect."

Spring book numbers do not yield a living and by June,
1921, Robert Frost accepted an offer from President Marion
Leroy Burton, of the University of Michigan, to become
Fellow in the Creative Arts for one academic year, 1921–1922.
The title signified what is now commonly called "Poet in
Residence."

That Frost had been alerted at the beginning of 1921 comes
to light in a letter to Harriet Moody:

South Shaftsbury, January 20, 1921

Dear Harriet Moody:

Elinor and I are to be in New York on and about the twentieth
(20th) of next month (February) We want to see you for the fun
of a good talk before we do or don't decide to take this step into
Michigan. Whichever we decide we'll be right. That's why we
find it impossible to treat anything as momentous. If you oppose
the step too much we shall think you have some reason for not
wanting us as near you and Chicago as the step would bring us.
Maybe you think there are enough poets within the first postal
zone from Chicago. We shall listen to you with respect and encouraging smiles. . . .

. . . I should be more pleased with your good opinion if you
hadn't told me that time that I might be the best poet in America,
but the best in America couldn't hope to come up to the worst in
England. Have a little national pride. Don't you know it's provincial to look up to England? So it is to brag about America.

What isn't provincial will be the question before the house at the next meeting.

Frost's playful tone with Harriet was based on frank understanding. He could say to her in a letter that people loved him because of rather than in spite of his insincerities, and she would get it. But Frost's humorous reference to English poets hid something of pique. Mrs. Moody loved celebrities from far lands. Back in 1917, when the Atlantic was at its most dangerous, she had entertained at some length in her Chicago house both John Masefield—no special friend of his —and he had found his own English friend and neighbor in Herefordshire, Wilfrid Gibson, there on his first visit.

R.F. has told me a little story of how he and Gibson, reunited later at the Browning Society in Philadelphia to read their poems, were subsequently entertained for the night by a poet whose wife put them in a double bedroom. When they retired, Gibson asked Frost to compare checks. The Yankee held his out reluctantly and found it exactly half the Englishman's!

Frost had rather desperately cast loose from Amherst. It was suffering from what he called "Meiklejaundice," and he knew every wheel as it ground and every academic resentment and yet had had, he felt, little money for his rather drudging labors. In Michigan he was offered $5,000 to do what he would be doing anyhow if he could—that is, write poetry. He referred to himself whimsically as Michigan's "Idle Fellow," and as he approached Ann Arbor, the future promised to be of his own making. Historically speaking, he was the second Poet in Residence in the world. Percy MacKaye, his friend, had been the first: appointed and invented by President R. N. Hughes of Miami University at Oxford, Ohio. With what Frost felt to be admirable daring, the redheaded, strapping politician-president of Michigan had adopted the same idea.

The *Michigan Alumnus* announced in advance that President Burton, by the appointment of Robert Frost, would make a place for the creative spirit in the world of literature and art in the University. "Mr. Frost will do no teaching nor will he be expected to accomplish anything definite unless he has something authentic to say." The declared aim of the University was to give him time and opportunity to do his creative work under favorable surroundings. There were those who said it was all Professor Tilley's doing. He was the Yankee's link with Ann Arbor.

Frost arrived with his eldest daughter—the rest of the family would come later. Lesley and he were warmly welcomed by the President and by Dean Bursley, who had got rooms for them at Mrs. d'Ooge's, the widow of the former head of the Classics Department. It was a pleasant old yellow Victorian house on Washtenaw Avenue, not unlike the Amherst houses they had occupied through years of subletting. Morris Tilley and Roy Cowden of the English department were on hand. Professor Cowden played a fostering role to the small circle of literary undergraduates who were destined to be Frost's chief illuminati. The professor's shy smile, his genuine upper New York State farm origins, his transparent preference for old-fashioned rectitude, as opposed to "city slicker" attitudes in students, endeared him to Robert Frost.

Lesley was a candidate for the Junior class. She had deserted Barnard College, after one year, to do book promotion for the Publishers' Association and with general approval was now returning to her studies. A year here and a year there, but not consecutively, was Lesley's idea of a college education.

While she was adjusting herself, Frost got his bearings in the world of the faculty and was in no time sharing family dinners, especially at the house of the professor of Greek, Campbell Bonner, who was also interested in another of Frost's passions—archaeology. In this house there was a high-school girl named Sue, with her whole heart and soul centered on this brightly shining campus genius. Frost had no car, walked far and near learning local geography, in shoes specially made and immediately ordered from a famed local shoemaker. Pretty soon the rest of the family arrived, and then he could be come on by some "prof" at the grocery store—say John Lewis Brum, now professor emeritus of Journalism—trying to remember by "looking around" the three things his wife had told him to get for lunch; but in vain, he could see but two.

"So let's go for a walk."

Brum recalls that the conversation during the walk ran to the many ways in which well-intentioned women frustrate men.

"Why, only last week," Frost said, "some women inveigled me into attempting to lecture before one of their literary clubs. As I stood there on the platform I heard a strange voice bellowing a lot of nonsense. I discovered it was my voice shouting to be heard in the back seats, and shame took possession of me. You simply can't bellow anything worth listening to!"

Ann Arbor had been settled by German people, small farmers and tradesmen, and many of them still served the college that had grown up to the east of them. Whoever in the University needed a laundress, cook, nurse, carpenter, walked across the bridge over the railroad to find them. The bridge was a regular line of social demarcation, surprising to a New Englander. The business section was west of the campus. The intellectual aristocracy lived east of it, and rejoiced in the quiet, prideful, old-fashioned town, very green then as now, and full of lovely trees. The college buildings were still mostly of brick or gray stone in 1921, like Amherst's or Dartmouth's—if not Colonial, at least Civil War or Victorian. English ivy grew thickly over all, and the Gothic building phase, illustrated by the Law Quadrangle of 1925, had not set in.

On the streets where the faculty lived, Frost was pleased to see many nice traditional white houses, set back in deep, well-kept lawns; and in the surrounding rolling hills, which he soon explored, old white farmhouses, probably built by men with New England roots.

He was reassured to discover a faculty that could, so far as its leaders went, live in big houses like the "best families" in New England, with cooks and even nurses. Women who never washed a dish or served less than three courses for dinner seemed in the ascendant. Though salaries were surely not munificent, many of the faculty had married into families with old Michigan backgrounds. The homespun and arduous life of the pioneer, still continuing in the New England states that Frost belonged to, had here yielded to the plenty of the plains.

It was a relief and a change. Even the more modest hostesses had a "caterer"—really a superior cook—when they entertained, and served their formal dinners on fine china to barenecked faculty wives, a-flash with real jewels. Amherst was not like this, and how well had the "Idle Fellow" understood and exemplified in poetry the fate of a woman with real poverty to deal with, something he knew at first hand.

> It's rest I want—there, I have said it out—
> From cooking meals for hungry hired men
> And washing dishes after them—from doing
> Things over and over that just won't stay done.
> By good rights I ought not to have so much
> Put on me, but there seems no other way. . . .

Elinor had had a lot put upon *her;* poverty for poetry's sake. Sometimes her husband felt so badly about it that he wept and reproached himself bitterly. But they had got to Michigan, were widely dined and loved, and he was free to plan his big Western lecture trip and to keep up his correspondence, about poetry, in addition to establishing a close connection with the informal literary life of the student body, then inter-woven with a college magazine called *Whimsies* (earlier and later *The Inlander*).

The *Whimsies* group, composed of the student staff and chief contributors, never more than twenty, met at the Cowdens', with Mrs. Cowden as kind hostess. In general, nothing was served to eat and nobody smoked—just a thoroughly satisfying feast of reason and flow of soul. The young folks, of course, felt that the new Fellow was created for them and they for him, and Frost made up to them roundly, asking them questions in the spirit of his Amherst teaching, reported by the *Michigan Alumnus:*

Long ago I gave up the idea of asking my students to tell me what I knew that I might discover if they knew as much as I did. Now in classes I ask questions in the correct sense of the word, for I want them to tell me something new, something I do not know.

An article in the *New York Times,* in 1939, quoted Frost as saying to his Michigan students:

Don't write for A's. Athletics are more terribly real than anything else in education because they are for keeps, for blood, and that is the way I want you to write. Studies are done just for practice. Write only when you have something to say.

A vital account from the student angle of what went on at the Cowdens' among these robust young Middle Westerners sitting alight about their Fellow with his seductive presence, mind and word, was written by a young woman, Frances Swain, in the spring of 1922, but not published until 1925 in *The Inlander:*

Beforehand we always set a big wicker chair directly under the reading lamp for Mr. Frost, then he comes and selects some unpretentious, dim corner far distant from the throne, and we are ready to begin—talking, and more, listening to him talk. Although he speaks lightly enough, with a whimsical, skipping surface over his comments, there is a lasting tang of significance in the stuff of them that puts one remotely in mind of that earlier luminary, Dr. Samuel Johnson. Except for that note of rugged sincerity, however, the two are extremely unlike . . . the conversation of

Frost sparkles, more lightly, more elusively, and is at its best in the pauses—when it is in his eyes, between words.

His talk proceeds so deliberately and informally that you might wonder, were you not too absorbed for wonderment, where it was leading anyway. When he was still a newcomer and a curiosity here, he launched his bolt against the academicians with the statement, "I like to see a woman take a sixty foot dive in the Hippodrome—and break her neck. . . . I like to be at a football game where five men are carried out on stretchers." There are successive strata of illumination. Rambling he interpreted: "I like to see the literary artist dare to risk his whole literary *life* just to say what he wants"—audacity, sincerity, tenacity! Then after an interval, his trick of making a clean breast of things forced him to add, "I know you're not all in sympathy with me. I'm glad—because I don't mean half of what I say. . . ." He makes you do the testing.

He is humorous and ruthless. . . . When you first meet him he appears to be quite a middling citizen—his build the least bit taller and stockier than the average, costume unostentatious. . . . Only his forehead, broad and majestic, marks him for an "intellectual." How he would despise the term! . . .

Once in the process of criticizing a "nice obscure poem" (he is a master in subtly discriminating between his *nices,* this one being strongly derogatory because coupled with the *obscure*) he said meditatively, "You know—there is a difference between fetching and far-fetching. . . ." He will often help tide over an emptiness thus, although he would much prefer to be exempted from the criticizing, and does manoeuver so as practically to obviate the impression that he is doing a thing. . . .

Such warm accessibility has its penalties. Professor Roy Cowden has spoken of this in a letter to me:

He [Frost] used to come to our house when students who were interested in *The Inlander* gathered for their meetings. He sat in a corner and listened to manuscript readings. Now and then he entered into the talk but never in a way to block the development of a talent.

Something he once said as we were walking home together has

remained in my mind. The University had put him in a house on Washtenaw Avenue next to a fraternity house. He had been there with Mrs. Frost for several weeks when he said to me, (I cannot quote him exactly)

"How can I write poetry beside a fraternity house? I like all those boys and they come over. I can't find myself!"

The periods during which he lived here were high lights in the lives of the students he came to know. He not only influenced their writing, but he was a great force for good in their lives. A great and good human being only needs to walk the earth, to be a help to mankind.

Yet Frost did find himself as poet in Ann Arbor as he had in Beaconsfield, and in his very first term—it must have been, for Miss Monroe published it in the January, 1922, issue of *Poetry*—wrote one of his major and most "New England" talk poems in blank verse, "The Witch of Coös," which has been called by Randall Jarrell the best poem of its kind since Chaucer. R.F. has told me that it came from "some scattered experiences and a dream," and that he remembers writing it at Mrs. d'Ooge's and showing it to Witter Bynner. He offered to swap it with Harriet Monroe for something else she had of his:

Coös is the next county above where you were in the White Mountains. If you were there in August, you could probably have found us there by looking for us. . . . Well, if we didnt meet in Franconia, probably we shall before long in Chicago unless you avoid me. Van Wyck Brooks has been telling me the future lies with the East in art. I don't know what he knows about it. But I thought I would look around Detroit and Chicago a little before I come to any conclusions for myself. Of course I am hopelessly Eastern in my accent; I have half a mind to call my next book The Upper Right Hand Corner; but that's no reason why I shouldn't view the landscape o'er more or less impartially for awhile yet. I'll let you know when I am ready to award the palm to any section.

Well, what do you say about the long poem?

246

In her well-bred autobiography, Harriet Monroe records a meeting with Robert Frost of this period. Speech rhythms were "a universal poetic principle" with her, as with him:

I remember one night, after a dinner I had given for Robert Frost, when he and I argued about poetic rhythms till three o'clock in the morning, against a background of cheers and jeers from three or four other poets who lingered as umpires, until at last Mrs. Moody called up my apartment and asked me to remind my guest of honor (her house guest) that she was waiting up for him.

How clearly one sees the rival Harriet, in her swing, expectantly, impatiently watching for one to whom time is of no import. Yet Frost's intimacy was with the more monumental Harriet, and Mrs. Torrence in her book quotes, among other letters of Robert Frost to Mrs. Moody, one that very much concerned Lesley and led to her interrupting her college career for the third time:

Dear Harriet:
I'm bringing Lesley instead of Elinor. Don't forget. I wouldn't have you take Lesley for Elinor. She calls for entirely different treatment. That is to say, she can be treated worse, though I shouldn't say there weren't bounds beyond which bad treatment ought not to go even in her case, young and tough as she is and of small account to her father.
If it could be arranged I should like to leave her a little while with you in Chicago for the good you would do her. The poor kid is rather sick of this institution and that through no fault of hers. She's had splendid marks and likes seventy five per cent of her teachers. But my line of talk isn't calculated to make her like any institution. You know how I'm always at it against colleges, in a vain attempt to reconcile myself with them.

Mrs. Moody invited Lesley to spend a few months with her as a sort of daughter of a house rich in visiting personages. She would have her share. Her parents assented, but now the older Lesley, Mrs. Ballantine, wishes they hadn't:

247

"I needed my degree, why didn't they *make* me see it?" she says in the manner of willful daughters.

In talking with Michigan friends of Robert Frost, I have noticed that they speak with especial pleasure of the poets and writers he drew there and brought to their *Whimsies* evenings. One of the first celebrities to turn up independently in November was John Collings—later Sir John—Squire of the *London Mercury,* reputed critic, brilliant parodist, and mildly conservative poet.

Mean thing I did [R.F. ruminated years afterward]—introduced Squire to Amy Lowell. He had taken her apart in print on her two-volume Keats study [of 1925] and when she asked him to dinner and twitted Squire with it, he refused to allow the "firstness" of her greatest treasure as a bibliophile—her original of Keats' "The Eve of St. Agnes."

Which is first? Even the poet doesn't know. I don't always know which version of my own poem is first.

As climax to the spring of 1922, he organized five college readings by Padraic Colum, Carl Sandburg, Louis Untermeyer, Amy Lowell and Vachel Lindsay. These were paid for by the students themselves.

Amy came to Michigan in 1922, bearing her special reading lamp which she made R.F. plug in for her, against the janitor's orders. Twenty-five hundred people sat listening to the quips of the two poets till the fuse was replaced.

"Please smoke your cigar, Miss Lowell!" plead a voice from the audience.

"Why don't you smoke?" Frost urged. "They'd like to see you do it."

"Don't I know it? Come on out behind the barn," she whispered to Frost.

When Carl Sandburg came to read, the Chicago poet stayed with the Frosts and retired early to his room.

"What's Carl doing? Priming for his lecture?" somebody asked.

"No," drawled the Yankee, "he's standing by his mirror

fixing his hair so it will look as if a comb had never touched it."

When Lindsay, that great, sweet, strapping fellow came, bringing the boom of "The Congo," "The Kalliope Yell," and "General Booth Enters Heaven," Frost stayed stubbornly in the background, relishing every line. Vachel he always trusted; other poets he sometimes strained to like.

"Slopping over isn't poetry," he had said to Tilley. But Vachel was Vachel and has remained one of Frost's genuine admirations.

Frost gave no public reading himself at the University of Michigan that first year. It presented him with its Honorary A.M. in June—a rather meager honor, he felt—and let him go home to South Shaftsbury with an invitation to return but so far no supporting salary. The incertitude was annoying.

Nevertheless, almost as soon as he set foot on Vermont soil, in June, 1922, Frost had one of the great, happy experiences of his poetic life. He wrote in one night at the Stone House the long colloquial-satirical blank verse poem "New Hampshire." As dawn came, he went out into the early light, then turned back indoors and "in one stroke of the pen," as he says, followed it with its very opposite, perhaps the most limpid and perfect of his lyrics, "Stopping by Woods on a Snowy Evening."

"New Hampshire" is a false-confidential confession, a dust-in-the-eyes satire in Horatian form, veering back and forth from double talk to good faith and candor on a dozen subjects as diverse as business—New Hampshire has nothing to sell, was his point—mountains; the wiry gang boss in the log jam; Matthew Arnold; and the artist:

> I'm what is called a sensibilitist,
> Or otherwise an environmentalist.
> I refuse to adapt myself a mite
> To any change from hot to cold, from wet
> To dry, from poor to rich, or back again.

I make a virtue of my suffering
From nearly everything that goes on round me.
In other words, I know wherever I am,
Being the creature of literature I am,
I shall not lack for pain to keep me awake.

The side notes in pencil that he wrote in my book read:
"Not so you'd notice it and still too much so for self-approval. I'm willing to sacrifice myself in my general contempt for artists."

"All through I have enjoyed confusion—contrariness—like a figure of speech."

Indeed he seems to be talking, in many tones of voice, to someone he has to oppose and controvert and fool—one of those he calls "enemy friends." He had given the first draft of these ideas as a speech to a lot of men in Michigan—a chamber of commerce group, and then, as he put it:

"I rattled it off at home—fact; I almost did that."

Latin forms he had used before, as in his young lyrical odes. But Horatian satire he had not tried till now, and so "New Hampshire" seems to initiate an era which stretched on into his older years when, not always but sometimes in Latin forms, he spoke from the wry, the bitter-gay, nonchalant, side of his mouth.

"Stopping by Woods," in contrast, is as if addressed to an unseen friend.

STOPPING BY WOODS ON A SNOWY EVENING

Whose woods these are I think I know.
His house is in the village though;
He will not see me stopping here
To watch his woods fill up with snow.

My little horse must think it queer
To stop without a farmhouse near
Between the woods and frozen lake
The darkest evening of the year.

He gives his harness bells a shake
To ask if there is some mistake.
The only other sound's the sweep
Of easy wind and downy flake.

The woods are lovely, dark and deep,
But I have promises to keep,
And miles to go before I sleep,
And miles to go before I sleep.

"A poem is never planned beforehand," Frost said to me, in discussing this moment in his life of poetry. "Many, many other poems of mine have been written in one stroke. Some have trouble in one spot and I may never get them right.

"But I always write with the hope that I shall come on something like a woman's last word."

Jean Starr Untermeyer has—for a possible unconscious reminiscence—referred me to a sonnet of Keats, published in 1817. The first four Keats lines run:

Keen, fitful gusts are whisp'ring here and there
Among the bushes half leafless, and dry;
The stars look very cold about the sky,
And I have many miles on foot to fare.

The speaker in "Stopping by Woods" is a man of middle years who knows himself, in the words of Origen, as "a second world in miniature. The sun and moon are within thee and also the stars." As in "Come In," he is resisting an almost overpowering siren appeal from nature; but as these lines from "New Hampshire" express it:

He knew too well for any earthly use
The line where man leaves off and nature starts,
And never over-stepped it save in dreams.

Long since, in the very first poem in his very first book—and this seems no accident—Frost had written of the haunting temptation to enter dark woods, stretching away unto the edge of doom:

251

I should not be withheld but that some day
Into their vastness I should steal away,
Fearless of ever finding open land,
Or highway where the slow wheel pours the sand.

But even then, the human fact, the human fate had brought him back. Now, after nearly twenty years of human promises to keep and kept, the poet who stops by snowy woods repeats a major life theme.

The great Frost family event of the summer of 1922 was a mountaineering trip in August, on the so-called "Long Trail" over the Vermont mountains—some two hundred and more miles of climbing projected, led off by the poet with Lesley, Carol, Marjorie, and Lillian La Batt, Marjorie's roommate when she attended Bennington High School.

Frost has told me how he started off alone in the rain, leaving the children behind to buy shoes somewhere, and reached the first shelter. There a couple already entrenched regarded him with unfriendly suspicion.

"I said I'd agreed to wait there for my children, who would come along at four o'clock. The couple didn't believe a word of it. But come the children did, streaming at exactly four around the bend. We were all hived up there in the rain."

Frost did over one hundred miles on the trail with a sore foot, then left the young people to finish by themselves while he hiked home via the White Mountains, sleeping on the ground.

Father Frost, *Tête d'Armée*, might be suspected of needing peace and quiet, for it was probable that with all the poems of the last several years, including those which were still to come out in magazines and reviews, there would be a new Frost volume, Book Four, in 1923. It was even all but sure it would be called *New Hampshire*. The project was as dear to Lincoln MacVeagh as *North of Boston* had been to Alfred Harcourt. MacVeagh was proving an excellent friend and able business agent, taking the lead in a second Frost project, a critical selection from his first three books, planned for March, 1923.

In September, 1922, when preoccupied with all this, both publisher and poet were stirred up by a sparkling satire on contemporary poets, Frost included, published anonymously and called "A Critical Fable." It was modeled, even to the rhymed couplets, on James Russell Lowell's "A Fable for Critics" of 1849. In spite of Amy Lowell's inclusion of herself among the satirized, the poets and the public were not long in recognizing the authorship. An excerpt, interesting to students both at Amherst and in Michigan:

> There's Frost with his blueberry pastures and hills
> All peopled by folk who have so many ills
> 'Tis a business to count 'em, their subtle insanities.
> One half are sheer mad, and the others inanities.
> He'll paint you a phobia quick as a wink
> Stuffed into a hay-mow or tied to a sink.
> And then he'll deny, with a certain rich rapture,
> The very perversion he's set out to capture.
> He's a foggy benignity wandering in space
> With a stray wisp of moonlight just touching his face,
> Descending to earth when a certain condition
> Reminds him that even a poet needs nutrition,
> Departing thereafter to rarefied distances
> Quite unapproachable to those persistencies,
> The lovers of Lions, who shout at his tail—
> At least so he says—when he comes within hail. . . .
> No wonder he cleaves to his leafy seclusion,
> Barricading his door to unlawful intrusion,
> The goal of the fledgling, a god in a thicket,
> To be viewed only Tuesdays and Fridays by ticket.
>   . . . he divides [she goes on] his life into two pieces,
> Keeping one for himself while the other he leases
> To various colleges. He's eclectic in choice
> And at least half-a-dozen have cause to rejoice
> That he's sojourned among them; for his unique duty,
> What they pay him to do and regard as their booty,
> Is the odd one of being on hand, nothing more.

He's an unexplored mine you know contains ore;
Or rather, he acts as a landscape may do
Which says one thing to me and another to you,
But which all agree is a very fine view. . . .

On top of this "The Witch of Coös" received *Poetry's* Levinson Prize of two hundred dollars in the fall of 1922. And the dissolving of the firm of David Nutt made possible the renewal in 1923—MacVeagh had arranged it—of the English publication of Frost's books through the reliable firm of William Heinemann.

With all this poetry "business" going on—it included the considerable pother over the leftover Nutt sheets of the first two books, which eventually were taken over by the Dunster House Bookshop in Cambridge, at Harvard's gates—Frost was uneasy about his responsibilities to the University of Michigan, which had raised $5,000 for him to "stay around" in 1922–1923, when actually he needed to write and revise undisturbed in the New England mountains, or keep reading engagements made before Michigan offered a salary for the second college year.

He was, as he wrote Whicher at the end of 1922, "not Mr. Frost formerly of Michigan but Mr. Frost formally of Michigan":

I expect to spend a lot of my time in South Shaftsbury this year writing little verses. I got started and my breaks ["double-take" again?] are burned out. It was in the agreement that I should be where I pleased to write. In theory they see that I should be in practice they are going to get cross unless I make it up to them for the lack of my smiling presence on the campus (my cane spats and bowler) by publishing a book of something this year and dedicating. Its a situation that can't last forever. . . .

In fact, though Robert and Elinor had dashed out, at President Burton's request, for his October, 1922, reception, they had as swiftly retreated again. Frost had lectures both in

New England and in the South and Southwest. He went to Fort Worth, Texas, and New Orleans. John Crowe Ransom, whom he already valued, drew him to confer with a rising poetic group at Vanderbilt University in Nashville, Tennessee, who called themselves the Fugitives. There he made more friends: the late Dr. Merrill Moore, who established himself in Boston and became known for his sonnets as well as for his psychiatry, was one of them; and another, Donald Davidson of Vanderbilt University, a professor of English and a poet who joined the summer Bread Loaf School of English which Frost had helped to found in 1921. To this day, Davidson spends his summers near R.F. in Vermont.

In Fort Worth, Frost has told me, he found himself very much out of character because he had slipped on—for the first and last time—a ruby-sapphire ring, William Vaughn Moody's wedding ring, in fact, which Harriet Moody had given him as earnest for some poetry fund she had asked him to administer.

A confederate veteran in the front row claimed contentiously that he could not understand poetry "without the beat of the tom-tom," and when the Yankee in gray-blue raised his hand and answered soothingly that they were both orphans and should get along, the local press took occasion to quote his remarks with a "said Robert Frost with a gesture of his jewelled hand."

The *Selected Poems,* dedicated to Edward Thomas, published March 15, 1923, gave evidence of Frost's imaginative care for the grouping of the poems as well as for the choices. It was important as the first selection of his published work. Elinor felt that there was much in it and brought out by it, in relation to Robert's poetry, that the public had not yet appreciated, and MacVeagh agreed with her. That would come, both felt sure.

In late May, Robert Frost read his own poetry to a full, glowing house in Sarah Caswell Angell Hall, the older and more intimate of the University auditoriums. This was his last contribution as a Fellow to his adopted university. Though he felt regret in leaving a group of intimates he had got sincerely involved with, he was too old (he said) to depend on provisional appointments; and there was then no prospect he could discern of a permanent seminar or professorship for him at the University of Michigan, with its twelve thousand students and its domination by engineers, scientists, and politicians.

The Fellowship in the Creative Arts was set up as a two year appointment, and there was talk of the next one going to the least "modern" of contemporary English poets, Robert Bridges, the Poet Laureate, whom Frost knew and had dared to argue with in England against fixed quantities in English verse. Had Michigan been unaware of the appearance of Eliot's "The Waste Land" in the *Dial* in 1922? Frost had noted it and "The Love Song of J. Alfred Prufrock," which Harriet Monroe, through Pound, had printed in *Poetry* in 1915. Had Edna St. Vincent Millay been noted? The poetic renascence was not untouched by these new events and personalities and the New Englander began to yearn for his Northeastern roots.

Things had, moreover, come to a crisis in Amherst College. He knew this through letters from his faculty friends and associates, who informed him that they were dismissing their president—a drastic, tragic, and embarrassing act—at Commencement, 1923.

Frost felt a deep stir of loyalty to the small New England college for boys that had first recognized his powers as a college teacher. But he believed in professors being "come after," and the Frost family, for the moment, was headed for South Shaftsbury, the poet for his summer's work of getting his forthcoming *New Hampshire* ready for November publication.

CHAPTER 12

THE AIM WAS SONG
1923–1927

The tranquillity of the Stone House in South Shaftsbury was soon disturbed by the discordant Amherst row. The dismissing of Meiklejohn—a brilliant, high-minded president—was the work of Amherst's faculty and trustees. But some seniors of the class of 1923 had, to demonstrate their disapproval and their sympathy, gone so far as to refuse their sheepskins, on the Commencement platform. Certain professors had resigned in protest; others had been dropped. The unanimous cry of the friends of Meiklejohn was that Amherst College would not tolerate liberal or radical thought.

Frost, who relied on his "wisdom of the commonplace," after taking his bearings wrote his friend Tilley, in Michigan, that no principle of radical or liberal was involved. Meiklejohn had gone (he said) because he had divided his house against itself, siding with the obviously clever as against the merely sound and able. Meiklejohn's faculty of this middle-of-the-road thinking caliber would have tolerated him if he had tolerated them. But he hadn't, Frost claimed. He had been "too high-minded for any *modus vivendi.*"

In fact Frost at this time, though admiring his courage, doubted his friend Meiklejohn as a thinker, doubted him as a practical man, and so doubted many of his brilliant young defenders among students who were also student friends of his own. One of them, Gardner Jackson, later a liberal lawyer

257

distinguished for his defense of Sacco and Vanzetti, tried to gain the ear of a poet who had "given him a soul." These two, so far apart in ideas, became lifelong friends and still meet to contend and disagree and admire one another.

Yet in 1923, for all the liberal and radical arguments to which he listened, Frost set himself firmly behind the faculty conservatives who were riding out the storm, and it was they who persuaded him that his loyal duty was to stick with them.

Their rock of strength was Acting President George Daniel Olds, a professor of mathematics, who had at Amherst already carried the administrative duty of dean along with his teaching. When Olds during the summer of 1923 confided in Robert Frost (after the latter's acceptance of an English professorship for 1923–1924), that he was in trouble through the sudden death of his professor of philosophy, Frost began to think up possible candidates and in the end found the philosopher he was in search of in himself, and put himself at the service of the philosophy department.

As he said in 1937, at Princeton University, he had had a great leaning toward philosophic thinking since the age of forty. Young people had insight, he thought—a flash here and a flash there—like the stars in the early evening sky. It was later, in the dark of life, that you saw forms, constellations, and these were philosophy.

He was to share the Amherst College duties with his friend Manthey-Zorn of the German department, who would give the regular course in German philosophy, while his own approach was to be, as ever, Socratic and based on "cases," which gave full scope to his life wisdom.

In English, Frost's single course, very fully attended, was to be in books off the main line of English literature.

He wrote Tilley that he wouldn't be expected to teach much. "You'll laugh. But such as I am I can't stay out of what interests me. I'm not very detachable."

Frost cared terribly that his good Michigan friends should understand the sincerity of his return to Amherst. Such caring to be understood is typical of him. To Tilley he wrote:

258

. . . You must wonder about my coming to Amherst after what I said to you about coming back to Michigan. But if you stop to consider you will see no great inconsistency. Michigan on year-to-year contract and no prospect of settling down and making myself at home was out of the question. . . . I was too homeless for my age out there and too dissatisfied with the way Burton conceived of the fellowship. If someone had asked me to give one seminar a week out there as long as I wanted to stay for $5,000 a year I should have taken him up. I liked the folks, I made more and closer friends than I ever did before.

In the South Shaftsbury house, during the summer of 1923, Frost was rarely released from his new Book Four, its concerns and correspondence. Lincoln MacVeagh, who was shortly to resign from Holt's and take over the direction of the Dial Press, was seeing it through. It was decided to have illustrations, woodcuts by J. J. Lankes, who became known to Frost through his delicately dour woodcuts for "The Star-Splitter," published in the *Century Magazine* for September. This plan gave Frost his first illustrated volume. His first Limited Edition had come in 1919 (*North of Boston*). He had a very keen personal interest in fine printing, aroused in part, in his youth, by the editions of Thomas Bird Mosher, and was pleased that *New Hampshire* would have a Limited Edition of three hundred and fifty copies.

But just before the college term began, the poet, to his dismay, discovered that some of the Amherst familiars who had read the title poem "New Hampshire" suspected him of making it a symbolic comment on the Amherst controversy, and of meaning Meiklejohn when he referred to "a New York Alec."

The passage in question runs as follows:

> Lately in converse with a New York alec
> About the new school of the pseudo-phallic,
> I found myself in a close corner where
> I had to make an almost funny choice.

"Choose you which you will be—a prude, or puke,
Mewling and puking in the public arms."
"Me for the hills where I don't have to choose."
"But if you had to choose, which would you be?" . . .

Finally the speaker with his Shakespearean words "mewling" and "puking" seems forced to a choice and the poem ends with a recognizable self-portrait:

> Well, if I have to choose one or the other,
> I choose to be a plain New Hampshire farmer
> With an income in cash of say a thousand
> (From say a publisher in New York City).
> It's restful to arrive at a decision,
> And restful just to think about New Hampshire.
> At present I am living in Vermont.

In the universal sense the speaker of the long autobiographical satire is a "natural man," who has experienced the lures and traps of sophistication and speaks of them sometimes in sly, double meanings and sometimes in sharp, moral denunciation and sober earnest. Here the debilities of the times, particularly the "pseudo-phallic," are let fly at with arrows tinged with gall. The poet felt that way.

A small a—alec for Alec—was in the end the only concession made to local gossip.

Frost's first seminar in philosophy in the autumn had for theme "What is an idea?" He sent the students out with lanterns to look for the human attitudes behind the major philosophies of the world. Teaching on these lines went on through two academic years: 1923–1925. A personal memory of Frost's Emerson class lingers with me from my first visit to him in Amherst. I noted in my portrait R.F.'s "vanishing and peripatetic look," on the platform; his "dry, sly, halting" speculative manner; and his request for comment on an idealist.

"What is an idealist? Is he a man who measures up from nothing, or one who measures down from everything? Might he be, especially if an artist, somewhere between the two?"

He spoke in a homespun voice (rather more "New England" than it really was), making his Socratic manner something like a farmer's interrogation of a neighbor—dropping his g's advisedly or subtly, apparently to keep the relationship on the level. No mask of superiority, no assumption that the man on the platform was wiser than the youth below. They might all have come from adjacent mountain farms.

R.F. said later to me: "I didn't realize what a dropper of g's I had become in my out-and-out farm days till I heard a boy mimicking me early in my return to the civilization of the schoolroom. It took me some time to recover my g's."

R.F. also said that the country characters of his poetry were about the same as he was. His father's people, around him when he was young in Lawrence, were all about the same.

In a talk on "Poverty and Poetry" at Princeton he has elaborated this theme:

For no matter how educated or poor a man is, a certain level up there in Vermont or New Hampshire stays the same. We people just sort of fountain up, jet up out of it.

Still, as I said in 1925: If Virgil had been a plain dirt farmer, he could hardly have written the Eclogues. So with Frost and his dramatic pastorals at Derry, Franconia, and South Shaftsbury, Vermont.

In his English class, at that time, Frost had asked his students, I recall, "How many things can you do to a poem besides read it or write it?" The class had found one hundred and eight.

> How had the tender verse escaped their outrage?
> By being invisible for what it was,
> Or else by some remoteness that defied them
> To find out what to do to hurt a poem. . . .

261

In discussing in the 1950s his method of teaching books off the main course of English literature, he used these words:

I said to the class:

"I'll be talking with you three times a week. You'll be reading off the main stream—Borrow, Cobbett, plays and things. You'll be sitting on a half sheet of paper. If your mind goes off to a bird outside the window, write a little item—leave it on my desk. If your insight is correct I'll read it. You're making your mark as in the world. I will know you from this, I'll respond—but not by *correcting* your work.

"Wait to write till something says something," I told them.

"The first thing you show will give you your year's mark. You can appeal from this."

He also told them that he wanted them to accumulate a library, to tell him of anything they found and to buy one hundred and fifty dollars' worth of books.

I escaped a lot of drudgery. I said:

"This is a class in seeing how long I can keep from reading what you write. Keep things till you have an accumulation and make a choice."

I always tried to escape the penalty of teaching by making the work more interesting to myself.

Such methods run the risk of failure with slackers; yet Frost had his own remedies: he might give a boy something so impossible to do, such misery, that the professor would award an A in compensation.

One rather roguish lad (he illustrated) was always saying how hard it was to get going *right*. Obviously he wasn't working. Finally the poet-professor said:

"You're a senior. You need my mark. Between us two you haven't written a thing. That puts you in an awkward place. You write me so many pounds of manuscript. I will weigh it and mark you by weight."

One night he came to see me in the library. I was talking with another boy, who told him to get out—but when we finall; groped our way out in the dark the rogue was lying outside the door, like the boy on the burning deck.

This sort of thing I did just for the symbol, to make them really do something. Always I was under the suspicion of the old-timers that I was dodging work. I was. I responded if something interested me.

Frost remembers that he had as students in his English class William Hasty, a distinguished Negro, later Governor of the Virgin Islands, and Charles Woolsey Cole, who became President of Amherst College, and a very close friend in Frost's elder years.

It was when the Frosts were living their first winter at Number 10 Dana Street—a house they could keep two years if they wanted—that the first family wedding occurred. Lillian La Batt had been Carol's girl since the Long Trail hike, and the couple had been engaged so young that Carol's father believed the romance would come to nothing. But—he told me—when Lillian, still only eighteen, returned from college, homesick, and "Carol went to her mother and got her," Frost found himself reliving his own early love and marriage, and gave them his blessing.

As it proved, the most unintellectual member of the younger generation had brought as steadfast and lasting a feminine influence into the family as his father before him. For a time the young couple shared the Stone House—they had it to themselves in winter. But soon the parents turned over their home completely to the youngsters who had decided to raise apples—and later also sweet peas—for a living. After a period in a shingled cottage, Rob and Elinor found themselves another farm, The Gully, which was their South Shaftsbury home until Elinor's death.

New Hampshire, the child of the mind, next claimed their devotion. It promised a wider sale than Frost had ever known. It had been seven years since *Mountain Interval,* and almost all the poems in the new book—not quite all—had been written since 1916 and were (though in no obvious way) the product of the wider, more cosmopolitan and less isolated life that the poet had led since his return from England. *New Hampshire* was appropriately dedicated "to Vermont and Michigan," and in the original edition—not in the *Complete Poems*—was divided into three parts: New Hampshire; Notes; and Grace Notes. The fourteen poems listed as "Notes" were poems with a story, full of vocal images, "the sound of sense," and the resonance of voices. The thirty "Grace Notes," as the musical term suggests, were shorter lyrical poems. Of these, the poem "Misgiving" dates from early Derry days (1900) and "To Earthward" was written in England. The masterly short dramatic lyric, "Fire and Ice," was written at Miss March's in Amherst:

FIRE AND ICE

Some say the world will end in fire,
Some say in ice.
From what I've tasted of desire
I hold with those who favor fire.
But if it had to perish twice,
I think I know enough of hate
To say that for destruction ice
Is also great
And would suffice.

This dramatic confrontation of opposite passions illustrates Frost's aesthetic creed that a poem must create situation as much as a play. "All we do in life," Frost commented to me on this poem, "is a clarification after we stir things up." The reader in search of cross references might look at the following lines from Emerson's "Uriel" which Frost, speaking through Job in "The Masque of Reason," has called "the greatest Western poem yet."

'Line in nature is not found;
Unit and universe are round;

> In vain produced, all rays return;
> Evil will bless and ice will burn.'

Since most of the poems in *New Hampshire* are very well known and dear to the public today, I mention here some that I have never heard Robert Frost read in public: as for instance "The Grindstone," which the poet told me had "many years of living" in its making. Here you find an adolescent boy, perhaps called Rob at home, helping a farmer—to help his mother —battling him all the time, meeting something tough in an older imposed will:

> I gave it the preliminary spin,
> And poured on water (tears it might have been),
> And when it almost gaily jumped and flowed,
> A Father-Time-like man got on and rode,
> Armed with a scythe and spectacles that glowed. . . .

Never knowing whether the skills involved had succeeded or gone too far:

> Mightn't we make it worse instead of better?
> I was for leaving something to the whetter.
> What if it wasn't all it should be? I'd
> Be satisfied if he'd be satisfied.

(These are lines one would recognize as Frost's anywhere.) The young boy could have found a better way, he implies, to pass the afternoon

> Than grinding discord out of a grindstone,
> And beating insects at their gritty tune. . . .

But where better could a poet have found those magic exact words, implanted by revolt in a mind of sensibility? Lankes, too, did for Frost his finest woodcut of that cumbersome grindstone, "symbol of the great round earth," in the thin shadow of the ruinous live apple tree.

265

Another poem from the "Notes" section, Frost's Paul Bun-yan story, which was written in Michigan and came from a Michigan lumberjack, is interesting as seemingly linked to the whimsical little stories the poet used to tell his children in Derry, the ones quoted in Part I from the old tattered copy-book.

"Paul's Wife" concerns metaphorically a man who refuses to share socially his spiritual possessions—in this case a wife who may not even be named by others without offense and vanishment. It is, like "The Witch of Coös," a mystery story, but romantic, concerning birth, not murder.

> . . . Paul sawed his wife
> Out of a white-pine log. Murphy was there,
> And, as you might say, saw the lady born. . . .

Actually wood became woman when Paul carried to water a delicate length of pith he found inside his hollow log. It seemed to have melted; then, beyond the open water, dim with midges, it slowly rose a person, rose a girl.

"Wild Grapes"—the only poem, Frost says, that he ever wrote "on assignment"—concerns the three ages of man, and is described by R.F. as a girl's version of "Birches." It had been given him by his dear old friend Miss Susan Ward, the stern preceptress, nurturer, and editor of his very early poetry. Old and blind she might be, and near her death as he sat beside her in the archetypal dignity of the Hayes family homestead in South Berwick, but anxious to contribute to the fine flow-ering of one she had known unaccredited, callow and yearn-ing.

It had moved the poet to visit the old Maine village where the Hayes house, on its hill, stands not far from the Sarah Orne Jewett house. The widowed brother and spinster sister, who had shared learning and intellectual energies at the *Independent,* were at this time, in old New England fashion, ending their lives happily together. As Miss Susan told her birches story about the little girl who had not, as the poem puts it, taken the first step in knowledge, to let go with the hands, and so was swung skyward on her birchtop like a bunch of grapes, the poet noticed that she kept clasping and unclasping her old veined hands.

> . . . but nothing tells me
> That I need learn to let go with the heart.

Another New Hampshire "Grace Note," with roots in early New England love and life, is the poignant "Two Look at Two." The boy and girl lovers of *A Boy's Will*, the young married folk facing their tragic discord in "Home Burial," the grateful, seasoned lovers of "To Earthward," are now, it seems, met as a tender, composed couple we somehow recognize, walking out at dusk on a mountainside and coming upon a doe across a wall:

> She [the doe] saw them in their field, they her in hers.
> The difficulty of seeing what stood still,
> Like some up-ended boulder split in two,
> Was in her clouded eyes: they saw no fear there.
> She seemed to think that two thus they were safe. . . .

After the doe, all unaware of the pregnant image she had given a poet, had "passed unscared along the wall," and this seemed all, an antlered buck of lusty nostril viewed them quizzically. Then he too passed unscared along the wall.

> Two had seen two, whichever side you spoke from.
> "This *must* be all." It was all. Still they stood
> A great wave from it going over them,
> As if the earth in one unlooked-for favor
> Had made them certain earth returned their love.

In the original editions of *New Hampshire* the opening satire is studded with little numbers referring to passages from the "Notes" section in the manner of a scholar referring to texts. This rather precious device was wisely abandoned in later collections. For the poems spoke for themselves, and the critics forecast truly that they would receive the Pulitzer Prize.

In the spring of 1924, Robert Frost, taking Elinor along, went back to Ann Arbor to stay with the Bursleys and give a reading of his own poetry to the University audience. He was, of course, again a guest of *Whimsies*, and saw again the girls and boys with whose efforts, aspirations, and personalities he had become involved as a teacher.

It was at this time that President Burton approached him on the subject of again renouncing Amherst teaching for a possible return to Michigan on a permanent basis. When Robert Bridges' time-period as Fellow in Creative Arts ran out, the President proposed to arrange some appointment for Frost, carried on the regular budget of the University and for an indefinite period. This would do away with financial worry and perpetual migration.

Frost listened, but his immediate concern was to get back to hold his Amherst examinations and help Lesley and Marjorie with the opening of a little bookshop, called The Open Book, in Pittsfield, Massachusetts. This had been Lesley's dream, and her adviser, Frederic Melcher of *Publishers' Weekly* (her father's friend), told her she was ready to break loose from the Hampshire Bookshop in Northampton, where she had been an apprentice, and put her own plan into reality.

Her youngest sister was happy to join her. They were both beautiful, poetical girls, Lesley as fair, blue-eyed and pink-cheeked and full of action, as Marjorie was dark and brown-eyed and full of poesie. The enterprise itself, owing to its parentage, made a stir in the Berkshire neighborhoods. Some Frost first editions were available and collectors were beginning to sniff around.

But the climax of 1924 was the presentation of the Pulitzer Prize to Robert Frost and *New Hampshire* in June at Columbia University, and just afterward, the presentation to him of honorary Doctorates in Letters by Yale University and Middlebury College. It is the first of everything that leaves the deep impress, like the first flowers and plants dug into a new garden. As time flows on, such adornments become too numerous to seem exceptional—in Frost's case, today a subject for the statistician.

One tiny little lyric only appeared in print in 1924, as if in protest that the past had been outlived or forgotten in a new, more splendid world. In its romantic identification of the subject with his flowers—its empathy—it seems as if saved out from *A Boy's Will:*

LODGED

The rain to the wind said,
"You push and I'll pelt."
They so smote the garden bed
That the flowers actually knelt,
And lay lodged—though not dead.
I know how the flowers felt.

In late June of 1924, Frost, rather worn from so much teaching and lecturing, settled down on a warm rock in South Shaftsbury from which he had a view of the young growing orchard. Lincoln MacVeagh had helped him and Carol with the planting of the trees.

It is no small burden, spiritual and even physical, to influence a campus by "presence," as R.F. had done in Michigan and in Amherst, too. He did it both unknowingly and knowingly, but never in the all-out manner of such campus favorites as "Billy" Phelps of Yale and "Copey" of Harvard, who deliberately influenced by personality and by their own almost compulsive interest in the young hopefuls. Frost, in a college, was just *there,* a bulky individuality, weighted with sheer being, human stature, and, above all, creative potency. As he had said to Jean Starr Untermeyer, he carried a jar of precious ointment on his head. Students with insight could catch the outline.

The release from his own bulk came to him through earth's

largesse. After due basking and "gloating," his senses might be relied on to return to him that instinctive acute responsiveness to the natural world from which his poetic impulses seem to spring. Frost lived with nature on many levels, including the relatively superficial one of infusing wind-crushed garden flowers with his own crushed feelings. He needed every level to bring himself back from college to poetry, and might be moved to exhume from some old notebook and publish in 1925 a poem composed in the late nineties:

ON GOING UNNOTICED

As vain to raise a voice as a sigh
In the tumult of free leaves on high.
What are you in the shadow of trees
Engaged up there with the light and breeze?

Less than the coral-root you know
That is content with the daylight low,
And has no leaves at all of its own;
Whose spotted flowers hang meanly down.

You grasp the bark by a rugged pleat,
And look up small from the forest's feet.
The only leaf it drops goes wide,
Your name not written on either side.

You linger your little hour and are gone,
And still the woods sweep leafily on,
Not even missing the coral-root flower
You took as a trophy of the hour.

"A queer unconscious one," R.F. commented to me. If so, of special interest to the student because its modern theme, man's minute dimension in a world of nature, existing in and for its own sake, is repeated in his later poetry, notably in one of his greatest later lyrics of the wilds, "The Most of It."

R.F.'s childhood, however tragic, had left him with a subjective certainty and positiveness of sheer being, almost animal in nature, that still, in old age, reassures students of post-war and post-postwar campuses that man's place in the universe does not need to shrink away from the human into the purely scientific proportion.

"I'm past my set teaching," Frost complained to his friend and colleague Manthey-Zorn, in a letter of the late summer of 1924: "I don't really want much to teach any more. Least of all do I want a losing fight in education with a lot of people who are good enough as they are." His attitude about his own children's education was of something the same sort. If they wanted one, all right, if they didn't—Carol and Irma hadn't and didn't—all right too. (Carol had a son now, William Prescott Frost again.) Lesley and Marjorie had wanted education; yet he could worry about that, too. In another letter he said that Marjorie's thinking was getting too much for her. She was apprehending everything at once, instead of in courses as at college. Absurd as such divisions of knowledge were, he wrote, they never hurt the docile.

He hoped to get through the academic winter (1924–1925) without resigning from Amherst, but not much more. In September he adjured Manthey-Zorn to help President Olds "keep his classes at bay." George F. Whicher, in one of his affectionate critical essays on Frost, puts such moods in their place:

. . . Frost . . . would not be fully himself unless there were an educational project somewhere in the offing for him to cherish and humorously despair of, for he is a born teacher with a knack of charging dry subjects with intellectual excitement and a large patience for struggling learners.

Teaching to him is a natural extension of his unfeigned interest in people. I have seen him ask friendly, insistent questions about the little country town where a man was born and brought up, and have watched the man, at first answering with diffidence because for years he had been apologetic about his simple beginnings and anxious to live them down, gradually warm to his memories, discover a fresh respect for the sources of his being, and go

271

out from the interview (as he said later) with a new dimension added to his personality. I doubt if Frost knew how much that conversation meant to the other man. He was just expressing an interest in the ways of little towns.

Young and fresh in teaching when he first came to Amherst, fifteen years Frost's junior, Whicher had risen to be full professor of English in 1922. He was becoming one of the leading professors in Amherst College, and later, after his Emily Dickinson studies and writings, and his translation of the Goliard Poets, one of the biggest "names." He had spice and wit and learning, was handsome, dignified, aloof by nature, and had a "touch of correctness," as Frost put it, that did not dismay one who liked to deal correctness a body blow now and then.

"He had a tendency to modify some of the things I said," Frost told me with a twinkle. "I lost a local friendship for standing by him in the Mickey rows. . . . Someone was going to get rid of Whicher . . . someone who had threatened to pick us off, fly by fly. . . ."

Now the two of them, Frost and Whicher, were seeing one another from door to door and back again on snowy-starry evenings, asking puzzling questions of life.

Frost's greatest personal, worldly puzzle that year was, first, whether the University of Michigan would really appoint him, considering that his most influential backer, President M. L. Burton, had died suddenly in October. When the money for the Fellowship in Arts was apportioned by the University, Frost had the puzzle of whether he wanted to commit himself once more, this time "all out" to the Middle West. On the money side it was tempting. Meiklejohn had started him at $1,200, moved on to $2,500. Michigan doubled this his first two years and had now offered him $6,000, something he could appreciate, since only Lesley of his children—possibly Marjorie too, but she had hardly started—seemed predetermined to successful independence. Carol, though happily married, and the most skilled of gardeners, was even less able to make a living than his father at the same age. To Elinor also, this was a concern. There was the grandchild.

In November, the Boston *Evening Transcript* announced Robert Frost's Michigan appointment, but even at Christmas time he himself spoke of it to Harriet Monroe as if the door were still open:

"I am thinking of concentrating my residence at Ann Arbor where you can put your finger on me."

Like all intuitives, more than most, Robert Frost wanted to remain vaguely uncommitted. It was borne in upon him and Elinor, however, that they *had* decided their fate and *must* begin to search for a suitable house. In his far-ranging walks two years before, Frost had been attracted to a charming little old white clapboard house with fluted Greek columns, on Pontiac Street in the German part of Ann Arbor. Would the neighborhood be too remote? Would it look as if they were running away from the obligations of the Fellowship? This worldly question bothered the unworldly Frosts as they sat in Dana Street, Amherst. What did the Tilleys and the Bursleys think? Would they consider it as if it were their own affair?

By present reckoning, Robert Frost was to be 51 on March 26, 1925. His friends, however, believed, as he did, that he was having a fiftieth birthday, and wanted to give him a dinner in New York.

"I won't say I don't like to be made of by the right sort of friends," he wrote Melcher, "if it is understood beforehand that I don't have to look or act my own age."

It was at about this time that I first talked with Frost in Amherst about his poetry and his life. So I was among the forty guests invited to attend the dinner at the old Hotel Brevoort. Subsequently I described him as he looked that night—"a good Greek out of New England":

The cast of feature bears out the cast of mind. If I could choose a sculptor from the antique world to mould Frost's head, I should vote for Skopas, who added shadows of human passion to calm Greek faces. In certain moods, this Frost face with its musing eyes, so deeply hollowed and shaded by sharp-drawn brows, seems touched by that pathetic hand. But again the poet's dream grows unified, grave, mystical-religious, and one says here are a brow and eyes like Dante's. At the dinner in honour of Frost's fiftieth birthday at the Hotel Brevoort, in New York, he wore at first the marble Dantesque mask; colored really like Carrara marble, with mauve and golden shadows, and shining with a clear Renaissance beauty of the Christian sort. . . .

Yet it took only a featherweight of affection—all that the friends dared offer, since they had come, for the most part, with the hands that bore gifts tied behind their backs—to make tenderness flicker like flame over the still features, and shape itself in facial line; only a quip of New England humor to bring a gentle cynic out of hiding. Or shall I say a rustic deity? Eyebrows arch roundly, cheeks draw into shrewd satiric wrinkles, eyes turn to flashes and darts of blue light, malicious or rejoicing, and as an unruly lock is tossed, one hears the stamp of a hoof—

> Pan came out of the woods one day,—
> His skin and his hair and his eyes were gray. . . .

An intimate simple, yet distinguished feast: the poet read "The Cow's in the Corn," his humorous one-page, one-act Irish verse play, to the Holts, the Harcourts; to James Chapin the painter, Arroldo du Chêne the sculptor, both of whom had beautifully captured his likeness as they saw it; to Fred Melcher, to Wilbur Cross who had led him into the *Yale Review;* to Jean and Louis Untermeyer; to Elinor Wylie, Sara Teasdale, Willa Cather, Dorothy Canfield Fisher; to the brilliant Van Doren twain—Carl was toastmaster but Mark, the poet, was the closer friend, often in R.F.'s company at this period.

Only Amy Lowell was absent—at home, recovering from the bitter diatribes of the English critics against her two-volume Keats biography and courageously preparing to sail off to confute them. In her own land, the book had gone into its fourth edition. A much more formal and glittery "complimentary dinner" than Frost's was to be given for her at the Hotel Somerset, in Boston, on the fourth of April. Though R.F. had said he "wouldn't go to hers unless she came to his," Amy expected Frost and asked him to make a toast.

"You and Louis come here first," she admonished him on one of her one A.M. telephone calls, *"and I'll tell you what you will each say at my dinner."*

This last imperial comment led Untermeyer to retire and Elinor to dispatch at once one of her tactful, wifely letters, from the Untermeyers' apartment:

My dear Amy.—

I am writing to say what we ought to have said decidedly in the first place—that it's simply out of the question for Robert to speak at your dinner. He just isn't able to. He is tired now, and has three lectures ahead of him this week, with much travelling. He is sorry, and we hope very much that it won't greatly disarrange your plans.

And we hope very much, too, that the occasion will be a happy and satisfactory one for you. I am sure it will be.

With love to you and Ada—

Faithfully yours,

Elinor Frost

Amy Lowell died suddenly of a stroke on May 12. She had recognized her condition instantly, through a reflection of her own face in her bedroom mirror, and with this flash of tragic consciousness and a cry to her dear friend and companion Ada Russell, had died in a few hours.

"All Elinor and I can think of at the moment is our personal loss and yours," wired Frost to Mrs. Russell. "We can hardly accept it."

Two days later Robert Frost spoke to his Amherst students on the poetry of Amy Lowell and the gist of this, gathered by a reporter from him, was printed on May 16 in the *Christian Science Monitor*. It said something that he was milling in his mind about the "immortal wound." But in the vista of time, the application to Amy Lowell seems to Frost exaggerated.

THE POETRY OF AMY LOWELL

It is absurd to think that the only way to tell if a poem is lasting is to wait and see if it lasts. The right reader of a good poem can tell the moment it strikes him that he has taken an immortal wound—that he will never get over it. That is to say, permanence in poetry as in love is perceived instantly. It hasn't to await the test of time. The proof of a poem is not that we have never forgotten it, but that we knew at sight that we never could forget it. There was a barb to it and a toxin that we owned to at once. How often I have heard it in the voice and seen it in the eyes of this generation that Amy Lowell had lodged poetry with them to stay.

The most exciting movement in nature is not progress, advance, but expansion and contraction, the opening and shutting of the eye, the hand, the heart, the mind. We throw our arms wide with a gesture of religion to the universe; we close them around a person. We explore and adventure for a while and then we draw in to consolidate our gains. The breathless swing is between subject matter and form. Amy Lowell was distinguished in a period of dilation when poetry, in the effort to include a larger material, stretched itself almost to the breaking of the verse. Little ones with no more apparatus than a teacup looked on with alarm. She helped make it stirring times for a decade to those immediately concerned with art and to many not so immediately.

The water in our eyes from her poetry is not warm with any suspicion of tears; it is water flung cold, bright and many-colored from flowers gathered in her formal garden in the morning. Her Imagism lay chiefly in images to the eye. She flung flowers and everything else there. Her poetry was forever a clear resonant calling off of things seen.

In May, 1925, Frost had to go to Ann Arbor to deliver an address: *In Memoriam* Marion Leroy Burton, and from then on it was clearly decided that he would move to Ann Arbor in September, 1925, as Fellow in Letters, and settle in a "Midwest Greek Revival house."

The only child to go along was Irma, and during October she too married a Michigan undergraduate, John P. Cone, a gifted student who soon took her to live with his parents on their Kansas farm. So, for the first time in many years, Robert and Elinor Frost were alone—or thought they would be. It was not long before Frost bought Irma and John a farm in North Bennington, close to South Shaftsbury.

For one who evaded tangibles in teaching, and said that the greatest test of a college student's chances is *"when we know the sort of work for which he will neglect his studies,"* Frost was lucky in his Michigan University supporters: regents' reports, president's reports, all the public documents praised his previous work and welcomed him again. So did the Detroit newspapers and those more local like the Dearborn *Independent*. Frost also certified his own attachment through a little poem given for publication to the young editors of *The Inlander* (January, 1926).

A MINOR BIRD

I have wished a bird would fly away,
And not sing by my house all day;

Have clapped my hands at him from the door
When it seemed as if I could bear no more.

The fault must partly have been in me.
The bird was not to blame for his key.

And of course there must be something wrong
In wanting to silence any song.

If anyone wanted to see it that way—said Sue Grundy Bonner—a metaphor about the effect of the poetry of the undergraduate on the poet's ear could here be dug up. What *did* Frost think of undergraduate verse, the editors his students sometimes wondered? He did not *teach* them; he just *talked*.

He did not *criticize* a poem submitted in his class—he just neglected it or just *read* it, or merely remarked:

"This is a nice little poem," or

"It does just what it is trying to do."

Things went along all right until news came that Marjorie was sick in hospital, under operation in far-off Pittsfield. Elinor dropped her new life in the making and hurried eastward.

Alone, deserted, jealous, half sick with flu himself in the Pontiac Street house, Frost (so he has recalled for me) built himself a great fire of black walnut logs and lay before it on a couch three days and nights writing a poem that has reminded me of the music of Mozart. Deaf, blind, and lost to anything but images and rhythms that surged up from within —images typical of New England in early spring—he would stagger to his feet and put on more wood and subside again. He could only write poetry with that degree of concentration and detachment.

The poem reads as if he were looking at something that he had lost his heart to, as Emerson with the Rhodora.

SPRING POOLS

These pools that, though in forests, still reflect
The total sky almost without defect,
And like the flowers beside them, chill and shiver,
Will like the flowers beside them soon be gone,
And yet not out by any brook or river,
But up by roots to bring dark foliage on.

The trees that have it in their pent-up buds
To darken nature and be summer woods—
Let them think twice before they use their powers
To blot out and drink up and sweep away
These flowery waters and these watery flowers
From snow that melted only yesterday.

When he reads this tender playful poem, Frost is likely to say that it is straight description, don't search for double meanings. Yet there is a secret warning in his

Let them think twice before they use their powers . . .

an implication of a darksome anthropomorphic plot in which he and the trees are involved—one that the reader has sensed since his early poetry. This tree fear is deep in Robert Frost. One feels it in "The Sound of Trees" and in "Tree at My Window." It is the converse of his love of trees and yet part of it, for he loves too the scare he invokes.

To replace Burton as president, the University of Michigan had appointed Clarence Cook Little, Bostonian, Harvard graduate, and distinguished research biologist.

It looks [wrote Frost to Manthey-Zorn] as though I had run into another exciting president to talk about. He's a youngster with no interest in noble sentiments. What he wants is something earth-shaking to do. Some think he doesn't realize how troublesome truth can be.

[In another letter] . . . I like him a lot in spite of his having for motto More mice and less men. I heard him tell his wife, he had a thousand mice born in his laboratory last week. That's going some in mice for the president of a society for human birth-control.

He hoped that a president who continued his own research in the midst of administrative concerns would see eye to eye with a poet who persisted in the composition of poetry while teaching. But the poet wasn't sure it would turn out that way.

In Ann Arbor as elsewhere, now that his poetry had received so much admiring critical notice, Robert Frost was expected to play, not side-step, the role of social lion, which became an annoying interruption unless some human or intellectual values were attached to it. As to students, there were those in his classes whose faculty fathers he knew well and who assumed themselves to be his special favorites, sticking like burrs, and exciting jealousies they made too little of. He liked them, of course, and urged them, in fact, to come and see him in Pontiac Street any time they wanted.

"He was our friend and our inspiration," wrote the geologist,

279

Mary Cooley, daughter and granddaughter of distinguished Michigan professors and at present head of the Hopwood Room at the University of Michigan. She was one of the three inseparable, gifted students who had in 1925 started a magazine of their own, *The Outlander*. The other two were Sue Grundy Bonner, a girl like a spring bulb, Frost described her; and Dorothy Tyler, of East Lansing, who soon was publishing her verse in the magazines. These were the leaders in Frost's class of twenty and its intimate nucleus.

The class was held at first in the library; soon it was divided into two sections. But before long Frost proposed abandoning any regular classes and asked the students to write poems and bring them to his home. There they found delight and excitement in poetic tea hours by the fire, with Elinor presiding and watching over her spouse "like a bright-eyed bird."

As for the actual class meetings, Mary Cooley has written me:

I can't remember anything that was said. . . . I remember that Mr. Frost would start talking and play with some idea, following wherever it led him, much as he sometimes does in his informal lectures. I remember being amused that some of the students seemed to be taking down everything he said into their note books, for it didn't seem to me he meant what he was saying to be frozen into permanent preservation. I remember one evening particularly when Sue Bonner and I decided to walk him home after the class. He was living way out on the other side of town. When we were well over half way, in the middle of the bridge over the river and the railway, he decided *he* ought to see *us* home so we turned around and walked back, and enjoyed that part of the evening much more than the class. The three of us . . . were rather spoiled by knowing him personally . . . and we preferred talking to him with just ourselves. . . . I'm afraid we were rather smug and inner-circlish. We had a wonderful time, anyway.

Frost believed that even lectures on literature should be narrative, and always had been in the habit of "beginning a course very present and then slowly disappearing."

Sometimes he would talk about form—for instance the sonnet, an old-fashioned thing he always intended to avoid, yet couldn't quite, and "hoped this wouldn't be noticed." He did vary his sonnets, not only in the traditional ways but by addition and subtraction of lines—"Hyla Brook" with fifteen (and the last the great one), for example.

We love the things we love for what they are.

"A sonnet is supposed to go eight lines, then take a turn for better or worse and go six more."

And those definitions of poetry itself, numerous and varied as the leaves of the trees, and not particular to Michigan:

A poem begins more felt than thought and ends more thought than felt.

A poem begins more ethereal and ends more material.

Poetry is a renewal of language, the dawning in you of ideas in their freshness—the freshness of having caught a feeling just as it comes over you—like mischief. . . . [he'd mischievously say, with those curving lines in his cheeks and around his eyes they all loved].

Don't hold an idea too long, don't idle along with it or it may be too well done for a poem. I use ideas I've been too lazy to put in verse for lectures. You write them for the *Inlander.*

Poetry is both prose and verse. Cicero was called a Roman *poet.*

When he had withdrawn largely from class work, in years of age, R.F. began to put his aphorisms into verse:

BOEOTIAN

I love to toy with the Platonic notion
That wisdom need not be of Athens Attic,
But well may be Laconic, even Boeotian.
At least I will not have it systematic.

In a letter of September, 1927, to Mary Cooley (for R.F. kept in touch with his favorites after he left Michigan) he was saying much the same thing:

. . . I'm less and less for systems and system-building in my old age. Some violence is always done to the wisdom you build a philosophy out of. Give us pieces of wisdom like pieces of eight in a buckskin bag. I take my history in letters and diaries, my philosophy in pensées thrown together like the heads of Charles the Bold's army after it was defeated and slain in Switzerland. You may have noticed them there this summer. . . .

Why don't you write some more poetry? I wouldn't question everyone thus incautiously.

Willa Cather, one of the first American writers to recognize and value Robert Frost as a poet, used to grumble sometimes that he was too consciously explicit in talking about poetry—why not just write it? There she was speaking against a modernity that Frost had in his bones. Even a University of Michigan senior or junior in 1926 could recognize that this troubling poetic intelligence was trying to humanize in a metaphor the inner poetic experience, often an awesome or fearsome, wracking thing, by thinking about it until it assumed the aspect of calm truth or wisdom.

By the end of the second semester of 1925–1926 the nomadic and incalculable Robert Frost had resigned from the University of Michigan and decided to return to Amherst College, where he had been offered a professorship of English on the Woodruff Foundation. The salary was to be $5,000—$1,000 less than his current Michigan salary. But the position was one of dignity and the salary good for the period, especially as it was promised that he was to have considerable time to himself—for himself the poet in solitude, and for his "barding around."

Life was moving to Frost, it was both tentative and final, it was exciting, despairing, dramatic but never dull or quiescent. He let it happen to him, rather than choose it, and yet he chose it, too, with a sense of rediscovery. He says he has never been able to appraise life as he lives it.

Yet Amherst was a real choice, and R.F. brought back to

it his genius for teaching a selected group, his poetic gifts in full flower, his irrepressible impulse, stronger with every year, to do, to fight, to triumph as a man of both action and word. The unseen pilgrimage of Frost's soul on this earth and his visible progression as a poet promised to be a long one.

PART IV

THE TRIAL BY EXISTENCE

1926–1938

CHAPTER 13

HOLDING THE CURVE OF
ONE POSITION

1926–1930

In the period from 1926 to 1938 Robert Frost, passing from the round, ripe age of fifty-two to the critical age of sixty-four, proved notably his staying power as poet, professor, and human being. The times were those of crucial social and political change, bringing new national and world trends with which both Elinor and Robert acutely disagreed—and a corresponding change, with which the poet could not sympathize, in the direction, tone, and content of modern poetry. But Frost again proved intellectually and spiritually challenged by difficulties and able to live his own freedoms. In the same cycle of years, increasing illness in his family and finally tragic loss by death ended the life, and even the kind of life, he had lived for forty years. But the world of his imagination as revealed in his poetry, sustained by the roots of the past and yet responding to the contemporary, declared itself as unchanged, indestructible.

Both the college and the publishing house in which he reposed his faith had the vision to "re-renew"—to use a Frostian word—the basic relationship after the Frosts' return from the Middle West. Frost's poetry must be supported as an art with hazards and personal idiosyncrasies. He must be "come after" rather than going after life's prizes and securities. Amherst College, emerging from its doldrums, heading for a reconstruction period, inclined to great tolerance and in fact held Frost to his professorship for twelve successive years. But the situation at Holt's was in the immediate sense unfavorable. The Holt sons who had taken over were not interested in poetry. Frost's books were not selling well; he would not have a new book for some years, and the charming, aristocratic MacVeagh, the personification to R.F. of the corporation, had gone.

It was really a ticklish moment and efforts were made to entrap him elsewhere. But Mrs. Frost, who was carrying most of her husband's business matters and correspondence at this time, talked of a new subsidy; and Richard H. Thornton, a new member of Holt's editorial staff, who had first met Frost during his fellowship at Michigan in 1925, sent up to South Shaftsbury to "think things over with the Frosts," showed insight.

Thornton's report led E. N. Bristol, Chairman of the Board at Holt, to arrange with the directors a new subsidy of $250 a month for five years—subject to renewal. This gave R.F. in Thornton a new friend at court who, for a decade, well fostered his gifts. Three books resulted. *West-Running Brook* (1928), a return to lyricism, received high critical praise. *Collected Poems* (1930), which Louis Untermeyer said established Frost as one of "the three bucolic poets of all time," received the Pulitzer Prize—Frost's second, as did *A Further Range* in 1936. The latter received also the Book-of-the-Month-Club award.

As to this last, I have heard that when Justice Felix Frankfurter, who, as a Harvard law professor had become one of Frost's "liberal" friends, vivaciously implored:

"Robert, do *not* accept the Book-of-the-Month Club!" Frost replied:

"You speak too late. It is accepted!"

The intimacy between liberal and conservative in this particular exchange had its origin in a chance earlier encounter at the Dunster House Bookshop in Cambridge. Two outstanding personalities, unintroduced, and as it were incognito, there flashed together spontaneously, into a common play of thoughts so absorbing that they wearied the bookseller, who left them the key and went home to bed. Frost said each protagonist knew darn well (secretly) who the other was and this added to the fun. The important thing to him and to the future Supreme Court Justice as well was the caliber of the opposing and adventuring mind.

Mr. Thornton, who now lives retired in North Carolina, has permitted me to quote him on the effects of the Holt's subsidy, which continued right through the financial crash of 1929, the Depression, and what Frost referred to in letters as "The New Deil":

Frost's royalties, permissions etc. took care of the monthly payments every year before I left the company, except one, and that was fully compensated for by the large amount of royalties paid him the year of the Book Club award. Holt has, since I left there, increased his monthly payment, and it is to continue for life . . . Holt has always given him the full amount of moneys received for permission to reprint. [Most publishers split permission fees, fifty-fifty.]

Frost still urges the value of poverty for the young. He does not regret that he and Elinor "lived poor," not just of necessity but "on principle," through their most creative and formative years. (To be sure they were early twentieth-century years.) But after they had turned fifty-odd, with their four then adult children, even the married ones, needing aid in illness, actual stand-by parental presence, moral support, and sometimes cash, their point of view changed. In the sum of their burdens, of which the incalculable duration of creative effort was one, money was not negligible. The poet who later wrote

289

PERTINAX

Let chaos storm!
Let cloud shapes swarm!
I wait for form.

and

THE HARDSHIP OF ACCOUNTING

Never ask of money spent
Where the spender thinks it went.
Nobody was ever meant
To remember or invent
What he did with every cent.

—this man began to respect money, praise it, find it, and enjoy
the liberalities he could make of it.

The remarkable freedoms that Frost exacted and received
from Amherst College have more than a personal meaning,
for they have paved the way for other American poets in other
colleges to wring from academic administrators unusual priv-
ileges for poetry. Discretion was used toward one who, tech-
nically and actually professor of English, bore the symbolic
role of Poet in Residence. The years in Michigan had enhanced this role for Frost, though Amherst, from well back
in the twenties, had required her star professor to teach only
three months a year, and not always the same months.

He was permitted to protect his health by Southern sojourns
in winter; to add to or subtract from his college duties by
reading, lecturing, and even teaching elsewhere, not only at
summer schools of writing like Bread Loaf, Vermont, and
Boulder, Colorado, but during the academic year. As, for example, in 1931, 1933, and 1935 at the New School for Social
Research in New York, and in 1936 at Harvard University,
where he gave the Charles Eliot Norton lectures, with the
status of professor.

For this Frost had to thank, in part, the large-mindedness
of the successive presidents of Amherst under whom he func-

tioned: first his friend President Olds, who resigned in 1927; then President Arthur Stanley Pease, a Latin scholar he admired, who resigned to head the Harvard latin department in 1932. The next President, Stanley King, an Amherst graduate, a brilliant businessman, liberal, and New Dealer, carried his college through the Depression and the war. Though proud of having R.F. at Amherst, King had less understanding of the subtleties of Frost's nature and of his contribution as a poet.

If colleagues tied to routines and salary incomes sometimes murmured at Frost's liberties, the poet always had ardent defenders, intimate friends on the faculty eager and ready to rescue him for poetry. He was as subject as any other human being to the inner ill satirized by Emerson in his epigrammatic translation from the French:

BORROWING

Some of the hurts you have cured,
And the sharpest you still have survived,
But what torments of grief you endured
From evils that never arrived!

Frost's rescuer was sure to be one who like "Tree at My Window"—in the new poem that recalls "The Sound of the Trees"—had seen him under the weight of "inner weather," and knew that inner weather was the seeding ground of poetry.

But, tree, I have seen you taken and tossed,
And if you have seen me when I slept,
You have seen me when I was taken and swept
And all but lost. . . .

Specifically, R.F. counted most at this time on his three close friends: Whicher, Elliott, and Manthey-Zorn. I find a typical informal letter to Whicher from South Shaftsbury of December 10, 1927.

. . . I was going to ask you for help. I'd like the freshmen on those terms. Only don't make too much of a point of their being writers. Why couldnt some of them qualify merely as readers who would be reading anyway whether under orders or not. Another thing: no one would object I suppose if sometimes I didnt see them more than once a week. I could call both days mine (Thursday and Saturday) but make them a present of the second now and then for effect—or for relief—"touch and remit after the use of kings." . . .

Frost was rather bluff about it all. He could trust the scholars, he hoped, not to treat poetry as if it were something else than poetry: as syntax, or language, or science. They, in turn, could trust him, he hoped, to "want poetry held as strictly to account as if it were science, philosophy or anything else that is solid and sound."

With them [the scholars—he wrote Sidney Cox later] everything must be cited or quoted. Every idea must be put in the mouth of an authority. The most they presume to be themselves is authorities on authorities. There is this to be said for their way, that they gain a certain objectivity by putting everything off on someone else dead or above them. It is the same objectivity I gain by putting everything into the mouths of characters. Only mine are characters while theirs are authorities.

It was acceptable to Amherst's conservatism that, although Robert Frost was a "modern poet," he did not figure with the avant-garde who were proud to be publishing their works in the fertile crop of *Little Magazines.*

"I'd as soon make love in Lover's Lane as write for the *Little Magazines,*" Frost declared.

He was satisfied to be sought by the conservative recognized weeklies, reviews, quarterlies, and by the anthologies which he regarded as affording the best critical estimates available.

But the poetic and intellectual climate of the late twenties and the thirties was not truly favorable to Robert Frost's unique genius. No matter what Untermeyer said, this was not an age of pastoral poets. T. S. Eliot's "The Waste Land" had made a rather precious but dramatic start in 1922. By 1925 the Imagists, with whom Frost was allied in good will at least, had bowed out as "influences" and vanished with Amy Lowell. Sandburg, Lindsay, and others who had shared the so-called poetic renascence with Frost were being somewhat super-seded in the public mind by Edna St. Vincent Millay, the gifted girl who in Frost's estimation had become too famous too quickly for her own good. Elinor Wylie and Marianne Moore, with her unique gifts, John Crowe Ransom, and many others were gaining influence. Even Frost's New Eng-land peer and rival, Edwin Arlington Robinson, publishing in 1927 his most successful "selling" book, *Tristram,* seemed to be deserting the region that he and Frost shared:

"What," said Frost—who esteemed "Mr. Flood's Party," Robinson's finest poem, "do I have to read *The Idylls of the King* all over again?"

Robinson's answer was:

"You have to."

Robinson might well have countered:

"Do I still have to read poetry deriving from Derry?"

And Frost might have answered:

"You do!"

For the Derry brook called "West-Running" named the new book, and a few of the poems in it are early in date or in subject matter. The volume was again dedicated to E.M.F. John Holmes, professor of poetry at Tufts University, a de-voted younger friend of R.F.'s, has told me what the poet told him—that a poem complete and final was Frost's intimate gift to Elinor. All the poetry, the long secret work was for her, for a woman whose mind, Frost had asserted ever since the tempestuous courtship, was "better than his own." Although his wife was not critical in the carping sense, she could hurt him by what she would not let pass in a poem. The hurt was excruciating, so he strove for perfection, held back until he could offer finality.

The same concern about the last and best word (in a poem) or the shape of a group of poems is shown in some letters to Mark Van Doren, who at this time was literary editor of the *Nation*. Frost had sent him three poems destined for *West-Running Brook*: "Blood," "The Armful," and "The Bear."

Dear Van Doren [he wrote from Amherst on January 18, 1928]:

If I seem slow with these things, its not from reluctance to keep my promise of that pleasant hour I had with you and your wife. It takes a long time for me to make up my mind to part with a poem, longer to part with more than one: Even now I'm not quite ready to let you have these three if for no better reason than that they dont make up into a set to print together. Why dont you choose one and send the rest back? "Blood" is in one vein and the others can't very well be in any vein and the figure kept.

We left the daughter, Margery, for the specialists to solve at Johns Hopkins. They've got nowhere in particular with her yet. ["Margery" seems to have been his private old English spelling for the daughter whose health was beginning to fail.]

It seems as if we folks ought to see more of each other. We must have you up to visit us when we get our new farm. I'd like your son to meet our grandson.

. . . The only excitement we've had is our own chimney on fire by a poem I was throwing away to spare you the reading of it. The fire company turned out and for the moment I felt reconciled with the place. Let them have it as they please—will. Anyway, Let the long contention cease, Geese are swans and swans are geese. Most teaching is mere correcting mistakes just as most loving is mere folly. Lud sing cuccu.

I have no typewriter and I often shrink completely from going to a public stenographer with poetry. Forgive the handwriting.

Sincerely yours

Robert Frost

The next letter pursued:

I must say you know how to make a fellow feel pleased with his own poems. Thanks for the good words.

You'll notice that I hadn't quite parted with poems when I sent them. There were a couple of lines written wrong in "Blood."

I am still writing them. I hope to have the definitive version before I mail this. Will you see to the alterations in the proof as
anxiously as if they were your own?

Sixty dollars is splendid. All I demand money at all for is to
compel respect for poetry in general.

We've had encouragement from Johns Hopkins. I'm hard to
elate.

Amherst January 23 1928

But Frost's next letter in May from South Shaftsbury, re-
lating to an anthology of world poetry, was cross-grained.

I confess a choice so perfunctory and slighting hurts my feelings.
[Van Doren had suggested "Mending Wall" and "The Runaway."]
It simply hurts them: I dont think it hardens them. If such is the
best you naturally do with or for me, what do you say if I stay out
of this anthology and turn my thoughts elsewhere?

Van Doren replied that in an anthology with translations
from fifteen languages he could use only a small, selective
list of poems in English. And he liked these poems of Frost's.

I'm too touchy [replied Frost on May 29]—particularly with
friends. Treat me well and you'll be expected to treat *me* better.
That's all the pay you'll get for treating *me* well. Such I am,
though I dont usually give myself away or get found out because
I live too far off in the country to speak on impulse and I'm too
lazy to write.

I could at least have asked you about the idea of your anthology
before getting unhappy.

But if this passage at pens hasnt lost me your respect and you
still want to further my poetry, why not leave "Mending Wall"
out of an anthology for once in a way and use in its place (of
those you name) "The Oven Bird," "An Old Man's Winter Night"
and "The Tuft of Flowers"? [In the anthology Van Doren used
the group Frost suggested.]

In quoting parts of these letters in his *Autobiography*
(1957) Mark Van Doren says:

I had found him [Frost] as nobody ever failed to do, a mixture of simple and complex, a man who simultaneously gave and withdrew himself; one, in brief, who could hide behind the very charm of his openness, his generosity in speech and act. So I could not be altogether surprised by a brief difference between us. . . . But . . . this correspondence occurred. In subsequent years nothing from him has revealed him any better, or in my mind to better advantage. . . . [Comparing Frost with E. A. Robinson, Van Doren says that Robinson never in conversation or letters dropped his guard.] Frost even more reluctant to "get found out," nevertheless could allow the thing to happen. Or it is truer to say in his case it sometimes simply happened. And then he was gone again. . . .

Frost, of course knows, and refers frankly to his "runaway" qualities. I have heard him call himself a "quitter," but I think his mind equates this with his loyalty, equally a character trait.

"I wanted Mark Van Doren's poetry alongside of mine, in my publishing house," he has told me more than once, and Van Doren was published by Holt for a time.

In January, 1928, the greatest living English literary figure died in his eighty-fifth year—Thomas Hardy. Robert and Elinor had long been prodding themselves to return to Europe, to revisit the England that had been a shaper of his poetic destiny. A war and thirteen years had passed. As early as 1925 Frost had published in the *Herald Tribune:*

THE PEACEFUL SHEPHERD

If heaven were to do again,
And on the pasture bars,
I leaned to line the figures in
Between the dotted stars,

I should be tempted to forget,
I fear, the Crown of Rule,
The Scales of Trade, the Cross of Faith,
As hardly worth renewal.

For these have governed in our lives,
And see how men have warred.
The Cross, the Crown, the Scales may all
As well have been the Sword.

By February, 1928, when "Blood"—in the *Complete Poems* called "The Flood"—appeared in the *Nation,* the poet's ironic disillusion was sharper:

And now it is once more the tidal wave
That when it has swept by leaves summits stained.
Oh, blood will out. It cannot be contained.

The new book was not to appear until November; so the poet, his wife, and Marjorie—whose health had improved— had plenty of time for a summer trip in 1928. Gibson had, in a sense, renewed their nostalgia for England by his poem of the midtwenties, "The Golden Room." I quote the first verse:

Do you remember the still summer evening
When, in the cosy cream-washed living-room
Of The Old Nailshop, we all talked and laughed—
Our neighbours from The Gallows, Catherine
And Lascelles Abercrombie; Rupert Brooke;
Eleanor and Robert Frost, living a while
At Little Iddens, who'd brought over with them
Helen and Edward Thomas? In the lamplight
We talked and laughed; but, for the most part listened
While Robert Frost kept on and on and on,
In his slow New England fashion, for our delight,
Holding us with shrewd turns and racy quips,
And the rare twinkle of his grave blue eyes?

The reality the three Frosts found in 1928 was that the handful of war-scarred survivors of that romantic group of "Georgians," with whom they had been so closely related, were scattered and had lost their special consanguinity. Gibson was still writing poetry, so was Davies, who had married, and diverted Frost by inquiring:

"You still interested in poetry, Frost? I'll give you a book with my autograph."

Abercrombie had (Frost said) largely turned away from poetry writing after 1919, to writing on poetic theory. He had become a professor in English—later Lecturer and Fellow of Merton in Oxford—in contrast to his American friend, who kept poetry and teaching in balance. Frost visited the Poet-Laureate Bridges, with his Michigan memories, and the solicitor-botanist Haines—still helping on the legal side the poets they had both frequented. But the American had, above all, to see Edward Thomas' widow, and walk, without E.T., in the shady lanes of Gloucestershire and Herefordshire. His poem, "A Soldier," quoted in Part II, about the heroic warrior whose spirit is shot on

> Further than target ever showed or shone.

owes, perhaps, much to the tragic meditations of that summer. It was published first, a few months later, in *West-Running Brook*.

Clearly in a downcast mood the Frosts went on to Paris. Marjorie wanted to improve her French. The parents did not know the country or speak the language and almost at once sought in the outskirts "tranquillity our life-long pursuit and occasional capture." "We are not sure we like anything yet," R.F. wrote to Otto Manthey-Zorn, and referred to "our pent-up powers of speech." But History was stalking Robert Frost and he wrote his Amherst friend about how he had met President Wilson who had never in the past been one of his heroes:

. . . they [the French] have arranged for his ghost to walk in their city for a long time to come. Here, overlooking the whole city, is a small treesy park called Place du President Wilson and there's a fine avenue named after him that runs right through the statue of George Washington. He shares the permanence with Washington and Franklin. (It must make Teddy jealous in Heaven.) It is a sad story—one of the saddest in history. And we saw it happen every step of the way. . . . I weaken now at the thought of him fallen with a crash almost Napoleonic. He had calibre, he saw as vastly as anyone that ever lived. He was a great something, if it was only a great mistake. And he wasn't merely his own mistake. He was the whole world's mistake—everybody's at one time there but Henry Cabot Lodge's—as much the whole world's as was Napoleon or Alexander. Some might think his failure was in missing a mark that someone to come after him will hit, but I suspect that it was worse than that: he missed a mark that wasn't there in nature or human nature.

As I read the foreboding "worse than that," I seemed to see in the gray Paris street the vigorous interrogating Yankee meditating incisively on the blind nature of the human race and its leaders.

Even as he stared at Woodrow Wilson's French embodiment, Frost had a poem ready for *West-Running Brook*, a pre–World War I poem that gave man, however trapped by nature, freedom through experience to shed the worn-out shells of his own making. It had been written with implicit faith in human intelligence:

SAND DUNES

Sea waves are green and wet,
But up from where they die,
Rise others vaster yet,
And those are brown and dry.

They are the sea made land
To come at the fisher town,
And bury in solid sand
The men she could not drown.

She may know cove and cape,
But she does not know mankind
If by any change of shape,
She hopes to cut off mind.

Men left her a ship to sink:
They can leave her a hut as well;
And be but more free to think
For the one more cast-off shell.

But read the poem on the limitations of man as knower—in the self-same three-stress verse and with similar sea images—that he published in *A Further Range*, his next small volume of 1936:

NEITHER OUT FAR NOR IN DEEP

The people along the sand
All turn and look one way.
They turn their back on the land.
They look at the sea all day.

As long as it takes to pass
A ship keeps raising its hull;
The wetter ground like glass
Reflects a standing gull.

The land may vary more;
But wherever the truth may be—
The water comes ashore,
And the people look at the sea.

They cannot look out far.
They cannot look in deep.
But when was that ever a bar
To any watch they keep?

In this later poem, which Frost calls "a California poem, derived from mixed memories," we get the sense of the restrictions, rather than the power of growth, of man's knowledge. Man is seen as a watcher, mesmerized into passivity, as before the television screen, and the reader, hypnotized by the purity and imagery of the verse, is drawn into the magicked company and led into meditation that will yield no answers. But he hardly knows it, his "watch" goes on. This is the sinister side of the poem, if you see it speculatively.

Humanly, R.F. was now approaching fifty-five, shorn of some optimism but deeply protected from human drought by human love and the depth of instinct. This is suggested by a less well-known poem (another sea image) from *West-Running Brook*.

DEVOTION

The heart can think of no devotion
Greater than being shore to the ocean—
Holding the curve of one position,
Counting an endless repetition.

Frost had—and gave—the devotion that holds the curve that many an artist loses because he will be only ocean. He kept the watch on earth. He held the view in life, the Puritan's view, that marriage is a long-time and lasting bond, and so told his young divorcing friends. Love, to Frost, was "something to be perpetually believed into existence." The title poem of *West-Running Brook* (the best part of which, R.F. has told me, was written in the upstairs Franconia room, facing Mount Lafayette) reveals this aspect of love. It is another of Frost's intimately moving dialogues between spouses which, though the dramatis personae differ, have a sort of common identity. Strikingly enough, rather confirming its autobiographical quality, it is the last such dialogue Frost published: the most intellectual and, in terms of poetic metaphor, the most ambitious since it tries through the one extended figure of the brook that runs counter to itself, to state matter in terms of spirit and spirit in terms of matter, and make a unity of the whole.

The "Fred" of the dialogue with his flashing needle mind, pushed by a brook to speculation about where life came from and where it is going has long since estimated the boundaries of "lady-land." His wife, though she may have suffered all the woes of Amy in "Home Burial," is now mistress of a tested human relationship and lives to give it serenity and playfulness:

She says to "Fred" that the brook can trust itself to go by contraries

"The way I can with you—and you with me . . .

"As you and I are married to each other,
We'll both be married to the brook. We'll build
Our bridge across it, and the bridge shall be
Our arm thrown over it asleep beside it.
Look, look, it's waving to us with a wave
To let us know it hears me." . . .

"Fred" gently flouts this feminine possessiveness of a force of nature and plunges quickly into his own fanciful, complex, strangely searching thought:

"Speaking of contraries, see how the brook
In that white wave runs counter to itself.
It is from that in water we were from
Long, long before we were from any creature. . . .
It is this backward motion toward the source,
Against the stream, that most we see ourselves in,
The tribute of the current to the source.
It is from this in nature we are from.
It is most us."

                    "Today will be the day
You said so."

                    "No, today will be the day
You said the brook was called West-running Brook."

"Today will be the day of what we both said."

The philosophic conclusion, the sinister running away of life into the abyss or the infinite is addressed to the ear of a woman who clearly knows earth's the place for love. That makes the dialogue all gay, flashing, redemptive as a fountain in the sun.

In the rest of the small volume, section headings—as FIAT LUX, FIAT NOX, MY NATIVE SIMILE—point to teasing subtleties of meaning and subject matter, to points of reference, recall, or even prophecy which should draw those who study Frost back to the small book that preceded the *Collected Poems* of 1930. Under OVER BACK, a little poem "The Times Table" opens:

> More than half way up the pass
> Was a spring with a broken drinking glass,

Is this not a humble forerunner of the famous "Directive" of twenty years later where a child's cup hidden in a spring becomes a sort of Grail, referring back to the feast of man's normal human fate? To Frost, the holiest, most heartbreaking memory and vision of the past is that of man's labor in high wild places, when it has been devoured by the return of nature to her own. He makes the raspberry-grown—or as in "Directive" *belilaced*—cellar hole of the humble Yankee farmer, mentioned first in the early poem "Ghost House," as sacred as the ruins of a temple or a Christian shrine.

"Acquainted with the Night"—naturally under the heading FIAT NOX—printed first in the *Virginia Quarterly Review,* October, 1928, and even then destined for immortality, seemed the quintessence of a lifetime of night walks.

R.F. has mentioned a further derivation:

"This poem," he told me in Ripton, "came to me after a visit from A.E. [George Edward Russell] the Irish mystic, who subtly murmured:

"'The Time is not right.'"

Randall Jarrell, in a fine essay on Robert Frost, has called it "a poem in Dante's own form and with some of Dante's own qualities."

ACQUAINTED WITH THE NIGHT

> I have been one acquainted with the night.
> I have walked out in rain—and back in rain.
> I have outwalked the furthest city light.

I have looked down the saddest city lane.
I have passed by the watchman on his beat
And dropped my eyes, unwilling to explain.

I have stood still and stopped the sound of feet
When far away an interrupted cry
Came over houses from another street,

But not to call me back or say good-by;
And further still at an unearthly height,
One luminary clock against the sky

Proclaimed the time was neither wrong nor right.
I have been one acquainted with the night.

In the *Collected Poems* of 1930 one more poem very much associated with Frost's past was added to *West-Running Brook*, "The Lovely Shall Be Choosers," first printed in 1929 as a broadside by Random House, in a series of pamphlets by contemporary poets: a touching, enigmatic, yet revealing poem, with a title in reverse meaning that moves us by its very dissembling.

It's my only poem in free verse—with a few iambics thrown in. The best of it—it wasn't all written at the same time—had its source in Franconia on that high chair perched on the platform I built to keep floor draughts off my feet in the middle of a cold winter.

It's a poem—well [he evaded], it has a lot to do with women. [He hesitated.] It's about my mother.

I have never heard R.F. read his poem about a mother. But once, after some fine piano playing by a composer at his farm, I heard him ask the younger man to put it to music.

The wonder of little loving children before a half-confession from their mother at the fireside about her early glamour and her drudging fate; the anger of a young man waking in maturity and trust to his mother's sacrifice: these are the poignant stuff of the poem and its inner music.

It opens with Voices that say "she" shall be hurled down seven levels of the world. One verse describes how she looked in youth:

> Invisible hands crowded on her shoulder
> In readiness to weigh upon her.
> But she stood straight still,
> In broad round ear-rings, gold and jet with pearls
> And broad round suchlike brooch,
> Her cheeks high colored,
> Proud and the pride of friends.

This hurling down shall be done by "joys," the tender ironic poem says, and later comes another humane revelation:

> "Give her a child at either knee for fourth joy
> To tell once and once only, for them never to forget,
> How once she walked in brightness,
> And make them see it in the winter firelight. . . ."

Still another, the climax of the poem:

> "Then send some *one* with eyes to see
> And wonder at her where she is,
> And words to wonder in her hearing how she came there,
> But without time to linger for her story.
> Be her last joy her heart's going out to this one
> So that she almost speaks.
> You know them—seven in all."

"Trust us," the Voices said.

So the heroine of the poem, who had almost spoken to *one*, has been revealed by one who has, in turn, almost spoken— keeping love as always just behind the page.

Frost, in his age, speaks of his mother's life in Lawrence sorrowfully:

"She sank right down, out of sight. And I never even realized that I should have earned more money for her. It was never more than fifty dollars a year. . . ."

Dear Melcher [Frost wrote on February 9, 1929, to the editor of *Publishers' Weekly* who was writing a bibliographical article about him for *The Colophon*]:

. . . My god I hate to have to listen to Cal and Henry laying it down to us spiritual and aesthetic. Some words ought to be copyrighted so that successful dufs shouldn't profane them. . . .

Marj has taken the plunge into the nursing. She may not be able to stand it. We all think it will do her good if she is.

I have a small edition of one copy of an early book of mine [*Twilight*] that nobody but Elinor and I and the printer ever saw. You'll have to say if it counts in my bibliography.

Ever yours,

Robert Frost

Then, on July 5, Elinor Frost wrote inviting Fred Melcher for a South Shaftsbury visit:

. . . We are still in the Shingled Cottage where you came to see us last, and shall not move to the farm until we return from Sugar Hill the last of Sept.

We go over to the farmhouse [The Gully], where repairs are going on, nearly every day, and putter around a little. Sometimes we feel that we were too hasty in buying, but I think we shall enjoy it when we are once settled and get over the homesickness that every move means to us.

Marjorie is just entering her sixth month at the hospital, [Johns Hopkins] and enjoying the work just immensely. She gets so tired that it's a wonder she can hold on, but she is doing good work. Her mark in elementary nursing at the end of the four months' probation period was 97 $\frac{5}{10}$, the highest mark in the class of 35.

Lesley's baby girl is a perfect darling. She is going to bring it here for a week or ten days during July. . . .

Sincerely,

Elinor Frost

[Lesley had married in 1928 a Pittsfield man, Dwight Francis.]

The *Collected Poems* of 1930, long awaited, for which Frost had taken his own slow time, contained five small books and commemorated a whole period. It stands today as a landmark, a sort of division between the poet's earlier and later work. Opening it with "The Pasture," set as a foreword, he stood by his early judgments. Six new poems were added, and only three—all from *A Boy's Will*—were omitted. "My Butterfly," was, however, included.

Only the book titles—in chronological sequence and without secondary headings—are given in the Contents. These book titles date the poems in a general way. But Frost occasionally added to a poem an "as of" an earlier year—a reference either to the date of the experience from which the poem took wing, or to the date of the writing.

Among bibliophiles and collectors the book was admired for the classic beauty of its typography and binding. Frost's own passion for fine printing had found a rare collaborator in Joseph Blumenthal of The Spiral Press, whose style was described by Ray Nash, R.F.'s friend and Dartmouth's specialist in typography, as "crisp, severe, venturesome." Both the limited edition of 1930 and the Holt trade edition employed the same plates.

Robert Frost was fast becoming what he now proclaims himself, "the best-printed American writer." Since there had been, from 1919 on, special signed, limited editions of his books of poetry, his work was produced, at one time or another, by the best book designers in the East—Bruce Rogers, D. B. Updike, W. A. Dwiggins, Harbor Press, and Spiral Press. This was done on the initiative of publishers who found the sales advantageous, but with the warm support and stimulus of the poet, who loved fine art, and nurtured the human endeavor.

"Particularly," Blumenthal said, "endeavors that go beyond the routine of things into the field of special performance." J.B. commented that he had printed many famous poets but only one who made a friend of the printer. On that hangs a little story that is worth telling because the "crisp, severe, venturesome" owner and printer of this press, who had always loved Frost's poetry, became, through their joint effort on the book, one of Frost's intimate circle.

307

The first Christmas card sent out with a Frost poem was the handmade, homemade one of 1915, with "Christmas Trees" in the poet's handwriting. In 1929 Blumenthal, on his own initiative, printed the same poem as a Christmas card for himself and his wife and certain members of the Holt firm. Frost had nothing to do with it. Poet and printer had not met in the flesh when they began their collaboration, by correspondence, on the *Collected Poems*. Blumenthal had chosen a new Dutch type face, Lutetia, which must be hand-set and proof-corrected in small lots. Frost had agreed, but proved impatient of his part of the detail. Both men, however, seemed to be playing "for mortal stakes," and when the deed was done the Yankee invited the young urban printer to Vermont.

Meeting him at the train, R.F. plunged J.B. into the novelty and surprise of his favorite country sport, sheep-dog trials, then took him home to Elinor and her supper; when she retired, inducted the dedicated Jew, with his liberal social ideas, into one of those long, intimate, all-hours Frostian talks, that, regardless of or because of divergent thinking, bring a friendship on several levels.

I'm what is called a conservative, very, not subversive at all [Frost said in 1958 in Cambridge],—you can tell by the way I talk. But the point is, that the worst radical in the world, if he's turned radical to get more meaning out of his life, that's all right with me. I'm with anybody that's seeking a life that has meaning.

Blumenthal has told me that he returned to New York exalted by the sense of having found a unique relationship; something that, even if it stopped right there, would nourish him for a lifetime. Later, as the connection went quietly on, he humbly realized that Frost gave similar deeply human friendship to many men with whom he had realistic association in life.

Shortly after the publication of the *Collected Poems*, Frost was on November 13, 1930, nominated a member of the American Academy of Arts and Letters. He had been a member of the lower body, the National Institute of Arts and Letters, since 1916.

Recalling in 1957 the earlier occasion R.F. said to me:

It was over the dead body of Robert Underwood Johnson, and with the backing of Wilbur Cross, Irving Babbitt and Paul Elmer More that I got in. . . . Johnson's resistance had its source in my early refusals by magazines. My backers could only bring me in as a Humanist—which means a Platonist. I'm actually so unhumanistic, so in tune with the nature piety of the scientist of today, that I'm more of an Aristotelian. I think there's probably nothing "up there" but a stockpile of nature observations that came from earth. I am often dismissed as just a nature poet. Well, my poems do have acute observations of nature, and if nature makes me a nature poet, it's all right with me.

Frost has rarely found time to occupy his seat at the Academy. But he did attend his own inauguration in 1930 and recalls also a meeting where the Old Guard were opposing the election of Steve Benét, and waspish little Judge Robert Grant "bearded" the bearded Nicholas Murray Butler in a fine, hot flare-up that Frost's bellicose humor and his friendship for Benét thoroughly enjoyed.

Frost, with no more tolerance than his lumberjack Paul for invasions of his private life, had had no biography written about him until Gorham B. Munson's *Robert Frost: A Study in Sensibility and Common Sense* appeared in 1927. Sidney Cox, whose letters from Frost have been quoted at some length in this book, and who was called to Dartmouth's English department in 1926, published in 1929 a small book of his insights: *Robert Frost: Original "Ordinary Man."* In 1930, Frederic Melcher's authoritative bibliographical article was published in the *Colophon*. These seem like premonitions and anticipations of the critical opinion formulated after the 1930 collection—which began to ask if the so-called New England poet was not as sure as Emerson or Longfellow of a permanent place in American literature.

Mr. Frost's place is and always has been singularly central [wrote Mark Van Doren in an essay, "The Permanence of Robert Frost," in the *American Scholar*]. He has had nothing to do with the extremes where most of our shouting has been heard. His range has been great enough to carry him close to all the corners, yet he has never quite crossed a line. He has always, in a kind of silence and with a most remarkable integrity, kept to his center. So has the criticism of him kept there, and so has his reputation. The result is a solidity of position almost unique in poetry today. . . . To say this of any poet is of course to praise him highly. But it is also to predict that he has a good chance of being read beyond his time. . . .

But there were other and younger American voices raised in the thirties, no-saying voices, which found the New Englander local, commonplace, too far from Baudelaire and from T. S. Eliot. The sad, frustrated, hypercritical, post-Great War Europeanized generation of young American poets did not then care for Frost, and though he took this with his typical phlegm and skeptical humor—for he had (he said) in youth learned to meet adversity half way—his contribution to magazines diminished to zero between 1928 and 1934. He was biding his time, ripening his fruits, writing and sending out poems in letters to friends: poems destined for *A Further Range.*

Frost's valued intellectual friend and associate of the *Seven Arts,* Van Wyck Brooks, who had seen himself and his generation as pathfinders in an America that was "coming of age" has movingly described, in *Days of the Phoenix,* how his own spirit failed him in the thirties after the collapse of these buoyant dreams of the twenties.

In contrast, Robert Frost had never joined a coterie of the elect. Primarily and finally he was an individual, a solitary, seeking his own salvation as poet: sure of poetry but never sure that reputation might not fail him in some changed critical standpoint. His surface was imperturbable but I can imagine his privately writing in a notebook something resembling G. M. Hopkins' epigram:

310

> Our swans are now of such remorseless quill,
> Themselves live singing and their hearers kill.

It irked him especially to have poetry in his world all of a sudden treated as a *corpus mortuum,* on which autopsies—critical exegeses—were performed. And he loathed the increasingly popular Freudian analysis of the poet's unconscious psyche:

"I do not want to read the biography of diseased authors."

He tossed aside with distaste the "new" subjective novelists, developing out of the "new" sociology and psychology:

. . . huge, shapeless novels, huge gobs of raw sincerity, bellowing with pain . . . [he wrote in 1936].

He warned his students and professional friends—his letters to Sidney Cox in the early thirties are full of this—not to dig up "complexes" as causes in poetry.

I grow surer I don't want to search the poet's mind too seriously [he wrote in 1932 to his friend]. I might enjoy threatening to for the fun of it just as I might frisk his person. I have written to keep the overcurious out of the secret places of my mind both in my verse and in my letters to such as you. A subject has to be held clear outside of me with struts and as it were set up for an object. A subject must be an object. . . . The idea is the thing with me. It would seem soft for instance to look in my life for the sentiments in "The Death of the Hired Man." There's nothing to it believe me. I should fool you if you took me so. . . . The objective idea is all I ever cared about. Most of my ideas occur in verse. But I have always had some turning up in talk that I feared I might never use because I was too lazy to write prose. I think they have been mostly educational ideas connected with my teaching, actually lessons. But I never reckoned with the personalities I keep to a minimum of such stuff in any poets life and works. Art and wisdom with the body heat out of it. You speak of Shirley [James Shirley]. He is two or three great poems—one

311

very great. He projected, he got, them out of his system and I will not carry them back into his system either at the place they came out of or at some other place. I state this in the extreme. But relatively I mean what I say. To be too subjective with what an artist has managed to make objective is to come on him presumptuously and render ungraceful what he in pain of his life had faith he had made graceful.

CHAPTER 14

FATE HAS NO CHOICE
BUT TO FULFILL
1930-1934

One of the good things in Sidney Cox's book of 1929 is a comment that Robert Frost "never could be, even by some future-perfected ultimate Behaviorist, quite reduced to *terms*."

I wish [Cox wrote] I could make that visible—as it is almost visible when you see him for a while—in a portrait of his lax but strong and masculine figure, his blunt but sensitive and interpretive, hairy-backed fingers, his massive oval head, his serene and passionate and changeful face, his tender, unsubdued blue eyes, with deep recesses and wild brows, his broad, slightly impudent nose, his thick sensuous, often mocking, oftener questioning lips, his tousled brown and gray hair deliberately rumpled, and his come-one-come-all chin, saved from being forbidding by the quizzical cock of head and eye, now and then.

This quizzical mood sometimes conveys the idea that R.F. is secretly fingering the hilt of a sword—as when he senses or imagines something adverse in the atmosphere. It is, however, but a conjecture that, in this mood, Robert Frost went forth to meet T. S. Eliot for the first time at a certain small literary dinner given in Eliot's honor at the St. Botolph Club in Boston on November 16, 1932.

The host, Mr. Robert G. Dodge, president of the Club, had

313

of course placed T. S. Eliot on his right, and down the two sides of the oblong table sat some twenty guests, among them half a dozen or more poets from Boston or Cambridge—Robert Hillyer, David McCord, Theodore Morrison, John Brooks Wheelwright, and others. Frost sat next to Professor John Livingston Lowes. Ferris Greenslet of Houghton Mifflin —my own first publisher and longtime friend, had arranged the whole affair.

Three of those present—Frost himself, Greenslet, and Mc-Cord—have given me accounts of the evening, and I have also read a "hearsay" account by the late Gordon Chalmers, then president of Kenyon College and one of Frost's intimates. From these the following possibly mythical composite is derived.

Mr. Dodge, the host, started things off by reading an early poem or two, "The Boston Evening Transcript" and "The Hippopotamus," by his guest of honor, the grave, distinguished and then most fashionable Mr. Eliot. Eliot seemed rather uncomfortable at the choice, and it was then proposed that both Eliot and Frost read some recent poem of their own. Eliot gallantly replied:

"I will if Frost will."

Frost said he was sorry but he had (as everyone knew) recently published his *Collected Poems*, and was "ready to loaf." But yielding to the general disappointment, he revised:

"Let Eliot read one and I'll write one."

"When," said Chalmers, "Mr. Frost writes something he is intent upon, his upper lip grows longer and longer, and the page seems to amuse him as if it were a small animal."

I suppose [said Frost with some contrition, when I asked for his memories], that I began the evening a bit antipathetic—with a touch of the old jealousy and suspicion that Tom Eliot had replaced me in the not too good graces of Ezra Pound. The jealousy that I felt after Eliot's poetry began to appear, and after Pound's efforts for him began to bear fruit. But I borrowed place cards and wrote out my poem, then said it—it was "A Record Stride."

314

It's a good guess that Eliot justly appraised this poem, which was to appear, several years later, in *A Further Range,* as no spur-of-the-moment effusion. In any case, a critical divergence between Eliot and Frost at once broke out on the subject of Robert Burns. Ferris Greenslet recalls this passage between them as the crux of an evening that he delights to remember as a witty and friendly-courteous meeting of rival minds.

However that may be, Eliot announced that Burns could not be considered a poet at all—in fact no poetry had been written north of the River Tweed except that of the fifteenth-sixteenth century William Dunbar, author of the gloomy lament that ends every stanza with the Latin refrain:

Timor Mortis conturbat me.

Frost, stifling in his Scotch blood, said:
"Eliot sounds like a Border name."
"We were Somerset Eliots."
"Might we consider Burns a *song writer?*" Frost pursued with irony.
"One might grant that modest claim."
"Then," said Frost, "it got into the papers that I'd risen from a sickbed to defend Burns. The opposite was true. After defending Burns I came down with flu—as I always had after a trip, from the Franconia days onward."
Lesley Frost Ballantine has spoken to me of the direful distress that on her father's return from a reading trip possessed the whole family in the earlier Franconia days. These readings helped their bread and butter. But after putting her spouse to bed Elinor would mourn, dirgelike, to her children:
"Your father *must* give this up. His health is failing. His life is being ruined. His poetry is suffering. It *can't* go on!"
The retirement to bed in the dignified, almost luxurious Victorian mansion on Sunset Avenue, Amherst, after the ironic triumph of the St. Botolph dinner, was almost a pleasure by contrast. For Frost proceeded to compose a poem—"just in my head. I had no pencil or paper."

It is getting dark and time he drew to a house,
But the blizzard blinds him to any house ahead.
The storm gets down his neck in an icy souse
That sucks his breath like a wicked cat in bed. . . .

Since he means to come to a door he will come to a door,
Although so compromised of aim and rate
He may fumble wide of the knob a yard or more,
And to those concerned he may seem a little late.

"That one rhyme 'house-souse'—it made the whole thing worth while!"

The poem realistically describes the struggle of a man in a snow storm to find his home door. Symbolically it may imply the stubborn intent of a poet, in adverse weather, to come into his own.

In short, destiny, as Emerson called it in a similar passage from the Journal of 1848:

Everything will come home and a man also. Where is his home. There thither, where he is incessantly called. He will surely come home, and, if long delayed, the more fiercely.

Speaking again of that St. Botolph Club meeting with T. S. Eliot of nearly thirty years ago, after his very pleasant and friendly re-connection with the distinguished poet in England in 1957, when called there himself to receive honorary degrees from Oxford and Cambridge, Robert Frost commented:

Eliot came everywhere I was, and showed me the most generous attention—at his home, at the English-Speaking Union, where he made an address for me—everywhere.

He had decided that there could be more than one kind of poet and so had I.

Eliot is a major poet . . . and does not want to be taken as deserting America with his English citizenship. He thinks about New England, as you can see from *The Four Quartets*. He was very willing that I'd understand that he hadn't made any repudiation of his native land. He doesn't detest America, as Pound does.

There the Yankee, who had chosen an extremely opposite fate from Eliot's in life and in poetry, paused and reflected before he chose these words, spoken with emotion:

We've seen more of each other recently. We've drawn closer together in the assumption that some sort of serious belief—or unbelief—is what lifts a poet out of the ruck.

The poet [R.F. said] must have something large it would break his heart not to have come true.

The Frosts, after years of subrentals, rejoiced to have at last a home of their own in Amherst. The house had been built by Stanford White, a genius among New York architects at the turn of the century, for the president of the agricultural college that preceded the present University of Massachusetts. High-ceiled rooms, tree shadows from expert plantings, marked the mansion. Strictly Victorian furnishings even to a zinc bathtub set in wood, and carpets of the 1870s were the Frosts' way of returning to the age of security, and having a lot of fun with it. After all, they had turned their eyes from aesthetic matters for poetry's sake all their lives.

But now the Depression was there, the New Deal coming on. Lesley was getting a divorce from Dwight Francis, facing life alone, with her two tiny girls, Elinor and Lee, to bring up and educate. After a reckless trip to the Baltic on a sailing ship as a sailor before the mast, she settled down to motherhood in Cambridge for two years. But by 1934 she was running Maddox House, a cultural center at Rockford College where Gordon Chalmers, her father's friend, was then president. After that she went to Mexico City to teach for a year in the University of Mexico, returning only in 1937 when her mother's health seemed shaken.

Meanwhile, Marjorie, the Frosts' youngest, had been established by her parents in Boulder, Colorado, to recover from

317

the tuberculosis that brought a sad end to her nursing studies. Irma, their second daughter, though Frost had helped her brilliant husband to an architectural career of promise and performance, was having troubles that worried them. Lillian, Carol's wife, whom they loved as a daughter had, like Marjorie, acquired tuberculosis and been sent by the Frosts, with Carol and little Prescott, to be treated in Monrovia, California.

The elder Frosts, bearing within them the burden of these events, in the summer of 1932 went out to Boulder, then to Monrovia, to see how things were going. As all was truly encouraging on the health side, on this, Robert's first visit to California since he had left it as a boy of eleven in 1885, he renewed some of his old Californian connections, and made some new ones—as with Louis Mertins, who later became a leading collector of Frost's work and the author of a critical bibliography. The Yankee poet, with relish, attended the Olympic Games of 1932—athletic feats are the next thing to poetry to him, he often says. And while once again on the Pacific ocean he wrote—very possibly, says Frost—a poem, one of his few "Californian" poems, which appeared in the *Yale Review* for March, 1934, and was sent out as Frost's 1935 Christmas card. This, now regarded as one of his greater poems, was "Neither Out Far Nor In Deep."

Frost, who continued to receive Litt. D's in profusion and had been made an Associate Fellow at Pierson College, Yale, in 1933, kept reminding himself that shocks are needed to keep human beings sane. As his childhood had endowed him with a keen interest in politics—an interest pugnacious to cantankerous—he was in his own poetic way drawn into political-philosophical thinking as the thirties came on. His letters as well as his poems betray his impatience with the beginning of the "welfare state," as introduced and incorporated into American law and life by Franklin D. Roosevelt. One of his witty sallies, perhaps of the 1940s, is that Mrs. Eleanor Roosevelt was "trying to homogenize American society, so that the cream would never rise again to the top."

He could still defend poverty as better for the poet and the citizen than dependence on the state:

Friends say to me "You should side with the poor. Your poems are about the poor." My answer is I wouldn't have written about them if I had thought anything was going to be done about their poverty. I didn't do it to get rid of the poor. I need them in my business. And anyway when I wrote about them I was poorer than they were.

Frost's major poetic expression of his fear of the trend toward socialistic government in the thirties was his poem "Build Soil—A Political Pastoral," delivered before the political party conventions at Columbia University on May 31, 1932. On June 1 he received Columbia's Doctorate of Letters.

The long philosophical dialogue or eclogue, published later in *A Further Range,* is a plea for individuation, for separateness, versus the growing trend to work with gangs and for social ends.

> "Keep off each other and keep each other off."

The argument is carried in a long ruminative conversation between Tityrus, a poet, and his alter ego, Meliboeus, a runout mountain potato farmer. Fellows so identical in mind that it is less easy than usual in Frost's poetic dialogues to recognize who is speaking.

> I may be wrong, but, Tityrus, to me
> The times seem revolutionary bad. . . .

says Meliboeus, early in the poem. After some "deep stuff," Tityrus comes in with Frost's mischief:

> Don't let the things I say against myself
> Betray you into taking sides against me,
> Or it might get you into trouble with me.
> I'm not afraid to prophesy the future,
> And be judged by the outcome, Meliboeus. . . .

I bid you to a one-man revolution—
The only revolution that is coming.
We're too unseparate out among each other— . . .

Meliboeus concludes:

We're too unseparate. And going home
From company means coming to our senses.

This and, again, "To a Thinker," so obviously a satire on
F.D.R. that Elinor begged Rob not to print it, are straight-
from-the-shoulder, challenging attacks on contemporary American official politics. By contrast, Frost's attitude to the European dictators of this period was astonishingly tolerant; like
George Santayana, he looked dispassionately upon them until
they proved themselves monstrous and depraved. He could
see them as believers in the Divine Right of Kings.

But let a youth of Amherst College, or of the New School
for Social Research, cry that he was born in an ill-starred age
of history, Frost would be after him. Take a rather angry
piece printed in the *Amherst Student* in 1936:

EVERYBODY'S SANITY

You often hear it said that the age of the world we live in is
particularly bad. I am impatient of such talk. We have no way
of knowing that this is one of the worst in the world's history.
Arnold claimed the honor for the age before this. Wordsworth
claimed it for his age and so on back through literature. I say
they claimed the honor for their ages. They claimed it rather for
themselves. It is immodest of a man to think of himself as going
down before the worst forces mobilized by God. . . .

All the ages of the world are bad—a great deal worse than
Heaven. . . .

Ages may vary a little, one may be a little worse than another.
But it is not possible to get outside the age you are in to judge
exactly. . . .

Fortunately . . . there is something we can be doing without
reference to how good or how bad the age is. There is at least so

much good in the world that it admits of form and the making of form . . . calls for it. . . .

Any one who has achieved the least form to be sure of it, is lost to the larger excruciations. . . .

The background is hugeness + confusion, shading away from where we stand into black and utter chaos. . . .

But—we were born to it, born used to it, and have practical reasons for wanting it here. To me, any little form I assert on it is velvet, as the saying is, and to be considered for how much more it is than nothing. If I were a platonist I should have to consider it, I suppose, for how much less it is than everything.

If one age is as good or bad as another, it must be granted that human "progress" for man and his society is an illusion. Frost felt that way, to the depths of his being, as he had made clear in his poetry. But he did believe in renewal. Mankind ever renewed and renewing was a faith. If man errs he will "build soil" again and come into his own again, always with the great mystery of his own beginnings and his ultimate future unknown and unknowable.

Frost himself was always building soil for poetry. At his first series of ten lectures at the New School for Social Research in 1931, an attempt was made to take down stenographically his colloquial words. He refused consent: the value of what he was saying, he insisted, was that it was "gone on the wind." (That is what some of the bright girls had thought he felt in Michigan.)

An analysis of the course to be given was printed in the 1931 catalogue of the New School.

The method of this course, as appropriate to an inquiry into pure poetry, will be one of soundings for meanings, rather than one of general analysis. Some attention will be given to the parties of poetry; since the poet cannot create in isolation, without co-operation in the spirit; to sense and music in poetry, to the truth of metaphor; to the capacity of poetry to transcend all boundaries. Because the truth about poetry is infinitely subtle, all formal requirements of the lecturer's procedure are excluded. The program of each session will remain tentative to the last moment, in order that the lecturer, after experiencing the needs of his audience, may have free choice among the means for satisfying such needs.

Again in 1933, there were three lecture-readings based on Frost's poems, with informal discussion of their genesis and meaning in the poet's own scheme of life and philosophy.

Frost was, all the while, of course, carrying his regular Amherst work. He has told me something about it. At one period he had no regular classes and carried someone else's course. In talking of this, he recalled for me an episode in a class of Professor Elliott's when they were studying the poetry of the sixteenth century. Specifically he remembered a poem— actually a madrigal—with a Latin title "Amantium Irae" by Richard Edwardes (1523–1566) with this refrain:

The falling out of faithful friends renewing is of love.

This is a theme Frost has tested out in life. Many a falling out has led to many a deeper renewal. So he was moved as he remembered:

Mother and babe fall out in this poem . . . you can't find many young boys able to read it. The student who volunteered was a country boy, son of a railroad man. Take the first verse:

In going to my naked bed as one that would have slept,
I heard a wife sing to her child, that long before had wept;
She sighèd sore and sang full sweet, to bring the babe to rest,
That would not cease but crièd still, in sucking at her breast.
She was full weary of her watch, and grievèd with her child,
She rockèd it and rated it, till that on her it smiled.
Then did she say, Now have I found this proverb true to prove,
The falling out of faithful friends renewing is of love.

Many a boy [Frost recalled] has had a black mark from me for one thing—I give no other chance. But one thing on the positive side will give him his year's mark or his life's mark.

Well, this boy—I gave him my mark for the discretion of voice with which he read an unusual meditative poem—his life's mark. I am always looking for singularity and felicity—sometimes I go wrong. In this case not. The man, Reuben Brower, has turned out a scholar in the field of poetry—one of the most distinguished professors at Harvard today, and Master of Adams House of which I am a Fellow.

Professor Brower, author of a critical book *The Fields of Light*, when I spoke to him of Frost's recall of his student reading, wrote:

. . . a day that I have not forgotten, one that he has mentioned to me many times. That poem and much else that I teach has been "marked" for me by Robert Frost. I do not go through many weeks of teaching without mentioning something he said, or without feeling his presence in something I am trying to say.

As to this question of marks [Frost went on as we sat by his log blaze], I once spoke to a class at the end of a year, at an examination:

"Do something appropriate to the course that you think would please me."

I gave them six blue books, and went to my office, saying threateningly:

"Don't write more!"

[He imitated himself speaking in that spurious flat voice which he hopes deceives only fools because it insinuates an opposite meaning—in this case]:

"Just a few sentences, please!"

Some wrote all six books. I gave the highest mark to one who wrote down a bit of Thomas Hardy and went out. He's a psychiatrist at Kenyon now.

I can be pretty sweeping. If you go the straightforward way students don't care, unless they want a row. They don't care if it doesn't bother the officers. I believe in marks. But it is *really* hard [he said with his clear, honest look] to know A from B and C. I know double A. The whole thing is a ruck. These assigned subjects. . . . Ask a child to compare Emily Dickinson with William Faulkner. . . .

Suppose [Frost wrote in an article called "Education by Poetry"] we stop short of imagination, initiative, enthusiasm, inspiration and originality—dread words. Suppose we don't mark in such things at all. There are still two minimal things, that we have got to take care of, taste and judgment. Americans are supposed to have more judgment than taste, but taste is there to be dealt with. That is what poetry, the only art in the colleges of arts, is there for. I for my part would not be afraid to go in for enthusiasm. There is the enthusiasm like a blinding light, or the enthusiasm of the deafening shout, the crude enthusiasm that you get uneducated by poetry, outside of poetry. . . .

But the enthusiasm I mean is taken through the prism of the intellect and spread on the screen in a color, all the way from hyperbole at one end—or overstatement, at one end—to understatement at the other end. It is a long strip of dark lines and many colors. Such enthusiasm is one object of all teaching in poetry. . . .

I would be willing to throw away everything else but that: enthusiasm tamed by metaphor. Let me rest the case there. Enthusiasm tamed to metaphor, tamed to that much of it. I do not think anybody ever knows the discreet use of metaphor, his own and other people's, the discreet handling of metaphor, unless he has been properly educated in poetry.

Frost also talked about metaphor to girl students. A Nyack friend, then Mary Ten Eyck Mosher, married long since, and a distinguished teacher herself, has preserved her notes on a Frost reading at Mount Holyoke College on February 13, 1931, when Gordon Chalmers was teaching there. She herself was a freshman at the time.

Robert Frost speaks on metaphor:
It used to be enough [she quoted him] to tell young writers about the forms of writing so that when they got old they would know how to say what they didn't have to say. All there is to writing is "the art of having something to say." Everything that happens to you is experience—unself-conscious. All there is to having something to say is making metaphors. There is no mental

324

action without metaphor [beginning with simile through allegory which he likes least of all].

[Mr. Chalmers is here looking worshipping. I think he wishes he were Robert Frost. He has on evening clothes.]

[Grace Luce is nuts about Frost. She has his *Collected Poems* to be autographed. I have *New Hampshire*.]

Draw a string of words through anyone's mind and you find registered emotion. A person managing words with his own influence may do things to people. "Running away"—stream of consciousness done well. Shakespeare good at it. "Mental sideslipping." Proximity stuff. The rest of mental action comes under the head of comparison. Only forward thrust of the mind through metaphor. Value always when you're feeling *like* something. No other freedom. The other "the going away of the mind." To be able to dip anywhere in time and connect anything in space with it. That's poetry, not only that but everything we are. "The scale of heaven is in trying to say matter in terms of spirit." Darts into perfect moments when we know unity. Matter and spirit—called the two great incommensurables. . . . Purity of all things and the force of all things lies in comparison. The mind will always be moving through fresh fields of comparison. The old-fashioned person thinks a metaphor a little ornament to hang on. *Saturday Evening Post* type. Metaphor—"essence of poetry."

[He's very dear. I understand Mr. Chalmers' adoration.]

I started calling myself a synecdochist when others called themselves imagists or vorticists. Always, always a larger significance. A little thing touches a larger thing.

[He reads (says he's going to, I mean). He says he's not in the mood for it. . . .]

[People have left—Emmy Low and Tracy for instance. I can't understand voluntarily leaving such delightfulness. We went up afterwards and he autographed my book. I'm in a spell. Mr. Chalmers was perfect with Mrs. Chalmers. It was raining when we came out. The others ran, but I slopped along alone and saw my shadow on the snow.]

Here is everyone's morning of life revealed, but the very last line is Mary's own poetic answer to life itself—complete communion!

Frost has never believed in talking the pain out of experience, or the joy either, by making it "copy" for a poem. But he once said to a friend that he wished things (he meant the depth of things) could be understood between them by just referring to poems. Even when the speaker of the poem seems to the listener closely to resemble the maker of it, Frost's poems are never literal autobiography. Thus I cannot refer, merely in the metaphorical terms of his verse, to this particular period of his life. Yet poems do come to mind in connection with human events.

The first poem I think of is "A Drumlin Woodchuck" (the poetic twin of "Departmental"): a witty satirical fable in rhymed couplets. Frost refers to it as "my most Vermontly poem." When I hear him read it from one of his old-age platforms in New York, I recall the homely, dusky, hospitable porch of the Gully, that white farmhouse which Frost had bought for himself and Elinor in 1931. There I spent a long quiet afternoon with them in the early thirties, after not having seen them for a time.

The Gully stood on the peak of a hill—that's what the geological word "drumlin" means—and was plagued with woodchucks which whistled in a queer little way that only a poet's sensitive ear could discern.

A DRUMLIN WOODCHUCK

One thing has a shelving bank,
Another a rotting plank,
To give it cozier skies
And make up for its lack of size.

My own strategic retreat
Is where two rocks almost meet,
And still more secure and snug,
A two-door burrow I dug.

With those in mind at my back
I can sit forth exposed to attack

326

As one who shrewdly pretends
That he and the world are friends.

All we who prefer to live
Have a little whistle we give,
And flash, at the least alarm
We dive down under the farm.

We allow some time for guile
And don't come out for a while
Either to eat or drink.
We take occasion to think.

And if after the hunt goes past
And the double-barreled blast
(Like war and pestilence
And the loss of common sense),

If I can with confidence say
That still for another day,
Or even another year,
I will be there for you, my dear,

It will be because, though small
As measured against the All,
I have been so instinctively thorough
About my crevice and burrow.

The woodchuck had definitely retired to his own pursuits,
leaving the younger folk to live in stone mansions. He enjoyed
being alone with his wife. The way Elinor and Robert sat
here on that deep porch, not needing to talk or even to exchange looks to share one another's thoughts, has remained
a long memory with me; it was in fact the last time I saw
Mrs. Frost.

These two were now close to sixty but living at the Gully
much as they always had anywhere, Elinor doing household
tasks that her spirit disdained and her fingers found awkward.
She was tending invalids, clasping to her heart children who

tagged after her just as much after their marriages as before
that kept her beautiful as nature is beautiful, when tested by
storms and then blessed by fair weather.

The next poem I recall that reflects the background of the
Gully is:

MOON COMPASSES

> I stole forth dimly in the dripping pause
> Between two downpours to see what there was.
> And a masked moon had spread down compass rays
> To a cone mountain in the midnight haze,
> As if the final estimate were hers,
> And as it measured in her calipers,
> The mountain stood exalted in its place.
> So love will take between the hands a face. . . .

Another lyric, where the speaker goes out into the night
to look at the mountains and the weather, and finds a human
tie, appeared also in *A Further Range*. Her father has told me
that the reference is to Marjorie, "sweet-cynical Marj."

VOICE WAYS

> Some things are never clear.
> But the weather is clear tonight,
> Thanks to a clearing rain.
> The mountains are brought up near,
> The stars are brought out bright.
> Your old sweet-cynical strain
> Would come in like you here:
> "So we won't say nothing is clear."

Soon after this, as I was to learn later, everything "cleared"
for Marjorie Frost. She recovered her health; a brave and
braw young Westerner, Willard Fraser, studying archaeology
at Boulder, triumphantly carried her off to live with him in
Billings, Montana, away from all illness and trouble. ["I Always Knew" Marjorie herself wrote, and the poem after her
death became part of a book.]

I ALWAYS KNEW

I always knew that you were there
Where eyes were dark, where skin was fair,
Where lay the dew of heated hair,
   Where curled sardonic lips;
While in my heart I had to bear
The scent of pollenated air;
To let the utter sweetness tear
   Like phantom finger tips.

Yet I would never let you be
Confused with sensuality:
For out of all eternity—
   My one immortal love—
I knew that you would come to me,
Like rock ascending from the sea,
The redwood from the aspen tree,
   The eagle from the dove.

Does this remind the reader of Frost's "To Earthward"?

Love at the lips was touch
As sweet as I could bear;
And once that seemed too much;
I lived on air

That crossed me from sweet things
The flow of—was it musk
From hidden grapevine springs
Down hill at dusk? . . .

Next look for an epithalamium by Marjorie's father, a poem referred to in the Introduction, also to be found in *A Further Range.*

THE MASTER SPEED

No speed of wind or water rushing by
But you have speed far greater. You can climb
Back up a stream of radiance to the sky,
And back through history up the stream of time.

And you were given this swiftness, not for haste
Nor chiefly that you may go where you will,
But in the rush of everything to waste,
That you may have the power of standing still—
Off any still or moving thing you say.
Two such as you with such a master speed
Cannot be parted nor be swept away
From one another once you are agreed
That life is only life forevermore
Together wing to wing and oar to oar.

But "the rush of everything to waste" overtook them. Only a year after her marriage Marjorie Fraser, after giving birth to a healthy baby girl, Elinor Robin, became mortally ill from a childbirth infection. A hundred young people in Billings offered blood for transfusions; a transcendent effort was made by her husband and her parents to save her through expert medical intervention at the Mayo Clinic in Rochester, Minnesota. A few letters and telegrams from the Frosts to the Whichers in Amherst tell the story briefly and bravely. I quote partially:

On April 12, 1934, a telegram from Robert:

NOTHING GOOD TO TELL OR PREDICT MARJORIE VERY LOW ALL WE HAVE IS HOPE

On April 22 a letter from Elinor:

. . . The days and weeks have passed by, and we are hardly aware of it, so much does this suffering and fear hold us apart from the world. . . . there is a faint hope that her resistance, which has proved so marvelous up to now, will pull her through. . . .

Then on April 29 a letter from Robert:

I musnt say it but I fear Marjorie loses ground. . . . Here at Rochester she has all that modern science and humanity can do

330

for her. . . . There are still a few things to be tried—one of them another serum, . . . That and Marjorie's tenacity and the devotion of Willard and Elinor and the mercy of God are my hope.

The last telegram from Robert on May 2:

ELINORS LOVE DIDNT SAVE HER FROM LOSS . . . BACK WITH YOU SOON

Elinor took her little grandchild Robin Fraser with her to the Gully for a short time, then returned her to the father and grandmother in Billings, saying to her friends that, though she believed in a future life, this loss, this suffering, this anguish of Marjorie's illness and death she could never forget or accept for even one hour—nor wanted to, the rest of her days.

Frost's attitude to death and fate is very different. One aspect of it is movingly expressed in a lonely poem of *A Further Range*, "Desert Places." But loneliness has always forced Robert Frost back into "the obscuration upon earth," as described in his early religious poem "The Trial by Existence." He never reads this poem to the public but never omits it from his collections.

> But always God speaks at the end:
> "One thought in agony of strife
> The bravest would have by for friend,
> The memory that he chose the life; . . ."

In another verse we read:

> Nothing but what we somehow chose; . . .

That was Frost's affirmative answer to sorrow, death, and human tragedy as early as his teens. He has told me that the lines about choice came to him, by themselves when, a high-school boy in Lawrence, he was walking to meet a friend. He recalls the exact spot.

"Trouble with the poem," he said, "it recalls Rossetti's 'The Blessed Damozel.'"

There is a little something similar in the mood, in the stanzaic form (though Frost used eight lines and Rossetti six), something in the mystic glimpse of heaven, and the contrast of earth and heaven. The young poet reads poetry, true.

But Frost's special originality is clear: he had, even as a lad, accepted the mature psychological perception—not always learned by human beings in a lifetime—that we are not merely pawns of fate; in some sense we *choose* our way, even if unconsciously and unaware of it at the time of choice.

There was one thing her parents could still do for Marjorie besides cherishing Willard and Robin. In 1935 Elinor wrote Joseph Blumenthal:

Our youngest daughter, Marjorie, died a year ago.

She had written poems occasionally, and though she had never offered them to magazines for publication, I am sure she looked forward to having a book sometime.

Robert and I think the poems are lovely and would very much like to have you make a book of them for us and for her friends.

This was done in 1936. The little books were not sold but given to Marjorie's and the family's friends. Here are two poems by a girl who had the dark in her, as well as the bright, like her father, and who was always poised for flight. Several of Marjorie's poems are full of birds and bird wings:

SPRING

To tangled grass I cling
When in the fields I lie,
For fear of taking wing.

332

When mountain torrents bring
The last of winter by,
To tangled grass I cling.

When maple tassels swing
Pure gold against the sky,
To tangled grass I cling.

Alighted robins sing
A song I dare not try
For fear of taking wing.

MY PLACE

Once up this slippery marble slab, stone blind,
I struggled seeking things I could not find;

Feeling my way with fingers bloodless cold
For this rough edge to mount my setting mould.

Now always sad from outside looking on,
But never from attachment wholly torn,

As raised alone to bear an endless strife,
I watch go by a Greek-like frieze of life,

Where beady eyes make impress as they pass,
And glance at me from surfaces of glass.

To keep from slipping back into that line,
I'll twist my feet in cracks like young wall vine.

In 1941, in *A Witness Tree,* Frost published "The Wind
and the Rain." I begin with the ninth line:

I sang of death—but had I known
The many deaths one must have died
Before he came to meet his own!

Oh, should a child be left unwarned
That any song in which he mourned
Would be as if he prophesied?
It were unworthy of the tongue
To let the half of life alone
And play the good without the ill.
And yet 'twould seem that what is sung
In happy sadness by the young
Fate has no choice but to fulfill. . . .

CHAPTER 15

ACQUAINTED WITH THE NIGHT

1934–1938

By the fall of 1934, a few months after his daughter Marjorie's death, Robert Frost was again teaching at Amherst and leading his usual life. He was now sixty years old and looked, as I remember him, handsomer than ever and stronger but with another depth. The photograph of him taken by a friend, sitting on a cracker box in South Shaftsbury, looking down at hands engaged with cat's-cradle strings, is almost perfect. His lower lip is characteristically pursed into a U-shape that, as Thornton Wilder remarked, "gives evidence of his being about to amuse himself without insisting on your participation."

But he could come out of his distance for a reading or a talk such as he gave at the convocation of the Massachusetts State College (formerly an agricultural college) in Amherst in October, 1934, and, in a simple unassuming way, say something he cared to say about his own relation to nature:

. . . I was going to say to you that deep down in me—I don't know how it is with you—deep down in me is a strong friendship in favor of basing imagination and judgment on a knowledge of country things. [He mentioned his poem, "The Need of Being Versed in Country Things."]

You have to be versed in country things to know anything about dirt. City people say "cheap as dirt." Let them try to move a lot of dirt and see how much it costs! . . . I had a city friend who bought a place in the Adirondacks. He had lots of trees, trees to burn. He wouldn't cut down any of the trees because he felt that all trees must be spared. This attitude is mere sentimentality. . . . I don't think any one understands people unless he has learned from country life that lots of people are smarter than they look. . . . And city people are not aware of it. . . . *I am always interested in unpromising looks.*

If you are going to understand what is going on in politics today, you must be versed in country things. If there is anything in the New Deal for me, it is an attempt to restore the balance between the country and the city.

Frost never wastes time on formalities. Being always *in medias res* himself, he plunges right in, as in this letter to Joseph Blumenthal from Amherst on November 23:

We've hesitated a moment longer. The picture for the title page is fine. My doubt of the design for the cover is perhaps due to the fact that no grain of any kind has been associated with the scythe in New England or anywhere else in America I think, for longer than my life time. If the wisp he used for binder had been weeds Joe Pye, Golden Rod or Turtle Head or even Timothy or Red Top hay I should have been easier in the mind. But I still cling to the idea of a bristle of three or four or five scythes, roughly circular as a whole like a handful grab of jack straws. None of this is too important, but it is a little to me.

This meticulous agricultural reference to the design offered by the Spiral Press for the cover of a new edition of *A Boy's Will* (Holt's, 1934) is quoted for its revelation of Frost's connection with what modern poetry calls "the symbol." Frost enjoys being unserious about the symbol on platforms, but he wants it accurate and realistic in a poem or on a cover.

The poet did a great deal of traveling at this period, lecturing or reading here and there. It was not his habit, then, to protect himself by Pullman seats in trains, but to sit down anywhere and see what could be made of the "unpromising looks" of the man across the aisle.

Once he had double-talked such a stranger into the query:

"Who are *you?* What do you do for a living?"

Usually [Frost said, in recounting the tale] I answer that I am a farmer. This time I said:

"I'm a poet."

"A poet? What's a poet?"

"A poet is a man to whom something happens or something occurs."

A good deal happened and occurred to Robert Frost in the winter of 1934–1935, when he and Elinor set up their winter quarters at Key West, Florida. Bankrupt since the previous July, the Key had been taken over by the Federal government through the administrator of public relief of the state.

This brought the workings of the New Deal right under the Frosts' critical eyes. The politics of it, the coconut palms and gentle surf, more dark than light-skinned people, no drainage system, and a great sea smell made Elinor a bit queasy. She wrote her close friend Mrs. Manthey-Zorn:

"So if you will I am living under a [local] Dictator. He wears white shorts and has very fuzzy legs."

This is a funny place to be [the poet wrote Joe Blumenthal]. It has been made a crown dependency. That is to say it comes directly under the Imperator at Washington without intervention of either city mayor or state governor. I expected to find it a busted cigar town. It turns out to be a busted land-boom town—all cut up into speculators lots, with hardly a house on them.

Frost, however, claimed that he felt the same anywhere: "my conditioning is wholly internal." His first act, here in the apartment which he rented for $38.50 a month, was to make himself, out of corrugated boxboard, a Yankee lapboard or kneedesk—"one of the chief creations of my mind," he called

337

it, with which he could sit himself down in any quiet spot to write poetry or communicate with friends.

Frost relishes his gifts as a Yankee inventor. The lapboard can be compared to the platform against cold that he devised in Franconia; and to his habit, before a trip to read poetry, of suspending his evening clothes on hangers and stepladders over a bathtub of hot water, instead of calling the tailor. Occasionally he forgets to turn off the spigot.

Carol and his little family were established down the road. Rob and Elinor were always trailed by their married children, or pulled them after them by magnetic attraction. Neither of the parents wanted to think of Carol and delicate Lillian left behind on the cold Northern farm. So the grandfather was soon taking little Prescott for after-lunch hours daily. Like his own father and indeed his grandfather Rob as a child, the boy had been withdrawn from his Key West school, almost as soon as entered.

But much of Frost's poetry had been written close to children, and like a lightning stroke illuminating a dusky landscape, "Departmental" made gay the somewhat dismal expanses of Key West in January, 1935. It is a witty and subtle satire on the academic administrator, in terms of the insect world. He had satirized himself as a woodchuck in the same verse form, so could venture a step further with the academic departmentalist.

A letter to Whicher [January 14, 1935] shows signs of diplomacy:

The enclosed went across my mind the other night like a cloud across the moon. There is nothing appropriate in it to anything down here—nothing particularly appropriate. The events recorded in it took place down here. But they might just as well have taken place in New England. Ants seem to be ants pretty much everywhere. Their characteristics are called forth by sugar on a table cloth equally north and south. If I could not by force or cunning wrest my poem to fit my being where I am cast away by the doctor on this 50 percent deserted island the question was how was I going to bring it in between me and anybody else. It wouldnt satisfy the requirements merely to print it in a magazine appropos of nothing. In my desperation casting about, I caught at the last word of the last line to connect it with you trying to be even feebly departmental with English at our Amherst College. You barely succeed. . . .

He goes on joking in prose (re ants) about the lack of perceptible step

. . . taken in evolution, human or animal. Fifty Years and Nothing Yet. . . . You remember how blithely Mrs. Charlotte Perkins Stetson Gilman . . . in a really brilliant poem makes fun of those of us who assume we cant change our natures. . . . The best thing in Pound's latest 'leven is the story of the two Afghans who turned up at Geneva to see if they mightnt pick up cheap any arms we were disarming ourselves of. . . .

Frost's flattest, jerkiest, most humoresque Yankee voice tones, and the malicious flash and play of his deep-set blue eyes are associated, for me, with "Departmental." I have sometimes wished he would follow it, on a platform, with "The Bear," which appeared in *West-Running Brook*. For the end of that presents another collegiate figure, the unredeemed pedagogue, with whom the poet had also a lifelong quarrel:

> He sits back on his fundamental butt
> With lifted snout and eyes (if any) shut,
> (He almost looks religious but he's not),
> And back and forth he sways from cheek to cheek,
> At one extreme agreeing with one Greek,
> At the other agreeing with another Greek
> Which may be thought, but only so to speak.
> A baggy figure, equally pathetic
> When sedentary and when peripatetic.

The above letter to Whicher actually enclosed not "Departmental" but "A Serious Step Lightly Taken." History now had taken over. I quote the fourth and the sixth stanzas:

339

It is turning three hundred years
On our cisatlantic shore
For family after family name.
We'll make it three hundred more . . .

A hundred thousand days
Of front-page paper events,
A half a dozen major wars,
And forty-five presidents.

The English have had the language six hundred years [he annotated the poem]. We have had it three—already half as long. When they have had it twelve hundred, we shall have had it three fourths as long. Thus their proportional advantage will grow less and less till I shant be surprised to see it lost sight of by history entirely and the language ascribed to us outright.

Thirty Presidents of eight years each + fifteen of four years each = three hundred years exactly.

The same theme was further elaborated to David McCord in a letter later in 1935:

. . . Three hundred years. One thing after another is coming of that age now. I have about made up my mind to help you celebrate Harvard's three hundredth birthday. Nineteen thirty-six will be the three hundredth year for my family in this country. . . . In three hundred more . . . it will take an effort of the historical mind to recall that the English language ever existed in Europe. We shall be holding the British Isles as an outpost against the German continent and as a summer resort for antiquarians. We moved in the seventeenth century but it may be some time before we get all our things moved. Don't say I said so.

On this seventeenth-century move and what followed it on the American continent, Frost has spoken finally in "The Gift Outright," his most eloquent and rhetorical short poem—one that shows his endowment as a Titan among Americans. Sidney Cox, in *Swinger of Birches,* says that, "The Gift Outright" was written in 1935, this year when Frost was learning

340

on a tropical island, the farthest reach of the United States, to live with grief.

THE GIFT OUTRIGHT

The land was ours before we were the land's.
She was our land more than a hundred years
Before we were her people. She was ours
In Massachusetts, in Virginia,
But we were England's, still colonials,
Possessing what we still were unpossessed by,
Possessed by what we now no more possessed.
Something we were withholding made us weak
Until we found out that it was ourselves
We were withholding from our land of living,
And forthwith found salvation in surrender.
Such as we were we gave ourselves outright
(The deed of gift was many deeds of war)
To the land vaguely realizing westward,
But still unstoried, artless, unenhanced,
Such as she was, such as she would become.

R.F. has called to my attention, as summing up his views about politics, what was said about Jefferson in "The Black Cottage"—written in 1905. The two poems are related in spirit. The crisp old lady about whom the minister is talking to his friend, as they peer into the windows of the deserted cottage, had lost her father "at Fredericksburg or Gettysburg." Her war was the Civil War and she had even "given outright":

One wasn't long in learning that she thought
Whatever else the Civil War was for,
It wasn't just to keep the States together,
Nor just to free the slaves, though it did both.
She wouldn't have believed those ends enough
To have given outright for them all she gave.
Her giving somehow touched the principle
That all men are created free and equal.
And to hear her quaint phrases—so removed
From the world's view today of all those things.

That's a hard mystery of Jefferson's.
What did he mean? Of course the easy way
Is to decide it simply isn't true.
It may not be. I heard a fellow say so.
But never mind, the Welshman got it planted
Where it will trouble us a thousand years.
Each age will have to reconsider it. . . .

In Key West thirty years later, R.F. was philosophizing about current 1935 politics to Manthey-Zorn:

. . . This country has gone crazy with the idea that it is big with revolution. But Roosevelt may get cured of any delusion of grandeur he may have had. . . . Democracy with all its faults is the world's best bet till the people's virtue all leaches out of them. Then we may start again with a monarch but only protem till we can get back with a chastened populace to the liberal ease of democracy. . . . No action is forward. . . . It is always a variable business between two limits. Security, for instance. How much may the state try to give of it. We have to determine, I say, what is its opposite so that we can know what we will be getting less or more of after we are getting more or less of security.

During the summer of 1935, when I was doing Pueblo Indian research under John Collier, the New Deal Commissioner of Indian Affairs with whom I had fought many a battle for the Pueblos against the government, R.F. came down from Boulder to Santa Fe, New Mexico, to read his poetry under the auspices of Writers' Editions, a regional group of poets and writers to which I belonged.

As R.F. came into my living room alone, the first evening, to meet the assembled group, he looked grave and drew me aside to explain that the return to Boulder and the University of Colorado where Marjorie had found her cure and her dear husband had been too hard for his wife. She was not well, he must hurry back to her in Boulder. But he said, with a sudden jest, would there be some way to fit in seeing a group of

Indians *who would spit in his eye?* Collier in Washington had promised him that I knew some.

Then he turned to greet Alice Corbin, who had been Harriet Monroe's assistant on *Poetry* when he first submitted his poems; to Witter Bynner, an old New England friend (the first to hear "The Witch of Coös" in Michigan), and to all the little Santa Fe group who were proud to have captured him for the reading. But Frost was no captive and, in one of his youngster moods, began to tousle his hair, laugh, shifting from foot to foot, and damning to hell some poet whom Hal Bynner admired.

But it happened that when a bigger group of artists and writers assembled at Bynner's for a formal lunch for the celebrity next day, the real man, who had a passion for archaeology, was eating cold fried chicken at the Puyé cliff dwellings. He just *had* to see them.

As, with a chosen few, we drove through the desert on that brilliant summer morning toward the Jemez mountains, along the sandy dry arroyos and waterless rivers, with their attendant rows of thin, trembling cottonwoods, my Indian secretary sang and beat on his hollow cottonwood drum, in honor of Robert Frost, the ancient Deer Dance song of his Winter People of Kapogé (Santa Clara). The second verse took us whither we were bound—to the Puyé cliffs, the prehistoric home of the Santa Claras. It was there that the bucks and the does, with their shepherd, had paused first on their descent from their Sacred Mountain to dance ritualistically in the Pueblo village.

Climbing up into the mesa country that lies below the peaks, with these rhythms in our ears I recalled also one of Frost's finest poetic passages, written out of pure imagination a quarter century earlier in "The Black Cottage":

>   . . . I wish
> I could be monarch of a desert land
> I could devote and dedicate forever
> To the truths we keep coming back and back to.

So desert it would have to be, so walled
By mountain ranges half in summer snow,
No one would covet it or think it worth
The pains of conquering to force change on.
Scattered oases where men dwelt, but mostly
Sand dunes held loosely in tamarisk
Blown over and over themselves in idleness.
Sand grains should sugar in the natal dew
The babe born to the desert, the sand storm
Retard mid-waste my cowering caravans— . . .

The Puyé caves are dug into the majestic curve of a canyon wall, spotted black with pinyons, grown with brilliant yellow and dull gray sage and rabbit brush. Sheer up the face of a cliff that rivals Delphi in beauty, we followed narrow stone paths still worn by the feet of little ancient men who lived that adage credited to Dickens:

"Life is given us on the definite understanding that we defend it to the last."

It did not occur to me that the hale and vigorous, hatless figure behind me, who lives a similar philosophy, was enduring the dizziness of the abyss. Only years later did R.F. say:

"I nearly died on that little path. I can't stand any dropping space."

Calmly, on the upper level, among the ruins of still other ancients, he gazed down a thousand feet into the great sweep of the Rio Grande Valley, backed by the Sangre de Cristo Range. He was discovering living Pueblo Indian villages, which to some might qualify as the "arrested" civilizations of Toynbee's classification—villages that were yet producing young progressives like my secretary, bound to make their way in the modern white world. Los Alamos, to the north of us, then the habitat of a boys' school lost among other cliff dwellings, cast no shadow that day.

Simple, massive, inscrutable as an Indian sun-priest, Frost seemed to contain all the ages of man at this moment, in his own person, and I wondered if a poem would come of it.

This is what I found, in 1942, in *Steeple Bush:*

344

A CLIFF DWELLING

There sandy seems the golden sky
And golden seems the sandy plain.
No habitation meets the eye
Unless in the horizon rim,
Some halfway up the limestone wall,
That spot of black is not a stain
Or shadow, but a cavern hole,
Where someone used to climb and crawl
To rest from his besetting fears.
I see the callus on his sole
The disappearing last of him
And of his race starvation slim,
Oh, years ago—ten thousand years.

It was nearly four o'clock when we got to Bynner's lunch with its disappointed company. But R.F. could and did dispel the gloom and I soon heard him asking John Sloan the painter *to show him an Indian who would spit in his eye.* But he left without having found one. Soon I heard that he was writing his perceptive preface to E. A. Robinson's *King Jasper* at the Fobes Place in Franconia. But Elinor and he could not face another summer there with its memories, and were buying, for the hay-fever season, a group of old farms, north of St. Johnsbury, Vermont—referred to, more or less, in "A Serious Step Lightly Taken." As Elinor took things hard, he was always playing up lightness while actually (as ever), being instinctively thorough about his own crevice and burrow.

Since they never, in winter, chose the same place twice, the Frosts were trying out Coconut Grove in the dark months of 1935–1936. The spring of this year promised a new significant connection with Harvard, and a new book, the sixth— Richard Thornton's concern—*A Further Range.* The year 1936 was one of those that Lesley as a child labeled "important."

. . . Let's want the greatest things [Frost wrote David McCord from 3670 Avocado Avenue in January], but let's not get caught wanting them. The Spartans were right. The only crime is in getting caught. I'd hate to have anyone know either by my uniform or the expression of my face that there was anything in particular I was waiting round for.

For the time involved he would be the Charles Eliot Norton Professor of Poetry at Harvard, though he accepted with misgivings about the Cambridge climate in March.*

. . . I shall—we shall—[he wrote McCord] be living near you for a few months. You probably know I have promised to have a poem ready for Phi Beta Kappa at the three hundredth anniversary. Looks like rather a Harvard year. I shall end sentimental like Dreiser, Menken, Hemmingway and Anderson, if people keep on being good to me. It isn't fair. . . .

Ten days later he wrote again:

An ode by me is going to be a novelty.

> Thou still unravished bride of Quietness
> Conspiring with him how to load and bless.

Do I get the tone? What? Is it all my own?

> "Or is it an echo of something
> Heard with a boys delight?"

Don't you like the idea of my using rhymed couplets where the subject is—well what it is? You don't think I will look too serviceable a boy-of-all-work doing all these poems and things round the Yard? I can leave my interests to you to protect. You will know if the demand for me comes from the right quarters (fore or hind). . . .

The Charles Eliot Norton Lectures ran from March 4 to April 15. Announced under the title "The Renewal of Words,"

---

* The chair was occupied before and since by T. S. Eliot, Igor Stravinsky, Sir Herbert Read, e. e. cummings, Aaron Copland, and others.

they were successively called: "The Old Way to Be New"; "Vocal Imagination—the Merger of Form and Content"; "Does Wisdom Signify?" "Poetry as Prowess (Feats of Words)"; "Before the Beginning of a Poem"; "After the End of a Poem."

To Robert Frost, who as a young married man had fled these Harvard halls of learning instead of completing proper academic studies, the return to Harvard was more than a return to personal honors on a rising tide of fame; it was a justification in generous terms of his having believed in experience more than in books. It was not a conventional following of educational tradition that had made him the brilliant teacher and poet he had become.

All this was implied, for him at least, in the great ovation he received at Harvard's New Lecture Hall on March 4. He was doubly introduced by Bernard DeVoto and John Livingston Lowes. As always, he spoke with no notes or merely casual ones. The audience of poetry lovers: teachers, professors, students, general public, overflowed and crowded in so that, as the course proceeded, lines were forming at four for a lecture at eight o'clock. It was, to the Cantabrigians and Bostonians, especially the brother poets, as if poetry and New England poetry had received an accolade.

The lectures, in the words of John Holmes who wrote warmly in the Boston newspapers about the series, were epigrammatic, pungent, sound, and wise. Each, in spite of casual marginal excursions, reached the exact point Robert Frost wanted to make. But what mattered most to a young poet like Holmes was that they were spoken as if directly to fellow poets.

Frost, Holmes has told me, came right out with the bases of his own integrity as poet:

Earn a living, have a life, Frost advised. But not the busyness of the usual American life, or its consuming demands. Frost illustrated in terms of his own life: he would not collaborate; would not teach where teaching was repetition; or stay where he could not grow—by which he meant, I think, follow and enlarge his own direction. This stand, taken almost

347

blindly in youth, had given him, he knew, the solid base for a creative, productive, mature life in his own mode.

The listeners may have divined that Frost's power of self-understanding, his ability to recognize and to stick with his own pattern, was not the least part of his genius. And Harvard University, as an institution, may have begun to look toward the Doctorate of Letters that followed along in 1937.

But this poet was nonconformist to the end. Norton Lecturers are expected to turn in their manuscripts to the Harvard Press for publication. Robert Frost did not do so. There was no manuscript. He had lodged something with his hearers that might be basic in their relation to poetry. But his actual words, except in a few notebooks, would again be unrecorded.

Those that he had cared to fix to the printed page were published in *A Further Range* in the month of May.

Book Six is dedicated, as others had been, but with a difference.

To E.F. for what it may mean to her that beyond the White Mountains were the Green; beyond both were the Rockies, the Sierras, and, in thought, the Andes and the Himalayas—range beyond range even into the realm of government and religion.

The hint given is that this book offers new geographical subject matter and a new range of meaning. It is true that under a Table of Contents heading, called "The Outlands," we go to the Andes and the Himalayas—and, more significantly, to the Malverns which gave "Iris by Night," taking us back to that English walk with Edward Thomas. There are two poems of California base: "Woodward's Gardens" and (much less obviously) "Neither Out Far Nor In Deep"; "Paul's Wife" from Michigan; no Florida poems. Actually the reader feels himself—or I do and want to—in the world of the poet's previous great creation. Can this world of Robert Frost change —should it change, since it is his? We simply make a few excursions, have new perspectives, and a number of varied forms.

The tone, the tones of voice, the colloquial idiom are struck across the sonnet, the lyric, the fable in couplets, the Socratic eclogue, the aphoristic couplet, which appears first here:

THE SPAN OF LIFE

The old dog barks backward without getting up.
I can remember when he was a pup.

"Got that right down Sunset Avenue," R.F. said. Others have looked back to the *Greek Anthology* or to Ralph Waldo Emerson, as in

I have an arrow that will find its mark,
A mastiff that will bite without a bark.

The variety of *A Further Range* might seem a little willful and ingenious, in a poet who most charms us when casual in tone, if the finest of the poems themselves were not so notable and wonderful. Besides those quoted in the last chapters, look for "Design," "Two Tramps in Mud Time," "A Lone Striker," "The White-Tailed Hornet," "Desert Places," and "Provide, Provide." If you regard a pure lyric like "The Pasture" as the best of Robert Frost, "Provide, Provide" must stand as its sophisticated, disillusioned, and worldly-wise opposite in tone and implication:

The witch that came (the withered hag)
To wash the steps with pail and rag,
Was once the beauty Abishag,

The picture pride of Hollywood.
Too many fall from great and good
For you to doubt the likelihood. . . .

Yet here too the voice of the spirit interposes:

Some have relied on what they knew;
Others on being simply true.
What worked for them might work for you. . . .

Frost enjoys reading the poem in a flatter-than-flat derisive Yankee drawl, and after the last lines

> Better to go down dignified
> With boughten friendship at your side
> Than none at all. Provide, provide!

He often adds, as he did once in Washington when he saw his friend Henry Wallace in his audience,
"And how will yer like that?"
Thus he subtly makes this a New Deal welfare poem—which in substance it is not. "Provide, Provide" was first published in 1933 in the *New Frontier*, a small Harvard student publication which Reuben Brower, then a Harvard graduate student, was editing.
All the poems named above and many more deserve quotation, for they are substantive, fresh, often challenging in meaning; and everywhere is found Robert Frost, with his cool lucidity and economy of phrase, his fine images and metaphors, his beautiful insight and perceptions, his immersion in nature as an element of living human life.

> Leaves and bark, leaves and bark,
> To lean against and hear in the dark, . . .

The stars are a little beclouded, in these poems—remember we are in the thirties—they do not, as in "Choose Something Like a Star," suggest Emersonian or Horatian aspiration. We cannot hitch our wagon to them. They may even be blank and stark, as in "Desert Places."

> They cannot scare me with their empty spaces
> Between stars—on stars where no human race is.
> I have it in me so much nearer home
> To scare myself with my own desert places.

The summer of 1936, in spite of the new book's getting the Book-of-the-Month-Club award, was something of a desert space. Frost had a case of shingles, sheer misery and ignominy, and had to give up his honorific rôle of Phi Beta Kappa Poet, and Commemoration Odist at Harvard's Tercentenary. The poetry of occasions, was, however, alien to him and he went back to Amherst work, now consisting of visits to English classes and "Babbott Room talks" on politics and literature, intended to encourage students to pursue their interests through visits to him on Sunset Avenue.

Later when he and Elinor went to San Antonio, Texas, for the winter with Carol and his family and also the baby, Marjorie Robin Fraser, in Lillian's care, he wrote to Sidney Cox (January 3, 1937):

. . . Talking is a hydrant in the yard and writing is a faucet upstairs in the house. Opening the first takes all the pressure off the second. My mouth is sealed for the duration of my stay here. . . . I'm not going to explain anything personal any more. I'm not going to explain my children, . . . My children are all good but rather offish with the human race. I myself am rather onish. I refuse to explain the discrepancy. . . .

Why shouldn't Frost feel "onish"? Book Six was to receive the Pulitzer Prize in May, and in June he would be honored by Harvard's Doctorate of Letters. In writing of this to McCord, in February, 1937, he joked about his age.

. . . A little more and I shall be getting self-conscious about my own age. It will spoil my pleasure in everything I say and think if I have to qualify it with a there speaks my seventy or eighty years as the case may be. You are old Father William. . . . . and yet you always are using your head. You ought to be using your heart. I can see now that could be all rhymed up into a poem, but I refrain from senile humility. It is a shame that a noble nature like mine right in the prime of life by Biblical standards should be brought in sorrow to such a standstill. . . .

In midsummer, Elinor and Robert had the adventure of settling into Concord Corners. A new place to live, a new height of country. Two village cultures fading into each other, as he said in "Directive," which seems to have been born out of this region.

> . . . Both of them are lost.
> And if you're lost enough to find yourself
> By now, pull in your ladder road behind you
> And put a sign up CLOSED to all but me.
> Then make yourself at home. The only field
> Now left's no bigger than a harness gall. . . .

This, had they known it, was Elinor's and Rob's last summer together. They did not need a piano, like the couple of "The Investment,"

> Not to sink under being man and wife,
> But get some color and music out of life . . .

In fact they never lost the freshness of their feeling, and a visitor who had brought others with her, and thus some inconvenience to the housewife in the kitchen, overheard this conversation,

He: "Woman, don't lose your head."

She: "How can I help it when you are around?"

One of their mutual concerns at this point was a book called *Recognition of Robert Frost,* edited by Richard Thornton of Holt's, and to be published in 1938. It brought together biographical and critical material which had never been collected, and they were concerned that it should not be "crudely a praise book."

I'm glad you got something from Jack Haines [Frost wrote Thornton on September 17, 1937, from Concord Corners]. I dont want those days at Little Iddens and the Gallows left out of the record. The Lord do so to me and more also if I forget who first called me a poet. Some times the British make me cross, but I have nothing against them that couldn't be settled by a good war now and then, and even in a war, if it should come to that, I should never cease to love them personally. I had nearly a perfect life over there—a romance such as happens to few. I mustn't neglect to emphasize it.

Are you going to have time to let Elinor see the sum total in some form before finality? . . .

For the next winter, 1937–1938, they had chosen Gainesville, Florida. R.F. had been persuaded by Harvard friends to run for the Alumni office of Overseer (the governing board of the university). He would be elected—or not—by Alumni vote in the spring. He called it "trial by ballot," and he had his doubts and reservations, some of which are expressed in a letter to David McCord:

. . . Politics will creep in on me in the most innocent of poems. I suppose we have to have politics if we are going to get the new deil out of office. But I don't see why I can't leave such matters to others as I did for forty years of my voting life. What's come over me that I can't get over?

I'm deeply affected by all these attentions from Harvard. You know I am. But wasn't the height reached last June and aren't we running the risk of spoiling it all . . . ? I'll bet the class I deserted will be against me to a man. And justly. I don't believe in forgiving renegades merely because they get away with it. I have plenty of sentiment about rounding out my educational career in some sort of relationship with my first college. I took my preliminary examinations for admission to Harvard in June or July of 1891. You didn't get that into your advertisement. But this appealing to the mob for sanction is a bit democratic for me. . . .

However, R.F. recalled his father's favorite poem "My Dear and Only Love":

> He either fears his fate too much
> Or his deserts are small,
> That dares not put it to the touch
> To gain or lose it all.

and had resolved to risk it when suddenly again, in the family circle, events took a tragic turn.

All was going as usual in Gainesville, in a new house shared with Lesley and her two youngsters; the elders lived upstairs so that the poet should hear no footsteps. Lillian, Carol, Prescott, and little Robin were in a larger house, nearby. Then Robert contracted influenza and while Elinor was tenderly and anxiously nursing him, as she always had, she herself died suddenly of a heart attack on March 20, 1938. Forty years of profound and extraordinary marriage had come to an end.

Through the illnesses, the poverty, the loss of children, Frost had continued to write, to teach, to read to audiences, with fortitude and courage. But after his wife's death, though never inactive, he was for some time despairing and reckless. He felt sure, at first, that he could not possibly live on. That black chaos which he sees as always close to the confines of man's adventure seemed to threaten him from every side.

"Elinor Frost," he wrote his young friend and collector, Howard G. Schmitt, in June, "is now more in my six books than she is anywhere else on earth."

PART V

I COULD GIVE ALL
TO TIME

1938-1959

CHAPTER 16

I COULD GIVE ALL TO TIME
1938–1941

Frost was sixty-four years old when Elinor died. For several years he knew what he called "wildness" of heart. "I lead a life estranged from myself." But his unhabitual way of perception—one of William James' definitions of genius—helped him to find new feet in the world again, and to make a new path as he went.

Frost in his eighties is a man of boulder strength, whose "age is as a lusty winter." By the time he was seventy-five, in 1949, he did not belong wholly to himself any more, to his family, or to his intimate friends.

He had something to say, and a way of saying it, to which the greater public wanted to listen. Like his country, he was gradually drawn from isolation into participation. The hot war challenged his spiritual and his physical resistance and he was ready for the challenge of cold war, when it came. The galloping changes in scientific discovery fascinated him too (his favorite "literary" journal, he says, is the *Scientific American*), and when you read Frost's poetry of the 1940s you realize that many of these changes of our time he had foretold or hinted at, in the poet's divining way. The ascent toward consciousness, "the most unnatural thing in nature," as Jung has put it, has taken hold of Robert Frost, endowing him with some aspects of the seer.

There are days of autumn rain at Ripton, R.F.'s realest home, when his sorrow emerges from the woods, as in that early poem "My November Guest." "The Wind and the Rain" is a late poem:

> I have been one no dwelling could contain
> When there was rain;
> But I must forth at dusk, my time of day,
> To see to the unburdening of skies.
> Rain was the tears adopted by my eyes
> That have none left to stay.

The private struggle between Frost's Promethean gift and his agonized Puritan conscience still goes on, as it has always done. But somehow the opposites in his nature have fused into mellowness, and he has found means to reconcile the passionate poet-dreamer and the man of action and of earth, and thus to externalize both his poetry and his wisdom. In youth or even middle age he might have feared, as a betrayal of his gifts, not the high critical recognition and true fame he has won but the sheer popularity that has come to him.

In his humanity and commitment to his chosen calling, Frost has also, by example, helped the destiny of all American poets in the Atomic Age. Where else in the world, as Auden has said, is a poet paid handsomely for reading his own works in public? Where else than the United States, in this scientific era, has the poet had such influence as a professor among professors? The answer seems to be "never, since the age of patronage." Frost has much in common, I have always felt, with Justice Oliver Wendell Holmes, who believed that a man of action and passion must live fully in tune with his times.

Frost's Amherst friends, after his wife's death and her sad collegiate funeral, wished in vain that they could *do* something for him. For, compelled by some inner force, in his aloofness and sorrow, he determined to renounce the immediate past that he and Elinor had shared at Amherst. He sold the Sunset Avenue house and simultaneously resigned his professorship. Even as President Stanley King had visited him in Florida during the illness, after his bereavement, that at the time seemed to him mortal, a rift had developed between them. Friends entered the crisis in vain. Frost refused compromise and severed the old and tried collegiate connection for, as it turned out, eleven years. He would not even read his poetry in his favorite college until 1945. A hurt with him could become a wound that must have time to heal.

One of the healing and indeed directive factors in Frost's new fate for the next few years was his election, in May, 1938, as Overseer of Harvard University by a larger Alumni vote than any alumnus, much less an alumnus by courtesy, had ever received. This share in Harvard's governing body was a strong confirmation of the influence and kudos he had acquired through his Norton lectures in 1936. Directly after Elinor Frost's death, in the spring of 1938, he was approached by his former Amherst president, Professor Arthur Stanley Pease, with regard to a unique post in the Harvard Latin department. Frost had had some ideas about it, which he had discussed with Robert Hillyer. But, averse to the burdens of scholarship, Frost shied away. Already two other Harvard friends, Howard Mumford Jones and David McCord, quite independently, were turning over in their minds means to offer a more suitable and creative opening. But the chief point in R.F.'s neglect, if so it was, of the Latin department possibility at the time was that the pivot of his personal life was lost and gone. The desolation of the summer of 1938 and its many empty houses was upon him.

He went to his son's in South Shaftsbury in June, and was able to write Richard Thornton that whatever he did, he did with some interest. When in Boston, he had been to three baseball games with the head of the Plimpton Press, Richard Mayo-Smith.

"I enjoyed my break-up with Amherst college while the somewhat mysterious row lasted. Now I am up here with Carol taking my memories as I must and can."

At The Gully the woodchucks still whistled, but he had loaned the house for the summer to his friend John Holmes and his little family; Holmes was a poet he appreciated and a man he cared for in literary society.

Every single evening, right after supper, Holmes has told me, R.F. would turn up at The Gully like a haunting spirit and burst into talk that lasted into the predawn. And every day, he would challenge Holmes to a game of pitching rocks into tin cans. Holmes still hears the vengeful echo.

By September or sooner, Frost went on to the last desolate house, Concord Corners, and wrote a long letter to David McCord that gives a concrete account of himself.

I feel as if getting away from a pen to a pencil would enable me to write. Sometimes a change of paper helps me get going again. I wonder what that would mean to the psychoanalysts. I would await their answer with composure. The trial would be of them not me. For I know what it means. Browning shows he knows in a passage in Pippa Passes.

You ask where I am. I am where the wind never ceases blowing. . . . That's a characteristic of our hill top: on the stillest day in the summer the air always draws knifelike across us up here. And in the fall it is almost too disturbing a foretaste of winter. No more nakedness mowing in the sun this year for me.

You haven't heard, but the prospects are that in spite of the way you have neglected me this summer, I am coming to live near you in Boston and attend Overseers' meetings when I am not all abroad lecturing the other colleges in Cimerian darkness. I seem to have had the narrowest escape from getting into the Latin department (har.) Pease took the suggestion I made to Robert Hillyer and was all for roping me in as an eleventh hour advertisement of a falling stock. He came to Amherst about it and wrote me a long letter. . . . My vice is that I will keep re-trying everybody and everything. Every little while I have another read at Queen Mab, The Revolt of Islam, Alastor, Prometheus Unbound or Epipsychidion. Personally I have never closed my mind on Franklin D. Grotonanharvard.

I am not going to stay up here in a bath of memories very long —I am damned if I am not for any hay fever. . . .

To show you how restless and reckless I am let me tell you what I paid for a pair of my books the other day to give to a friend to whom I owe almost my life. I thought it would be romantic to pay the market price or the latest auction price. By special favor and with some discount I am getting from a very friendly dealer a copy of the first *North of Boston* out of his bookshop for $150. and a copy of *A Boy's Will* out of his private collection for $100. I could have bought the two books together twenty-five years ago in any English bookstore for exactly one dollar, from my publisher for half that. How many commodities have risen in value from fifty cents to two hundred and fifty dollars in that time? I think it's fun to be so commercial about poetry. Tell it in your funeral oration over me. To hell with living on a sound financial basis or with running a country on a sound financial basis. My adventures with money make it look ridiculous. . . . But don't worry about me: this gallop will level off into the same old trot in a minute.

Glad you are having a book.

Ever yours

Robert

A Witness Tree, the volume of 1942, has a poem, "November"—dated "1938"—desolate and ambiguous as a waning moon, in which somebody is taking farewell of basic stocks of values that seem to be sweeping to waste:

NOVEMBER

We saw leaves go to glory,
Then almost migratory
Go part way down the lane,
And then to end the story
Get beaten down and pasted
In one wild day of rain.

We heard " 'Tis over" roaring.
A year of leaves was wasted.
Oh, we make a boast of storing,
Of saving and of keeping,
But only by ignoring
The waste of moments sleeping,
The waste of pleasure weeping,
By denying and ignoring
The waste of nations warring.

1938

"November" recalls another poem of farewell, "Reluctance,"
in which dead leaves lie also on the ground. But in the poem
of 1912, the speaker hopefully, youthfully, almost romantically bows and accepts the "end of a love or a season," whereas
a cry from age's very vitals rings out in "November":

" 'Tis over"

In a sense, however, a liberating cry, for before the end
of January, 1939, Frost had published his second *Collected
Poems;* received the Gold Medal for Poetry of the National
Institute of Arts and Letters, found an intrepid and accomplished secretary, Mrs. Theodore Morrison, to help him make
order out of his business papers, neglected since his wife's
death; and had moved with her aid to live alone, for the first
time in his life, in a pleasant small apartment, at 88 Mt. Vernon Street, Boston.

Not entirely alone, for he had with him a new companion,
a great black-and-white sheep dog, Gillie, who took the poet
under his watchful charge. Very close by in Louisburg Square
lived that early friend of his poetry, Mark A. De Wolfe Howe,
the last remaining Bostonian to look back to the age of Longfellow. The golden dome of the Boston State House again
shone on Rob Frost's despairs, as in his floundering, lyrical
young manhood. The purple panes of the colonial swellfront
brick houses on Beacon Street, opposite the Common, again
tied him to the men of the Revolution and the Constitution.

The poet did not yet have the senatorial neck that he has acquired in his eighties, but when he walked out, hatless and open-throated, with Gillie behind his right heel, the old ladies and gentlemen of Beacon Hill felt reassured that one of the great New England line had come to them again.

But Frost was not a re-embodiment. If he had said to them (wickedly), as he did to his Cambridge intimates: "Know what the difference is between me and T. S. Eliot? I play euchre. He plays Eucharist. We both play," what would they think?

He didn't especially belong in a dignified flat with no trees or dooryard on Beacon Hill—at least it did not fit R.F. like an easy shoe. But for his renewed ties with the Morrisons he might have found the loneliness unbearable. Mrs. Morrison, as Kathleen Johnston, one of his Bryn Mawr students in the early 1920s, and her husband, Theodore Morrison, Lecturer in English at Harvard University, a man of creative and poetic gifts, after the Norton lectures had opened their house to the older couple and their crowding circle of poetry lovers. Now Frost wanted all his circle to know how much he owed them.

I had a wretched time in Florida [he wrote to Sidney Cox as the winter ended]. One friend, my secretary has taken me in hand to keep me lecturing and talking as of old. But I am very wild at heart sometimes. Not at all confused. Just wild—wild. Couldnt you read it between the lines in my Preface nay and in the lines? All the more reason for your being objective with me. Nothing can save me for any more verse but unscrupulous reality.

The early part of the letter to Sidney Cox, just quoted, deals with the long-lasting personal relationship between them (begun in Cox's early twenties and Frost's late thirties at Plymouth) which has been approached here largely from the literary standpoint. Frost's letters to friends waste no time on "thanks for yours" but, like his conversation, plunge straight to the heart of things. Cox had evidently announced his coming appointment to a full professorship at Dartmouth College. Frost replied:

. . . One more thing to say and then I shall have done with indoctrination forever; the agreement to date from the day of your promotion to fullness. I should think you could afford to be a little easier in the spirit without any risk of losing your invaluable effrontery. Positively that's my last. Lets lay off being personal with each other. Let our object be to be objective. Lets tell each other ideas we have. I have always hoped you might sometime publicly remember me in writing, but I got discouraged with the way you started off on my having sought you at least as much as you sought me. What the hell has that kind of inferiority superiority got to do with two people like us? . . .

There is only you left to be uniquely mental with me mind to mind. Maybe I ask too much too vaguely. . . . What Henry Holt printed was all right. But you could go still higher into the thought realm for my taste. You know if any one knows I talk on some interesting subjects rather freshly. . . .

This needs a footnote. Cox did go further into the thought realm than he had in 1929, in *Robert Frost, Original "Ordinary Man."* One book was discarded, but he left behind him, when he died in 1948, greatly mourned by Dartmouth students, *Swinger of Birches* published posthumously in 1957. It is "uniquely mental" and seems in its cerebral intensity almost to wrestle with the psychic secrets of Frost's poetry, his obiter dicta, and his personality.

The preface referred to in the letter to Sidney Cox was "The Figure a Poem Makes," a significant piece of Frost's thinking in prose about poetry. Dated in the *Collected Poems* of 1939 "Boston, January 11th, 1939," we may guess it to be the first piece of work done on Beacon Hill, and a last-minute contribution to a very distinguished book, the first printing of which was January 29, 1939. William M. Sloane 3d, director now of the Rutgers Press, but then Richard Thornton's successor as manager of Holt's trade department, still glows when

364

he talks of how he elicited the preface from a beloved and sorrowing poet. Frost, for his part, took to this young man, a "literary guy" and lover of the classics, and soon relied on his friendship, judgment, and fine literary taste, which owed something to the Latin classics. When the first collection since 1930—containing, of course, the new book, *A Further Range*—appeared, Sloane sent Frost the following telegram in Latin:

EXEGISTI MONUMENTUM AERE PERENNIUS

This is a near-quotation from Carmen xxx Liber III of the Odes of Horace. Singing audaciously of his own work, Horace wrote: *Exegi monumentum aere perennius*—"I have erected a monument more lasting than bronze."

Sloane, who revered Frost as a Latinist, changed the verb to read *exegisti*—"*you* have erected a monument more lasting than bronze."

Frost was moved by the omen and the faith.

In May, 1939, Robert Frost was offered and accepted for two years a post newly created for him at Harvard, the Ralph Waldo Emerson Fellowship in Poetry. His group of devoted friends, among them Howard Mumford Jones, Archibald Mac-Leish, Robert Hillyer, David McCord, had raised a little over four thousand dollars. To accept the Fellowship, Frost had, by Harvard ruling, to resign from the Board of Overseers. The work started with the fall semester of 1939, shortly after the Nazis entered Poland. It actually continued three academic years, by a grace on the part of the poet, for no more money was available.

But the work was arranged just as he wished—one seminar a week for one semester only, leaving his Southern winter at his command. No formal program was imposed—he could educate by poetry exactly as he chose and had won again the freedoms achieved first at Amherst.

Harvard, however, did not solve his economic problem. He was cumbered also by an oversupply of real estate and other cares. Therefore he was tempted, so he has told me, by the

sudden increased interest shown by collectors in his manuscripts and notebooks. A dubious excitement, it proved, that
fermented his inner "wildness."

"It went to my head for a time."

One collector in particular by "putting Christmas presents
down my chimney," persuaded R.F. to part with items he now
wishes he had kept: notably the only remaining copy of his
first two-copy, self-published book of poems, *Twilight*. The
first copy he had destroyed at a moment when he did not know
"what love was all about" and was repulsed, as he felt, at
Elinor's St. Lawrence University. His plunge South on that
desperate lonely walking trip is picked up again in a recent
poem "Kitty Hawk" which in theme is reminiscent of "Reluctance."

> Kitty Hawk, O Kitty,
> There was once a song,
> Even a rather great
> Emblematic ditty,
> I might well have sung
> When I came here young
> Out and down along
> Past Elizabeth City
> Sixty years ago.
> I was to be sure
> Out of sorts with Fate,
> Wandering to and fro
> In the earth alone,
> You might think too poor-
> Spirited to care
> Who I was or where
> I was being blown
> Down along the coast
> Like a crumpled better-
> Left-unwritten letter
> I to waste had thrown—
> Given up for dead.

One friend of Frost's recalls being asked to do the mailing of the parcel containing *Twilight*, as it lay by the poet's bed, after an operation. The friend refused to do the deed, and rightly. For in 1949 the collector sold his whole Frost collection, after having obligingly offered *Twilight* back to the author for ten thousand dollars.

He did not *promise* not to sell [mused Frost, looking in his habitual whimsical way at both sides of the case]. It was I who lost my head. Why, I must have thrown away twenty thousand dollars in two–three years. Well, not quite. It wasn't all wasted because it went into real estate—the Homer Noble Farm and the house on Brewster Street, Cambridge.

But I was crazy-reckless in that Boston period. I'd walk along Charles Street, and round the Hill at night with Gillie, my Border collie, throwing all the change I had (under a quarter) in my pockets into school yards. If George Washington could shy coins across the Potomac, I figured I could throw my quarters into the Charles River. But now—well, the collectors still come to me but I assure you that one of my favorite freedoms is freedom from what I am in the market.

The unprecedented relationship between poet and dog was noted by friends who joined his walks. The poet never raised his voice in giving orders, just made them a part of his general conversation about something else. "Poetry is—Gillie, you may run," soft and unemphasized as a leaf falling, and Gillie would instantly vanish into the dark; yet return as silently if his name was absently mentioned, in a further definition. If R.F. got into a friend's car, Gillie would jump in the back seat and sit quietly alone. If his master unlocked a home door, after hours of absence, Gillie would not fawn, lick, bark, jump up— he knew better than to make his love overt.

It happened that, in the fall of 1940, when in the Boston region for a few days, I met my old friend by chance on Beacon Hill, with this noble beast at his side. I had not seen him for five years—not since his reading in Santa Fe, not since his wife's death.

He explained at once, in his simple forthright way, that two weeks before, just as he began his second year of Harvard teaching, he had lost his son Carol. By suicide.

"Come over tonight after supper and I will tell you about him and about Elinor. And read you some new poems."

It seemed to be an imperative and I telephoned my friend in the suburbs who would send her son to Mt. Vernon Street to bring me home.

I thought I'd talked Carol out of it [the poet said, as he quietly let me in to his apartment]. I'd made a trip up to see him in South Shaftsbury. He refused to see a psychiatrist. I talked a night through with him. He saw me off on the train, remarking: "You always have the last word." But a couple of days later he shot himself.

Lillian, Carol's wife, whom her father-in-law had always loved as one of his own, was away in hospital for an operation. Carol and his sixteen-year-old boy, Prescott, were alone in the Stone House. When the end suddenly came, the schoolboy became a man; called the neighbors and the police and telephoned his grandfather in Boston.

"Don't know where the boy got it," Frost spoke with warm gratitude and admiration for Prescott's courage. "Must be from his mother."

Whence your own courage, I silently wondered. From your mother, too?

Carol [his father explained] had, all his life, avoided books, as if they were dangerous to him. Parents skeptical of formal education had never pressed him to study. His schooling had truly been negligible. He had not achieved economic independence in maturity, but in the last few years had been writing poetry and sending it to magazines. This might have had some value—his father couldn't tell. One thing was sure—Carol had a romantic, almost Byronic sense of his own destiny as poet, and had felt defeated by editorial refusals.

"God's stress in whatever He's up to is our distress," Frost remarked with oblique stoicism.

"Lord, I believe. Help Thou mine unbelief."

R.F. was reading some of the prophetic books of the Bible —not, he said, for the "poetry" as some did, but to find their meaning. For instance, the Promethean challenge to God's justice in the Book of Job. What was the Creator after when he used Job as he did? What was he after when he allowed Marjorie to die of septicemia in an age of science?

The Book of Micah states it (so Rabbi Reichert, Frost's Cincinnati friend, told me) as Frost felt it and still feels it:

Will the Lord be pleased with thousands of rams *or* with ten thousands of rivers of oil? Shall I give my first-born for my transgression, the fruit of my body *for* the sin of my soul?

He hath shewed thee O man, what *is* good; and what doth the Lord require of thee, but to do justly, and to love mercy, and to walk humbly with thy God?

The impersonality that a poet can eventually bring to his greatest personal tragedies is one of the debts humanity owes to poetry.

Before I left his flat that evening, R.F. "said" for me and then wrote out a new poem, which became his Christmas card poem for 1941. I think he wanted me to know that despite these three deaths in six years, he had come out of chaos into safety. He had given sorrow its tragic due, but was wasting no fiber in nostalgia or useless regret. What was, *was*. He had accepted it. And what the future would hold, he was on the eve of finding out.

I COULD GIVE ALL TO TIME

To Time it never seems that he is brave
To set himself against the peaks of snow
To lay them level with the running wave,
Nor is he overjoyed when they lie low,
But only grave, contemplative and grave.

369

What now is inland shall be ocean isle,
Then eddies playing round a sunken reef
Like the curl at the corner of a smile;
And I could share Time's lack of joy or grief
At such a planetary change of style.

I could give all to Time—except—except
What I myself have held. But why declare
The things forbidden that while the Customs slept
I have crossed to Safety with? For I am There,
And what I would not part with I have kept.

CHAPTER 17

A WORLD TORN LOOSE
WENT BY ME
1940–1950

A world torn loose went by me.
Then the rain stopped and the blowing
And the sun came out to dry me.

The 1940s—his sixties–seventies—though afflicted with war and not devoid of further grave family illness, were for Robert Frost years of bounty and mastery. Continuity in change again showed itself the very basis of his human and poetic life. The dramatic in the man embraced with heart and mind, and with the flow of poetry and a renewal of teaching, his dramatic times: World War II, the Korean War, the dawn— or damnation—of the Atomic Age.

Frost, however, in spite of his curiosity and keen apprehension of the discoveries of modern science, did not accept the domination of science in today's world without contradictory and skeptical feelings that are reflected especially in his later poetry. In reading the lyrics and the masques I am sometimes reminded of the equivocal, daemonic laugh heard by the speaker of his first poem on science, "The Demiurge's Laugh," in *A Boy's Will*.

. A sleepy sound, but mocking half,
As of one who utterly couldn't care. . . .

371

This speaker, says the poem, was hunting "no true god." In corroboration of the doubt still lurking in the poet's heart in the forties I cite a passage from *A Masque of Reason* which R.F. wrote on the flyleaf of a student's book in 1945. God is speaking:

> . . . My forte is truth,
> Or metaphysics, long the world's reproach
> For standing still in one place true forever;
> While science goes self-superseding on.
> Look at how far we've left the current science
> Of Genesis behind. The wisdom there though,
> Is just as good as when I uttered it. . . .

Then he added, below:

> Really Robert Frost's
> though by him ascribed
> To Someone higher up.

The life background, in this new period, was again a Vermont farm and an unassuming Victorian house in a college town.

When, in 1940, Frost acquired first the Homer Noble Farm in Ripton, with its nearly three hundred largely wild, wooded, or deserted acres, its crystal brooks, verdant heights, old cellar holes, three dwelling houses and log cabin; and again in 1941 his half double house in Brewster Street, Cambridge, he was acting out of a conscious experience of his personal needs. Most of all, he needed freedom. Had he been somebody other than R.F., he might have demanded that Lesley give up her life to live with him so that he could fill a house with his grandchildren and his innumerable eager friends.

What he did, being himself, "a man of sovereign parts," blessed with powers of self-renewal, was to live alone on his "Sabine farm" in the rustic log cabin just big enough for one and Gillie; to make his own iron bed and cook many of his own meals; and to follow the same pattern of late night walks, night work, reading or impassioned talking and slow morning rising that he had practiced since his twenties. Wood-cutting and vegetable planting and tending were a natural part of any day at Ripton. And if some idea took hold of the poet as he walked or cut down a tree, there was the solitary, comforting log fire where the lyrical-speculative-meditative muse of later years could be received and entreated with due honor and alacrity.

This detachment would not have been possible, at Robert Frost's age, if his devoted friends the Morrisons had not continued to live, in Cambridge, a few streets away and, in Ripton, where he had found them as "renters" in 1939, in the Homer Noble farmhouse, a green lane and sharply downhill, wild-flower-grown stretch below the log cabin. This farmhouse is an old simple one, with very steep stairs rising from the front door, living rooms on either side of the entry, and a kitchen and pantry wing "out back." The professorial family from Cambridge had two children, young when he settled there. They were forming close connections with Middlebury College and Bread Loaf where Frost's own ties went back to 1920. So there was a happy mingling of interests. Meals, drives, and fine human society were available as well as secretarial and practical help if the poet needed them. But nothing or nobody was "underfoot," and he had no telephone in the cabin.

Indeed, when I first saw him in Ripton—not until 1949—I was struck by the calm with which he was accepting the diastolic-systolic motion of his being, which took him forth into the wider world to read, to teach, to receive an academic honor, or give a radio broadcast, and then as calmly returned him to his Vermont base. In the past, as I had known it, every one of these dates with the world had to be wrestled out and paid for with human agony and even illness. Now, with Mrs. Morrison keeping calendar time for him, the poet—as if it were always afternoon or evening for his work, his thinking— was released into Timelessness.

Frost has always said that to write poetry he must have the sense of leisure, and if in the 1940s he did write and publish

four more small books—bringing the number of them to ten—
A Witness Tree (1942), *A Masque of Reason* (1945), *Steeple Bush* and *A Masque of Mercy* (1947), it was because his new form of life was for that decade centrally dedicated to poetry and protected.

Two of the new books proved that lyric poets do not necessarily die young; while the two masques, major works in intent and full of good things, revealed Frost's continuing experimental interest in the colloquial dramatic-dialogue form and in the Bible as a source book on the subject of man's fate.

But, as Frost has written:

The groundwork of all faith is human woe. . . .

The transformation and transmutation into first the creator, then the exuberant, outgoing figure of the 1950s were not accomplished without inner and outer stress. Since Elinor, Carol, and Marjorie were gone, the welfare of the remaining family brood, though now at a certain remove from R.F.'s daily life was, all the more, the father's and grandfather's care.

Lesley, to be sure, could take care of herself and her girls. Her activities were interesting and varied too. A director for three years in the King-Smith Studio School in Washington she then founded a school of her own there for adult cultural education; and, as the war encroached on private undertakings, became an electric mechanic at the Air Transport Command's Washington airport. Next she worked in the Office of War Information, then was sent by the Cultural Office of the State Department to the Casa Americana, for two years, in Madrid; and on her return in 1948 was sent to Latin America under the same auspices. But the family tie remained close-drawn and she was never out of touch with her father, her children, and her sister Irma, who was divorced and became a chronic invalid in the late 1940s.

Lesley's two spirited daughters, Elinor and Lesley Lee, who shared the Frost heritage of beauty, had had their years of "progressive" schooling at Putney, Vermont, not too remote from Ripton and, in successive years, went on to Radcliffe College—just round the corner from their grandfather's Cambridge home. Elinor, in 1947, after two years of college, married Malcolm Wilber of Fairfield, Connecticut, and had three children before a serious illness in the polio epidemic of 1952, from which she recovered and now has a family of four. Lee, the scholar of the family, after a brilliant record of summer teaching performance in Central America and elsewhere during her undergraduate years, graduated when just under twenty. Following in her mother's footsteps, she worked for the International Cooperative Agency (ICA) in Spain for several years.

Lesley herself married in 1952 Joseph W. Ballantine, then a member of the Foreign Service Studies of the Brookings Institute in Washington, after having been thirty years in the Foreign Service in the Far East, and eight years director of the Far East Division of the State Department as a close associate of Cordell Hull.

Frost himself, taking up his new life in the wartime world, contained the seeds of his own resurrection: soundness of body, youth of heart, clarity and acuteness of mind, and beyond the intellectual that extra something, discovering and mercurial, that keeps the human spirit in motion and evokes the magical utterances of the poet.

Old poets formerly wrote epics. In our time, some of them write novels. But R.F. returned to lyricism. *A Witness Tree*, the poetic first fruits of the new way of life, suggests a breakthrough of heart, mind, senses from some cold prison. As "All Revelation" puts it:

> But the impervious geode
> Was entered, and its inner crust
> Of crystals with a ray cathode
> At every point and facet glowed
> In answer to the mental thrust. . . .

Geode-cathode: word rhymes from the realm of science. A little "obscure" for Robert Frost? Just what he needed for his poem.

The times were similarly going through a molten process, a period of deep national arousing to the implications of the European war, and to the increasing American part in it.

The speaker in "The Lesson for Today" says to the medieval scholar, his auditor and counterpart:

> We can't appraise the time in which we act.
> But for the folly of it, let's pretend
> We know enough to know it for adverse.

The tone of this poem, a twin of "Build Soil" in form, read before the Phi Beta Kappa Society of Harvard University in 1941, is that of an Horatian satire—the accomplished man of the world discussing with familiarity, wit, concern, and a hint of didacticism the questions of the hour.

Frost felt these world-wide troubles threatening to the freedom of Americans. Freedom to him meant Emersonian freedom: sturdy resistance to pressures from mass opinions at home as well as from other nations. Since he was so aware that the war god fights on both sides at once, he was often blamed for his "isolationism," his quips at the British, his dislike of our then allies the Russians, and his supposed tolerance of dictators; all of these attitudes somewhat relative, and skeptical in general.

Van Wyck Brooks has told me that Frost, as our own war came on, with the reminiscent guilt that would come up in him, spoke of his conservatism and skepticism—which surely he possessed inherently—as the only reparation he could offer to Elinor for all that he had made her suffer for poetry. She had been fiercely Republican, sternly armed against the New Deal. Well, he could and did follow the same line of thought [he said] for her sake. This penitential tone seemed later to yield to a certain veering of his mind on Franklin D. Roosevelt. The poet admired, for instance, F.D.R.'s private religious

376

attitude toward the high office of the presidency, and joined him in his belief in war. Frost was never against war, far less so than most Americans, as his students well knew.

The whole objective of Frost's teaching anywhere, and so at Harvard, was to get men—young men, in the latter case—to see a little further than they "just naturally do." Certainly at Harvard, his Ralph Waldo Emerson seminar emphasized enlightenment rather than the acquisition of knowledge. Even at this august university (but that was before the war) Frost had said something like this:

Learning should come in an off-hand, cavalier fashion. An artist, especially, should be able to go right through college with one brain tied behind him. . . .
You need not read all of Wordsworth—or all of Shelley. I just read till it clogs. Of course—if you're going to be a scholar. . . .

In the last year of his Emerson Fellowship, they would sit at Adams House, one evening a week, a large number of predestined soldiers, listening spellbound. Many had enrolled, some came as listeners, nobody went home. The Harvard Corporation has made Robert Frost an Honorary Associate of Adams House, and the house cherishes today a letter from the poet to the then Master, David Mason Little, fearing he had kept the janitor up late.

"Bring in next time," he said to the students, "a 3 x 5 card written on one side only. You are asked to state one thing that interests you—one little idea, however small."

Anything could be the subject of the seminar, even, hilariously, the poet-professor's morning mail.

"*Don't work—worry,*" he dismissed them at the end of the course.

"Best thing ever said to students," commented Professor Perry Miller.

That the Emerson Fellowship money had more than run out seemed to many no reason for Harvard's losing Frost. But

President Conant was reorganizing the curriculum on a war-time basis, giving more weight to science than to humanities. There was talk of another Fellowship, this time in the History of Civilization. For Frost was known to feel that the arts did not stand alone, were part of a nation's enterprises, and had made a permanent record—the only one there was, very often, of a nation's past and its traditions. The soldiers of today, the advocates of this fellowship said, should be reminded of their past to do their best in battle. Frost could inspire them. He accepted the new Fellowship for 1941–1942.

Other friends, especially the poets among them, felt that, as an institution of learning, Harvard was insufficiently aware of Robert Frost's already deeply assured place in American letters. In his own world of poetry, his value was known. But he cared and needed also to teach, and the requests from colleges poured in. So he cut the Cambridge tangle by positive action, and 1943 proved a good year of new adventure.

He was appointed Poet in Residence at Indiana University from March 25 to April 15, and more happened there than teaching. A letter of April 2 from Bloomington to Professor Whicher confesses:

. . . Last night I finished writing the Forty-Third Chapter of Job, *A Masque of Reason*. You may have to listen to it sometime when I have done its companion piece The Whole Bible, *A Masque of Mercy*. Neither may ever see the light. I *will* dabble in drama.

Come In, a book of selections for young people, named for the great poem of 1941 and edited by Louis Untermeyer, was published in April also. Frost received the Pulitzer Prize for *A Witness Tree* in May. In July he was appointed to the George Ticknor Fellowship in the Humanities at Dartmouth College, which President Hopkins, and his special friends like Stearns Morse, Harold Goddard Rugg (who first brought him back to Dartmouth in 1916), Ray Nash, Sidney Cox, and others had urged on him for some time. This would start in October, 1942.

At Dartmouth I dealt largely with GI's [he told me in 1949]. I said:

"You've got to have something to say for yourself if you are going to hold your own with your teachers. Presuppose something to hold—don't drop it at the first word—don't chuck everything you had at home—for instance, God.

"Get up a rigmarole to throw at them—something to laugh them off. See, here's what I use about science:

Let me not to the marriage of true minds
Admit impediments. Love is not love
Which alters when it alteration finds,
Or bends with the remover to remove:
O, no! It is an ever-fixèd mark,
That looks on tempests and is never shaken;
It is the star to every wand'ring bark,
Whose worth's unknown, although his height be taken. . . .

"With that last line (I told 'em) of his famous sonnet Shakespeare divides the world. Science measures height, but can't measure worth. Science will never know.

"Take this other Shakespearean line:

Most friendship is feigning, most loving mere folly:

"Is it true? How true is anybody's love? There is no measure for it. Science will never know."

Then I drew a circle, dividing it in half horizontally.

"Science has half the world—the lower half. All science is domestic science—domesticated on earth. Here I place the practical men, gadgeteers and engineers—here, in the upper right hand corner, pure science, creative science, because curiosity is the highest thing in man. The loveliest part of science is the courage to *know*—for we can't *see* what is the matter.

"It's hard to see forward and almost as hard to see back. But it's necessary to have glimpses, to know what is going on."

379

One of our great freedoms [I heard R.F. say at the New School in 1957] is in abusing each other genially. It may come over me as I walk at night on a lonely road—something quite disagreeable to say to a neighbor—of course in a genial way! The reason you can't have peace lies right there. . . . Every once in so often a Karl Marx or a Jesus Christ—or a Mohammed [he added later] —some man with followers comes along and upsets the whole business. They would level us down to just no emotion. I am all for stand-offs. They develop into showdowns, and the result is bloodshed.

All nations are always on the brink of war.

There it is in all its grandeur.

Frost has told me of "run-ins" he had with Louis Untermeyer on the subject of the dictators. Untermeyer had wanted him actively to propagandize. His answer was that he wasn't interested in heaving his poetry at Hitler from Manhattan! If he did anything, it should be to risk his life. Say, if he were asked by the military to be dropped from a plane over Germany to make a try to kill Hitler, he would do it. War was and must be dangerous. He respected the young men who went forward dauntlessly into danger—like his college students; like his friend Bill Sloane of Holt's who out of personal conviction volunteered in the OWI and was sent to the Pacific.

You know my sentiments [he wrote Sloane on May 21, 1943]; Nobody's war effort counts much that doesnt get him into danger. Port wardens are all very well, but they dont inspire my interest. All the way to Chungking in times like these! I knew you would take risks if you had the chance. Me, what can I do? It would not take any courage for me to write articles against Hitler in this country. It would take some to write articles in his favor. But even for the sake of risking my life on an equality with the soldiers I admire so much, I can hardly bring myself to do that. There is no use in being foolhardy. And anyway we could see Hitler from the first. . . .

Frost himself felt that he best stated his own patriotic convictions in "The Gift Outright." This poem he first read publicly on December 5, 1941—two days before the Japanese attack on Pearl Harbor—to the Phi Beta Kappa Society at William and Mary College; then printed in the *Virginia Quarterly*. It was his poem of the Revolutionary War, his shield and buckler, his pledge to his native land.

Another poem he often read, in his tone of light humor, is also interpreted by some as a war poem:

ONE STEP BACKWARD TAKEN

Not only sands and gravels
Were once more on their travels,
But gulping muddy gallons
Great boulders off their balance
Bumped heads together dully
And started down the gully.
Whole capes caked off in slices.
I felt my standpoint shaken
In the universal crisis.
But with one step backward taken
I saved myself from going.
A world torn loose went by me.
Then the rain stopped and the blowing
And the sun came out to dry me.

The poet spoke to me of the concrete origin of the poem, what set it going in his mind. For, as Picasso has said of his symbolic painting, as Goethe spoke of his poetry to Eckermann, so Frost feels about his poems: every one is a departure from the concrete.

I got the idea [said R.F.] when, from a train window in Arizona, I watched a violent storm in an arroyo. Just as a car drove onto a bridge over this dry river bed an avalanche of water from the height above flooded under it. The car backed off barely one second before the bridge was carried away. . . .

He chuckled and called my attention to the rhymes, especially "dully-gully." He said too that he had first called the poem: "I Felt My Standpoint Shaken." But almost any line would have served as title since there was an abundance of slogans.

The poet-speaker with his subtlety puts up a wonderful bluff there of just describing visually a dramatic escape from a crisis in nature, a terrifying flood that nearly sweeps him away, while all the time he is talking about landslides in thinking.

"Choose Something Like a Star," with its tone of grace and elevation, suggests how a retirement from the contagions of the hour may be achieved. I quote the beginning and the end:

> O Star (the fairest one in sight),
> We grant your loftiness the right
> To some obscurity of cloud—
> It will not do to say of night,
> Since dark is what brings out your light.
> Some mystery becomes the proud.
> But to be wholly taciturn
> In your reserve is not allowed. . . .
> Tell us what elements you blend.
> It gives us strangely little aid,
> But does tell something in the end.
> And steadfast as Keats' Eremite
> Not even stooping from its sphere
> It asks a little of us here.
> It asks of us a certain height,
> So when at times the mob is swayed
> To carry praise or blame too far,
> We may choose something like a star
> To stay our minds on and be staid.

Note that there is a group of speakers, here "we"—perhaps transcendental inheritors of Concord and Emerson who separate themselves from "the mob" and turn to the stars' enduring fires as moral or religious symbol.

Frost is speaking here from the depths of his profoundly religious nature. In a prose Sermon, preached in 1946 on the

First Day of the Feast of the Tabernacles at his friend Rabbi Reichert's Temple in Cincinnati, the poet defines religion as "a straining of the spirit to a wisdom beyond wisdom." This poem, of relatively the same period, implies a similar trust in the "something over us" that sees further than the clashes on the worldly plane in which we humans are involved. Indeed, the use of the word "stay" as Rabbi Reichert commented to me in Ripton, suggests a direct reference to Isaiah, 26-3:

Thou wilt keep *him* in perfect peace *whose* mind *is* stayed on thee; because he trusteth in thee.

"Come In," another famous and enchanting lyric poem of this period, has been read by Professor Whicher in a felicitous essay, "Out for Stars," as a repudiation of the dark lamenting note of modern poets—the poets who followed T. S. Eliot in dealing with the world's despairs.

COME IN

As I came to the edge of the woods,
Thrush music—hark!
Now if it was dusk outside,
Inside it was dark.

Too dark in the woods for a bird
By sleight of wing
To better its perch for the night,
Though it still could sing.

The last of the light of the sun
That had died in the west
Still lived for one song more
In a thrush's breast.

Far in the pillared dark
Thrush music went—
Almost like a call to come in
To the dark and lament.

But no, I was out for stars:
I would not come in.
I meant not even if asked,
And I hadn't been.

Emily Dickinson revealed a similar shiver of apprehension in "What Mystery Pervades a Well":

But Nature is a stranger yet;
The ones that cite her most
Have never passed her haunted house
Nor simplified her ghost.

Whicher described his friend as "a stocky figure, but alert in motion, wearing an old suit and scuffed shoes, freshly laundered soft shirt, open at the throat, his white hair tousled in the wind, his seafarer's blue eyes twinkling." There'd be the vegetable patch to plant, if the cold was out of the ground, with the aid of R.F.'s farmer-caretaker-friend, Stafford Dragon, one of a big family of ballad-singing Vermonters, descended from a French dragoon, whom he had established in "the Iry Dow place," one of his "marginal" farms a mile off through the woods.

With R.F. as he walked, alone or in company, from meadow to wood to "upland pastures, whence as from a shelf hung high up on the slope of the Green Mountains one may look off westward across a narrow strip of Lake Champlain to tumbled Adirondack masses on the rim of the world," was his personal shadow, the responsive, vigilant, intuitive Gillie, who watched over him by closing screen doors tight against disturbing mosquitoes, and was bellman to R.F.'s Yankee contraption that connected him with the dinner hour and the telephone at the Homer Noble farmhouse.

The invention was a clothesline, with a bell, stretched from below up the hill to Frost's log cabin. When the bell pealed, Gillie would give a brisk *wouf;* if Frost did not immediately emerge from cabin or woods, then one more *wouf*. That usually did the trick.

Oscar Williams, poet and anthologist, once told me a story about dog and master's indivisible relationship. Williams is a thin, slight, urban, spectacled man and on a visit to R.F. in the evening, from Bread Loaf, seating himself by invitation at the log-cabin fireside, he felt his shoulders terrifyingly pinned down by Gillie's powerful paws.

> I gasped:
> "Frost—I don't know if I can stand this. I'm afraid of dogs."
> Frost's response was to make a sound—not a word but a sort of grunt, and Gillie slipped down and away into a corner. From then on, he stayed there, watching me.
> That [Williams said] was when I found that Frost had some special faculty with animals—believe me, he *speaks dog*.

Family visitors, including Lesley, Elinor and Lee, Lillian and Prescott, and Marjorie Robin from Montana, came and went during the forties. Some intimate friends like the Whichers—they were the first—James Chapin, Hyde Cox, and for some years Lawrance Thompson of Princeton during this period occupied the fourth house, the so-called "U-Bar" (Euber) place over the ridge, and set up for this companionable purpose. Professor Thompson soon had a growing family, and his fine courtesies and responsive mind and his scholarship, added to the special gifts of the family below in the Homer Noble house, helped to make Frost's farm a place where life glowed and moved about an abiding center.

As the poet wrote in "Too Anxious for Rivers":

> What set us on fire and what set us revolving
> Lucretius the Epicurean might tell us
> 'Twas something we knew all about to begin with
> And needn't have fared into space like his master
> To find 'twas the effort, the essay of love.

The first section of *A Witness Tree* seems to me to be all about love in diverse forms. "The Subverted Flower," a—for

Frost—startling poem about sex in a pair of young Puritans; "The Discovery of the Madeiras"—adult illicit love defeated; "The Quest of the Purple-Fringed," the love of a budding youth for

> . . . the buds in the copse's depth
> That were pale as a ghost.

"The Most of It," the love of the ego-driven seasoned man who "thought he kept the universe alone"—"that's the soul of the poem," Frost said—for nature's unasked, living, sensuous gift:

THE MOST OF IT

> He thought he kept the universe alone;
> For all the voice in answer he could wake
> Was but the mocking echo of his own
> From some tree-hidden cliff across the lake.
> Some morning from the boulder-broken beach
> He would cry out on life, that what it wants
> Is not its own love back in copy speech,
> But counter-love, original response.
> And nothing ever came of what he cried
> Unless it was the embodiment that crashed
> In the cliff's talus on the other side,
> And then in the far distant water splashed,
> But after a time allowed for it to swim,
> Instead of proving human when it neared
> And someone else additional to him,
> As a great buck it powerfully appeared,
> Pushing the crumpled water up ahead,
> And landed pouring like a waterfall,
> And stumbled through the rocks with horny tread,
> And forced the underbrush—and that was all.

This reminds me of an interesting but far less magical poem of Gerard Manley Hopkins, which begins:

> It was a hard thing to undo this knot.
> The rainbow shines but only in the thought
> Of him that looks. . . .

386

and again recalls a passage from Sir William Temple's *Mis-cellanies:*

   . . . 'tis not always beauty gives love but love gives beauty to the object that raises it; and if the possession be strong enough, let it come from what it will, there is always beauty enough in the person that gives it.

There is always beauty enough in Frost to convey it without using the word: as in "The Silken Tent," a sonnet quoted later, which gives us the delicate portrait of a lady who rules and is ruled by the silken strands of protective relationship. We who go to Frost's readings know it well and also its companion piece:

NEVER AGAIN WOULD BIRDS' SONG BE THE SAME

> He would declare and could himself believe
> That the birds there in all the garden round
> From having heard the daylong voice of Eve
> Had added to their own an oversound,
> Her tone of meaning but without the words.
> Admittedly an eloquence so soft
> Could only have had an influence on birds
> When call or laughter carried it aloft.
> Be that as may be, she was in their song.
> Moreover her voice upon their voices crossed
> Had now persisted in the woods so long
> That probably it never would be lost.
> Never again would birds' song be the same.
> And to do that to birds was why she came.

This is not only a poem about the voice of Eve but illustrates Robert Frost's whole theory of his own poetry as based on spoken, overheard tones of meaning. A third in the same group is "Happiness Makes Up in Height for What It Lacks in Length," a lyric written in Florida in 1935 and read first to the Cambridge audience at the Norton Lectures. The one that begins:

Oh, stormy stormy world,
The days you were not swirled
Around with mist and cloud, . . .
Were days so very few
I can but wonder whence
I get the lasting sense
Of so much warmth and light.
If my mistrust is right
It may be altogether
From one day's perfect weather,
When starting clear at dawn,
The day swept clearly on
To finish clear at eve.
I verily believe
My fair impression may
Be all from that one day
No shadow crossed but ours
As through its blazing flowers
We went from house to wood
For change of solitude.

All three of these lyrics have, in relation to womankind, the quality of what Frost calls synecdoche, "skirting the hem of the goddess." What the young squander with reckless prodigality the old reserve and can often but imply and cherish behind "the curtain of the inner soul."

Love poetry [wrote Edward Thomas], like all other lyric poetry, is in sense unintentionally overheard and only in part understood, since it is written not for anyone, far less for the public, but for the understanding spirit that is in the air round about or in the sky or somewhere.

A *Witness Tree* forgets women as it proceeds, and leads on into the mind of the man constantly aware of the age in which he lives; seeking a moment to meditate, as in the exquisite sonnet, "Time Out"; or throwing out skeptical jets of thought from fires inner and outer that burn and consume. Some of these fires are political: as in "An Equalizer" and "A

388

Semi-Revolution"—New Deal ironies, to which might be added an unpublished merry couplet, especially apt in 1959, though made for Frost's liberal friend Mrs. Thomas Lamont in the years between the wars:

> It would take a first class believer
> To take any stock in Geneva.

In *Steeple Bush* (1947), the last of Frost's small volumes, women have all but vanished, except the one who kept her night light burning, and the lady moon, and the young lady birch, a Yankee's "thing of beauty"—a reference to Keats' "Endymion."

That *Steeple Bush* was influenced by the ominous facts of the war, and the aftermath of wars, the common reader will discern, for nature and man are contending, the poet—here modern man—is reaching for the universe as caul, the bomb is exploding, and doubts are raised as to whether, with the darkening of the world, man's humanity or science's destructive side will win. Even the lyrics concern man's discovering but limited intellect. In writing in my copy of the book, R.F. said:

We mustn't stop with saying poetry is the sound of vowels and consonants: it is the sound of sense—meaning.

So we find the ironic

A CASE FOR JEFFERSON

> Harrison loves my country too,
> But wants it all made over new.
> He's Freudian Viennese by night.
> By day he's Marxian Muscovite. . . .
> With him the love of country means
> Blowing it all to smithereens
> And having it all made over new.

and the sardonic

389

> Sarcastic Science she would like to know,
> In her complacent ministry of fear,
> How we propose to get away from here
> When she has made things so we have to go
> Or be wiped out. . . .

"The Planners," "The Broken Drought," "Bursting Rapture," and "U.S. 1946 King's X" all spring from the same set of ideas. The poet who saw further than most Americans in 1946 now in the 1950s reads these to unresentful audiences—listeners at last knowingly in the same boat with him. Though he usually keeps his comments in lighter vein, talking subtly and allusively, he may suddenly, like an Old Testament prophet, give warning that man's spiritual verities and discoveries tend to become tools of careless power. In a poem of the *Steeple Bush* volume, "The Fear of God," he begins menacingly

> If you should rise from Nowhere up to Somewhere,
> From being No one up to being Someone, . . .

and urges this "You" to stay humble, to attribute his success to mercy, and not to use for "apparel" what was meant

> To be the curtain of the inmost soul.

The word soul does not affray Robert Frost and in "To the Right Person," the designedly last poem, under the heading *Editorials,* he confronts us with a deserted, old-fashioned schoolhouse where school isn't keeping any more:

> Unless for penitents who took their seat
> Upon its doorsteps as at mercy's feet
> To make up for a lack of meditation.

The note of penitence or remorse marks the deeper resonance of *A Masque of Reason* and *A Masque of Mercy,* especially the latter. They are complementary works, published in 1945 and 1947. In them Frost returns to the dramatic dialogue form, even to the dialogue between spouses, in this case far more complex and sophisticated spouses than in the farm poems. The debate concerns the problem of good and evil, justice and mercy, opposites in Frost's view, in terms of two familiar Old Testament characters, both sorely and unjustly tried by God: Job and Jonah.

"I can't resist my own cleverness," Frost said at Ripton in 1949, referring to the psychological hail of quips, puns, humor, wit, and paradox by which his characters are, as it were, assailed in the Masques. "Wherever I set my foot there's a smell of brimstone."

This daemonic smell does pervade the dramatic Masques, but the poet also uses them to state the essence of a serious personal philosophy, even belief. Historically the masque form has sought to do just this.

God knew he could trust Job but still refuses, in Frost's *A Masque of Reason,* to clarify the why of it. Still the riddle is somewhat resolved.

God explains to Job's wife:

> . . . Job and I together
> Found out the discipline man needed most
> Was to learn his submission to unreason;
> And that for man's own sake as well as mine,
> So he won't find it hard to take his orders
> From his inferiors in intelligence
> In peace and war—especially in war. . . .

Job's wife says, and we are reminded of "The Trial by Existence":

> Job says there's no such thing as Earth's becoming
> An easier place for man to save his soul in.
> Except as a hard place to save his soul in,
> A trial ground where he can try himself
> And find out whether he is any good,
> It would be meaningless. It might as well
> Be Heaven at once and have it over with.

391

This prompts God to come out with the finality:

> I was just showing off to the Devil, Job,
> As is set forth in chapters One and Two. . . .

God can't exist without evil, or Satan without God. Satan was even a son of God in Job's time, says the Biblical text, and the show-off side of it comes out in Job One and Two in fact, and keeps their rivalry in *A Masque of Reason* in the vein of comedy.

A Masque of Mercy, a very urban piece, intended to annoy the liberal "who talks so Roosevelt and so Freud," is nevertheless on the tragic side and brings us the poet's conviction that God's injustice is only bearable if "mercy-crossed." The chief protagonist, Jonah, had many trials, including that of being swallowed by the whale, before he got around to prophesying, as God had commanded him, the destruction of Nineveh. Then God spared the city for the sake of the women and children, thus giving the first example of mercy in the Old Testament, but letting his prophet down.

The final passages of *A Masque of Mercy*—which the poet says came to him while preaching in Cincinnati—declare that the fear of God is necessary to human beings. Keeper (otherwise known as "My Brother's Keeper," here a bookstore owner or collector) and Paul (the Apostle) are talking:

Keeper   And I can see that the uncertainty
> In which we act is a severity,
> A cruelty, amounting to injustice
> That nothing but God's mercy can assuage. . . .

Paul   Yes, there you have it at the root of things.
> We have to stay afraid deep in our souls
> Our sacrifice, the best we have to offer,
> And not our worst nor second best, our best,
> Our very best, our lives laid down like Jonah's,

392

Our lives laid down in war and peace, may not
Be found acceptable in Heaven's sight.
And that they may be is the only prayer
Worth praying. May my sacrifice
Be found acceptable in Heaven's sight. . . .

Though the Masques are authentic and highly sophisticated
Robert Frost in his seventies, I turn from them with gratitude
to "Directive," in which the poet seems to me to have fulfilled
the aim he expressed to me at the age of fifty: the "undrossing
of himself"; the "purification of his quality."

This poem of great imaginative power fuses the sights and
insights of a lifetime into a whole that can be read as parable
or revelation. It is clear as a dream and dark as a legend.

Since it is too long to quote in full, I must remind you that
you are invited, indeed commanded, to climb alone—not in
a small group of the elect as in "Something Like a Star," but
alone like the human soul—to a height of land described with
startling beauty of figure and image. You are to find a house
that is no more a house, on a farm that is no more a farm,
a place familiar from Frost's earliest lyrics but here enhanced
and elevated. The speaker, a sort of high shepherd or spiritual
guide, points your way with authority.

Your destination and your destiny's
A brook that was the water of the house,
Cold as a spring as yet so near its source,
Too lofty and original to rage.
(We know the valley streams that when aroused
Will leave their tatters hung on barb and thorn.)
I have kept hidden in the instep arch
Of an old cedar at the waterside
A broken drinking goblet like the Grail
Under a spell so the wrong ones can't find it,
So can't get saved, as Saint Mark says they mustn't.
(I stole the goblet from the children's playhouse.)
Here are your waters and your watering place.
Drink and be whole again beyond confusion.

But who are *you*, led to this arcane spring, perhaps Pierian? Some late wandering Arthurian knight? Some Christian disciple, worthy to know truth from parable? Some poet of our time who, in his heart, feels art and religion identical at the deep source of human emotion? The colleges where Frost goes to read and those that he doesn't reach are all debating these points in the classroom. I shall not expound my answer, if I have one, because in a later published selection of his poems, *Aforesaid,* which was distributed as a special gift to the guests at his eightieth-birthday dinner, he wrote into my book: "with special attention to subversive Prerequisites." The preface to the collection is called "Prerequisites" and the poet tells in it some of the troubles of his own with Emerson's poem "Brahma," where as a youth he got stuck for a meaning he did not find for years. It says:

Success in taking figures of speech is as intoxicating as success in making figures of speech. . . . The heart sinks when robbed of the chance to see for itself what a poem is all about. . . . Being taught poems reduces them to the rank of mere information. . . . Approach to the poem must be from afar off, even generations off. . . . The thing is to get among the poems where they hold each other apart in their places as the stars do. . . .

So I have already said too much about "Directive." What he said about it himself happened one summer evening in 1949 when dusk, his time of day, had taken over, and his eyes were sunk in deep sockets, and his fine old hands with the square-tipped fingers, very effective, useful human hands with a delicate tracery of gray-purple veins, held open at page 520 of the *Complete Poems,* the book of 642 pages that is the poet's personal sacrifice to God.

"This is the poem that converted the other group. The one these fellows have taken to build my reputation on. The boys [followers of T. S. Eliot] call it great. They have re-estimated me. This is great and most of the rest, trivia." His voice had those husky-hurried tones, teasing-mourning tones, that require the listener to listen seriously. For Frost is, as he often says, never more serious than when he is fooling.

He laid down the thick green volume on the arm of his morris chair. Then, after a moment, jerked his elbow in that direction, remarking:

There I rest my case.

CHAPTER 18

TRIPLE BRONZE
1950–1959

> Life borders on the joy
> Of joyful things.
> If we grow old, it is not with our age
> But with our youth: the hive too full,
> The soul too mattered with divine content.
> —"A Bucket of Bees" by David McCord

The *Complete Poems,* on which Robert Frost "rested his case" in 1949, introduced a new era in his life, that of real old age and world-wide fame. His eighties have reversed the "retreat" pattern of his youth; he has opened his arms warmly to the increasing mobility and exposure to the public that, in our time, celebrity and fame try to impose.

Climatic diversity and the steady instinctive connection with nature and human nature seem to give R.F. "the life to go on living" with male vigor. When I first knew him his skin was marble-pale. Since he acquired his permanent winter retreat (a couple of modest small houses) in South Miami and his own pines and orange trees, he returns with the mien of a rosy Poseidon; or again of a tanned and wrinkled Greek sage who has long discoursed wisely with fellow philosophers among the columns of an agora.

His multifarious connections, East, West, North, South, with colleges prolong the connection he has with professors, many of them poet-teachers whose work he has followed for years —as Richard Wilbur, Robert Hillyer, Robert Penn Warren, John Holmes. When he starts north in March, he is anticipated in the colleges on the way like a homing bird of fine plumage. Since 1949 he has held the Simpson Fellowship at Amherst— for life, if he wants it that way—and in the fortnight to month of his sojourn spring and fall, offers himself and his metaphoric wisdom to those who need him most. Though he resigned his George Ticknor Fellowship at Dartmouth in 1949, he lectures and reads there twice a year, as if with the old titular connection.

. . . Poetry has been a great concern of school all down the ages. A large part of reading in school always has been and still is poetry; and it is but an extension from the metaphors of poetry out into all thinking, scientific and philosophic. . . . [Frost wrote in an introduction to an anthology of 1957: *The New Poets of England and America.*]

He has greatly cared to share that wider, newer, scientific thinking, which gives perspective on our age. Another of his comments on this subject is: "Science cannot be scientific about poetry, but poetry can be poetical about science. It's bigger, more inclusive."

As to the significance of the humanities, he likes to say, from a platform, as at Columbia University, that in the United States today the universities and colleges "as if they had bad consciences" take the place of the old nobility of Europe, who fostered the artist and the arts. "I owe much to this," he assures audiences that greet him as a sort of American Poet Laureate. This term, however, does not fit a poet who never wrote but one poem ("Wild Grapes") on an assigned subject, and who enjoys writing complex rebel rhymes on his Christmas cards. We must find a more appropriate honorific epithet.

The Resolution of the United States Senate, honoring, in 1950, Frost's seventy-fifth birthday in the national sense, was another affirmation that seems increasingly appropriate. In telling me that Senator Robert A. Taft had something to do with this senatorial recognition, Frost remarked candidly that when he spoke of this to one of Senator Taft's sons, the answer was:

"Well, it couldn't have been because you were a poet!"

The National Academy of Arts and Letters—honoring Frost as a poet—asked him to deliver the Blashfield Address on May 25, 1950: a poem entitled, "How Hard It Is to Keep from Being King When It's in You and in the Situation." Frost used to ponder and find lines for this poem, Walker Hancock, the sculptor, has told me, while in Gloucester sitting for Hancock's strong sculptured head of him. This bronze embodiment, which the poet loves especially, again brings out in him an aspect of the elder statesman which one catches intermittently, as for instance, when he recites "The Gift Outright."

When he accepted the Emerson-Thoreau medal of the American Academy of Arts and Sciences in Cambridge in 1958, Frost named as his list of the "four greatest Americans" —not an artist's choice, but a statesman's: Washington, Jefferson, and Lincoln—with Ralph Waldo Emerson as fourth, a philosopher-poet, also passionately concerned to mold the deeper life and hopes of Americans. Frost's luminous converse with his great audiences today strikes the note of patriotism in no narrow or flag-raising sense.

This attitude of mind, no doubt, had some part in his acceptance of a quasi-political appointment, Consultant in Poetry to the Library of Congress for the year 1958–1959. Frost deliberately approached his official business at the Library in his own character, fitted into no pigeon holes, tore down a few contemporary idols. Further, he read his own poetry to chosen groups which included high-school children, exchanged wisdom with friends of the Supreme Court—especially with Justices Warren, Frankfurter, and Douglas—and even discoursed with congressmen (after all his was The Library of Congress) as to where poetry and politics might fruitfully meet. Even in one year, Robert Frost has left on what might have been taken as a routine honor or sinecure the stamp of his fertile humanity and poetic authority.

In consequence Quincy L. Mumford, Librarian of Congress, in the spring of 1959 appointed Robert Frost Consultant in the Humanities for three years. At the end of his happy acceptance Frost wrote:

"It sets me up mightily that my venture into the capital of my country wasn't for nothing."

Frost's eightieth-birthday dinner was celebrated four years after his seventy-fifth: setting his birth date definitely as March 26, 1874. Two official dinners were given on two successive days: the more public occasion by Holt and Company at the Waldorf in New York; the more intimate one by the professors and poets in Amherst. As one of the few survivors of the fiftieth-birthday dinner, I had the privilege of being among the hundred Amherst guests who, if my arithmetic is correct, numbered ninety-one men and nine women—the latter mostly detached poets and members of R.F.'s family. "Wives" in general could not be included in the intimate quarters of the Lord Jefferey Inn. These figures, I think, illustrate the fact that in spite of Frost's delicate perception in his poetry of woman and her nature, his life-long friendships have as a whole been with men. One of those he loved best, Professor George F. Whicher, had died a few weeks earlier, but his affectionate words were read by Curtis Canfield.

The shrewd, benign, robust hero of the evening, looking happy-sad, as in the drinking songs he admires, sitting at the center of the raised head table between Thornton Wilder and Archibald MacLeish, loomed before us all that night on an eminence where he has since remained constantly in view. But I recall that he stepped quietly down to the floor to "say" his poetry, and that one of his first choices was the rarely read eclogue "West-Running Brook," the long colloquy between husband and wife about the brook where

> . . . the white water rode the black forever,

and

> . . . trust itself to go by contraries
> The way I can with you—and you with me—

That poem brought another woman into the room, at least to the elder guests and her descendants like Lesley, Elinor Wilber, and Prescott: one of the permanently absent, the dear and admired; one who had been the essence of the poetry and shared the sheer daring and brave fighting, the doubts, precariousness and serious setbacks, the narrow margins between success and failure that had preceded the rich and great rewards so shiningly clear this particular evening.

The poet's depth [wrote Frost in the introduction just named] is the lightsome blue depth of the air . . . Maturity will come. We mature. But the point is that it is at best irrelevant. Young poetry is the breath of parted lips. For the spirit to survive, the mouth must find out how to firm and not harden.

That aspect of the poet dominated the reading. But there was more to observe. At the dinner thirty years earlier, I had named Frost a "good Greek out of New England," thinking chiefly of his relation to the evasive Pan. At the eightieth, I found him almost an Athenian, living for prowess, for honor, for renown, playing his part among men by making the most of his gifts, and surpassing others by the mellowness and excellence of his performance. His performance is a complex thing. As Lydia Lyon Roberts, who had charge of the Robert Frost records in the Poetry Room of the Harvard College Library, put it:

"His very simplicity is complex, his clarity is deep."

But surely, I felt, noting the volume of *Complete Poems* held tight under an arm, hugged to him, surely the one closest to him on earth in this banquet room or away from it is the "person" exemplified by his poems. "Frost's poetry is a person," Mark Van Doren says, and I warmly agree. Without this per-

400

son, this double, who is a little more than Robert Frost, who speaks through him, not only to us, but for us, this evening would not so stand apart in memory.

"I note that Robert Frost is now called a 'popular' poet by critics to whom this word is the last word of contempt," writes Van Wyck Brooks in *From A Writer's Notebook.* "It is a fixed idea with them that, as Edwin Muir says, 'The imaginative writer today can be widely popular only by writing falsely' and the fact that a writer appeals to a large number of readers is in itself sufficient to condemn him.

". . . How can we feel that the question of numbers means more or less in our time than it meant fifty or a hundred years ago? As often as not, the best books have been the most popular books."

In fact, Frost's books alone earn him what would be considered a sizable income for a poet. Though his sales are not so large as were Henry Wadsworth Longfellow's, they are approaching the half-million mark. Frost is, I am told on authority, "the most read American poet after James Whitcomb Riley!"

Frost has not sought the radio or the television screen but he has sought to *communicate.* Both the inspired and inborn teacher in him and the inspired and witty conversationalist and aphorist have, in this, helped and governed him more than the poet—who always has his needs of solitude, his doubts of what Frost has called "publicality": a self-made word, which has a different meaning than "publicity." The reader will recall how much the Franconia poet resisted and agonized over the exposures he underwent when he began to read to small literary and collegiate groups, after his return from England in 1915.

In his new, expansive relation to the larger public, Frost has been advised and sustained by the executive vice president of Holt's, A. C. Edwards, who came to the firm shortly before Frost's editor, William M. Sloane 3d, left after World War II to found his own firm, as Harcourt had done before him. In the internal shake-up that ensued, R.F. made Edwards his chosen friend in his chosen firm of Henry Holt and Company, and so it has been in the fourteen years that followed, years that have gradually transformed Robert Frost into a "presence," an elder statesman, a Socratic humane philosopher to millions who do not know his poetry intimately. Edwards, for his part, with Mrs. Morrison's warm support and insight, has fought to see that the expanding public vision of one he regards with veneration as sage and "greatest living poet" should not become distorted, that the poet should not become prey, that poetry should always come first.

Frost unquestionably enjoys being able to parry the most wily onslaught of reporters into privacies he does not wish to share. When asked on the incisive program "Meet the Press" whether he is happy or not, he replied that he didn't know. He got up in the morning, made his bed. . . . Asked on another occasion whether he would define poetry as "escape" he answered hardily:

"No. Poetry is a way of taking life by the throat."

This dramatic statement found a kind of corroboration when Frost, in April, 1958, in his quality as poet who is also a man of action and a cavalier, made a bold personal effort to get his old enemy-friend, Ezra Pound, author of the first review of the English edition of *A Boy's Will*, released from a closely restricted ward of St. Elizabeth's Hospital. There Pound had lived many years awaiting trial for treason for broadcasts made in Italy during World War II; all these prison years writing his *Cantos*, which received the praise and prizes given fine poetry.

This is an excerpt from the "Statement of Robert Frost," made in the United States District Court for the District of Columbia:

I am here to register my admiration for a government that can rouse in conscience to a case like this. Relief seems in sight for many of us besides the Ezra Pound in question and his faithful wife. He has countless admirers the world over who will rejoice in the news that he has hopes of freedom. I append a page or so of what they have been saying lately about him and his predicament. I myself speak as much in the general interest as in his. And I feel authorized to speak very specially for my friends, Archibald MacLeish, Ernest Hemingway and T. S. Eliot. None of us can bear the disgrace of our letting Ezra Pound come to his end where he is. It would leave too woeful a story in American literature. . . . I rest the case on Dr. Overholser's pronouncement that Ezra Pound is not too dangerous to go free in his wife's care, and too insane ever to be tried—a very nice discrimination. . . .

There is probably legal precedent to help toward a solution of the problem. But I should think it would have to be reached more by magnanimity than by logic and it is chiefly on magnanimity I am counting. . . .

There is still a chance for the literary and intellectual public to "meet" Robert Frost, as living man and poet, at the poetry readings given for some years, not only to the many Town and Gown audiences that he says he still prefers to all others, but in the auditoriums of great urban centers like the Young Men's Hebrew Association or The New School in New York City, where hundreds of listeners of many American races and stocks await him eagerly. They are not just straight readings of poetry but have inimitable prose introductions, full of insights that do not lose themselves in the empyrean; insights that have feet, that walk the earth.

R.F. has told me that in the early days he first read the poetry, then made a few laconic remarks that would screen him a little longer from the onset of his hearers.

But things are different now:

I start in anywhere [R.F. said], a relation to history or education or science . . . what a boy may think. It's all a part of my inner web of thought and feeling. I cut off a piece anywhere; cut it but don't tailor it. [Then as an afterthought:] These rigmaroles I say are not tentative but they're not insistent.

You remember what I said in a preface:

"All I would keep for myself is the freedom of my material, the

403

condition of body and mind now and then to summons aptly from the vast chaos of all I have lived through."

Frost is likely to come to New York from Boston on the same day as the reading. He likes train travel, always did, as one of the least known poems in *North of Boston*, "The Generations of Men," tells. The speaker is a young man, making up to a girl cousin near the cellar hole of a vanished ancestral home:

> "We have seen visions—now consult the voices.
> Something I must have learned riding in trains
> When I was young. I used to use the roar
> To set the voices speaking out of it,
> Speaking or singing, and the band-music playing.
> Perhaps you have the art of what I mean. . . .
>
>   . . . I mustn't feel too hurried,
> Or I can't give myself to hear the voices."

Since the poet-speaker can't feel too hurried, he retires alone to his hotel room to rest and think out his program for the evening while taking his tea and raw egg. That's all he'll eat till midnight.

When he emerges on the platform at the appointed hour, his step is confident and alert, and his countenance warms to the packed auditorium. Not an empty seat!

Frost sits down quietly, while his introducer says a few words, but with eyes that sparkle and anticipate an enjoyable, combative evening. He likes animus in the air. Then he rises, stocky, solid, benevolent. Swaying a little to right and left, he reaches the central desk and to gain a minute more temporizes with the lamp, which he rarely uses later, for his recall of his own poetry is almost total. At this moment he exposes some convexity of neck, some bumpiness of chin, and if the auditorium suddenly darkens to spotlight the celebrity, he shakes his head warningly:

"Turn them up, please: I like to see the faces of my audience."

404

This done, aware of the faces (he can tell you later what the woman in the second row thought when he made a certain reference and how often another went out for a glass of water), he starts right in with his prose prelude which, though in simple plain conversational English, has a beauty of sound suggestively like the poetry that will follow—something "more overheard than heard," as Mary Cooley of Michigan said in a poem, that inspires the imagination of his hearers and their inward thoughts. Despite the jokes which may border on hokum or the flights of wit, the words, as in the poems, cut through to the depth of the fateful, the meaningful, and sometimes the fearful in our world of today.

It has been my privilege to attend many of his New York readings of the fifties, making pencil notes in my lap, when I could, that are by no means tape recordings. Here are a few samples I caught on the fly at the Young Men's Hebrew Association (April 11, 1954).

I used to talk so to see if I couldn't get over being scared. . . . Now I just do it as a matter of course.

I thought I'd try to say what the poems are to me. Like quips, little things I've arrived at. Each poem is a surmounting of something in life.

For instance I said in "Birches"

"It's when I'm weary of considerations, . . ."

What I try to give is the sound of meaning, as you get it when people are talking in the next room (through the intonation of their voices). You don't hear what they are saying but you get their meaning—a quarrel or something happy. . . . You must have the words, too, in poetry, but it has to go deeper than the words.

A line—is a triumph over something that bothered me.

A poem is a momentary stay against confusion.

But what about this confusion they talk about? I say I'm not confused, I'm just well mixed.

Then he talked about the opposites—their value to us.

405

Someone said to me once, years ago: "I hope you have a soul above buttons." That means that the material and the spiritual are opposites.

Take freedom and equality—they are as opposed as spirit and matter.

Freedom means justice. Equality means mercy. It's unmerciful to be as strong as we can. A judge has to be juster than an executive. [And then the Emersonian in him]:

As to the conflicts of our age, I *am* the conflicts, I *contain* them but the society I've grown into takes care of most of it.

"Now what shall I say to you?" he asked with ruse, and started right in with "Never Again Would Birds' Song Be the Same." He read it twice, to assure that his hearers understood what he meant by

Her tone of meaning but without the words.

He was reading to a world that had not lived up to anyone's hopes, where suffering and war and pessimism are oppressive, and the young, in New York, are wary and skeptical.

"Turn your head and look at the audience," whispered Joe Blumenthal. I saw a sea of faces all eyes bright and burning with one thought:

"This is just for me!"

"That's the way I feel myself!"

On another occasion (New School, December 3, 1957) R.F. said in his prelude, after a quip or two:

Randall Jarrell thinks poets aren't helped enough. But I say poetry has always lived on a good deal of neglect.

The seven cities claimed Homer dead. Homer in his life was probably eating under the table.

[Then he dropped his bantering tone]:

Self help. Helping each other. The issue is drawn between them. *Nearly all my poetry has something to do with that.*

People say Mr. Frost holds that life is cellular. I don't "hold."

It just *is* cellular, that's all. Everything has a skin. Here is a poem about that. It's a pendant to "A Drumlin Woodchuck," and has a Horatian title.

TRIPLE BRONZE

The Infinite's being so wide
Is the reason the Powers provide
For inner defense my hide.
For next defense outside

I make myself this time
Of wood or granite or lime
A wall too hard for crime
Either to breach or climb.

Then a number of us agree
On a national boundary.
And that defense makes three
Between too much and me.

See? You can't be anything but a nationalist.

Then he read "Closed for Good," which he pointed out raised the same question of people "being together and not together." It describes a road now left only to him, where men of the past have walked.

This poem has six stanzas in Frost's *Complete Poems*. In 1958 the poet told me he was trying out a new version of four stanzas and changing one word.* Though he reads the poem both ways, I salute the new:

And come not back with steed
And chariot to chide
My slowness with their speed
And scare me to one side.
They have found other scenes
For haste and other means.

* *Note:* "spread" is the new word, instead of "shape."

407

They leave the road to me
To walk in saying naught
Perhaps but to a tree
Inaudibly in thought,
"From you the road receives
A priming coat of leaves.

"And soon for lack of sun
The prospects are in white
It will be further done,
But with a coat so light
The spread of leaves will show
Beneath the brush of snow."

And so on into winter
Till even I have ceased
To come as foot printer,
And only some slight beast
So mousy or so foxy
Shall print there as my proxy.

My favorite moment in all the seasons is shown in this poem:
when you can see the shape of leaves under snow.

Mousy, foxy, proxy—lucky strikes.

In 1956 in New York R.F. read on consecutive days at the
Metropolitan Museum, the Y.M.H.A., and New York University where he received a medal. He had chosen a common
subject:

I reached a point lately where I could finally divide life into
three parts, the three greatest things in human thought: Religion,
Science, Gossip. At the top, the exaltation part, they are close
together.

Religion, belief, the great God question. It's always had philosophy right there, rationalizing it, pruning its shape, purifying it.
No woman has ever made a great name in philosophy; that's
against it. (They are on the belief side. They could not waste

408

their time on it.) The top of religion is pure sainthood; the top is where you get crucified.

He did not refer to his *Masques* or to Eliot's *The Cocktail Party* but he must have had them in mind. Man is the indispensable means of God's becoming in all three.

Science . . . first for glory not for use. The top is discovery for discovery's sake.

Gossip. I venture to say that the greatest of the three is Gossip. It may be defined as our guessing at each other in journalism, novels, poetry in that order. Gossip exalts in poetry. Poetry is the top of our guessing at each other. We are shy of the word glory. That is due to the modesty of soldiers. The beauty of gossip is that it is the whole of our daily life. It has flashes of insight. The height of imagination is there.

Frost is more and more concerned with the conflict of spirit and matter in our nuclear age.

He told me once at Ripton how he ran head on into this topic in Brazil, when sent there to represent the State Department in the summer of 1954.

I was constantly being blamed for our American materialism, our leading the whole world down the road of materialism. Finally I got annoyed about it. So I made a joke of it, and said we were worried, too. We had scales in all our bathrooms. But [he said slyly]

It takes all kinds of in and out door schooling
To get adapted to my kind of fooling.

Think . . . ours is a Christian adventure into materialism . . . the first time it's been tried. In Brazil they are trying Marxism with Christianity. There's danger of communism winning.

He did not care much for this trip, but kept on wrestling with the spirit-matter question. At the Poetry Society, when presented with a medal in 1958, R.F. talked to this theme, as reported by Jack Hagstrom.

We have to duff into the material at the risk of the spirit. . . .
Our religion, our country, God himself by descending into the
flesh showed this duffing into the material. . . . Poetry is the
preservation of the spirit in the material.

When I read that sentence to Harriet Whicher, her comment was:

"In the Christian church that definition would be an accurate description of a sacrament."

At the Y.M.H.A. in the same year Robert Frost's subject was
"Into the Material."

My great complaint of education is that it is so loaded with
material you never move in the spirit again. You've got to
get into it but no more than you can swing and sing.

When I get to the next world they'll ask me: "Did you live
modern?" I'll answer "a little" and go on to say: I flew a little,
went on TV a little and then someone will ask me "Did you smoke
the right cigarette?" and I'll say I don't know about that.

Misery loves company and if we go together, it'll be a grand
affair. We'd say to each other after we got there:

"Wasn't that somep'n?"

It was comments of this sort that took our Yankee poet so
deeply into English hearts when he was there to receive honorary degrees from Oxford and Cambridge in the summer of
1957—degrees never since Lowell and Longfellow given to
one person. The English have always loved their Americans
free, unsubservient, and vernacular-spoken. The public lecture
Robert Frost gave in Cambridge, at the invitation of Mr. Basil
Willey of Pembroke College, about a month before the honorary degree ceremony, created a lasting impression on all who
met and heard him. He held a vast audience spellbound just
talking about how he wrote his poetry, and recited a number
of his poems.

I'd rather receive an honorary degree from your University
than be educated here. Writing free verse is like playing tennis

without a net. It's like this [counting the fingers of one hand] one, two, three, four, five. And then you play a tune on top of that, see?

This (Mr. Willey said) was translated in the Cambridge press:

"Mr. Frost discussed the manner in which speech rhythms could be super-imposed contrapuntally upon a basic metrical pattern."

According to the press and to private information, the English young folks called for more and more, as they do in New York. At the degree ceremony in June there were no speeches, but Robert Frost exceeded in interest the Archbishop of York.

The Public Orator, in presenting him inserted into his Latin speech:

Ubi boni limites, ibi boni vicini.
["Good fences make good neighbors."]

When all the ceremonial doings were over [Mr. Willey wrote to Jack Hagstrom], and the Vice Chancellor's luncheon, Mr. Frost said with obvious relief to the Cambridge professor who had invited him to lecture:

Well, the war's over.

Are you over-tired?

I shall be all right once I get back to Vermont.

During a visit to Ripton in 1957, R.F. told me how he had split up the approximately 300 acres of the several farms he had bought and put together in 1940. He had (futuristically) divided 200 acres with the Morrisons, giving them also the Homer Noble farmhouse. His friend and caretaker, Stafford Dragon, would receive his house and farm, in lieu of later pension. The Euber place he had already sold to the Donald Gordons of Miami, parents of the wife of his only grandson, Prescott, of whom his grandfather is so proud. This brilliant naval architect, in whom the family genius has taken a scientific direction, took his A.B. degree at Miami University and married a Miami girl. The Gordons, who are teachers, have taken care, in his long yearly absences in the North, of Robert Frost's Florida pine land and now live next door to him on a piece of it he has given them.

Next him also, among the pines and fruit trees, the Ballantines have built a beautiful modern house, big enough to include for holidays their branch of the Frost family, the Wilbers from Connecticut with their four children, and, of course, Lesley Lee Francis, the scholar of the family. Joe Ballantine, after many years in the United States Foreign Service, teaches at the University of Miami. Lee took her M.A. and received her Phi Beta Kappa key at the University of Miami in 1958. She reminds her grandfather of his daughter Marjorie, writes poetry and consults him, as Marjorie did. Lee flew from the American Embassy in Spain to England to be with Robert Frost in his 1957 summer, so adorned with honors and degrees.

Thus the clan of the Titan grows, holds together and comes together summer and winter. Since all four of Robert Frost's children married and had children of their own, he now, at eighty-five, has six grandchildren and eleven great-grandchildren. The poet refers to great-grandchildren as "my distant relatives"—not just humorously either. For, as he told a French professor who wrote of him in a Paris newspaper in 1957, he had played so much with children and grandchildren and sat beside so many sickbeds that he could no longer bear to witness the sufferings of little children.

I doubt if the "greats" realize this, for he does so much to contribute to their play. At the Vermont farm I noted one little "spitting image" (male, with blue-blue eyes and familiar features) riding in a pony cart and coddling a burro in the Ripton lane. Another descendent (female, about two) made a bold attempt to climb to an indifferent knee, firmly rooted under a tree, and when successful, beamed to all:

"Now I belong."

Robin Fraser, the handsome, tall, dark granddaughter from Billings, Montana, Frost's daughter Marjorie's child, who had been such a concern to her grandmother—she is now Mrs.

David Hudnut, with a baby of her own—completed her education at Smith College, near Amherst and not too far from Ripton. Her grandfather gave her Commencement address. R.F. has told me about the conversation they had when Robin was considering her future.

"Grandfather," said Robin, "I'd like to do good."

"I'd rather do well, if I were you."

"I'd like to do good well," she retorted, as neatly as he might have done. His comment to me was:

"There are two groups: those who do good and those who do well. The second are the artists."

This set me thinking of R.F.'s statement that in most of his poetry the issue was drawn between self-help and helping each other. Many, many poems come to the mind of the lover of Frost's poetry in this connection; they would make a small book in and by themselves. He cited one in particular, "The Lost Follower."

The speaker is a philosophic observer-adviser of a bride and groom. One stanza runs:

> The muse mourns one who went to his retreat
> Long since in some abysmal city street,
> The bride who shared the crust he broke to eat
> As grave as he about the world's defeat. . . .

The speaker tells the couple, in beautiful and famous lines, that the millennium to which they bend is not involved with politics:

> But right beside you book-like on a shelf,
> Or even better god-like in yourself. . . .

R.F. was writing, he told me

. . . about a couple I knew in the thirties and others like them. Nobody leaves poetry for money; the anti-lure has been the wish to help humanity by social settlements and social change. Some of those youngsters who went overboard for Russia in the thirties were lost poets. I think I showed my sympathy for them here. But when I published "Provide, Provide" my good friends Wilbur Cross and Helen MacAfee of the *Yale Review* were worried:

"Don't throw cold water on the young!" they warned me.

On the contrary, one of Frost's joys of later years has been his growing connection with the really young of the United States, through the teaching of his poetry in the junior high schools and high schools. Even in the Girl Scout camps (where poetry isn't "sissy") the paper "Pocket Book" edition of Frost's poetry, first designed for the Armed Forces, lies about and gets dog-eared as the children choose their favorites, beyond the Frost selections they have come to know in their school textbooks.

A great deal of water has flowed under the bridge since Oliver Wendell Holmes, in 1883, wrote the following letter to the pupils of one of my aunts. It begins in good Victorian fashion, "My dear Young Friends":

I am told that some of you intend doing me the honor of hanging my portrait with those of my friends living and dead with whose names it is a pride and a pleasure to find my own associated.

I think also you are to read something from my writings on the occasion. I hope you will choose such of them as will be most creditable to me, for there is a good deal of difference, and you must not forget that many were written when I was a very young man, and had a good deal of the boy left in me. If any of my earlier poems amuse you, I am glad they can do it, but I hope some of the later and more serious ones, like "The Chambered Nautilus" and "Sun and Shadow" may leave a lesson after them which may be of use to some of you.

When Robert Frost, in his guise as New England autocrat, speaks to eighth-grade urban or suburban children—not in a handwritten letter but from first-rate recordings, in his own voice, of his poetry that go straight and aptly to their ears, and from television films that reveal to their eyes a magnificent old grandfather bard in person, he is not imparting moral lessons but realizations of how the world and poetry are to be taken in 1959.

One teacher told me that Frost's greatest contribution was in the knowledge of country things, sadly fading from the experience of our urban civilization, barely glimpsed by the luckier of the young during summer motor trips to New England. Leaves and trees, wild flowers, woodchucks, deer, bears, ants, wasps, stars, he makes them all important and vibrant in lives with no vistas but of concrete city canyons.

Another teacher, of the generation familiar with the complex college exegesis of poetry that Frost, ironically enough, has banned and even derided in his own college teaching, tells me that the urban child learns something significant about poetic form and symbolic meaning from studying Frost's poetry.

For instance, at a noted "pilot" junior high school on Manhattan's upper West Side, social studies and English are "integrated" in the eighth term in a course called "American Heritage," in which Robert Frost and his old urban crony, Carl Sandburg, are taught as contemporary American poets. The children—their teacher, Mrs. Frances Lyman says—buy the Pocket Books, listen to the records, and learn from "The Road Not Taken" that it needs courage to be an artist; and from "Mending Wall" that they must think beyond the stone walls of New Hampshire to walls in themselves and in the world, which in our day are breaking and re-forming.

Sometimes one finds a teacher in the heart of Manhattan who is himself a poet and inspires the children in secret ways. One, a friend of mine, Michel Farano, has told me about a period of practice-teaching in a slum area of the lower East Side, where he was permitted to read a selected list of Robert Frost's poems to seventh-grade children of polyglot origins. Among them was a slim sage little Chinese boy who came from a family partially supported by public welfare but with

415

an old father who had told his children that paints and brushes and books were more important than food.

The children had no texts—this was some years ago—but were good listeners and able, after several readings by the teacher, to commit "Stopping by Woods" to memory. Then Ferrano tried them out with another brief lyric, quoted first in Part III of this book:

DUST OF SNOW

The way a crow
Shook down on me
The dust of snow
From a hemlock tree

Has given my heart
A change of mood
And saved some part
Of a day I had rued.

"When I asked Jimmy Y. to give his reactions to 'Dust of Snow,'" Ferrano said, "my Chinese pupil remarked on the elements of opposition, called it 'a poem in blacks and whites —the black crow, the white snow,' which he said might be 'yes' and 'no' in this poem.

"He connected it with another poem I'd read in class, 'Tree at My Window,' calling attention to the 'inner weather' in that poem and the 'outer weather' expressed in 'Dust of Snow.'

"I asked him what he thought the most important word in this lyric.

"'Heart,' said the young philosopher, 'because with that word the poet tells how a little thing like fallen snow changes the poet's mood from a sad one to a glad one.'

"Why do you like Robert Frost's poems, Jimmy?

"'Because Mr. Frost, he's got balance,'" said the wise child.

It is not only children, however, who sense this quality in Robert Frost. The same point was made to me, in her special sophisticated tongue, by Marianne Moore, her thin face flashing wit, wisdom, conversational complexity, and kindness under a black felt tricorne that reminds me of the wide shiny-black sailor hat she wore in the twenties, when editor of the *Dial Magazine*. She had been sitting beside Frost on a sofa at the Blumenthals' flat in Chelsea, for a moment of human respite and gossip after one of R.F.'s New York readings. I had seen that they were favorite friends. Indeed this had been noted long before, as they sat together, like a pair of legitimate elderly monarchs, at a Poetry Society dinner, guarding undying values.

But now Miss Moore and I were in an elevator at one or two in the morning, and I said:

"I have just read in a critical book that Robert has not fulfilled his early promise in his later poetry. Do you agree?"

"No! It isn't true," she retorted vigorously, and spoke of her admiration of Frost's "pithy use of counterpoint. His verbal and psychic complementary juxtaposings."

"I'll write you," she said as we went in opposite directions, "how consistently this skill persists in his later poetry."

When the letter came, it explained that her examples were drawn from the poetry of the thirties because the later poems, those that have in some cases been sent out as Christmas cards and will help to make the new book we are promised some time, which may be called *The Great Misgiving*, were not at hand.

Robert Frost's "continuity" in spirit and performance [she wrote] is a thing for which to give thanks in our unending battle with materiality. His "complementarity" has a vigor that never wears thin; the verse, a dexterity that never seems forced—that never loses its craftly fascination:

(A Lone Striker—1934)

He knew another place, a wood,
And in it, tall as trees, were cliffs;
And if he stood on one of these,
'Twould be among the tops of trees, . . .

His e's and be's and he's and trees do more than keep out of one another's way; they say something. His consonants and rhymes [she wrote,] do more than chime neatly:

(Two Tramps in Mud Time—1936)

But yield who will to their separation,
My object in living is to unite
My avocation and my vocation
As my two eyes make one in sight. . . .

The letter had a postscript which cast a light on earlier contacts.

In 1934 or 5 after he had read at the Brooklyn Academy, I thanked him. He had a heavy cold, was being solicitously and rapidly conducted along the corridor from the offices to an elevator, implored not to delay on any pretext. He insisted on stopping, however, and said, "I want to say something" and asked me if anything of mine had been printed as a book. I said no. He said, "Well, I am going to do something about it." I said, "O but I must explain; I *am* going to have a book. Macmillan and Faber & Faber—at the same time—say they would like to issue for me a book of Selected Poems. So you mustn't do anything about me." "O well then," he said (and in a very unhurried manner as he turned away with his guide) "that's all right."

CHAPTER 19

THERE I ELECTED TO DEMUR
1959

Few poets of our time have given so many cogent prose definitions of what a poem *is,* as Robert Frost. One of the best discourses on how a poem is made is given in the introduction to the *Collected Poems* of 1939, repeated in the *Complete Poems.* It boils down to words like this:

. . . The figure a poem makes. It begins in delight and ends in wisdom. The figure is the same as for love. . . . Its most precious quality will remain its having run itself and carried away the poet with it. . . .

The mystery of the act of creation, the stroke of the divine fire remains unexplained. The carrying away of the poet by what is conventionally called "inspiration," instead of his painfully seeking it, is surely an important point. For the prophets and seers of myth and history often went into the wilderness deliberately to find the burning revelations that the poet also relies on. In Frost's "An Unstamped Letter in Our Rural Letter Box," a dual individual, the everyman of our time, described as a "tramp astrologer," just happens to be wandering under the stars near an occupied farmhouse in "a suite of spruce glades" and is tempted to trespass for the night:

> There I elected to demur
> Beneath a low-slung juniper
> That like a blanket to my chin
> Kept some dew out and some heat in,
> Yet left me freely face to face
> All night with universal space.
> It may have been at two o'clock
> That under me a point of rock
> Developed in the grass and fern,
> And as I woke afraid to turn
> Or so much as uncross my feet, . . .
> The largest firedrop ever formed
> From two stars' having coalesced
> Went streaking molten down the west. . . .

That is the outer vision. Then the equivalent happened:

> Only within. Inside the brain
> Two memories that long had lain,
> Now quivered toward each other, lipped
> Together, and together slipped;
> And for a moment all was plain
> That men have thought about in vain. . . .

William James, I recall, describes a similar illumination on one of his mountain trips; and I know very well another camper who, sleeping out under the brilliant New Mexico stars on a riding trip in the Jemez Mountains, experienced for one second the wisdom of the ages. But the tramp astrologer of the poem, no more a mystic than Frost himself, takes pains to let the farmer whose sleep was disturbed by the barking of his dog know—through the "Letter"—that he claims no uniqueness for his star-brain revelation of balance: the farmer, in his own way, might have experienced something similar.

Granting that Frost's major poetry, poetry spoken by a man, to an auditor, you or me, comes from the center where opposites meet and often, paradoxically, says both yes and no,

420

he has also been impelled to pull these conflicting elements apart, live them apart in a poem. As in one voice and mood, he has lived his sense of the portentous in the human fate in "Once by the Pacific"; and in another his burning earth affirmations in "Birches" or "Putting in the Seed"; or his cosmic courage in "Riders" and "I Will Sing You One-O." The *Complete Poems* offer abundant examples and many subtle skeptical nuances of negation and affirmation, tragedy and comedy. But if the reader inclines to arithmetic, he can surely prove that in this poet, drawing strength and sturdiness from the positives of the nineteenth century and profoundly aware of the explosives of the twentieth, the positives prevail. He can walk to the very edge of an abyss, stare into it, quietly and unobtrusively realize its psycho-pathological and scientific horrors to a point beyond despair, and with courage or humor retire to his meditative aphorisms: all in a few fine lines.

An example of his integrity in balancing the opposites is—so I feel—shown in his discrimination and separation of the male and female elements which, so the psychologists say, work together or in opposition in the psyche. Frost knows these voices in life as well. When he feels like it, as notably in some of his eclogues, he lets each sex speak so true that there is no confusing the identity or the accent. William Dean Howells, long ago, noticed how perceptive and forgiving he was about women.

Can you point to any other poet who in his sympathy or empathy permits a frantic, stricken woman to speak as Amy does in "Home Burial" to her unnamed spouse (unnamed because to her he is just Man, Man Unregenerate)? Not to beguile, please, or even convince, but from outraged mother-loss, from a flagrant woman-truth that the average male flees in terror. Not Amy's husband, however; he is man enough to listen, to plead, to draw his wife by his steady voice, his reasonable mind, aided by a heart buried out of her sight, to the center where one and one make one.

In "The Death of the Hired Man," by contrast, the issue is in Mary's hands. Her voice so gently enforces her compassionate insight that Warren, her husband, impatient and un-realizing, is persuaded to her view that the least of the farmer's human world needs acceptance on his own terms. But it is too late—Silas, the unwanted, has died by the stove, as they talked their dear intimacy together.

The half-cracked, wily, "crone" tone of "Mother" in "The Witch of Coös," responded to subserviently by her captive "Son," is creepy to blood-curdling, especially as Frost reads it. Possibly only an elderly New Englander who in childhood, up near the White Mountains, has known "crones" and their button boxes, and spied under their attic eaves a some hundred-year-old adult-sized cradle for rocking the feeble of mind, can fully savor the power of the compounded essences, voices, and visual images of this Puritan murder-ghost story of vital female evil. The witch was no ghost herself.

But Frost has also spoken one-sidedly from the maleness of men. In some of the epigrams, in the New Deal ironies which drive at the pretenses of the "do-gooders," above all in "Build Soil" and "The Lesson for Today," where two philosophic wise-heads talk of their times, it is as if there were no women in the world. In the Masques too, men (from God down) so prevail that women grow sharp-voiced in trying to be heard. "God will be God," warned the young minister, "whether you like it or not," and somehow that is the tone of the *Masques*.

Frost's early and indeed his middle-aged love poetry talks from the center where the fact of married love is "the sweetest dream." In love at sixteen, married at twenty-one, he did not begin, like Shakespeare, saying,

> Who is Silvia? What is she?
> That all our swains commend her?

It was later, during his twenty years alone, that the influence which is in the wood and the air and the birds' song brought the poetry into the more universal chorus of men's voices.

Robert Frost has said, over and over, that in his poetry he did not aim to keep to any particular speech, unliterary, vernacular, or slang.

What I have been after from the first, consciously and unconsciously [I repeat from one of his comments of 1925] is tones of voice. I've wanted to write down certain brute throat noises so that no one could miss them in my sentences. I have been guilty of speaking of sentences as a mere notation for indicating them, I have counted on doubling the meaning of my sentences with them. They have been my observation and my subject matter.

"Mowing," he told me in 1925, was the first "talk-song" which he was aware of having made; and this led in the direction of the New Hampshire material. In October, 1958, in accepting the honor of the Emerson-Thoreau medal of the American Academy of Arts and Sciences, Frost, who rarely discusses his "sources," gave a valuable suggestion of when and where he was early struck by such voice tones.

Since he recast his informal conversation with friends into one of his admirable prose essays, published in the October, 1959, issue of *Daedalus* (the Journal of the American Academy of Arts and Sciences), I am privileged to quote something final:

Some of my first thinking about my own language was certainly Emersonian. "Cut these sentences and they bleed," he says. I am not submissive enough to want to be a follower, but he had me there. I never got over that. He came pretty near making me an anti-vocabularian with the passage in "Monadnock" about our ancient speech. He blended praise and dispraise of the country people of New Hampshire. As an abolitionist he was against their politics. Forty per cent of them were states-rights Democrats in sympathy with the South. They were really pretty bad, my own relatives included.

> The God who made New Hampshire
> Taunted the lofty land
> With little men;—

And if I may be further reminiscent parenthetically, my friend Amy Lowell hadn't much use for them either. "I have left New Hampshire," she told me. Why in the world? She couldn't stand the people. What's the matter with the people? "Read your own books and find out." They really differ from other New Englanders, or did in the days of Franklin Pierce.

But now to return to the speech that was his admiration and mine in a burst of poetry in "Monadnock":

> Yet wouldst thou learn our ancient speech
> These the masters that can teach.
> Fourscore or a hundred words
> All their vocal muse affords.
> Yet they turn them in a fashion
> Past the statesman's art and passion.
> Rude poets of the tavern hearth
> Squandering your unquoted mirth,
> That keeps the ground and never soars,
> While Jake retorts and Reuben roars.
> Scoff of yeoman, strong and stark,
> Goes like bullet to the mark,
> And the solid curse and jeer
> Never balk the waiting ear.

In his informal talk, as reported to me, R.F. paused at the end of his quotation from "Monadnock" and said:

Well, now that had more influence in my life than you'd think —just that kind of talk about it. . . .

And I run into people who say: Of course you don't mean, the great Emerson you speak of, you don't mean him as a poet? And that's just what I do mean. . . . Cut these sentences and they bleed. . . . There's a way of saying every sentence that's different, though the sentences all look short and about the same. You see, they're alive to the ear, and that had something to do with my career. . . .

"Rob was always interested in queer characters, he always wanted to stop and *listen,* when we walked," one of the companions of his early Lawrence youth said to me. The truth is Frost was born with an ear—the best gift a poet can have—that might be said to have the musician's "absolute pitch" in another realm than music. Later Rob said that he had liked people for their voice tones before he liked them for themselves. And hasn't he done more listening than most poets to the "voices of nature"? I am not thinking only of the animal voices, like the fascinating "little whistle" of the drumlin woodchuck. Take just the sound of leaves—you get it in poem after poem. Green leaves, as in "Tree at My Window":

> Not all your light tongues talking aloud
> Could be profound.

Dry leaves as in "Reluctance" and "Bereft" ("creeping and scraping," "hissing and striking").

"They spoke to the fugitive in my heart as if it were leaf to leaf," he wrote in "The Leaf Treader" and the same idea is expressed in "The Sound of the Trees":

> I shall make the reckless choice
> Some day when they are in voice
> And tossing so as to scare
> The white clouds over them on.
> I shall have less to say,
> But I shall be gone.

When Ezra Pound wrote that first review of *A Boy's Will,* he cited as an imaginative figure a sound made by birds:

> The whimper of hawks beside the sun.

Eliot's description of the world ending "not with a bang but a whimper" conveys a dog-like sound, but Frost's whimper—arresting to the ear and even eye when associated with birds of prey—fits with Audubon's realistic "liquid gurgling notes of varying pitch."

425

Frost is equally attentive to the sound of brooks.

> . . . the grist of the new-beginning brooks
> Is blocks split off the mountain mass—

Through the word "grist" we hear the grinding by resonant mountain waters of rock masses which turn to the round grains of cobblestones that, below, make a "wide-spread brawl," a loud, confused noise with a hint of the quarrelsomeness of the human race. Even a dried-up brook is recalled by our poet through the shrill, startling sound of the hylas:

> That shouted in the mist a month ago,
> Like ghost of sleigh-bells in a ghost of snow . . .

A Japanese author, C. Maeda, in an article in English in a Japanese review, discusses Frost's voice tones in this fashion:

Japanese is an unaccented language, its verse forms syllabic, and its natural speech and poetic rhythms dactylic and exclamatory—more suited to Hogg than to Frost, whose natural speech and poetic rhythms are iambic. For that reason, Maeda urges, Frost should be read and studied *as written*, by Japanese students of English, because, more than any other contemporary poet, he has "reconciled conversational speech to the demands of traditional metrical patterns." Further, he deals with common things but gives them symbolic and metaphoric meaning that leads the awakened student into meditation and thought. Maeda illustrates Frost's originality by setting the sing-song of the iambic quatrain of Tennyson's "In Memoriam":

> 'Tis better to have loved and lost
> Than never to have loved at all.

beside the conversational tones, identical metrically, of:

> Whose woods these are I think I know.
> His house is in the village though;

426

David McCord made a similar comparison of the Puritan sophistry of:

> Better to go down dignified
> With boughten friendship at your side
> Than none at all. Provide, provide!

with that soft-spoken passage of the *Merchant of Venice:*

> Tell me where is Fancy bred,
> Or in the heart or in the head?
> How begot, how nourishèd?
> Reply, reply.

This is an illustration of R.F.'s unconsciously, most likely, dipping anywhere in time and connecting anything in space with it—as he advised the Mount Holyoke students and many others to do. The liberties he has taken with traditional forms —and even, as Glenway Wescott once said at the American Academy of Arts and Letters, with syntax—are what make the poet himself. Some of his finest effects are gained by ending sentences with prepositions, as:

The white clouds over them on. ["The Sound of the Trees"]

Was it some money suddenly come into?
Or some extravagance young love had been to? ["The Investment"]

The trees are all I'm afraid of,
That flowers can't bloom in the shade of;
It's no more men I'm afraid of; ["The Last Mowing"]

Best of all, the last line of "The Pauper Witch of Grafton":

> I might have, but it doesn't seem as if.

"Have you thought," wrote McCord, in a comment he should expand into an essay, "of the prime function of the

427

monosyllabic line in Frost? It looms like a ridgepole from which the poem itself may depend:

> Love has earth to which she clings . . .

> Some say the world will end in fire, . . .

"Or as the granite sill—the first stone last: the solid, the inevitable as—

> We love the things we love for what they are.

> Oh, yes, he showed John the wheel-pit all right.

"Or sometimes the monosyllabic line runs across the vertical somewhere in the middle of the poem—like backbone upholding and suspending at once:

> But just to ask us who we think we are . . .

"And there are poems that begin and end with monosyllables—'Hyla Brook,' for example."

The progression "My Butterfly"—"Storm Fear"—"After Apple-Picking" shows the liberation of a strict and often stiff form, the ode, into a free mastery that makes a masterpiece. Lawrance Thompson has pointed out a similar series in the rather rigid "The Trial by Existence" through the comic-dramatic "Brown's Descent" to the joyous freedom and "juxta-posings" noted by Marianne Moore of "Two Tramps in Mud Time"—all written basically in octo-syllabic quatrains.

In a very touching "new" poem of the past decade, "One More Brevity," sent out as a Christmas card in 1953 (in disguise, it seems an elegy for Gillie, Frost's Border collie), the poet describes a dramatic, slightly supernatural encounter between a wise old stray dog "of the carriage breed" and a man who offers him food, shelter, adoption. R.F., the crafts-man, craftily asserted to me that the Dalmatian was chosen for a poetic sound effect:

His *hard tail loudly smacked the floor* [italics mine]
As if beseeching me, "Please, no more
I can't explain—tonight at least."
His brow was perceptibly trouble-creased. . . .

A symbol was all he could hope to convey

the poet reflects, when the dog vanishes after one night's
lodging. And the symbol is sublime—no less than Sirius, the
Dog Star, the brightest in the heavens of the constellation
Canis Majoris.

An unusual footnote refers the reader to two earlier Sirius
poems. "Choose Something Like a Star" had been suspected
of being Venus but now we know. "Canis Major" was composed in the twenties. Under the title "The Great Overdog,"
Frost wrote it on the flyleaf of my copy of *A Boy's Will* in
1925, and only one word of the poem was changed in the final
version, which appeared in 1928 in *West-Running Brook.*

He dances erect
All the way to the west
And never once drops
On his forefeet to rest.

The final adjective is "upright":

He dances upright

This recalls another familiar and captivating star portrait at
the beginning of "The Star-Splitter":

"You know Orion always comes up sideways.
Throwing a leg up over our fence of mountains,
And rising on his hands, he looks in on me
Busy outdoors by lantern-light with something
I should have done by daylight, and indeed,
After the ground is frozen, I should have done
Before it froze, . . ."

Why did R.F. omit from his footnote a third Sirius poem "Bond and Free"? Remember:

> Thought cleaves the interstellar gloom
> And sits in Sirius' disc all night,
> Till day makes him retrace his flight,
> With smell of burning on every plume,
> Back past the sun to an earthly room.

Opposite this passage R.F. wrote in my *Selected Poems* in 1925:

"If it isn't flowers its stars."

And opposite a reference to ferns in "A Servant to Servants":

"Consumed with stars when I was fifteen, with flowers when I was twenty. Matter of history."

Many of the other star poems, quoted, or not, in this book—for instance "I Will Sing You One-O"—seem, like the above, to symbolize the human poet's relation to thought, to the abstract, the religious, the cosmic; they are associated with those long, lifelong night ramblings in which he has walked off his passions and his moods. If there is one figure that runs consistently through Frost's poetry it is the star. In his scholarly book *The Dimensions of Robert Frost*, writing of "Image as Signature" Professor Reginald L. Cook of Middlebury College finds the star is identified with Frost as the tower with Yeats, the moon with Keats, the cave with Shelley, the sun with Blake. He has even calculated that 10 per cent of the *Complete Poems* refer to stars.

Flowers, from *A Boy's Will* on—from "Rose Pogonias" to ". . . the last remaining aster flower" and

> . . . the faded flowers gay
> That could take me from beside you
> For the ages of a day?

to "Lodged" (the poet knew how the flowers felt) seem associated with heart feeling, with the earth and earthly life.

So is the image of the web, which is more rare but recurs, I think, in a striking enough way to remind the reader that threads, the web of threads, have a fascination for this poet. I have never seen him engaged with the old solitaire game of cat's cradle, which all New England children knew in my childhood. But old friends of his have spoken of his fascination with it, his fondness for weaving his two hands skillfully together with fingers and string—as "his two eyes make one in sight." In the poems the spider weaves evil webs (as in "Design"), webs of indifference to the human fate (as in "Range-Finding"). In "Pea Brush," a poem in the same verse form as "Two Tramps," the brush draws up the curling tendrils of the budding vegetables to their consummation for man's use. But the climax of this symbol is the web woven by woman to keep man to his normal orbit—to temper his abstractions to the human heart.

> . . . She [Mary] put out her hand
> Among the harp-like morning-glory strings,
> Taut with the dew from garden bed to eaves,
> As if she played unheard some tenderness
> That wrought on him beside her in the night.

Then there is the mill worker in "A Lone Striker":

> Her deft hand showed with finger rings
> Among the harp-like spread of strings.

Here is that beautiful sonnet in one sentence and one incomparable metaphor, the height of Frost's metaphoric imagination, in which man's tender relation to woman is exemplified:

THE SILKEN TENT

> She is as in a field a silken tent
> At midday when a sunny summer breeze
> Has dried the dew and all its ropes relent,
> So that in guys it gently sways at ease,

And its supporting central cedar, pole,
That is its pinnacle to heavenward
And signifies the sureness of the soul,
Seems to owe naught to any single cord,
But strictly held by none, is loosely bound
By countless silken ties of love and thought
To everything on earth the compass round,
And only by one's going slightly taut
In the capriciousness of summer air
Is of the slightest bondage made aware.

Another deeply imaginative figure comes from the little-known epigrammatic poem in heroic couplets called "Riders."

The surest thing there is is we are riders,
And though none too successful at it, guiders,
Through everything presented, land and tide
And now the very air, of what we ride.

What is this talked-of mystery of birth
But being mounted bareback on the earth?
We can just see the infant up astride,
His small fist buried in the bushy hide. . . .

The affirmation in this bold image of the infant alone, clinging for dear life to the bushy hide of a rugged world, sailing through space and yet headed, even as a babe, for being a "guider," is to me the very essence of Robert Frost. Like the soul descending to earth in the "Trial," the babe will experience "nothing but what he somehow chose." He will choose poetry but, for many years, almost as if he had not, as if he had to hide the flame, in order to entangle himself with the humblest aspects of the web of life.

If now this great, witty, complex, endearing personality so loved by the American people is involved with the extreme opposite of early poverty and obscurity—with fame, honors, platforms, prizes, degrees, medals and millions of readers —nobody should forget that for his first forty years he was wholly engrossed in finding his own way and his own voice as a poet. His sacrifice to do this was both voluntary and involuntary. Where another man with his gift for vigorous and original prose would have turned to journalism or letters or a place in some urban literary group, Frost just stuck with his farm, his humble teaching and his poetry.

> . . . Why, it doesn't seem
> As if a man could move that slow and move.

—a passage from "Snow" that he once marked for me, writing beside it:

"The way it feels when a poem creates itself as you write."

When he went to England in that old freighter, with his family of five, to be poor without prejudice to friends, it was almost as if they were taking a space ship to Mars, so little did they know the future. But the poet had written "Reluctance" and "The Pasture." He had written "Mowing," "The Death of the Hired Man," and "The Black Cottage"—he had "had it out with himself," and because of this inner maturity, he was sure of a new fate, which fulfilled itself recently at his eighty-fifth birthday party. This was celebrated by his publishers and some hundred of his many friends at the Waldorf in New York.

From his honored place in the middle of the head table Robert Frost did not look venerable, or nostalgic, like some of his older friends among the guests. "Within" [said Emerson], "I do not find wrinkles and used heart, but unspent youth." He looked vigorous, with that "crooked straightness" he advocates. When compared by Lionel Trilling, the distinguished critic, to Sophocles, he assumed "an absolutely abandoned zig-zag that went straight to the mark." As his eye caught mine, he pursed that lower lip of his with a faint humorous smile and I seemed to catch again the words of the letter quoted in the Introduction. When I got home I looked it up:

And still I can't say that I didn't always know it was coming. My prophetic soul told me I was in for it forty five years ago come yesterday on the cliff house beach at San Francisco. Is it not written in a poem of mine. The one thing I boast I can't be is disillusioned. Anything I ever thought I still think. Any poet I ever liked I still like. It is noticeable, I go back on no one. It is merely that others go back on me. I take nothing back. I don't even grow. My favorite theory is that we are given this speed swifter than any stream of light time or water for the sole purpose of standing still like a water beetle in any stream of light time or water off any shore we please.

ROBERT FROST
SELECTIVE CHRONOLOGY

1874

Born in San Francisco, California, March 26. Son of William Prescott Frost, Jr. (of Lawrence, Massachusetts) and Isabelle Moodie Frost (of Edinburgh, Scotland).

1885

Moved to Lawrence, Massachusetts, with his mother and sister, after death of his father.

1890

Published his first poem, "La Noche Triste," in the Lawrence High School *Bulletin*.

1892

Graduated from Lawrence High School. Co-valedictorian with Elinor Miriam White. Author class hymn.

Student in Dartmouth College for a few months.

1894

Twilight, privately printed in Lawrence.

"My Butterfly," first published poem, in the *Independent*, November.

1895

Married Elinor Miriam White.

Taught in mother's private school.

1897–1899

Undergraduate student at Harvard.

1900–1909

Farmed and wrote poetry near West Derry, Rockingham County, New Hampshire.

1906–1911

Years of poetry writing. Taught, chiefly English, in Pinkerton Academy, Derry Village, New Hampshire.

1911–1912

Taught psychology New Hampshire State Normal School, Plymouth, New Hampshire.

1912–1915

Went to England with wife and four children: Lesley, Carol, Irma, Marjorie. Wrote and farmed in Buckinghamshire and Herefordshire.

A Boy's Will, 1913, London: David Nutt.

North of Boston, 1914, London: David Nutt.

1915

February, returned from England.

Settled on a farm, Franconia, New Hampshire.

North of Boston, New York: Henry Holt and Company.

A Boy's Will, New York: Henry Holt and Company.

Phi Beta Kappa Poet, Tufts College, May.

1916

Mountain Interval, New York: Henry Holt and Company.

First college readings: Bates College, Amherst College; Phi Beta Kappa Poet, Harvard College.

Elected to National Institute of Arts and Letters.

1917–1920

Professor of English, Amherst College.

1918

First academic honor: M.A. Amherst, May.

1919

Moved to new farm, South Shaftsbury, Vermont.

1920

Co-founder, Bread Loaf School of English, Middlebury College. Annual lecturer, 1920–

1921–1923

Poet in Residence, University of Michigan.

1922

A.M., University of Michigan.

1923

Selected Poems, New York: Henry Holt and Company.

New Hampshire, New York: Henry Holt and Company.

L.H.D., University of Vermont.

1923–1925

Professor of English, Amherst College.

1924

Pulitzer Prize for *New Hampshire.*

First Litt.D.'s: Middlebury College, Yale University.

1925

Fiftieth Birthday Anniversary honored by friends, Hotel Brevoort, New York City, March 26.

1925–1926

Fellow in Letters, University of Michigan.

1926–1938

Professor of English, Amherst College. John Woodruff Simpson Foundation.

1928

West-Running Brook, New York: Henry Holt and Company.

Revisited England. Went to Paris.

1929

A Way Out, New York: The Harbor Press.

1930

Collected Poems, New York: Henry Holt and Company.

Elected to American Academy of Arts and Letters.

1931

Pulitzer Prize for *Collected Poems.*

1933

Litt.D., Dartmouth College.

1934

Death of Marjorie Frost Fraser.

1936

A Further Range, New York: Henry Holt and Company.

Charles Eliot Norton Professor of Poetry, Harvard University.

1937

Litt.D., Harvard University.

Pulitzer Prize for *A Further Range.*

1938

Death of Elinor Frost.

Sold Amherst house. Resigned from Amherst College.

Elected to Board of Overseers, Harvard College.

1939

Collected Poems, New York: Henry Holt and Company.

The Gold Medal for Poetry, National Institute of Arts and Letters.

1939–1942

Ralph Waldo Emerson Fellow in Poetry, Harvard University.

1940

Death of Carol Frost.

Buys Homer Noble Farm, Ripton, Vermont; house in Cambridge, Massachusetts.

Phi Beta Kappa Poet, Tufts College. (Twenty-fifth anniversary of first public reading.)

1942

A Witness Tree, New York: Henry Holt and Company.

1943

Pulitzer Prize for *A Witness Tree.*

1943–1949

Ticknor Fellow in the Humanities, Dartmouth College.

1945

A Masque of Reason, New York: Henry Holt and Company.

1947

Steeple Bush, New York: Henry Holt and Company.

A Masque of Mercy, New York: Henry Holt and Company.

1948

Litt.D., Amherst College.

1949

Complete Poems, New York: Henry Holt and Company.

Appointed Simpson Lecturer in Literature, Amherst College, October.

1950

Resolution of United States Senate on seventy-fifth birthday. (Correct birth date, March 26, 1874, established after this.)

1952

Litt.D., Durham University, Durham, England.

Delegate to World Congress of Writers, São Paulo, Brazil.

1954

Eightieth Birthday Anniversary honored by publishers and friends, New York City, Amherst, Massachusetts, March 26–27.

1955

LL.D., Dartmouth College.

1957

Trip to England, summer.

Litt.D.'s at Oxford and Cambridge Universities and National University of Ireland.

1958

Consultant in Poetry to Library of Congress.

1959

Eighty-fifth Birthday Anniversary honored by publishers and friends, New York City, March 26.

Resolution of United States Senate on eighty-fifth birthday.

INDEX

INDEX

444

445

449